a CENTURY of THEATRE

a CENTURY *of* THEATRE

RUTH LEON AND SHERIDAN MORLEY

First published in 2000 by Oberon Books Ltd.
(incorporating Absolute Classics)
521 Caledonian Road, London N7 9RH
Tel: 020 7607 3637 / Fax: 020 7607 3629
E-mail: oberon.books@btinternet.com

British Library Cataloguing-in-Publication-Data
A catalogue record for this book is available from
the British Library.

ISBN: 1 84002 058 X

Cover design and book design and layout: Jon Morgan

Cover and author photographs: © John Timbers

Printed in Great Britain by Alden Press Limited, Oxford.

Plays of the Year

1900 Uncle Vanya
1901 The Dance of Death
1902 The Importance of Being Earnest
1903 Man and Superman
1904 Peter Pan
1905 The Voysey Inheritance
1906 Major Barbara
1907 The Playboy of the Western World
1908 Peer Gynt
1909 Strife
1910 Grace
1911 Trelawny of the Wells
1912 Hindle Wakes
1913 Mary Goes First
1914 Pygmalion
1915 The Widowing of Mrs Holroyd
1916 Hobson's Choice
1917 Dear Brutus
1918 Exiles
1919 Heartbreak House
1920 The Skin Game
1921 The Circle
1922 Six Characters in Search
     of an Author
1923 Anna Christie
1924 Juno and the Paycock
1925 Hay Fever
1926 On Approval
1927 Thark
1928 Show Boat
1929 Rope
1930 Private Lives
1931 Of Thee I Sing
1932 Dangerous Corner
1933 A Sleeping Clergyman

1934 Murder in the Cathedral
1935 Waiting For Lefty
1936 French Without Tears
1937 Amphitryon38
1938 Our Town
1939 The Little Foxes
1940 The Corn Is Green
1941 The Man who Came to Dinner
1942 Antigone
1943 Oklahoma!
1944 The Life of Galileo
1945 Perchance to Dream
1946 All My Sons
1947 A Streetcar Named Desire
1948 The Lady's Not For Burning
1949 Lost in the Stars
1950 Come Back Little Sheba
1951 A Penny for a Song
1952 The Pink Room/Absolute Hell
1953 A Day by the Sea
1954 The Boy Friend
1955 Waiting For Godot
1956 Look Back in Anger
1957 West Side Story
1958 The Birthday Party
1959 Roots
1960 A Man For All Seasons
1961 The American Dream
1962 The Pope's Wedding
1963 The Workhouse Donkey
1964 The Royal Hunt of the Sun
1965 Loot
1966 Rosencrantz and Guildenstern
     are Dead
1967 A Day in the Death of Joe Egg

1968 Forty Years On
1969 Christie In Love
1970 The Philanthropist
1971 Follies
1972 Butley
1973 The Changing Room
1974 The Norman Conquests
1975 Chicago
1976 Sexual Perversity in Chicago
1977 The Kingfisher
1978 Buried Child
1979 Bent
1980 The Dresser
1981 Noises Off
1982 Master Harold...and the Boys
1983 Run For Your Wife
1984 Breaking the Silence
1985 Les Miserables
1986 Broadway Bound
1987 Serious Money
1988 Our Country's Good
1989 Aspects of Love
1990 Racing Demon
1991 Six Degrees of Separation
1992 Dancing at Lughnasa
1993 Angels in America
1994 Love! Valor! Compassion!
1995 New England
1996 Two Trains Running
1997 Stanley
1998 Art
1999 Summerfolk

For Barnaby and Tom, who already have a new century to chronicle.

It would take several volumes to write a complete Theatre Chronicle covering the entire 20th century of plays and players, births and deaths, openings and closings, news and notices. Any single volume such as this must be a personal selection. Furthermore, in dealing with such vast amounts of information, we came across certain problems which we resolved by using a system and layout adopted after considerable trial and error.

Plays of the Year: these are sometimes not plays at all, but musicals. Moreover, they have been chosen in order to allow us to write about the playwright or composer/lyricist, as well as the play or musical. To take just two examples, as we had written extensively about Arthur Miller in the context of *All My Sons*, there seemed little point in returning to him a mere three or four years later for his *Death of a Salesman*. Equally, we have selected Edward Albee's *The American Dream* as a Play of the Year over his other and more important work simply because 1961 gave us a good window in which to examine his plays with no other conflicting claims from other major American and British dramatists in that year.

Thus, our Play of the Year may, for the above calendar reasons, not be the most significant, or important, or even successful of that writer or twelve month period; it is simply a way into his or her work, and in order to be able to include all the writers we wanted to cover, we have sometimes opted for their London premieres, sometimes those on Broadway, and sometimes even the year when a play was first written. Precisely which of these options we have chosen is, of course, always indicated in the text.

Where a major play or musical does not appear as a Play of the Year, details of it will often be found in the text, Calendar and/or Notable Premieres section for that year. Space would not allow us to be comprehensive in these areas of the book, and we had to settle for a broad sketch of events that would place the plays in their wider cultural context.

Births and Deaths: death dates are usually reliable, birthdates rather less so, as many actors and actresses choose to shave a year or three off their ages in later life. Where there is reasonable doubt, we have simply opted for what we thought was the most plausible of the many dates we often had on offer.

As for geographic scope, this is centrally a book about English-speaking theatre, and therefore its main focus is London and New York. We have tried however not to ignore Australia or English-speaking Canada, (as far too many theatre surveys always do), and we have of course included non-English writers from Ibsen to Ionesco where their work seriously influenced or affected the English-speaking theatre at any time this century.

Finally, last but by no means least, the authors would like to express their gratitude to James Hogan, Torben Betts, Humphrey Gudgeon, Mike Allen, Dan Steward, Peter Coller, Richard Mangan and Donna Percival whose patient enthusiasm and co-operation have ensured that this book is now before you.

Above all Paul Webb, without whose persistent and cheery knowledge and helpfulness we would never have made it through the century.

Ruth Leon and Sheridan Morley
London, 2000

Curtain Up

The British theatre, like almost all other performing arts, does not correspond to strict calendar rules. Just as we talk of the Royal Court revolution of the 1950s, meaning precisely what happened there and elsewhere after 1956, and just as we talk generally of the 1960s, meaning precisely what happened between 1963 and 1972, so the curtain actually went up on 20th century British theatre in 1895.

This was the year in which Oscar Wilde, (although his *Lady Windermere's Fan* had been premiered three years earlier), achieved an amazing treble – *An Ideal Husband, The Importance of Being Earnest* and *A Woman of No Importance* all had their West End premieres between January and April.

This was the year when George Bernard Shaw, having already seen private or one-off matinee productions at home and abroad of his *Widowers' Houses* and *Arms and the Man*, effectively decided that his future lay in playwriting, rather than in music and drama criticism.

This was the year when, largely thanks to Shaw's writing, Ibsen became a figure on the international theatrical landscape. His *A Doll's House* had been seen in London as early as 1884, admittedly in an unrecognisable adaptation by Henry Arthur Jones and H Herman which, entitled *Breaking a Butterfly*, solemnly gave the piece a "happy ending". Other Ibsens had also been seen briefly in London and hailed, often in isolation, by Shaw in his critical role. *The Pillars of Society* had achieved one London matinee in 1880; *Ghosts* had run briefly in 1891; *An Enemy of the People*, again in a very revisionist translation, had been at the Haymarket in 1883; and *The Wild Duck* had a more successful production at the Royalty in 1894. *Rosmersholm* had been tried twice in London in 1891 and 1893, as had *The Lady from the Sea, The Master Builder* and *Hedda Gabler*.

Five years after Shaw had published his *Quintessence of Ibsenism*, this was also the time when the work of both TW Robertson (*Caste*) and Sir Arthur Wing Pinero (*The Magistrate, Dandy Dick, The Second Mrs Tanqueray* and, in 1895, *The Notorious Mrs Ebbsmith* all began to introduce a new kind of "problem play" realism to the West End, suggesting, albeit gently, to audiences for the very first time that it might not be an entirely bad idea for a play to make them think instead of simply laugh or cry. And it was in 1895 that the cumulative effect of all these brief stagings really began to influence, if not yet audiences, then the other young playwrights of Shaw's generation. In this year it suddenly became, for the first time in almost a century, not just fashionable but almost compulsory to go to the theatre on anything more than an occasional basis.

Theatre began to be discussed outside the review columns and outside the pubs and clubs of the few who were then professionally involved. Theatre became a real element of London life: controversial, discussed at dinner parties and other social and professional gatherings by audiences clearly torn between the safety of the old shows and a future suddenly looking decidedly as if the British stage was, however reluctantly, going to join the European avant-garde.

So, the West End of 1895 was at a kind of crossroads: still controlled by a prudish and puritanical if hypocritical late Victorian establishment, but now firmly marching towards a future which would not be to the liking of the old guard. Indeed, the storm which was about to break out over the homosexuality of Oscar Wilde, because 1895 was also the year of the Marquis of Queensberry's infamous calling card branding him a 'somdomite' (sic), could also be seen as the last great battle between the old and the new, the British and the European, censorship and freedom of expression, suppression and honesty. A theatre of safe costume drama was giving way to the reality of sexual disease (Ibsen's *Ghosts*) and social/feminist revolution (Ibsen's *A Doll's House*). And now, for the very first time, one or two actors even began to dress and behave on-stage as they might in real life. The age of the strolling player was rapidly coming to an end.

Indeed, 1895 was also the year when the very first actor, Henry Irving, was knighted by Queen Victoria for services to the theatre, a gesture which, overnight, bulldozed a tradition that for more than four centuries had placed all actors beyond the social pale. And again, 1895 was the year when the American theatre first became a force to be reckoned with in London; one or two American playwrights and comedians began to reverse the transatlantic tide which had thus far allowed Wilde and Gilbert and Sullivan to barnstorm America, but very few Americans to make any kind of a mark in the West End. It also needs to be noted that this year in Paris, Adolphe Appia published his first crucial, influential and prophetic treatise on stage scenery, *La Mise en Scene du Drame Wagnerien*.

Sir Henry Irving

But in the end, the best guide to the sheer and sudden wealth of the West End in 1895 can best be gained by briefly flicking through the plays noticed by Bernard Shaw for his theatre column in the *Saturday Review*. They included: Pinero's *The Second Mrs Tanqueray* and *The Notorious Mrs Ebbsmith*; Wilde's *The Importance of Being Earnest*; the March visit to London of the Parisian Opera Comique company with Ibsen's *Rosmersholm* and *The Master Builder*, and Maeterlinck's *Pelleas et Melisande*; the first showing of *Living Pictures*, a primitive kind of cinema; a dramatisation of *Vanity Fair*; Pinero's *Bygones*; the debut of Lillah McCarthy as Lady Macbeth; *The Prude's Progress*, a farce by Jerome K Jerome and Eden Phillpotts; Sardou's *Gismonda*; Robert Louis Stevenson's melodrama *Macaire*; Dumas' *La Femme du Claude*; simultaneous London seasons by the two greatest actresses in the world, Eleanora Duse and Sarah Bernhardt, both playing *La Dame Aux Camellias* at rival theatres; Rostand's epic romance of chivalry *La Princess Lontaine*; *The Two Gentlemen of Verona*; *Twelfth Night* played in the manner of the 16th century; Forbes Robertson and Mrs Patrick Campbell as *Romeo and Juliet*; Arthur Bourchier in a new musical *The Chili Widow*; the stage premiere of *Trilby* with Gerald du Maurier, Rosina Filippi and, as the definitive Svengali, Herbert Beerbohm Tree; a revival of *The Rivals*; and finally, Seymour Hicks' dramatisation of the recent Dreyfus affair, *One of the Best*. It would be hard to think of any year in the subsequent century that could seriously claim a better or

Herbert Beerbohm Tree

more varied diet of the ancient and the modern theatre in one capital city at one time.

I want some more hock in my selzer
And Robbie, please give me your hand –
Is this the end or the beginning?
How can I understand?
(John Betjeman, *The Arrest of Oscar Wilde
at the Cadogan Hotel*)

In January 1895, Oscar Wilde, in his prime at the age of 41, was all set to become the most successful British dramatist in the 300 years since William Shakespeare, with three new plays *An Ideal Husband*, *The Importance of Being Earnest* and *A Woman of No Importance* all set to go into rehearsal. By the end of May, he was starting a prison sentence of two years' hard labour, which was to end with his immediate exile to France and his death there in 1900. In the century that has elapsed, there have been hundreds of books, countless radio and television programmes and three major movies, all trying to explain the context of Wilde's amazingly rapid fall from grace and, as we open the Millennium with virtually all his major plays being filmed, in many cases for the third or fourth time and of course revived on stages all over the world, the topicality of (for instance) their debates on political sleaze or domestic intrusion is as breathtaking now as when these were first seen and heard a century ago. In 1937, Lord Alfred Douglas, the direct cause of Wilde's imprisonment said, "Let England bear the responsibility for what she did to Oscar," and at least it could be said that we have not borne our responsibility in silence. Somehow, one suspects, that silence is what Oscar would most have dreaded; and all that really needs to be recalled here is that there were in fact three Wilde trials within less than three months.

The first was the result of Wilde suing the Marquis of Queensberry, Lord Alfred Douglas's father, for the 'somdomite' card left at his club. When that resulted in a verdict of innocent for the Marquis of Queensberry, the police were left with no choice but to arrest Wilde for gross indecency, though they did leave him several hours in which to flee the country, an opportunity Wilde declined for reasons still unclear.

The second trial, for offences under "the blackmailer's charter", dealing with the protection of minors, resulted in a hung jury but the judge, refusing now even to allow Wilde bail, so hostile had the public mood become towards the playwright, announced that there would immediately be a re-trial – making it clear by his very speed that the establishment was now determined to get a conviction, come what may.

The third trial opened on May 20th, lasted just five days and resulted in the hard-labour conviction. "And I, my Lord," Wilde called from the dock, "am I to say nothing?" For once in Wilde's life, the answer was in the negative, and he was taken to Pentonville to begin the sentence which famously ended in Reading Gaol. It was just thirteen weeks since

he had found Queensberry's card at the club, and he was still only in his 41st year.

The four remaining years of the 19th century, although less eventful in London terms than 1895, nevertheless reflected all around the world a sudden rebirth of interest not only in theatre generally but specifically in a new form of psychological and character-led drama. These were the years of Ibsen's *John Gabriel Borkman*, Chekhov's *The Seagull*, Rostand's *Cyrano de Bergerac*, Shaw's *Candida*, and Pinero's *The Gay Lord Quex*.

So at the turn of the century which we now chronicle, the modern theatre had already in four short years become a reality.

Unc/e Vanya

Although first seen at the Moscow Art Theatre in the closing weeks of 1899, it was in this year that word of Chekhov's masterpiece began to spread around the world; although London would have to wait until 1914, and New York until 1924, by 1901 it was already in Prague and Berlin, and of all Chekhov, this was the most frequently revived in Britain during the twentieth century.

The production that immediately springs to mind is the 1963 Laurence Olivier staging at Chichester with an all-star cast headed by Olivier himself and Michael Redgrave which effectively saved the theatre from closure at the end of an otherwise disastrous first season. Later, it came to London's Old Vic where it became one of the very first pillars of Olivier's National Theatre. Many of us reckon this to have been the definitive English-language version, largely because of the Olivier/Redgrave Astrov/Vanya double-act and a quite amazing supporting cast which included Sybil Thorndike, Lewis Casson, Joan Greenwood, Joan Plowright and Max Adrian. Notable productions since have included Paul Scofield at the Royal Court in 1970, Albert Finney and Leo McKern at the Manchester Royal Exchange in 1977, Michael Bryant and Dinsdale Landen at the National in 1982, and Michael Gambon in the West End in 1988 with Jonathan Pryce as Astrov. This was in a new translation by Michael Frayn who has now brought all the major Chekhovs to new English life.

As Kenneth Tynan noted of the Olivier revival, "There is a tide in the affairs of men, and Chekhov's people have all missed it." What keeps *Uncle Vanya* alive and eternal is that sense of yearning loss for a pre-revolutionary world, coupled with a very real fear of what is about to come. In *Vanya*, above all, it is the discrepancy between what is and what might have been that holds the attention. The final agony lies in the way Chekhov forces his people, and by extension us, to see them not as they would like to be, but as they really are. There have been several screen *Vanya*s, including a photographic record of Olivier and Redgrave at the National, and, more recently, three intriguing variants:

the Anthony Hopkins Welsh Valleys version, the Michael Blakemore relocation to the wide open spaces of the Australian outback at the end of the First World War, and Andre Gregory's *Vanya on 42nd Street*.

Michael Gambon and Jonathan Pryce at the Vaudeville Theatre, 1988

CALENDAR

• Bernard Shaw publishes *Three Plays For Puritans*

• The Japanese Court Theatre company from Tokyo, en route to the Paris Exhibition, make their London debut with three traditional dramas described by one local critic as, "so odd, so bizarre, and so sincere that any description can only faintly reflect the absurdity and the excellence"

• Herbert Beerbohm Tree opens one of his longest-lived roles, as the title character in a play suitably enough entitled *Rip Van Winkle*

• Irving returns to his Lyceum from a triumphant American tour with a revival of *Olivia* starring his beloved Ellen Terry

• Bernard Shaw swears, "Never again will I cross the threshold of a theatre. That subject is exhausted and so am I." In the next 10 years he will write 20 plays

• Beerbohm Tree reopens his Her Majesty's Theatre in the Haymarket with a *Julius Caesar* in which he stars as Mark Antony

• In Paris, the first screening of a short silent film, *Hamlet's Duel*, starring Sarah Bernhardt

• Very primitive cinematic colour and sound systems are demonstrated at the Paris International Exhibition

• Marconi receives first radio signals transmitted from Cornwall to Newfoundland

• In New York, James O'Neill, father of playwright Eugene, opens yet another long-running revival of *The Count of Monte Cristo*, the play that, in *Long Day's Journey Into Night*, his son was effectively to blame for his mother's drug addiction and his father's descent into alcoholism

BIRTHS

Jed Harris Broadway director and producer

Luis Bunuel Stage and screen director

German composer **Kurt Weill**

Spencer Tracy Hollywood film star

Louis Armstrong Trumpeter and singer

German actress **Marlene Dietrich**

Mildred Dunnock American actress

Tyrone Guthrie British stage director

John Mason Brown Theatre critic

American stage actress **Helen Hayes**

Lotte Lenya German actress and singer

Singer and early black star **Ethel Waters**

Arthur Schwartz American songwriter

DEATHS

Oscar Wilde Poet and playwright

Carl Bechstein German piano maker

Critic and social reformer **John Ruskin**

Sir Arthur Sullivan Creator with WS Gilbert of the Savoy operas

Sir George Grove First director of the Royal College of Music

NOTABLE PREMIERES

Charles Ives' **PRELUDE**

Puccini's **TOSCA**

Debussy's **NOCTURNES**

Mahler's **FOURTH SYMPHONY**

Boston Symphony Hall opens

First jazz clubs open in New Orleans

Philadelphia Orchestra inaugurated

HIT SONGS

I Never Liked A Nigger With A Beard

All Coons Look Alike To Me

Strike Up The Band, Here Comes A Sailor

The Dance of Death

Although completed in Stockholm in the early weeks of 1901, the two parts of Strindberg's *The Dance of Death* were destined as usual for a German premiere. The first Swedish production would not be until 1909, and London would have to wait until 1924.

Part One of the play concerns an army captain, Edgar, and his wife Alice, who have been married for 25 years and hate each other deeply. She had been an actress who gave up her career for marriage and it is her cousin, Kurt, first attracted to her plight, who finally realises that she is as evil as her husband and leaves them to their own mutual self-destruction.

Set in contemporary Sweden in the year that Strindberg married the Norwegian actress, Harriet Bosse, 29 years his junior, the first part of *The Dance*, at least, can be seen as a terrible forecast of the marriage to come. Part Two, in which the children of the characters in Part One search for the happiness which had eluded their parents, was only written because Strindberg had been told by his German translator that Part One alone would be far too gloomy to sell.

Nevertheless, this has become the part which has been far more frequently revived, most notably in a 1966 National Theatre staging starring Geraldine McEwan and Laurence Olivier. In this production, Olivier found the character many of us reckoned alongside Archie Rice (*The Entertainer*) to be his greatest non-Shakespearean role. Olivier recognised that Edgar was "ten per cent love and ninety per cent hate" and his evil, cruel, vain, and devious performance was recognised by JW Lambert for *The Sunday Times*, "The man's spiritual means seems to glitter from every glance and to rasp in every word... His dance, starting as an endearing little mazurka, ends in a humiliated collapse to the floor amid the pathetic whimpers of a spiritually crushed man." "Even Sir Laurence," added Harold Hobson, "has never done anything better."

None of us who saw that production could forget it, although it is arguable that in O'Neill's *Long Days Journey into Night* Olivier achieved the same kind of total physical breakdown.

Strindberg himself always thought this his finest play and would frequently perform the Captain before stunned guests at his house. His own description of the Captain is a textbook for any actor: "He is a refined demon! Evil shines out of his eyes which sometimes flash with a glint of Satanic humour. His face is bloated with liquor and corruption and he so relishes saying evil things that he almost sucks them, tastes them, rolls them around his tongue, before spitting them out. He thinks of course that he is cunning and superior, but like all stupid people he becomes at such moments a pitiful and petulant wretch. First and last, the Captain must look old. His ugliness, age and whisky must always be visible." Olivier went lightly on the "ugliness, age and whisky" but his manic Prussian military turn harked back intriguingly to a little known 1947 film in which Erich von Stroheim played the role.

Other notable Edgars in our time have included Emrys James for the Royal Shakespeare Company (RSC) and Alan Bates. Edward Fox starring with Jill Bennett were similarly unforgettable.

Deeply indebted to Freud, whose ideas about the interpretation of dreams and the sexual basis for human motivation were just beginning to achieve widespread currency throughout Europe as Strindberg was writing *The Dance of Death*, his "Dream" plays and the preoccupation he had with what he considered to be an elemental and unchangeable conflict between men and women, made him the first truly 20th century dramatist. By the time he died, in 1912, he was one of the most famous writers in the world and although his plays have seldom been box-office winners, his vision of human beings as tortured and alienated showed the way forward to many later playwrights who were also keen to use the subconscious and to find ways of staging psychological states and spiritual intuitions.

When the National Theatre production of *The Dance of Death* was filmed just after it closed at the Old Vic, Olivier himself noted, "I have been married a bit

Gemma Jones and John Neville at the Almeida, 1995

myself and the play seems to me still utterly realistic – there isn't a line in it that I haven't said to at least one of my wives."

Indeed, Kenneth Tynan, Literary Manager of the National, watching Olivier and McEwan's Edgar and Alice draining each other of self-respect, their life together a dreary round of endless card games interrupted by acts of sudden violence – the Captain shoots six bullets through a portrait of his wife, throws bottles at closed windows, sobs and wails only at the close to wrench himself out of his wheelchair so as to spit at his wife full in the face – was heard to murmur backstage, "So like the dear days at Notley." The reference was to Notley Abbey, the house that Olivier had shared with his second wife, Vivien Leigh, during the flamboyant melt-down of their marriage a few years earlier.

Olivier went on to say, "A new young actor in the company of obviously exceptional promise was understudying me and when I was hospitalised during the run walked away with the part of Edgar like a cat with a mouse between its teeth. His name was Anthony Hopkins."

CALENDAR

• The death of Queen Victoria: the Lord Chamberlain closes all London theatres for a week
• Opening of the Apollo Theatre
• Several actors arrested in New York at the Academy of Music for wearing stage costumes on Sunday
• Sir Henry Irving and Ellen Terry depart for their first major tour of the USA
• In Paris, the author of the scandalous *Claudine* novels is revealed to be a young woman, known only as Colette. Fifty years later, she would write *Gigi*.
• In New York, a 21-year-old Ethel Barrymore makes a triumphant Broadway debut in *Captain Jinks of the Horse Marines*

BIRTHS

Walt Disney Animator and film-maker
Andre Malraux French poet and playwright
American actor **Clark Gable**
Gary Cooper American actor
Frederick Loewe Composer who with Alan J Lerner wrote MY FAIR LADY, GIGI, CAMELOT
Israel (Lee) Strasberg Founder of The Method school of acting

DEATHS

PT Barnum Showman
Henri de Toulouse Lautrec French painter of the theatre
Richard D'Oyly Carte Impresario
Opera composer **Giuseppe Verdi**

NOTABLE PREMIERES

Florenz Ziegfeld stars his wife in THE LITTLE DUCHESS. During the 17 week run he eliminates the entire plot to allow for the musical numbers
BECKY SHARPE with Marie Tempest in the title role was the first dramatisation of Thackeray's VANITY FAIR
The two great Parisian classical actresses set up rival London summer seasons. Sarah Bernhardt played CAMILLE and PHAEDRE, while Mme Rejane opened with LA COURSE DE FLAMBEAU
For the first time, players from the Imperial Court Theatre in Tokyo performed in London. The play is entitled THE SHOGUN
Arthur Wing Pinero's IRIS

HIT SONGS

The Stars and Stripes Forever
Goodbye, Dolly Gray
Tell Me, Pretty Maiden
Ain't Dat a Shame
She's The Flower of Mississippi

The Importance of Being Earnest

The arrest and imprisonment of Oscar Wilde in 1895 led immediately to the closing and blacklisting of all his plays, three of which were actually running to packed houses in the West End at the time. But it is some indication of his sheer power as a dramatist that less than 18 months after his death five years later, they were nearly all back in the West End and the provinces; as for his best, *The Importance of Being Earnest*, that made its triumphant New York debut early in 1902.

The most frequently revived in later years of all Wilde's comedies of bad manners is about a lot more than the most perfectly constructed dragon lady ever invented. Premiered on 14th February 1895 in one of the worst snowstorms of the London century this "a trivial comedy for serious people", as Wilde described it, did not have immediate acclaim. Bernard Shaw thought it "Oscar's first really heartless play; it amused me, of course, but unless comedy touches as well as amuses, it leaves me with a sense of having wasted my evening."

Decades later, the American critic Mary McCarthy reckoned, "written on the brink of his fall, *The Importance* is Wilde's true 'De Profundis'. The other was mere false sentiment. Wilde's dialogue is peevish, fretful and valetudinarian; it is the tone of an elderly recluse imprisoned by her comforts…like a piggish old lady, it combines the finnicky with the greedy."

So why, after more than 100 years, is the play still in regular production all over the world with dramatists as diverse as Tom Stoppard and Alan Bennett able to parody it in their own work totally secure in the knowledge that its landmarks will be recognised by audiences everywhere?

For a start, of course, we get some of the greatest one-liners ever written: "The truth is never pure and rarely simple", "In married life, three is company and two none", "To lose one parent, Mr Worthing, may be regarded a misfortune, to lose both looks like carelessness", "All women become like their mothers, that is their tragedy. No man does, that is his", "The good ended happily and the bad unhappily – that is what fiction means", "I never travel without my diary. One should always have something sensational to read in the train".

Far more importantly, as always with Wilde, the sub-text is what always fascinates. The idea of John Worthing creating a mythical brother and then going away for a weekend's Bunburying can clearly now be seen as a metaphor for the necessarily secretive life of the homosexual in 1890s London and throughout the play it is easy to read a coded attack on the hypocrisy of high London society.

As most actors burn to play Prospero so is the wondrously snobbish Lady Bracknell a benchmark for the great and near-great actress. The many Lady Bracknells in living memory range from Maggie Smith through Judi Dench and Barbara Leigh Hunt to Irene Handl (who for Jonathan Miller played her as a wealthy German immigrant) but they are all to this day overshadowed by the 1939 memory of Dame Edith Evans on stage and screen giving her legendary line, "A handbag?" several additional octaves and syllables.

But the fact that Lady Bracknell is now often played by a man in drag and there have even been entire plays speculating on what happens to her in later life stressed that *The Importance* is strong enough to withstand anything that directors or other playwrights can now throw at it. Sometimes, of course, as in the cases of Coral Browne and Dame Maggie Smith, the player can be as witty as the character. Asked to take a recent London staging to New York, Dame Maggie replied, "Take this to Broadway? I wouldn't even take it to Fulham Broadway." It is indeed not a production one always approaches with utter glee; sometimes I think I must have seen it in English, French, German, American, modern dress, period dress, under glass, under water, in school, college, field and even on one occasion on ice. And yet the play still haunts us from beyond Oscar's grave of which there is even a terrible portent here: "He wished to be buried in Paris," says John of his mythical brother, "that scarcely indicates soundness of mind at the last."

Maggie Smith
at the Aldwych,
1994

CALENDAR

• Ellen Terry makes her debut at Stratford-upon-Avon
as the Queen in *Henry VIII*. Intriguingly, the Stratford
season also features such non-Shakespeares as *The
Rivals* and *Richelieu*

• In New York, major variety theatres now start
playing three or four shows a day of 8 to 12 acts each.
Ticket prices run from 5c to 25c and chorus salaries
start at $6 a week, although a visiting star like Lily
Langtry commands up to $3,500

• Vaudeville workers frequently have to share dressing
rooms with live animal acts and discrimination against
black artists is still rampant

• Meyerhold founds the Society of New Drama in
Russia. He eliminates all scenery and treats the actor
as a puppet in the hands of a director

• Thomas Edison invents the electric storage battery
which, along with his other inventions, the
phonograph and the electric lightbulb, was to
revolutionise theatre technology

• Eighty-two acres of land surrounding the Earl's
Court Arena are sold at auction for £560,000

BIRTHS   **Cheryl Crawford** Founder of the New York
Theatre Guild

Wolcott Gibbs Critic

Actress and teacher **Stella Adler**

Donald Wolfit British actor/manager

Richard Rodgers American composer

British actor **Ralph Richardson**

Vittorio de Sica Italian film director

Anthony Asquith British film director

DEATHS   **Emil Zola** French writer

Samuel Butler British author

NOTABLE PREMIERES

JM Barrie's THE ADMIRABLE CRICHTON
scandalises Mayfair by suggesting that when a
wealthy family is wrecked on a desert island their
butler is the only one fit to take charge.

Stephen Phillips' great poetic drama ULYSSES
opens at Her Majesty's Theatre with Herbert
Beerbohm Tree and wins a rave review from the
Times: "It is something at this time of day to find a
great world-story told for the first time on the
English stage in the language of true poetry and with
all the resources of this age and the arts of plastic
and music." Tyrone Power led a less triumphant
Broadway premiere some months later.

Edward German's MERRIE ENGLAND opens at the
Savoy where it becomes a marathon hit, despite the
fact that night after night audiences come purely to
jeer at its amazing awfulness.

David Belasco's THE DARLING OF THE GODS
produced on Broadway, starring George Arliss.

Lily Langtry stars in her own play THE CROSS-WAYS

THE GIRL WITH THE GREEN EYES by Clyde
Fitch, starring Lucile Watson

MUSICAL NOTES

Enrico Caruso records VESTI LA GIUBBA on a wax
cylinder in his hotel room which sold a million copies

Premieres of Debussy's PRELUDE DE L'APRES-
MIDI D'UN FAUNE

Jelly Roll Morton announces, "I have invented jazz"
although he was merely the most popular of many
ragtime musicians to extend the form

HIT SONGS

Bill Bailey, Won't You Please Come Home?

In the Good Old Summertime

If Money Talks, it 'Ain't On Talking Terms With Me

Man and Superman

Although it had been a work in progress for some three years, *Man and Superman* was first published in August 1903 and first performed two years later at the Royal Court with Granville Barker and Lillah McCarthy. The first American production followed two years later and since then there have been more than 100 productions on both sides of the Atlantic. At first reading the critic Max Beerbohm exclaimed, "In swiftness, tenseness and lucidity of dialogue no living writer can touch the hem of Mr Shaw's garment… In *Man and Superman* every phrase rings and flashes. Here, though Mr Shaw will be angry with me, is perfect art."

High praise indeed for the work which Shaw himself concluded was "as long as three Meyerbeer operas and no audience that had not already had a Shaw education could stand it."

The story, a contemporary retelling of *Don Giovanni*, tells of Jack Tanner, a socialist millionaire who falls in love with his ward, Ann Whitfield and her sister, imagining that she is more interested in Octavious. A blind idealist, Jack misunderstands every emotional signal and misjudges every motive, especially Ann's and those of her friend, Violet. It takes his chauffeur to explain to him that she intends to marry and subdue him and a romantic secret elopement to Spain is foiled by Ann's invitation to her family and friends to join them. Once there, in the often-deleted Act Three, Jack dreams that he is Don Juan arguing in Hell with the Devil and expounding the theory of creative evolution to him and Ann, with Mozart's Commendatore making a surprise appearance. The subsequent disillusionment prepares him for his capitulation to Ann in the end.

As Beatrice Webb noted, this was the script in which Shaw at last found his true voice, "It is a play which is not a play, but only a combination of essay, treatise, interlude and lyric – all these different forms illustrating the same central idea." That central idea is at the same time a statement and a mockery of the theory that life can be lived according to a single set of ideals. Shaw makes it clear, especially in Act Three, that only in a fictional world can ideals be maintained intact.

Even Shaw thought *Man and Superman* useless as a stage play and it wasn't until long after Shaw's death, in the late 1940s in fact, that the 20-year old Peter Brook brought it together at the Birmingham Rep and, for the first time the critics came around to it. "The performance

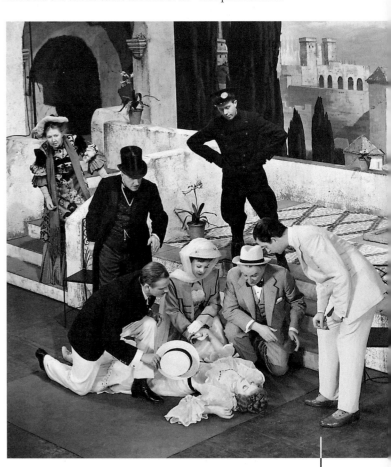

The New Theatre, 195

was lucidity itself," wrote JC Trewin, first noting that it was madness to put such a terror of a play into the hands of a boy his age, "and if (Paul) Scofield's Tanner had to depend now and then upon the charm that can be a bloom on Shavian actors… it was clear that he and Brook understood one another."

In more recent years, Peter O'Toole at the Theatre Royal Haymarket in 1982 made a bizarre return to the barnstorming, eye-rolling, scenery-chewing, stellar flamboyance that may well have been a feature of touring actor/managements in his Irish youth. Both Micheal MacLiammoir and Donald Wolfit would have been the first to recognise what was going on at the Haymarket. In an otherwise desperately slow and deadly dull production, Mr O'Toole strode firmly into a walk-in deep-freeze full of ham, taking the play in there with him.

Ironically, the greatest success of *Man and Superman* has always been the *Don Juan In Hell* sequence performed in isolation. For many years Charles Laughton, Charles Boyer, Vincent Price, Agnes Moorehead would travel across the United States in recital of it, thereby inadvertently inventing the platform performance which has now become a standard and sizeable part of theatre repertoires all over the world.

As Benedict Nightingale was later to write: "The impression with which the play leaves us is both ambiguous and teasing. A man's ideals have been dented, yet so have his myopia, complacency and folly; Tanner has lost himself but he now has the opportunity to find himself in a new and perhaps profounder way; marriage may yet mar him or it may yet make him. There is reason to feel pessimistic about his future, reason to feel optimistic, and reason to respect a play that ends by making us feel both at the same time. Shaw himself told his European translator Trebitsch to leave it alone, "as you would get six years in a fortress for the preface alone."

CALENDAR

• London County Council names two new streets – Kingsway (now home to the Peacock Theatre) and Aldwych (where the Aldwych Theatre and the Strand now are)

• The new Gaiety Theatre opens in the Aldwych with *The Orchid*. King Edward VII and Queen Alexandra are in the audience

• First news service between London and New York is established using Marconi's wireless

• The exotic dancer Isadora Duncan causes a sensation in Paris with the premiere of her *Danses-Idylles*

• Americans are fascinated by the first ever action movie. *The Great Train Robbery*, an 8-minute film made by the Edison company dispensed with captions and cut rapidly from scene to scene, even including a shot where a pistol is fired directly at the audience.

• More than 600 people killed on Dec 30 when the brand-new Iroquois Theatre in Chicago burns down during a performance

• Oscar Hammerstein builds Drury Lane Theatre in New York, later to become the Manhattan Opera House and the Lyceum Theatre opens with *The Proud Prince*

• Granville Barker publishes his first ever plans for a National Theatre

• Founding of the Abbey Theatre in Dublin

BIRTHS

American actress **Tallulah Bankhead**

Harry L Crosby (Bing) American crooner

Al Hirschfeld Theatrical cartoonist

French actress **Claudette Colbert**

Elliot Norton American critic

DEATHS

Hugo Wolf Austrian composer

Paul Gauguin French painter

James McNeill Whistler Painter

NOTABLE PREMIERES

Dorothy arrives on Broadway with the premiere of the first stage adaptation of L Frank Baum's book THE WONDERFUL WIZARD OF OZ.

IN DAHOMEY, the first black musical in a legitimate Broadway house, opens at the New York Theatre

COUSIN KATE by HH Davies inaugurates the new Hudson Theatre with Ethel Barrymore in the title role

John Barrymore makes his NY stage debut in GLAD OF IT by Clyde Fitch. It runs for only four weeks

At one point this year all three acting Barrymores are on Broadway for the first time with Lionel in THE BEST OF FRIENDS by Cecil Raleigh for Charles Froelich at the Academy of Music

MUSICAL NOTES

Enrico Caruso makes his Metropolitan Opera debut in Verdi's RIGOLETTO

Arnold Schoenberg premieres his opera PELLEAS UND MELISANDE

Verdi's ERNANI becomes the first complete opera to be recorded

HIT SONGS

Ida, Sweet As Apple Cider

Sweet Adeline

Always Leave Them Laughing When You Say Goodbye

Toyland

In The Merry Month Of May

Peter Pan

"Oh dark and terrible man". Peter Pan, of course, addressing Captain Hook at the start of their final shipboard duel but it could, we have always believed, be an equally accurate definition of the author, JM Barrie himself.

Nina Boucicault as the first Peter, 1904

Born in 1860, he started out from Edinburgh University as a journalist but soon moved to London where he made his name as a playwright first with *The Admirable Crichton* and in this year *Peter Pan* which, although always considered a children's play, strikes us as one of the most fearfully adult ever written.

Essentially, it is the story of a young girl, Wendy Darling, waking up one night in the safety of her Kensington home to find a boy fairy at the end of her bed asking her to fly away with him to the Neverland, where she is to become not his lover but his mother. Insisting on bringing her younger sister and brother, she agrees. At the end of the flight she is shot down by the bows and arrows of Peter's "Lost Boys" and only brought back to life by yet another fairy known as Tinkerbell, an irritable flying candle who can herself only be saved from death by the applause of children in the audience, confirming their faith in the existence of fairies.

If we add to this a public-school-educated pirate captain with a hook for an arm and a decidedly sexual interest in *Peter Pan*, a captain moreover always played by the same actor who doubles as Wendy's father, the latter spending much of the play quite literally in the doghouse, and if finally we add the facts that while Wendy back home ages normally to the point where the ageless Peter no longer recognises her, and that until very recently Peter was always played by a girl, it is not hard to detect the Freudian bi-sexual nightmare into which the play is all too eager to plunge us. Indeed, *Peter Pan* has always said far more about the incredible complexity of its author's sexual, mystical and social neuroses than even Barrie's own more secretive autobiography.

But, from the time of the nearly simultaneous *The Wizard of Oz* right through to Roald Dahl, the great children's hits of the 20th century were always as dark as Peter's suggestion that "To die will be an awfully big adventure."

In 1898 James Barrie met five children by the Round Pond in Kensington Gardens and, always uneasy in the company of adults, encouraged them to become his lifelong friends. Of the five Llewellyn-Davis brothers for and about whom James Barrie wrote the stories which became *Peter Pan*, two were to die by their own hand, and one in the First World War.

You do not have to be unusually perceptive to see, in the way that Peter literally flies into the Darling household through a window and imposes himself on all their lives, changing them forever, an exact parallel with the way in which Barrie erupted into the lives of the Llewellyn-Davis's. Nor is it difficult to see, in the utter sexlessness of Peter's demands on Wendy, a reflection of Barrie's own recent divorce where the cause was widely believed to be his impotence, nor again is it hard to perceive a connection between Barrie's passion for the children he could never have and the idea of a magical kingdom where children never age and adults never arrive to take them away. Their only friends and enemies are therefore the pirates and the indians who have always been at the heart of children's games, and in the many and various last acts which Barrie was to continue re-writing for years to come the message was always the same – never grow up, never give in to the grown-ups and move as swiftly as you possibly can from birth to death.

Again, as in *The Wizard of Oz*, there is somewhere over the rainbow where dreams are born. And if, in Barrie's case, they were also the nightmares of sex and age and impotence, he was a great enough playwright never to allow his largely youthful audiences to assume that they had wandered by mistake into Strindberg.

For all its dark brooding majesty, *Peter Pan* is also a masterpiece of childish high spirits which would perhaps explain why, from 1904 for more than half a century, it was performed annually on the London stage.

Radical changes first set in immediately after World War II. On Broadway, first Leonard Bernstein and then, more successfully, Comden and Green with Jule Styne wrote musicals, the second of which became a staple of American Christmas television for more than thirty years.

Back in England, the RSC became the London producer of *Peter Pan* and adopted the revolutionary casting of a male actor in the leading role, a tradition which was continued when its directors, Trevor Nunn and John Caird, moved it to the National Theatre in 1997.

Peter Pan has since then had one last and extraordinary political triumph. JM Barrie died in June 1937, leaving the rights in the play to the Great Ormond St Hospital for Sick Children in London. When the copyright on the play was about to elapse, thereby putting an end to the thousands, if not millions of pounds in royalties earned for the hospital, the former Prime Minister James Callaghan forced though the House of Lords a special Bill extending the copyright in perpetuity – an extension which has never before or since been granted to any published work. *Peter Pan* lives; second star to the right and straight on 'til morning.

CALENDAR

• In *The Southerners*, an otherwise white cast is joined by what the NY Times calls "A chorus of real live coons" the first such interracial mix on the American stage

• The Vedrenne-Barker seasons start at the Royal Court making it effectively the first London theatre with a social conscience

• Sir Herbert Beerbohm Tree founds the Academy (later Royal Academy) of Dramatic Art

• Opening of the Abbey Theatre in Dublin

• Frequent arrests of women for smoking in theatres (it was legal for men)

• Opening of the London Coliseum in St Martin's Lane. Frank Matcham's building in the Italian Renaissance style is now the largest theatre in London with 2358 seats

BIRTHS **Archibald Leach** (later Cary Grant) **American film star** British classical actor **John Gielgud** American character actor **Ralph Bellamy** **Harold Hobson** Drama critic **Moss Hart** American playwright/director **George Balanchine** Russian born choreographer and founder of the New York City Ballet **Anton Dolin** the first British born ballet star

DEATHS **Antonin Dvorak** Bohemian composer **Anton Chekhov** Russian dramatist

NOTABLE PREMIERES First New York production of Ibsen's **ROSMERSHOLM** Moscow premiere of Chekhov's **THE CHERRY ORCHARD** Premiere of Jerome Kern and Henry Darnley's **MR WIX OF WICKHAM**

MUSICAL NOTES Puccini's new opera **MADAMA BUTTERFLY** is a flop at its first Italian production Formation of the Boston Symphony Orchestra, which dedicated its first concert to the memory of Dvorak Buddy Bolden, an early jazz pioneer, plays cornet in the style that will later come to be identified with New Orleans

HIT SONGS **Give My Regards to Broadway** **I Can't Take My Eyes Off You** **Meet Me in St Louis, Louis** **Come and Take a Trip in My Airship**

The Voysey Inheritance

Though largely neglected today Harley Granville Barker was in the early 1900s far and away the most famous and respected director in the British theatre while his reputation as an actor stood almost as high. But as early as 1916 he wrote a "Farewell to the Theatre" and although he lived on until the end of World War Two, the second half of his life was spent almost entirely abroad as a professor of theatre, writing his famous *Prefaces to Shakespeare*.

Of his dozen or so major plays, only *The Madras House* and *The Voysey Inheritance* have achieved any real afterlife and what is fascinating about *The Voysey Inheritance* is the cynicism with which Granville Barker tries to convince his audience that conventional morality may not in the end be very moral.

Not only is the play one of the very few of its time to attack Edwardian smugness and middle-class respectability but it also persuades an audience that a satisfactory outcome could often justify criminal ways of achieving it and even that a swindler could well live on a much higher moral plane than the man whose money he has stolen.

The plot is complex. It starts with a retiring solicitor suddenly confessing to his upright son and partner that he has for many years been speculating with his clients' trust funds. Old Voysey maintains that this speculation has allowed his large family to live well, kept many others afloat and by paying the interest (though never the capital) he has ensured that no client has ever asked a single question nor lost a single night's sleep.

His son, won over by the old man's buccaneering spirit, not only perpetuates the system but also takes up a life of gambling. Inevitably, the system eventually crashes and Young Voysey now demands that his family make good his debts. They, after all, have been living for years on what is for all practical purposes borrowed money. The play never reaches any obvious conclusions. The last act is effectively a debate on the nature of wealth. Where, in the end, does it really come from, who really has a right to it, and shouldn't it perhaps end up in the hands of those who can do most good with it, regardless of original ownership?

These ideas did not, of course, meet with the immediate approval of a still censorious early Edwardian audience but what has been most impressive about the scattered revivals over the years has been the way in which critics and audiences alike have gradually come around to Granville Barker's demands for a more liberal attitude towards good and bad. What Granville Barker really wrote about was the futility of higher ideals; liquidity of cash was what he argued for and a much broader concept of borrowing and mortgaging assets rather than leaving them lying in dust-covered vaults.

In the end, says Granville Barker, we are all living in a compromised world and what we have to measure is the balance between the kind of idealism which longs for absolute right as a moral imperative and the inevitable compromises and tricks that belong unavoidably to the murky transactions of everyday life. As one of his characters says, "Fine feelings, my dear, are as much of an unnecessary luxury as clean gloves." Eric Salmon has noted that *The Voysey Inheritance* celebrates anarchic moral assertions and the moral claims of the individual soul over and above the strict laws of contemporary society. Harley Granville Barker is careful to prosecute no one and to give every member of a very large cast his or her absolute moral defence of their own behaviour.

Of the few revivals of *The Voysey Inheritance* last century, one at the National Theatre in 1990 won an Olivier Award for Jeremy Northam as Most Promising Newcomer; an award that kick-started his Hollywood career. This production seemed to have the absolute measure of the moral complexity of the *Inheritance* and of the Voyseys themselves. Less than five years after the death of Queen Victoria here for the first time is a major play by a major playwright telling us that not only are Victorian values themselves both suspect and hypocritical but that honesty may very well not be the best policy and the play reverberates through the decades like a time bomb.

The Shaftesbury Theatre
production in 1934

CALENDAR

• Nickelodeons open in many American cities offering short silent films and live vaudeville acts at 5c a ticket

• Theatre curtains start to have advertisements painted on them

• The $1,750,000 New York Hippodrome opens with a new musical extravaganza called *A Yankee Circus On Mars*

• The first six-play season of GB Shaw opens on Broadway but during *Mrs Warren's Profession* two actors are arrested on stage for performing an immoral work. The play would not receive its London premiere until 1926

• Picture postcard machines first appear on boardwalks

• Russian composers Rimsky-Korsakov, Rachmaninov, and the operatic bass Chaliapin sign a public protest against the oppressive regime of the Tsar

• London's first permanent cinema opens

• Designer/Director Gordon Craig (son of Ellen Terry) publishes his *Art of the Theatre*

• Lillian Russell becomes the first star to get $100,000 for thirty-week vaudeville season

• First celebrity commercial – Fatty Arbuckle endorses Murad Cigarettes

• Founding of the American showbusiness bible *Variety*

• First double-sided gramophone record coincides with the invention of the jukebox

• Sarah Bernhardt pelted with rotten eggs in Canada after she criticises lack of culture there

• WC Fields, then a juggler, makes his Broadway debut in *The Hamtree*

• Abolition of stage censorship in France

• Opening of new Theatre Royal, Haymarket and Royalty Theatre after major renovations

• A freak accident causes the collapse of Charing Cross Station killing six and injuring 26 occupied in rebuilding of the Playhouse Theatre

• Typhoid epidemic closes East End music halls

• Sam Shubert, founder of the American theatre chain, killed in train crash

• English actress, later longtime resident of the United States and wife of Alfred Lunt, Lynne Fontanne, makes her debut in chorus of *Cinderella* at Drury Lane

• Oscar Wilde's *De Profundis* finally published five years after his death

• William Gillette brings triumphant American *Sherlock Holmes* to London as Conan Doyle bows to reader pressure and brings his detective back to life

BIRTHS American choreographer **Agnes de Mille**

Margaret Webster British actress/director

American actor **Henry Fonda**

Mildred Natwick American actress

Lillian Hellman Playwright

Dorothy Fields Librettist

Swedish actress **Greta Garbo**

Emlyn Williams Welsh actor and playwright

Russian ballet dancer **Serge Lifar**

Michael Tippett British composer

Sam Levine Actor

Character actor **George Voskovec**

Jule Styne London born composer of musicals

Audrey Wood American theatrical agent

Sanford Meisner Acting teacher/ director

Hyman Arluck American songwriter

(later Harold Arlen)

Marc Blitzstein German born American

composer

DEATHS **Sir Henry Irving** First actor to be knighted

Maurice Barrymore Father to Ethel, John

and Lionel

Jules Verne French writer

NOTABLE PREMIERES David Belasco's **GIRL OF THE GOLDEN WEST**

Shaw's **MAN AND SUPERMAN**

MUSICAL NOTES **THE MERRY WIDOW by Franz Lehar**

Debussy's **LA MER**

SALOME by Richard Strauss

HIT SONGS **How d'you Like to Spoon With Me?**

Major Barbara

Apart from one or two tentative matinee performances late in 1905, the first sustained run of what many of us still think of as Shaw's greatest play opened under the new Granville Barker management at the Royal Court on January 1st 1906, with Annie Russell as Barbara and Lewis Casson as Cusins.

The story of the struggle between the armaments millionaire, Andrew Undershaft, and his salvationist daughter, Barbara, gives a sometimes didactic and static drama two of the greatest characters in all 20th century theatre. Actresses from Sybil Thorndike to Joan Plowright and actors from Charles Laughton to my father, Robert Morley, have found on stage and screen a power of language which exists almost nowhere else even in Bernard Shaw.

In many ways Barbara is the forerunner of Eliza Doolittle in *Pygmalion*, written seven years later; but for Undershaft, the devil who seems to have all the best songs, there is really no challenger until we get all the way to Lambert Le Roux in David Hare and Howard Brenton's 1985 *Pravda*.

When *Major Barbara* first opened, however, critical opinions, as so often with Shaw, were sharply divided. Max Beerbohm, Shaw's successor as drama critic of the Saturday Review, wrote of "an intense vitality… as valid and close-knit a piece of craftsmanship as any conventional playwright has ever achieved, and a cumulative appeal to the emotions which no living playwright has ever touched." For William Archer, however, "there are no human beings in *Major Barbara*: there are only animated points of view…the play is one long discussion between Barbara, standing for beneficence through love, and Undershaft, standing for beneficence through power, and it is to Undershaft that Shaw resolutely gives the upper hand. He is an admirable figure. There is a passionate and even poetical conviction in many of his sayings that is intensely dramatic and thrilling."

Because my father played Undershaft in the 1940 movie with Wendy Hiller, and because he always believed that Shaw was the only living Saint he had ever met, I (who was born in 1941) grew up with this play and have never failed to be moved by the extraordinary battle of wills between father and daughter.

The first stage revival I ever saw was the 1970 Clifford Williams production for the Royal Shakespeare Company at the Aldwych – a clean, crisp and inventive staging from which the play emerged as a cynical variation on Wilde, The Importance of Being Undershaft, perhaps. But already it was clear to me that Shaw's lust for the English language would carry the play safely around all the pitfalls of a conversation piece, and lead it safely to its anti-Messianic conclusion. What, after all, is human contact but the daily selling of our souls to the highest bidder, always providing, of course, that he doesn't happen to be criminal, or foreign, or anything dangerous like that?

For many years it was believed that the inspiration for Undershaft was the armaments manufacturer and prize-giver, Nobel. But the play is, of course, more timeless than that. Undershaft is anybody who has ever sold arms for profit, even to the enemy.

Judi Dench was my first Barbara to the Undershaft of Brewster Mason, but in 1958 there had been an equally acclaimed revival at the Royal Court with Joan Plowright, Alan Webb, and a young Vanessa Redgrave.

Shaw's own favourite Barbara was Wendy Hiller on film to my father's Undershaft, but the Undershaft that I would most have loved to have seen was the one played by Charles Laughton in New York, 1956, with Glynis Johns as Barbara and a young Eli Wallach as Bill Walker.

This was the play with which Shaw confirmed his success among the intellectual and political audiences he most wished to reach. The Prime Minister even attended the opening night at the Court, and although he himself called it "a discussion in three acts" there is in fact rather more going on in the background of the Undershaft-Barbara struggle for supremacy. Shaw himself had been inspired to write the play by Willam Booth's work among the poor of the East End in the founding days

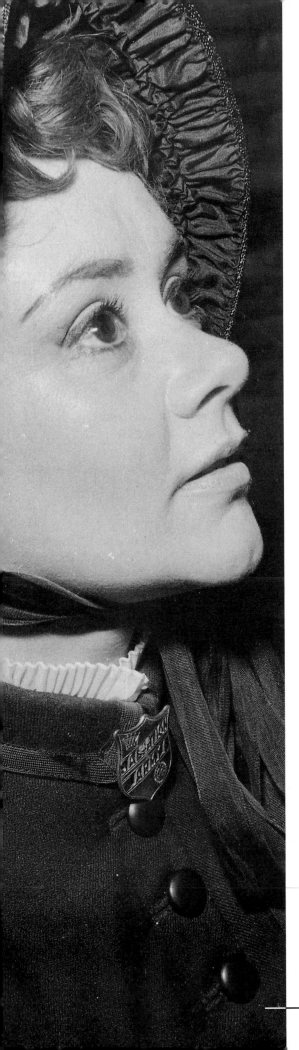

of his Salvation Army (the inspiration not only for this play, of course, but also for that greatest of all Broadway musicals half a century later, *Guys and Dolls*) but he gets as carried away by the devil's disciple in Undershaft as Barrie had recently been carried away by the equally magnificent evil of Captain Hook.

    As Benedict Nightingale has noted, "not many English plays have managed to be simultaneously serious about politics and religion"; *Major Barbara* is one of those, and coming in precisely the same year as *The Doctor's Dilemma*, with Louis Dubedat's great speech about his belief in the power of art over all else, it remains a sharp, perhaps the sharpest, reminder of Shaw's infinite ability to debate with himself from either side of the argument. *Major Barbara* is ultimately about money and gunpowder and the impotence of goodwill alone; *The Doctor's Dilemma* is about art over life itself. The miracle is not the consistency of the arguments, but the fact that they came from the same author in the same year.

CALENDAR

- In London this year there are 57 theatres for the production of plays of which two, Drury Lane and Covent Garden are "Royal"
- It is estimated that 39 million Americans see at least one vaudeville show this year
- In London Charles Frohman organises a benefit for the victims of the San Francisco earthquake in the presence of the American Ambassador at the Duke of York's Theatre
- At the Theatre Royal, Drury Lane, Ellen Terry celebrates her Golden Jubilee in the theatre with a gala benefit
- The American/Canadian theatre chains expand and merge, with hundreds of theatres spread throughout the US and Canada, East and West Coasts

BIRTHS

Irish playwright **Samuel Beckett**

Roberto Rossellini Italian film director

Gracie Allen American comedienne

Dancer and singer **Josephine Baker**

Billy Wilder American film director

American playwright **Clifford Odets**

Otto Preminger American film director

American film director **John Huston**

Dimitri Shostakovich Russian composer

DEATHS

Henrik Ibsen Norwegian dramatist

Paul Cezanne French painter

NOTABLE PREMIERES

Shaw's CAESAR AND CLEOPATRA in New York

THE THREE OF US, Rachel Crothers' first Broadway hit

Edith Wharton's THE HOUSE OF MIRTH

On Broadway, Thomas Dixon's THE CLANSMAN causes riots

Ethel Smyth's opera THE WRECKERS

Charles Ives' THE UNANSWERED QUESTION

MUSICAL NOTES

The young Russian pianist Artur Rubinstein makes his New York debut

A Mozart Festival is started in Salzburg, Austria

Scriabin performs his own piano concerto in New York

HIT SONGS

You're a Grand Old Flag

In Old New York

Why Do They Call Me a Gibson Girl?

Chinatown, My Chinatown

Joan Plowright in the title role at the Royal Court, 1958

The Playboy of the Western World

Fashion in theatre, as elsewhere, is curiously unpredictable; by the turn of the 20th century into the 21st, major productions of JM Synge's *The Playboy of the Western World* were coming in about once per decade; yet in 1960 Kenneth Tynan was complaining for the *Observer* that "it is possible to have too much of a good Synge; in the past four years I have seen the play five times, including a musical comedy version and one by the Berliner Ensemble, who changed the title to *The Hero of the Western World* and linked Christy Mahon's Ireland to Mike Hammer's America, by means of a front-cloth decorated with Mickey Spillane dust-jackets (Message: in decadent societies, murderers are idolised)."

Christy is of course the young man who arrives at a country inn on the Mayo coast boasting that "in a windy corner of high distant hills" he has killed his own father, whereupon he is treated as a hero until the father suddenly arrives on the scene. Synge was in 1907 only two years away from his own early death at 37, but his supporters were already out in force: Yeats wrote of a

Donal Donnelly and Siobhan McKenna at the Piccadilly Theatre in 1960

genius who "made his own selection of word and phrase, choosing what would express his own personality; above all, he had word and phrase dance to a very strange rhythm".

But the rhythm was not to everyone's taste; the Dublin premiere of *Playboy* led to a week of Dublin rioting by "a veritable mob of howling devils" as the Abbey's manager WG Fay saw it; what they were objecting to was not just the unprecedented use on the Abbey stage of the word "bloody" but those who found, in the scene where Christy really does try to murder his father in order to live up to his own false reputation, a satire that had gone much too far towards a destruction of the hitherto lovable Irish rogue.

Synge had already said that his ambition was to annoy his audience, and through the character of Pegeen Mike he had the courage to question a community in which official morality is established only by the local Catholic priest. *Playboy* though officially billed as a satire, was in fact a devastating attack on the hypocrisy of village Ireland, and it foreshadowed by more than a decade the rows that were eventually to drive Sean O'Casey into exile.

Synge's attack on the ignorance and crass hero-worship of the Irish character did not play any better when *Playboy* opened in Boston four years later; in New York, 100 police were required to quell rioters in the theatre, where the disturbance on the first-night began suitably enough with the hurling of an Irish potato. A judge later noted that the play was "the nastiest, vilest, most scurrilous and obscene thing I have ever seen" and fined a man ten dollars for hurling eggs at the cast.

Playboy satirises Irish parents, priests, drinkers and wastrels; for the first time, it asks whether there is really anything very lovable or even admirable in the Irish peasant character, and in that sense Synge was already seen as a threat to what all too soon became the Celtic heritage industry. Tynan admired the way that a reputation for patricide could transform a weakling into a sex-symbol, but he too had trouble with the language: "I concede its soft lyricism, but where is its hard meaning?"

He went on to a brief but brilliant parody: "The was you'd be roaring and moiling in the lug of a Kilkenny ditch, and she with a shift on her would destroy a man entirely, I'm thinking, and him staring till the eyes wuld be lepping surely from the holes in his head". The revival that provoked that was the one in 1960 with Siobhan McKenna confirming her reputation as the greatest of all Pegeen Mikes; by the time I saw Bill Bryden's National Theatre revival fifteen years later, Susan Fleetwood was playing Pegeen Mike with Stephen Rea as Christy, finding within himself a wondrous mixture of bemusement and deception, so that when he falsely admits to the killing of his own father, he seems as amazed as anyone that he should be believed. By now, revivals had become somehow more picturesque, losing the sharp original edges; but the real joy of this revival was predictably that band of Irish Abbey veteran players (Liam Redmond, JG Devlin, Eddie Byrne, PG Stephens) who seemed to carry on stage with them the whole weight of turn-of-the-century Ireland.

CALENDAR

• 71 British authors write to The Times demanding the end of the Lord Chamberlain as censor after he has banned Shaw's *The Shewing Up of Blanco Posnet*

• British actors register themselves as a trade union – aims are: fair minimum wages, freedom from management abuse and peaceable negotiation

• In view of the State visit of the Crown Prince of Japan, the Lord Chamberlain bans all performances of Gilbert and Sullivan's *The Mikado*

• Granville Barker refuses to remove references to a fatal abortion from his new drama *Waste*. As a result, it is not licensed until 1920

• Start of the London "Music Hall Wars" – a number of stars go on strike claiming they are getting a raw deal from the hall managers

BIRTHS **Daphne du Maurier** Novelist/playwright
Christopher Fry British playwright
Broadway producer **Herman Levin**
Broadway star **Katharine Hepburn**
Laurence Olivier British actor
British actress **Peggy Ashcroft**

DEATHS **Richard Mansfield** First actor to present Ibsen and Shaw in America
Alfred Jarry French playwright

NOTABLE PREMIERES Galsworthy's THE SILVER BOX is the modern theatre's first attack on social injustice

Gerald du Maurier opens a near-lifelong run as RAFFLES, the gentleman detective

Broadway opening of CAPTAIN BRASSBOUND'S CONVERSION by Shaw, starring Ellen Terry

THE SHOO-FLY REGIMENT, an all-black musical intended for white audiences, closes in 10 days.

ZIEGFELD FOLLIES opens on the roof of the New York Theatre at a cost of $13,000.

MUSICAL NOTES Puccini's opera MADAMA BUTTERFLY first performed in London in English
New York Metropolitan Opera bans Richard Strauss's SALOME as obscene.
Nellie Melba sings LA TRAVIATA in New York
First production of Delius' opera A VILLAGE ROMEO AND JULIET

HIT SONGS Merry Widow Waltz
There Never Was A Girl Like You
Marie From Sunny Italy – first song which names co-author as Irving Berlin (until now he has used his original name Israel Baline)

Peer Gynt

Although written in 1867, Peer Gynt only received its first British production at the Queen's Hall Edinburgh on February 14th 1908. Intriguingly, when it first reached London five years later, a woman, Pax Robertson, was to play the title role. Since then, the great British Peers have included Russell Thorndike (1922), Ralph Richardson (1944), and Leo McKern (1962).

Set in Norway, Africa, and Norway again late in the 19th century, *Peer Gynt* tells of a peasant boy closely bound to his mother until he finds in Solvieg a pure girl who loves him. Leaving her and Norway because he feels unworthy, he ends up a wealthy and cynical tycoon in a madhouse. But the last act, I believe the greatest Ibsen ever wrote, has him returning from a shipwreck to meet his own angel of death, the Button Moulder, who wishes to melt him down since he has never been true enough to himself to allow for either heaven or hell. It is now the aged Solvieg who saves him because she alone has kept her memory of Peer as the "self that bore God's stamp upon his brow."

From the very first production in Norway *Peer Gynt* was widely attacked for its self-hatred and contempt for humanity. The real objection, however, was that Peer was an all-too-accurate reflection of the Norwegian character, lacking in idealism and unable to meet the demands of either art or reality.

But Ibsen never thought of *Peer Gynt* in performance. The way the play moves freely in time and space, the way it ignores the barriers between reality and fantasy and the dreamlike quality of confused pantomime led Ibsen always to talk about *Peer* as his book of poetry. Others would have to grapple with the myriad staging problems not least its length. Its five acts often take up the best part of five hours.

The first *Peer Gynt* I ever saw and in many ways the most remarkable was a student production which starred the director Sam Walters at Oxford in 1960. Right in age for the early scenes and surprisingly plausible for the later ones, Sam caught the rare mix of outward

William Devli and Vivienne Bennett at th Old Vic in 193

panache and inner nervous breakdown which has defeated many more accomplished players.

On to the next crossroads, as the Button Moulder tells Peer, and then we'll see. What we see is a man in total meltdown trying to correct the mistakes of his middle age and get back to the dreams of his youth. Like much of Ibsen, it always seems to be a work in progress and the fascinating appeal of the play is that every time you go back to it you find something you never knew was there. Just as Peer tears away at the skin of the onion to find nothing but emptiness in the middle, so he takes off mask after mask only to find at the last that his face is somehow no longer there.

In 1970, Peter Coe staged a Chichester revival using a new and radical adaptation by Christopher Fry. In what was still a complex travelogue, Peer had now become the Billy Liar of his day and all that happens in the play after the abduction of the bride became merely a figment of his fevered imagination. This was a production of shreds and patches, with Roy Dotrice as Peer. There were some magical moments here but in general the adaptation only served to underline rather than camouflage the failings and eccentricities of the play itself.

You could just about make the case for *Peer Gynt* as the Scandinavian *Peter Pan* who had first taken flight in London barely four years earlier. Both men are chronic fantasists with an ability to take off on wings of their own imagination; both men collect and corrupt a community of admirers and both men finally come home to the girlfriends they have originally abandoned, hoping finally to discover who they are and where their lives have gone so wrong.

As late as 1950, *Peer Gynt* was still being described in Scandinavia as "the great national poem of Norway" and its lasting achievement was often seen to have been Ibsen's request that Edvard Grieg (who died just a year before the British premiere) should write his *Peer Gynt Suite* which quickly became more popular and widely familiar than the original play. Early American productions usually abandoned the fourth act travelogue

entirely but even so, the *New York Times* referred to the first American production in 1906 as "A hodge-podge of mere madness." By 1923, opinions had radically altered. Heywood Broun wrote of "The most beautiful thing on Broadway…the death of Ase is one of the most moving scenes ever written for the theatre." Alexander Woolcott was less impressed, "*Peer Gynt* is an undisciplined, unedited play. A tremendous unfiltered stream fed from the springs of Norwegian folklore and carrying with it no end of rubbish that fell in by chance as it was being written." When Sybil Thorndike as Ase, Ralph Richardson as Peer, and Laurence Olivier as the Button Moulder opened at the Old Vic in 1944 James Agate noted, "There is neither iota nor scintilla of jollity in this cavernous and gloomy masterpiece."

CALENDAR

• In London actor Sir John Hare leads a committee which calls for creation of a National Theatre to commemorate the 300th anniversary of Shakespeare's death which is coming up in 1916

• In Manchester, Annie Horniman establishes the first provincial repertory company

• The Irish National Theatre of Dublin make New York debut

• Hans Christian Andersen produces short season of German-language theatre in London

• A deputation led by JM Barrie, Gilbert Murray, Pinero, Henry James and Granville Barker confronts Gladstone at the Home Office with an unsuccessful petition demanding the ending of stage censorship by the Lord Chamberlain

• In Britain, opening of the new Watford Palace of Varieties. Early stars include Charlie Chaplin, Stan Laurel, Marie Lloyd, and Bob Hope

• Opening of the new Brooklyn Academy of Music on Lafayette St

BIRTHS American actor **James Stewart**
Rex Harrison British comedy actor
Michael Redgrave British classical actor
American producer **Leonard Sillman**
Robert Morley British actor
American comedian **Milton Berle**
Jacques Tati French comic mime
Burgess Meredith American actor

DEATHS **Nikolai Rimsky Korsakov** Russian composer

NOTABLE PREMIERES JM Barrie's **WHAT EVERY WOMAN KNOWS**
Tiller Girls make first appearance on London stage
GB Shaw's **GETTING MARRIED**
Jerome K Jerome's **THE PASSING OF THE THIRD FLOOR BACK**
Beerbohm Tree's production of **THE MERCHANT OF VENICE**, considered offensively Jewish by several critics
WS Gilbert appears as Claudius in his own new play **ROSENCRANTZ AND GUILDENSTERN**, a distant forerunner of the Tom Stoppard classic

MUSICAL NOTES Gustave Mahler makes Metropolitan Opera debut
Elgar's **FIRST SYMPHONY**
Bartok's **FIRST STRING QUARTET**
Strauss' **THE CHOCOLATE SOLDIER**

HIT SONGS Shine On Harvest Moon
Oh Oh, Antonio
Take me out to the Ballgame
Golliwogs' Cakewalk

Strife

Though now recalled, if at all, mainly for *The Forsyte Saga*, John Galsworthy (1869-1933) was also a prolific and successful dramatist at the head of a line which can be directly traced from Pinero through W Somerset Maugham to Terence Rattigan. Unlike Granville Barker or Shaw, when Galsworthy wanted to write a political pamphlet he simply did so, leaving his plays to be less didactic or overtly political. In many of them (such as *The Skin Game* and *Loyalties*) there is indeed no real way of working out where the playwright's own sympathies lie. *Justice* (1910) does have considerably more commitment to the idea of prison reform but it was in this year, with *Strife*, that Galsworthy really wrote his masterpiece.

The story is simply of a battle between two intransigent idealists: Roberts, who is the Union leader at a large tin factory, determined to win higher pay and better conditions for his men and, ranged against him, Anthony, the chairman of the board of directors, who is equally convinced that he is right not to give in to any of his workers' demands.

On both sides are people eager to compromise, but their leaders are so bull-headed that a strike becomes inevitable. Both men suffer terribly, the union leader's wife dies, and in the end the compromise that is reached is precisely the one that the moderates were urging at the very beginning. By the end of the play, with one woman dead and the two best men broken simply by their refusal to negotiate, the question of 'justice' remains unanswered. "Do you know, Sir, these terms, they are the very same we drew up together, you and I, and put to both sides before the fight began? All this – all this – and – and again – what for?"

Galsworthy's even-handedness means that we leave the theatre unaware of his own real sympathies. He is as usual on the side of the moderates, but that doesn't stop him depicting the extremists with equal power and sympathy. He is never a playwright to intrude or manipulate, and his style is utterly naturalistic. When *Strife* had its last major revival in 1978 at the National, it seemed as topical as in the time it was written; but

Galsworthy's message now seems commonplace where once, in 1909, it was revolutionary in its refusal to side automatically with the ruling classes.

It was DH Lawrence who pointed out (of *The Forsyte Saga*) that all Galsworthy's characters are economic beings, defined only by their money or their lack of it, but in *Strife* he does seem to be pushing forward the idea of social justice.

The parallel with Rattigan is striking. Both dramatists wrote well-made scripts over a long period of time (Galsworthy was still playwriting when he won the Nobel Prize for Literature in 1932), and both men refused to have any part of the international theatrical revolutions raging around them. Just as Rattigan had no dealings with the Royal Court of George Devine, so Galsworthy maintained a little-England position which resolutely refused to take into account the coming of Ibsen or Chekhov or even Bernard Shaw.

Yet precisely because Galsworthy was so firmly rooted in his own country and time and class, his plays (though now shamefully neglected in production) retain a considerable social and historical as well as dramatic fascination. Nor should it be thought that he was politically impotent because of his usually centrist views; a year later, in 1910, his *Justice* caused such an arousal of public indignation about the penal system that Winston Churchill (then Home Secretary) after seeing the play reduced the allowable period of solitary confinement in English prisons from nine months to four weeks. It would be hard if not impossible to think of any subsequent Home Secretary in almost 100 years being equally inspired by one single theatrical experience to change the law.

From industrial relations to prison reform Galsworthy, like Shaw, had an unerring instinct for targeting issues that have remained unresolved for a century. But unlike Shaw, Galsworthy seldom, if ever, preached or pontificated. Like the master craftsman he was, he threw spotlights onto his causes simply by detailing their fallout on ordinary people living apparently ordinary lives in time of stress. For more than thirty years

Industrial
warfare at the
Comedy Theatre
in 1913

as a playwright, he remained remarkably clear-sighted and detached. His plays were often tragedies in which an audience could participate, because time and again they recognised people acting and sounding just like them but up on a stage.

In that sense, Galsworthy was a pioneer of theatrical naturalism, and even when he was satirising the upper classes it was done with such subtlety and quiet good taste that the victims hardly felt the knife. His writing may never have been hugely provocative, but he maintained the decent, moderate, liberal traditions of his time. His plays have few villains or heroes, and over all his characters he exerts equal understanding and compassion, for all the world like a baffled county court magistrate trying to do the right thing in impossible circumstances. As Benedict Nightingale summed up for *The Times*, "A Chekhov or a Gorky would have put these characters into a deeper perspective, and asked larger questions about the fate of the society to which they belonged. Galsworthy has no cosmic vision. His interest is early 20th century English society, and his concern is the practical ordering and humanising of it. But within those self-imposed limits, he is both trenchant and assured."

CALENDAR

• New York Times announces the birth of Broadway: "It will be the Great White Way in reality, for there have been added several electric displays and with theatres in full swing the site will surely dazzle visitors"

• Helen Hayes makes Broadway debut at the age of 9

• Edward Sheldon's *The Nigger* opens on Broadway; "The nigger problem," says the NY Times, "is not one the American public wishes to see on stage"

• Diaghilev Russian Ballet opens a season of Russian opera and ballet in Paris starring the Russian ballet dancer Vaslav Nijinsky

• W Somerset Maugham has six plays running in London and New York this year

BIRTHS **Ethel Zimmerman** Musical comedy star (later Ethel Merman)

American director **Joseph Losey**

James Mason British actor

Elia Kazan US director

Robert Helpmann Australian ballet dancer

Howard Da Silva American songwriter

Tom Ewell American stage and screen star

British actress **Jessica Tandy**

DEATHS **John Millington Synge** Irish playwright

American playwright **Clyde Fitch**

Helena Modjeska Classical actress

NOTABLE PREMIERES Maeterlinck's THE BLUEBIRD

In Paris, Ballets Russes de Monte Carlo gives first performance of LES SYLPHIDES

John Barrymore opens in THE FORTUNE HUNTER: "Let us hope", says the NY Times, "that he is now lost to musical comedy forever"

MUSICAL NOTES Controversy over Gustave Mahler's reorganisation of the New York Philharmonic at Carnegie Hall.

Sidney Bechet joins Buddy Bolden's New Orleans band

First performance of Richard Strauss's opera ELECTRA

Mahler's SYMPHONY NO 9 premiered

HIT SONGS Moonstruck

I Wonder Who's Kissing Her Now

Has Anybody Here Seen Kelly?

By the Light of the Silvery Moon

Grace

Now recalled firstly for his short stories, secondly for his novels, and only thirdly for his plays, William Somerset Maugham nevertheless wrote 26 full-length comedies and dramas of which four were running simultaneously in London by 1908 – a record equalled in later years only by Noël Coward and Alan Ayckbourn.

Trained as a doctor, Maugham was at his best when simply anatomising the concerns of his audience. Unlike Ibsen or Shaw or even Pinero, he had no real interest in social or political reform. But unlike Barrie, nor was he there purely to entertain. Maugham's talent as a dramatist was essentially psychiatric and photographic, but his themes were surprisingly wide-ranging – everything from euthanasia (*The Sacred Flame*) to miscegenation (*The Letter*).

For many years he was effectively the resident dramatist at the Playhouse under the management of Gladys Cooper, for whom he wrote four of his greatest hits: *The Letter, The Sacred Flame, Our Betters*, and an adaptation of his novel *The Painted Veil*.

After one of his other great hits, *For Service Rendered* (1932), a forerunner of Priestley's *An Inspector Calls* in the way it despairs of cynical British middle-class morality, he abruptly abandoned playwriting in a famous handover: "For us English dramatists, the younger generation has assumed the brisk but determined form of Mr Noël Coward. He knocked at the door with impatient knuckles, and then he rattled the handle and burst in. After a moment's stupor, we older playwrights welcomed him affably enough and retired with what dignity we could muster to the shelf which, with a sprightly gesture, he indicated to us as our proper place."

Coward later repaid the compliment by writing several short stories in the Maugham manner, dedicating one play (*Point Valaine*) to him, and making him the subject of his last play, *A Song At Twilight*, about an old novelist of immense distinction whose worldwide fame is threatened by revelations of a homosexual past.

Of all Maugham's plays, *Grace* (written and produced in 1910 and revived a year later under its original title *Landed Gentry*) was by no means the most significant, but it is a useful guide to his prolific dramas of this period, of which he wrote later "most neither lost nor made a fortune; they simply served their purpose". This one tells the story of two women, one the wife of a country squire debating whether or not to reveal to him her infidelity, while the other is a girl on the estate who eventually commits suicide rather than face the shame of eviction from her farm cottage when, unmarried, she becomes pregnant.

Ironically it is the suicide of the land girl which convinces the lady of the manor that she must never reveal her own illicit affair to her husband, but instead stay with him and make amends by unceasing devotion to a loving but unloved husband. By any contemporary standards *Grace* is laughably antiquated and unfeminist, which perhaps explains its total lack of any revival; but here as in so many other of his country-house dramas Maugham was raising an issue which had just begun to become of some concern to his middle-class West End audiences: just what were the boundaries of tolerance and self-fulfilment, and just when did duty and honour still matter more than personal happiness?

Maugham, often his own best critic, thought the trouble with *Grace* was "that it fell between two stools; I knew the narrow, hidebound life of country gentlefolk was about to change but I also knew that my play had to interest, move and amuse the very people it attacked. So the play was neither frankly realistic nor frankly theatrical; my indecision was fatal." Here, as so often, Maugham was issuing the correct prescription but the patient still died. His plays are now usually dismissed as "snobbish and dated" but what makes them to me of constant fascination is that he seems always somehow to have been in at the death of the old Victorian certainties. Like the good doctor he was, he often hid the truth behind a veneer of social acceptability but as often as not he was the doctor at the deathbed, administering the fatal dose with a reassuring smile. Maugham knew that his audiences did not wish to see themselves as they really

Lillah McCarthy, Leslie Faber and Irene Vanbrugh at The Duke of York's in 1910

speech you could very often find the centre of his philosophy. "My dear, I don't know that in life it ever matters so much what you do as what you are. No one can really learn by the experience of another, because no circumstances are ever quite the same. If we make rather a hash of things, it is perhaps because we are rather trivial people. You can do anything you like in this world if you are prepared to take the consequences but consequences depend on character."

Over his thirty years of playwriting, Maugham as a craftsman added considerably to the prestige of the English theatre. He has given three or four plays to the permanent repertoire. He never failed to tell us a story, and until the end of his playwriting career he was a successful and practical dramatist, always there to take the pulse of the public.

CALENDAR

• Enrico Caruso makes first wireless broadcast from the Metropolitan Opera. It goes to 50 receiving sets and ships at sea

• Irving Berlin, hitherto a singing waiter, makes his first theatrical appearance in New York singing his own songs in the revue *Up and Down Broadway*

• Ziegfeld is brave enough and powerful enough to include in this year's *Follies* the first black performer, comic singer and dancer Bert Williams

• No less than three West End plays of this year concern the problems of American Indians married to whites

• Death of Edward VII marked by closing of all theatres except the Abbey in Dublin; its patron Annie Horniman resigns in protest

• Opening of the London Palladium, Frank Matcham's 2325-seat theatre which opens with a mixed bill of variety and one-act plays

were but he found a way of turning the well-made play into something infinitely more threatening than might at first have been expected.

There was always an icy glitter about Maugham. He was far more of a stage technician than most of his contemporaries and in the most apparently throw-away

BIRTHS

French dramatist **Jean Anouilh**

Adelaide Hall American cabaret singer

American songwriter **Frank Loesser**

French playwright and novelist **Jean Genet**

Constance Cummings American actress

EG Marshall Hollywood character actor

DEATHS

Samuel Clemens (Mark Twain) Novelist

Count Leon Tolstoy Russian novelist

Julia Ward Howe US women's campaigner

NOTABLE PREMIERES

THE FIREBIRD, Ballets Russes' sensational new ballet, with music by 28-year old Igor Stravinsky, premieres in Paris

John Galsworthy's JUSTICE

THE MADRAS HOUSE by Harley Granville Barker

NAUGHTY MARIETTA, Victor Herbert's operetta

In London Conan Doyle dramatises his own THE SPECKLED BAND

Abbey Theatre in Dublin premieres WB Yeats' THE GREEN HELMET

MUSICAL NOTES

In New York, Toscanini conducts Puccini's THE GIRL OF THE GOLDEN WEST

Elgar's VIOLIN CONCERTO

Russian dancer Anna Pavlova makes her Metropolitan debut dancing Swanilda in COPPELIA

HIT SONGS

Ah… Sweet Mystery of Life

Every Little Moment

Put Your Arms Around Me, Honey

Down By the Old Mill Stream

Some of These Days

Yiddle on the Fiddle

Trelawny of the Wells

Sadlers Wells Theatre Company. As the play starts, she is about to marry a young man from a totally untheatrical and very hidebound Victorian family. After a miserable 'probation period' as his fiancee, she eventually flees back into the theatre and all ends happily enough; not only does her future husband join her as the company's new leading man, but the old uncle and aunt who have brought him up are finally reconciled to the idea of a life on the boards.

As so often with Pinero, the subsidiary characters are often more fascinating than the leads. Here we have not only Tom Wrench, as a very close approximation of the real-life playwright TW Robertson (the first naturalist writer of the British theatre) but at the same time we also have the loveable, irritating old Telfers, a couple of lifelong character actors who suddenly realise that their safe if impecunious world, that of Victorian strolling players, is coming to an abrupt end.

Then again, there is the initially anti-theatrical uncle, Sir William Gower, whose moment of revelation and change comes when he is suddenly reminded of his own early years watching Edmund Kean – "Ah, Kean, he was a splendid gypsy." Not only is this, I think, the first-ever use of "gypsy" to mean player (now in current Broadway parlance a show dancer), but it also captures the magical ability of theatrical memory to transcend all generational and class differences. While Rose finds life with the Gowers unbearably dessicated and unhappy, the theatre is where there is love and laughter and life itself.

Although it was written and first staged in London in 1898, it was the first Broadway production of 1911 which truly established *Trelawny of the Wells* as the classic it is. There had, of course, been earlier plays about the theatre (notably John O'Keeffe's hilarious 1791 *Wild Oats*, triumphantly rediscovered by the RSC in 1976) but *Trelawny* has always been, for our money, quite simply the best backstage play ever written. It is also now a fascinating historical document about the abrupt changes that had already started to transform the London and British theatre at the moment when the play was first seen.

The story is straightforward enough: Rose Trelawny is the rising young star of a thinly-disguised

From the year of its very first production, *Trelawny* has always been, for very obvious reasons, beloved of actors. Its only ever film version was a 1928 Norma Shearer silent called *The Actress* which had the distinction of opening the old Empire Theatre in Leicester Square. Twenty-five years later, under the same title, Ruth Gordon wrote a screenplay based on her own beginnings, how she first became an actress against the wishes of her stubborn sea-faring father, which bore a remarkable real-life resemblance to *Trelawny*. That movie was made by George Cukor with Jean Simmons and Spencer Tracy.

The stand-out theatrical revivals, in our lifetime, include a very early National Theatre staging at the Old Vic; a wonderful Julian Slade musical version at the Bristol Old Vic (with Gemma Craven as Rose and Max Adrian in his last role as the old uncle), shamefully never revived; and more recently, a memorable double in the early 1990s when there were two simultaneous productions, one of which starred Sarah Brightman.

Precisely because it is written nostalgically of the 1860s, *Trelawny* is both a history and a prophecy about the British theatre. On the one hand, through the Telfers, (loosely based on Squire and Lady Bancroft, the most famous acting couple of their day), it celebrates what would now be called a world of luvviedom. Pinero, lovingly but painfully accurately, shows us the humiliation of the old couple as with age they become marginalised from the modern theatre of their time, ending up as something of a laughing stock even within their beloved Wells. At the same time, the dramatist introduces us to Tom Wrench as the first "angry young man", perfectly pinning down a moment of crucial transition in the 1860s.

Tom is not only the first playwright we ever get to meet on a stage in modern times, he is also the first to demand some kind of control over how and where his work is performed. The real life Robertson plays are now forgotten, with the possible exception of *Caste*, but he lives on in *Trelawny* as the first realist, the first dramatist to insist upon not only naturalism in acting but also recognisably contemporary characters.

Though Pinero was to write virtually one play a year from the 1880s through to 1910 (his last play was as late as 1922), he had in fact started as an actor in Henry

Irving's company at the Lyceum and because of that *Trelawny* was the first 'insider' play ever written about the British theatre. Its themes of sudden success, slow failure and the transient nature of audience loyalties, run right through the 20th century – you can find them as easily in Clifford Odets' *The Country Girl* (1950) as you can in all three Hollywood movie versions of *A Star Is Born*.

The enduring fascination of *Trelawny* is what it shows and tells us of backstage life – we learn about the coming of realistic scenery and props, the role of the stage manager, about the hierarchy of a theatrical company, about the tension between the old sentimentalists and the young radicals. By putting Rose into the middle of all this we see through her eyes one of the most exciting transitional periods in all theatre history. Pinero had seen the greasepainted future, but he also realised at what cost to the old guard it was to be achieved.

Even Bernard Shaw, usually one of Pinero's sternest critics, found in *Trelawny*, "a certain delicacy which makes me loath to lay my fingers on it."

CALENDAR

• New York State law forbids "any representation of Jesus Christ" on stage
• First *Folies Bergère* company opens in New York produced by Jesse Lasky
• Sir Frank Benson takes over complete control of the Shakespeare Memorial Theatre at Stratford-upon-Avon
• Opening of Victoria Palace Theatre in London, 1565 seats
• First performance of Stravinsky's *Petrushka*, starring Vaslav Nijinsky for Diaghilev's Ballets Russes de Monte Carlo

BIRTHS **Thomas Lanier Williams** (Tennessee) American playwright
Swiss writer **Max Frisch**
Terrence Rattigan British playwright
Virginia McMath Dancer/actress/singer, later Ginger Rogers
Television and film comedienne **Lucille Ball**

DEATHS **David Merrick** Broadway producer
Savoy opera writer **WS Gilbert**
Joseph Pulitzer US publisher

NOTABLE PREMIERES Max Reinhardt directs OEDIPUS REX with Sir John Martin Harvey and Lillah McCarthy at the Royal Opera House, Covent Garden
KISMET by Edward Knoblauch opens long London and Broadway runs

MUSICAL NOTES Schoenberg publishes first manual of 12-tone scale theory
First major American tour of Puccini's THE GIRL OF THE GOLDEN WEST breaks all previous box-office records
In London, Aolian Hall opens for concerts
American premiere of SWAN LAKE
Mahler's DAS LIED VON DER ERDE
Strauss's DER ROSENKAVALIER
Franz Lehar's COUNT OF LUXEMBOURG
Ravel's DAPHNIS ET CHLOE

HIT SONGS Oh, You Beautiful Doll
Roamin' In the Gloamin'
Woodman, Spare That Tree
Goodnight, Ladies

Hindle Wakes

Like so many dramas of this period, Stanley Houghton's *Hindle Wakes* has now fallen into almost total oblivion, but in 1912 it was crucially important for two reasons: it was the first play to give Sybil Thorndike a major role in modern dress and it was also one of the very first to establish the significance of British regional drama. It later became famous as a movie (1931, remade 1952) for which the advertising slogan was the classic "Should Fanny marry Alan?".

Many of Houghton's plays were set in "Salchester", an obvious amalgam of Manchester and Salford but the title of this one refers to the town of Hindle in Lancashire which every year would take the traditional "Wakes" holiday by the sea at Blackpool. This was a major play about class distinctions. It told the story of Fanny, a Lancashire mill-girl who spends a week at Blackpool with her boss's son, Alan – in love with her but engaged to another girl – and then refuses to marry him. In that sense, it was also an early feminist tract. For Sybil this was the beginning of a remarkable career. "She had," wrote the dramatist Eden Phillpotts, "a rare sense of humour in comedy and yet she was able equally to play stricken heroines with every apt and poignant emotion, mien and gesture, even to the expression on her face and the woe in her voice. Comedy and tragedy are alike to her and always were, for she has that protean gift to lose herself in any character, having grasped its intrinsic nature."

Like her only real successor, Wendy Hiller, Sybil thrived on playing "ordinary women" even if they were to become as extraordinary as Bernard Shaw's *Saint Joan*. But what is always forgotten about *Hindle Wakes* is that Sybil did not in fact play the mill-girl (that was a long forgotten actress called Edyth Goodall); instead, Sybil established her London reputation with the character who takes over the whole of the last act, "a determined, straightforward girl of 23" who, engaged to the wealthy son, has to convince him to sacrifice her happiness and go off with his lower-class love.

Stanley Houghton was the leader of what became known as the Manchester School of regional dramatists. Much influenced by Ibsen, already devoted to the radical *Manchester Guardian* (Houghton was briefly its drama critic), these were writers who specialised in revolt against parental and indeed any kind of male authority, demands for workers' rights, and the struggle between the generations.

At a time when it was still unusual for dramas to focus on a girl "from the wrong side of the tracks", the central lesson of *Hindle Wakes* was the nobility of the girls of both classes contrasted with the cowardly, vacillating rich man's son who has seduced the one from the mill.

This plot, of course, was a staple of Victorian melodrama but the great change here is that we are asked to see both girls not simply as victims but as highly intelligent and motivated northern cousins of Bernard Shaw's New Woman.

Scenically, the plays of the Manchester School gave their audiences (for almost the first time on stage)

Leonard Mudie, Ada King and Edyth Goodall at the Playhouse in 1912

kitchens, small sitting rooms and rebellion in middle-class streets. This was a tough non-London reply to Pinero's belief that the new middle-class theatre audience really didn't want to see on-stage characters lower down the social scale than themselves.

The driving force behind this Manchester School was a remarkable, wealthy English woman, Annie Horniman, who had started out in London as the first great sponsor of WB Yeats. She had then gone back with him to Dublin and in 1904 created the Abbey Theatre for the Irish National Theatre Society. Shortly afterwards, having fallen out with the Dubliners, she moved to Manchester and set up there the Midland Hotel Theatre, which under several later names, was to inaugurate and sustain the provincial repertory movement well into the 1930s.

In Shakespearean terms, this Manchester School, as Allardyce Nicol once noted, was "the rising in the North". It posed a deliberate and direct threat to the always cosier and less confrontational West End theatre, and had Houghton not died of meningitis at the age of 32, only two years after the premiere of *Hindle Wakes*, there cannot be much doubt that he would have become one of the most successful playwrights of his generation.

As it was, the legacy of *Hindle Wakes* lives on in everything from *Hobson's Choice* to *Room at the Top*. The idea of a woman from the working classes finding a rich young man not good enough for her was the laying of a bomb by Houghton which was to detonate regularly through all 20th century drama, initially and perhaps still most famously in the *Pygmalion* which Bernard Shaw started to write a few months after the premiere of *Hindle Wakes*. The relationship there, between Eliza and Freddy Eynsford-Hill, is almost an exact Covent Garden replica of that between Alan and Fanny here in Manchester, a debt which characteristically was never acknowledged by Shaw himself and has seldom if ever been noted by his critics.

CALENDAR

- Britain establishes first Board of Film Censors
- Eighty years before Sam Wanamaker was finally to establish it on the South Bank of the Thames, a replica of Shakespeare's Globe opens in the Exhibition Hall of Earl's Court
- Irene and Vernon Castle become America's most popular dance act with their "Castle Walk". Irene gives John D Rockefeller tango lessons at $100 an hour
- Revolutionary backstage machinery allows trains to run across stages, thunderstorms to pour rain onto sets, and shipwrecks to be achieved by swiftly moving scenery
- Invention of the scrim, the translucent curtain
- Opening of London's first Yiddish language theatre in London's East End
- Founding of American Actors' Equity
- Marie Lloyd banned from Royal Variety Performance for "unsuitable material"
- Broadway star Fanny Brice meets gambler Nicky Arnstein, a relationship which was to be the source of the musical *Funny Girl*

BIRTHS

Gene Kelly American dancer/choreographer

British actress **Wendy Hiller**

Eugene Ionesco Romanian playwright

American actress **Eunice Quedens** later known as Eve Arden

Rosalind Russell American actress/singer

DEATHS

August Strindberg Swedish dramatist

WT Stead Radical drama critic and early defender of Ibsen

George Rignold English actor/manager

NOTABLE PREMIERES

John Barrymore opens on Broadway as ANATOL, the first American staging of Schnitzler's provocative Viennese sexual predator

London premiere of Franz Lehar's GYPSY LOVE

Parisienne Yvonne Arnaud becomes a star in the West End musical THE GIRL IN THE TAXI

MUSICAL NOTES

Al Jolson has first million-selling recording of RAGGING THE BABY TO SLEEP

James Europe's CLEF CLUB ORCHESTRA become the first black band to play Carnegie Hall, but only because they hire it

Bessie Smith and Ma and Pa Rainey join CHATTANOOGA MINSTREL TROUP

First American appearance of London Symphony Orchestra shocks audiences with Bruckner's FIFTH SYMPHONY

HIT SONGS

It's a Long Way To Tipperary

When Irish Eyes are Smiling

Melancholy Baby

When I Lost You

Waiting for the Robert E Lee

Mary Goes First

Mary Goes First, a minor drawing-room comedy which opened this year, has vanished without trace and for very good reason, although it did make a star of Marie Tempest. But its otherwise unimportant premiere gives us the opportunity, in the nick of calendar time, to look at the career and significance of the last major dramatist of the turn of the century whose work we have not yet considered.

everything from melodramas through European translations to light comedies. For most of his lifetime he was considered, with Pinero and Bernard Shaw, to be one of the three greatest dramatists writing for the British theatre, which makes his subsequent and almost total disappearance all the more intriguing, especially when you consider that his work gave major starring roles to Beerbohm Tree, Charles Wyndham, Forbes Robertson, George Alexander, Fred and Marion Terry, and Sybil

It was back in November 1882 that Henry Arthur Jones, a commercial traveller who had been trying to get his plays staged since 1869, hit the West End headlines with a hugely successful melodrama called *The Silver King*, all about the plight of a man who wrongly believed himself to be a murderer. Jones was very soon after that linked to the arrival in the British theatre of Henrik Ibsen, not least because it was his own very free and much softened adaptation of *A Doll's House*, the one with the infamous happy ending, which ran successfully all through 1884 as *Breaking a Butterfly*.

What is interesting about Jones is the sheer range of his work between the 1890s and his death in 1929 –

Thorndike. He was sometimes splendidly scandalous, as when his *Michael and his Lost Angel* was withdrawn in 1896 after less than a dozen performances, essentially because of a scene in which a priest, standing before his own altar, makes a public confession of adultery. For the first time since Tom Robertson in the 1860s (see *Trelawny of the Wells*) here was a playwright eager to drag his audiences into a new world and a new sensibility; to reconsider almost everything they held as either dear or sacrosanct. As he wrote in an 1883 letter to *The Times*, "The truth is that audiences want literature and poetry, but they are now tired of unactable, intractable imitations of Shakespeare without his vitality. They want life and

The Playhouse production in 1913

they want reality; they demand that the characters they see on stage should not be the ghostly abstractions of somebody's thoughts, but living, breathing human beings with good, warm, red blood in their veins."

And then, in a paragraph which has lost none of its topicality after more than 100 years, he added, "Drama is today no longer merely an art, but the competitor of circuses, music halls, Madame Tussaud's and the Westminster Aquarium…drama is an uneasy Siamese twin

with two bodies – dramatic art is lean, pinched and starving and has to drag about with it, wherever it goes, its fat, puffy, unwholesome, dropsical brother, popular entertainment…these twain waddle on together in a path leading nowhere; but the demand for truth, for reality, for thought, and for poetry, difficult as it may be to rear, is perennial, constant, assured, and eternally fruitful. Every worthwhile actor, manager, or author has achieved his position in the theatre not by the base idea of catering to every passing appetite of the multitude, but instead by unflagging appeals to the nobler instincts of the few. We must coax, watch, allure and guide, but we must resolutely refuse to pander to the public."

It would be hard to think of any call to dramatic arms from this period, even including the lengthy prefaces of George Bernard Shaw, which goes more directly or timelessly to the heart of the problems of theatre. Sadly, however, none of Jones's plays (always more popular with audiences than critics, even in his own time) have survived into the repertoire of the 20th century except for such brave revivals as a late 1990s *The Case of Rebellious Susan* at the Orange Tree on the London fringe. His two great hits, that one and *The Triumph of the Philistines* (1895), were both comedies of manners which also attacked the prudery and the hypocrisy of the average Victorian when faced with anything remotely Bohemian.

CALENDAR

• Controversial Broadway opening of Eugene Brieux's *Damaged Goods*, first play to deal with venereal disease

• Both of Isadora Duncan's children drown in the Seine

• Barry Jackson opens the Birmingham Repertory Theatre

• Lillian Gish makes her Broadway debut with Mary Pickford in *A Good Little Devil*

• In England, formation of the Critics Circle

• Opening of London's Ambassador's Theatre

• Laurette Taylor breaks the record for continuous performances by an actress when she plays *Peg O' My Heart* for the 600th time

• George Abbott makes Broadway debut in *The Misleading Lady*. His will be the longest career ever sustained on Broadway

• Mrs Patrick Campbell opens long-running revival of Pinero's *The Second Mrs Tanqueray*

BIRTHS

US comedian **Danny Kaye**

British classical stage and screen actor **Anthony Quayle**

Burt Lancaster American film star

William Inge American playwright

British actress **Vivien Leigh,** born Vivien Hartley

American musical comedy star **Mary Martin**

DEATHS

Actor **Herbert Wilson** dies of gunshot wounds sustained on-stage as part of the plot of a Broadway drama

Stanley Houghton Author of HINDLE WAKES

NOTABLE PREMIERES

In London, Shaw's ANDROCLES AND THE LION

First ever London staging of Oscar Wilde's novella A PICTURE OF DORIAN GRAY

Sybil Thorndike stars as JANE CLEGG at the Gaiety, Manchester

The German Kaiser bans both his army and navy from dancing either the tango or the two-step

MUSICAL NOTES

French composer Camille Saint-Saens, 78, gives his farewell concert in Paris

Oscar Hammerstein starts to build an American National Opera Theatre in New York

Opening of Century Opera in New York with production of AIDA

HIT SONGS

You Made Me Love You

Hello, Hello, Who's Your Lady Friend?

Trail of the Lonesome Pine

Danny Boy

Pygmalion

Written in 1912/13, Bernard Shaw's "Romance in Five Acts" has a curious production history, in that it was first seen at the end of 1913 in a German translation at the Hofburg Theatre in Vienna. This production was also seen on Broadway a few weeks before the first British staging with Herbert Beerbohm Tree as Higgins and Mrs Patrick Campbell as Eliza Doolittle.

The two stars had frequently clashed in rehearsal with Shaw himself as an equally belligerent bystander, but from that first night on April 11th 1914, it was clear that here, alongside *Saint Joan* and *Major Barbara*, was to be one of the most triumphant of all Shavian scripts.

Even before the coming of *My Fair Lady* in 1955, there had been three film versions in the 1930s (one German, one Dutch, and the famous Wendy Hiller/Leslie Howard British picture), and of all Shaw's plays this is the one most frequently in worldwide revival.

Why, exactly? As we have noted (see *Hindle Wakes*), there was nothing especially new in the idea of a flower-girl rejecting an upper-class suitor. What was new here was, of course, the relationship between the professor of phonetics and his recalcitrant pupil. The title refers to the classical legend of the sculptor whose statue is brought to sudden life. But there was nothing Greek about the play itself, which took on a number of contemporary concerns – from the increasing independence of women, long a Shaw interest, to the way in which, almost uniquely, the English define class barriers by the way people speak.

Wilfred Hyde-White, Audrey Hepburn and Rex Harrison in the film version of Pygmalion; My Fair Lady, 1955

The survival of *Pygmalion* across almost a century is also to do with its wondrous gallery of supporting characters, from the dustman, Doolittle, forced into middle-class respectability, through the harridan housekeeper, Mrs Pearce, to the languid, ineffably English officer and gentleman, Colonel Pickering to the oily Hungarian rival, Zoltan Karpathy, and Higgins' wise old mother who always knows him best.

Opening only a few months after a suffragette had actually killed herself by throwing herself under a racehorse at Royal Ascot, *Pygmalion* is also a savage attack on the idea of male supremacy. Eliza is carelessly and contemptuously cut off from her family and friends, held more or less captive to satisfy Higgins' and Pickering's gambling instincts, constantly patronised for her humble origins, and ultimately educated to be a lady with, as Higgins admits, no real idea of what will happen then.

Shaw's lifelong indecision about whether, at the last, Eliza should return to the chauvinist Higgins or run away with the amazingly feeble Freddie Eynsford-Hill reflects the conflict at the heart of the play itself. Is this, in the end, a savage social and linguistic satire, or an odd-couple love story in which the central characters overcome frequent hurdles to get together?

It is precisely that tension which keeps *Pygmalion* fresh. Not surprisingly, both the 1938 movie and *My Fair Lady* settle for the happy ending, but there is no sign that Shaw really objected to this. Indeed, he worked on the first English screenplay.

Although now it is Rex Harrison on stage and screen in *My Fair Lady* who dominates all memories of the script, it's important to remember how many leading actors had tackled the central roles without ever having to sing them. Beerbohm Tree and Mrs Campbell were followed by the likes of Gwen Ffrangcon-Davies through Diana Wynyard, Robert Morley, Alec Clunes, Peter O'Toole, Alec McCowan, Diana Rigg, and Leslie and Alan Howard. They all brought something of their own time and character to a play that has a reasonable claim to remaining in the top twenty of the century.

More recent stage productions of the play, notably those starring Alec McCowan and Alan Howard, have gone back to the idea of Higgins as someone fundamentally unlovable and trapped in his own chauvinist misogyny, a reading that would never have worked in a Broadway musical.

It is not difficult to see in *Pygmalion* Shaw's own Cinderella – the girl from the wrong side of the tracks gets to go to the ball and once again slippers are a part of the plot; but although Shaw always claimed that he wrote the play "merely to call attention to the importance of the study of phonetics", it is precisely because *Pygmalion* is about so much more than that, and finally about the importance of being true to yourself, that it finds a new resonance with every staging and for every audience.

CALENDAR

- Sarah Bernhardt receives the Legion of Honour
- US President Woodrow Wilson on Broadway theatregoing:" If you get a bad act at a vaudeville show, you can be reasonably secure that the next one may not be so bad; but from a bad play, there is really no escape"
- Four Marx Brothers make stage debut in Chicago
- Eugene O'Neill announces that rather than be "a mediocre journeyman playwright" he has decided to become "a great artist or nothing"
- American Equity tries to limit the number of British actors working on Broadway
- After the outbreak of World War One, several stars including Elsie Janis demand payment in gold bars because of world currency uncertainties
- Variety warns that American actresses working abroad during the war will inevitably "be stripped of their health, their jewels, their innocence, and even their belief in God"

BIRTHS **Loretta Young** American actress

British stage and screen actor **Alec Guinness**

Dylan Thomas Welsh poet

American movie star **Tyrone Power**

William Gibson Playwright

Revolutionary stage designer **Tanya Moiseiwitsch**

DEATHS Henry Irving's younger son **Lawrence** author of PETER THE GREAT, drowns in St Lawrence River

NOTABLE PREMIERES First London staging of Wagner's PARSIFAL

In New York, WATCH YOUR STEP, the first musical by Irving Berlin, opens at the New Amsterdam

Mrs Patrick Campbell and Philip Merivale open PYGMALION on Broadway

First public performance in London of Ibsen's GHOSTS

MUSICAL NOTES Wagner heritage is presented to the German people in perpetuity

At Drury Lane, a brilliant season of Russian opera and ballet, introducing Chaliapin and the ballerina Karsavina, where Thomas Beecham makes his conducting debut

Holst begins to compose THE PLANETS

HIT SONGS They Wouldn't Believe Me

St Louis Blues

Keep The Home Fires Burning

Love's Own Sweet Song

By The Beautiful Sea

Sister Susie's Sewing Shirts For Soldiers

The Widowing of Mrs Holroyd

Curiously, DH Lawrence, now recognised as one of the major playwrights of this period, had to wait so long for posthumous recognition as such that as late as 1970 he has no entry in the *Oxford Companion to the Theatre*. Two years earlier, in 1968, 38 years after his death, what we now know as the Lawrence Trilogy was first staged at the Royal Court by Peter Gill. So strong were these three plays – *A Collier's Friday Night* (1909), *The Daughter-in-Law* (1912) and *The Widowing of Mrs Holroyd* (1914) – that it seems extraordinary they should have had to wait more than half a century for any kind of attention.

Lawrence himself wrote in 1913 that it was "time for a reaction against Shaw and Galsworthy and Barker and everything Irishy", but the only people who would then have agreed with him were the Manchester School of Annie Horniman's writers and for some reason Lawrence never made contact with them.

As a result, he was remembered only for his novels, *Sons And Lovers* and the scandalous *Lady Chatterley's Lover* and ironically it was the same Royal Court Theatre which led his rediscovery as a playwright that had in 1914 abruptly rejected *The Widowing of Mrs Holroyd*.

When it did finally open 12 years later, *The Times* found it "stagnant and tormented". The story dealt with an eternal triangle – Jack Holroyd is a "tipsy and lawless miner", his wife Lizzie, better educated than her husband and frustrated by their marriage, falls in love with a young electrician but before they can run away together, Holroyd gets killed in a pit disaster which Lizzie decides is a judgement on her intended infidelity.

Like the other two plays in this sequence, *The Widowing of Mrs Holroyd* is about a strong and educated woman who has married beneath her, thus precisely echoing the story of Lawrence's own family – the drunken and violent father and the long-suffering mother who only finds emotional fulfilment in her children and, in particular, the sickly gifted son who was a reflection of Lawrence himself.

The general theory about Lawrence's failure as a playwright in his own lifetime is that although he wrote so specifically about his Nottinghamshire origins, he was spending so much of his adult life abroad that he was never in touch with any coherent theatrical movement; and the irony is that the most famous Lawrence films (*Women In Love* and *Sons and Lovers*) are based not on his dramas but on his stories.

It was Sean O'Casey, who himself knew a thing or two about dominant mothers and violent fathers, writing in 1934 who claimed that "had Lawrence got the encouragement he called for and deserved, England might have had a great dramatist." In the end, we may have got one after all: there's no doubt that the low-level plotting and the 'slice of life' dialogue central to Lawrence was to foreshadow the northern rebellion of the British cinema in the late 1950s. It's also true that in Lawrence, 40 years before *Look Back In Anger*, we see ironing boards and kitchen sinks on the stage as well as a family at war with itself.

When the men bring Holroyd's body back from the mine, they tell his widow that he made no effort to escape from the rockfall. On the one hand, this could be the proof of her earlier complaint that "There's nothing at the bottom of him – no anchor, no roots." On the other hand, did he perhaps welcome his death precisely because she had taken his place at the head of the household, and then planned to leave him for another man? What keeps

Programme of 1926 production

us interested now in Lawrence are not just the power struggles, the class distinctions, and the sense of a brave new world (Mrs Holroyd's husband is a miner but her lover is an electrician at a time when the tradesmen were already taking over from the labourers) but also we never quite know where the author's sympathies really lie.

It would be tempting to draw a direct line from DH Lawrence through Clifford Odets in America to Joan Littlewood at Stratford East, the rise of the workers' theatre movement. Unfortunately, because Lawrence's plays suffered so much neglect for so long, this theory only works with the wisdom of hindsight.

CALENDAR

• Opening of the San Francisco "Universal Exposition" including exhibits from warring European states
• Sarah Bernhardt has her right leg amputated in Bordeaux and is back on stage within months
• Jerome Kern and Guy Bolton invent the "Princess" musicals. They have three new musicals this year, two of them at the Princess Theatre including *Very Good Eddie*
• First appearance of Charlie Chaplin's Little Tramp
• Opening of the Neighborhood Playhouse in NY's Greenwich Village
• Closing of The Little Theatre in London, not to reopen until 1920
• The Broadway season includes 80 dramas, 43 comedies, 21 musicals, two revues, eight operettas, and two Shakespeares
• Formation of the Provincetown Players who became famous for premiering the plays of Eugene O'Neill

• The popularity of the cinema begins to have an impact on the live theatre: in December 1900 there were 392 theatre productions on the road; in the same month this year there a total of 95
• Opening in Baraboo, Wisconsin, of the $100,000 Al Ringling Theatre, an exact copy at one third the size, of the opera theatre at the Palace of Versailles
• Employers of vaudeville performers warned them not to make movies as they are considered "an opposition business"
• Ziegfeld opens the roof of the New Amsterdam as the first ever intimate revue nightclub
• Alexander Woollcott drama critic of the NY Times, banned from Shubert Theatres for hostile reviewing. He gets a court order reversing the ruling
• In London, first German Zeppelin raid halts Laurette Taylor's 1000th performance as *Peg O' My Heart*
• Marion Davis meets William Randolph Hearst backstage while she is playing in Irving Berlin's *Stop! Look! Listen!*
• In London, because of the war, many theatres go over to musical revues and there is a huge increase in the number of French comedies and dramas reflecting Allied interests
• Broadway debut of Ruth Gordon as one of the lost boys in *Peter Pan*
• DW Griffith releases his masterpiece *Birth of a Nation*

BIRTHS
American singer **Frank Sinatra**
Yul Brynner American actor
American comedy star **Patricia Morison**
American actor/director/writer **Orson Welles**
Ingrid Bergman Swedish actress
American playwright **Arthur Miller**
Eli Wallach American actor
French singer **Edith Piaf**
Billie Holliday US blues singer
Hedwig Keisler born in Austria, later the moviestar Hedy Lamarr

DEATHS
Charles Frohman American theatre producer, in the sinking of the Lusitania
Tommaso Salvini the leading Italian actor of the 19th century
American Playwright **Charles Klein** also in the Lusitania

NOTABLE PREMIERES
Maurice Ravel's PIANO TRIO at the Salle Gaveau in Paris
Richard Strauss's ALPINE SYMPHONY
NY premieres of three Bernard Shaw plays on Broadway – MAJOR BARBARA, THE DOCTOR'S DILEMMA and ANDROCLES AND THE LION

MUSICAL NOTES
Toscanini retires from the Met and returns to Italy
Paul Whiteman leaves classical music in order to form his own orchestra to perform syncopation jazz

HIT SONGS
Pack Up Your Troubles in Your Old Kit Bag
Back Home in Tennessee
I Love a Piano

Hobson's Choice

The most successful and long-lasting of all the plays of the Manchester School, Harold Brighouse's *Hobson's Choice* rather surprisingly was premiered in New York in 1915 and only opened in London a year later, having never in fact yet played Manchester, largely because Miss Horniman's company there was now near to collapse.

Brighouse himself was a prolific Manchester dramatist who lived until 1958, though this was his only real success. It tells of the hard-drinking Hobson and his three daughters, one about to get married against her father's wishes, the second dangerously intellectual, and the third, Maggie, an old maid who decides to marry one of her father's workers, the unpromising Willie Mossop.

As in so many Manchester plays of the period, the reversal here is that it is Maggie who takes charge not only of her father but also of young Willie, forming a marital partnership with him which is to revolutionise the shoe business. Old Hobson has always been seen as the "Salford King Lear", rejected at the last by two of his daughters and only saved from madness and death by the third. Indeed, two of the greatest classical actors of the century, Charles Laughton (on stage and screen) and Michael Redgrave (on stage) found some of their best reviews here. The reasons for the survival of *Hobson's Choice* across the century have been neatly summarised by Benedict Nightingale, "It clinches several themes characteristic of the more enlightened British drama of the period. The play chronicles a shift in the balance of power between the generations and between the sexes. Its view is that parents have no prescriptive rights over their offspring, and that heavy fathers must be resisted. It suggests that women, as much as men, must assume responsibility for their destinies and it insists that intelligence, determination, strength of will, and even business acumen can no longer be regarded as male prerogatives."

What also was to ensure the supremacy of *Hobson's Choice* is that quite simply and unlike most other plays of its genre, it is a broad comedy and therefore always inclined to be more audience-friendly than a sombre feminist drama. Audiences of the First War in search of escape from death by Zeppelin warmed to *Hobson's Choice* and its long London run, as surely as did those of the Second World War to *Blithe Spirit*.

Although it is inevitably Charles Laughton in the 1953 film who still dominates the memory of the tyrannical 1880s Lancashire bootmaker, other notable Hobsons since the Second World War have included Donald Wolfit, Leo McKern, and Frank Thornton.

But it is still the 1964 National Theatre staging which predominates. Michael Redgrave as the old North Country Lear with the young Joan Plowright in one of her signature roles as the feisty no-nonsense Maggie with Frank Finlay as the hapless Willie Mossop, a production which also went to Moscow and Berlin in 1965.

CALENDAR

• Two actors with the Abbey Theatre in Dublin are killed in the Easter Rising

• CB Cochran opens St Martin's Theatre

• Columbia University's Varsity Show *The Peace Pirates*, has a cast including Lorenz Hart and Oscar Hammerstein II, who backstage is introduced to a 14-year old Richard Rodgers

• Picasso designs *Parade*, a circus ballet by Jean Cocteau with music by Erik Satie and choreography by Leonide Massine. It was the first musical entertainment to be described as 'surrealisme'

• Prime Minister David Lloyd George rejects petition to have all German music banned from Britain for the duration of the war

• At the end of the season, the Memorial Theatre in Stratford-upon-Avon becomes the wartime home of amateur army productions. It will also house two pageants and a patriotic melodrama but no Shakespeare until 1919

The Funniest Comedy in the World.

"HOBSON'S CHOICE"

from the Apollo and Prince of Wales Theatres, London.

"*Maggie*"

After a drawing of Miss Edyth Goodall, by "Fish."

Edyth Goodall, drawn by 'Fish' in 1916

• Bernard Shaw publishes prefaces to *Androcles* and *Pygmalion*

• Alfred Lunt, 24, makes Broadway debut with Lillie Langtry, 64, in short-lived drama *Ashes*

• On the first night of *The Harp of Life* on Broadway, Lynn Fontanne hears that her fiance Edmund Byrne has been killed in the war. She later marries Alfred Lunt forming one of the enduring partnerships of theatrical history

• Lenin, poet Tristan Tzara and artist Max Ernst all take part together in Zurich amateur theatricals

• James Joyce's semi-autobiographical novel *Portrait of the Artist as a Young Man* is published in NY after being banned in Britain for "blasphemy"

• Variety complains that there is too much "yiddish" in show business

• Fanny Brice, Theda Bara, Ina Claire, Bert Williams, and WC Fields, who speaks on stage for the first time, are all in Ziegfeld Follies

• BM Giroux patents a volcano-painted curtain containing the means to simulate tremors, smoke and landslides

• Pre-figuring the computerised stage lighting of the late 20th century, a device is patented by which intensity of light can be controlled by electrical contacts operated by piano keys

• To commemorate the 300th anniversary of Shakespeare's death, the company from the Memorial Theatre in Stratford present Frank Benson in a matinee performance of *Julius Caesar*, followed by a pageant of Shakespearean characters at Drury Lane. Three days later Benson presents Gladys Cooper, Irene Vanbrugh, and Ellen Terry in a special gala of nine scenes from Shakespeare's plays

BIRTHS

Violinist **Yehudi Menuhin** American-born, long resident in the UK

Playwright/critic/educator **Eric Bentley**

American actress **Irene Worth**

June Hovick later June Havoc, sister of Gypsy Rose Lee

DEATHS

Playwright and novelist **Henry James**

Novelist and sketch-writer **HH Munro** better know as Saki

NOTABLE PREMIERES

Oscar Asche's **CHU CHIN CHOW** at His Majesty's Theatre, London, the greatest theatrical success of WWI, runs 2238 performances

Eugene O'Neill **BOUND EAST**, his New York debut

W Somerset Maugham's **CAROLINE**, a light comedy starring Irene Vanbrugh, opens at the New Theatre. It is to run for 141 performances

MUSICAL NOTES

Hubert Parry composes **JERUSALEM**

Ukeleles and Hawaiian music become hugely popular

George Gershwin publishes first song **WHEN YOU WANT 'EM YOU CAN'T GET 'EM AND WHEN YOU'VE GOT 'EM YOU DON'T WANT 'EM**

Baltimore becomes first city to finance municipal orchestra through taxation

HIT SONGS

Roses of Picardy

If You Were the Only Girl in the World

Pretty Baby

You Belong To Me

Dear Brutus

Most theatre critics cart around with them lists of long-lost plays that they would love to see revived; but whereas most of these turn out to be obscure classics loosely translated from the Hungarian, our list has always been headed by *Dear Brutus*. Apart from the perennial *Peter Pan*, and a rare RSC revival of *Mary Rose* with Mia Farrow at the Aldwych in the late 1960s, the only play of Barrie's to have achieved any kind of permanence is *The Admirable Crichton*. But *Dear Brutus*, written and first staged in 1916, is, it seems to us, of considerably more interest.

The title, which caused considerable confusion at the time since nobody called Brutus is ever referred to in the play, is of course taken from *Julius Caesar*, "The fault, dear Brutus, is not in our stars, but in ourselves that we are underlings." And *Dear Brutus* also owes a considerable debt to *A Midsummer Night's Dream* – there is an enchanted forest, and the character of Lob is unmistakably Shakespeare's Puck grown ancient and the play takes place on Midsummer's Eve.

The reasons why Barrie has fallen so far out of favour are not hard to discern. The more we learned about his private life, the more we discovered that his devotion to young boys was, to say the least, questionable and the fey charm which was his stock-in-trade has become curiously politically incorrect.

Yet there is no doubt that his time-travelling (he lived after all in the same world as HG Wells) was the forerunner of Priestley's 'time' plays and, you could even argue, a certain amount of contemporary science fiction. It is also by no means difficult to trace a direct line from *Dear Brutus* to Ingmar Bergmann's *Smiles Of A Summer Night* and therefore also to Stephen Sondheim's *A Little Night Music*.

All that really happens in *Dear Brutus* is that the magical gnome-like conjuror Lob shows the houseparty guests a glimpse of the alternative life they might have led and proves in so doing that their real-life disappointment and failure comes from their own characters rather than anything which happens to them.

WYNDHAM'S THEATRE.

CHARING CROSS ROAD, W.C.2.

LEICESTER SQUARE Underground Station is next door to this Theatre.

Under the Management of
FRANK CURZON and GERALD du MAURIER.

On Saturday Evening, May 6th, 1922, at 8.30

DEAR BRUTUS

A Comedy, in Three Acts, by
J. M. BARRIE

Mr. Dearth	..	..	..	..	GERALD du MAURIER
Mr. Coade	..	..	..	..	.. NORMAN FORBES
Mr. Purdie	..	..	..	..	.. RONALD SQUIRE
Matey	..	..	..	..	..	ALFRED DRAYTON
Lob	..	..	..	..	..	ARTHUR HATHERTON
Mrs. Dearth	..	..	..	..	MADELINE SEYMOUR
Mrs. Purdie	..	..	..	..	.. MOYNA MACGILL
Mrs. Coade	..	..	..	..	MABEL TERRY LEWIS
Joanna Trout	..	..	..	..	JOYCE CAREY
Lady Caroline Laney	..	..	..	.. AUDRY CARTEN
Margaret	..	..	..	..	..	FAITH CELLI

ACT I.	...	...	...	Lob's House
ACT II.	...	...	...	The Wood
ACT III.	...	...	...	Same as Act I.

MATINEES WEDNESDAY AND SATURDAY AT 2.30.

MUSIC.
ERNEST BUCALOSSI'S STRING QUINTETTE will play the following :—

1. SUITE—" JOYOUS YOUTH "	...	...	...	...	Eric Coates
2. {a. NUMBERS from "CAIRO"	...	...	...	...} Percy Fletcher
{b. "SYLVIA DANCES" from "SYLVAN SCENES"	...	...	...} Percy Fletcher
3. SELECTION—"THE BEGGAR'S OPERA"	...	arranged and composed by Fredk. Austin
4. NEW VALSE	...	...	...	...	Sibelius

Stage Manager	...	...	...	...	...	...	...	W. T. LOVELL
Acting Manager	...	...	...	...	...	...	...	J. E. HOUSTON
General Manager	...	...	...	...	...	...	...	T. B. VAUGHAN

The final stage direction of Act Two is as frightening as any in contemporary drama. Margaret, the imagined daughter of the failed artist who finds his true self in the magic wood, disappears into the darkness: *We begin to lose her in the shadows, and out of the impalpable that is carrying her away she cries in hopeless anguish* "*Daddy, please come back; I don't want to be a might-have-been.*"

That fear of being a might-have-been underlies almost all of Barrie's writing as does the denial that life ever gives you a second chance. As one of the characters in *Dear Brutus* says, "Our lives have nothing to do with

Fate. Fate is something outside us. What really plays the Dickens with us is something in ourselves. Something that makes us go on doing the same sort of foolish things, however many chances we get."

Barrie always called his plays "uncomfortable tales" but *Dear Brutus*, like *Mary Rose*, is really about the redemptive power of the supernatural in everyday life. For a while, after its first triumphant production, it was in regular West End revival, five major productions between 1920 and 1940. After the Second War, changing theatrical times took it off the map and precisely what had most appealed to audiences under threat of imminent wartime death, the idea that time and life itself could somehow be rearranged suddenly ceased to be of much interest in peacetime.

In the original cast was Gerald du Maurier, Barrie's first Captain Hook, and even then many critics recognised a weird connection between Lob and his author – both men were hospitable, observant, mysterious, silent, mildly mischievous, child-like, cunning, strange and different, young and old all at the same time.

Alongside *Chu Chin Chow*, *Dear Brutus* was the greatest stage hit of the First World War, running well into 1919. In 1937, *Dear Brutus* became the first play to be broadcast by the BBC three times in its entirety, on three consecutive nights. As usual, Barrie was technically ahead of his time and emotionally way behind it.

CALENDAR

• Fred and Adele Astaire make their Broadway debut in the revue *Over The Top*
• Eugene O'Neill briefly arrested in Provincetown on the false report that he is a German spy
• A 16-year old Tallulah Bankhead takes up residence at the Algonquin Hotel in NY for $21 a week to try her luck in the New York theatre. She finds work in a non-speaking role on Broadway
• First Pulitzer Prize for Drama is awarded to Jesse Lynch Williams for *Why Marry?* about a New Woman who wants to mate but not marry
• Oscar Hammerstein II abandons the law to follow his father into the theatre
• Two new Broadway theatres open – the Morosco, specially built by the Shuberts to house the work of West Coast producer Oliver Morosco; and The Bijou, smallest theatre on Broadway with only 650 seats which was razed to make way for a hotel in 1982
• Marguerite Zell, a Javanese Broadway dancer, is shot in France as spy Mata Hari
• Shuberts offer to put up in lights outside Winter Garden Theatre, the name of any performer willing to pay them $25 a week for the privilege
• First women directors hired by Hollywood

BIRTHS   Broadway musical comedy star **John Raitt**
Lena Horne American singer
British actor **Donald Pleasance**
Broadway and Hollywood comedian
Ray Walston
Oliver Smith Set designer
Jazz trumpeter **Dizzie Gillespie**
British writer **Anthony Burgess**

DEATHS   Ragtime pioneer composer **Scott Joplin**
Opera composer **Ruggiero Leoncavallo**
Shakespearean and classical actor/manager
Herbert Beerbohm Tree

NOTABLE   Igor Stravinsky's ballet **A SOLDIER'S TALE**
PREMIERES
Otto Hauerbach, whose **KITTY DARLIN'** opens in November, changes his name to Otto Harbach
A hugely popular long-running musical, **THE MAID OF THE MOUNTAINS** with a book by playwright Frederick Lonsdale
Jerome Kern has three musicals on Broadway this year including **OH BOY!**, **LEAVE IT TO JANE** and **MISS 1917**

MUSICAL   As America joins the War, Irving Berlin writes the
NOTES   official naval recruiting song **FOR YOUR COUNTRY AND MY COUNTRY**
In New York the Original Dixieland Jazz Band, an all-white group from New Orleans, takes New York by storm
New York debut of 16-year old violinist Jascha Heifetz
In London, Bechstein Hall, closed as a German concern in 1915 is reopened as the Wigmore Hall
German and Austrian composers deleted from concert programmes

HIT SONGS   Till the Clouds Roll By
Yellow Ribbon
For Me and My Gal
Goodbye-ee
We're Gonna Take the Germ Out of Germany
The Bells of Saint Mary's

Exiles

Completed in 1918, James Joyce's *Exiles* was first staged unsuccessfully in Munich a year later. First productions on Broadway (1925) and in the West End (1926) were equally unsuccessful and it wasn't until Harold Pinter revived the play with John Wood at the Mermaid in 1971 that its true importance became clear.

Not only is *Exiles* the only produced play by the writer of *Finnegan's Wake* and *Ulysses*, it is also the first 20th century psychological drama to challenge Ibsen on his own territory. This is not entirely surprising; as early as 1900 Joyce was lecturing on Ibsen while still a student at University College, Dublin and in the "noble and bare"

living after almost fifty years. It is a play so close to the nature of Pinter's own work that his production of it became an act of homage. The three principal characters, caught in some eerie formation dance, are exiles from home, country, parents, and lovers. Their interlocked relationships form the basis for an exquisitely mannered, intricately cross-fertilised and highly sophisticated conversation piece which Pinter loaded with the pregnant pauses and sombre stares that are part of his own dramatic stock in trade.

To think of James Joyce as the contemporary of Sean O'Casey, which of course he was, is all but

Programme from the Torch Theatre production of 1945

11 SEPTEMBER, 1945

Programme 3d.   (Tel. SLOane 4424)

TORCH THEATRE
(Club under the management of Hilda Maude)

LONDON THEATRE GROUP
IN

"EXILES"
By JAMES JOYCE

Tuesday, September 11th till September 30th

Every Evening (except Monday) at 7. Matinee: Saturday 2.30

style of *An Enemy of the People*, Joyce began to see his own future as a writer. Ironically, however, even the English Players in Zurich, of which Joyce was a founder member, rejected it in favour of Synge's *Riders to the Sea*.

There can be no doubt that the story in *Exiles* is at least partly autobiographical. It concerns two old friends, Robert Hands and Richard Rowan, both fighting for the love of Bertha, just as Joyce himself and Vincent Cosgrave fought for the love of Nora Barnacle.

In 1971 it was easy to see what had inspired Harold Pinter to bring the play back into the land of the

impossible; *Exiles* has about as much relevance to the Irish Troubles of the time as Noël Coward's *Private Lives* has to the worldwide depression in which it was written.

Yet *Exiles* retains its value as a wry, melancholy exploration of the individual's freedom to act for himself, heightened by a plea for the immunity of passion from all social laws which must have amounted to mere blasphemy in its time.

In writing this doctrine of freedom, Joyce sets up an interesting conflict. We are never really told whether Robert gets into bed with Bertha but there is no doubt that the possibility of this excites Richard to the point where (as in *Design for Living* written 15 years later) the two men may be as in love with each other as they both are with Bertha.

So this is a play about the pathology of sex and if you were looking for some kind of historical or political connection then it could just about be argued that Robert, the intellectual, and Richard, the sensualist, represent the two sides of the Irish character which can never be reconciled.

At the last, it is the sensualist who goes into exile but Joyce's constant suggestion that Richard is secretly turned on by the possibility of an affair between Bertha and Robert leads us directly on to Pinter's *Old Times* and *Betrayal*.

The constant surprise of *Exiles* is its cutting-edge modernity, even after eighty years. Rather than the traditional sexual triangle, Joyce puts forward the possibility that three in a bed are better than two and that uncertainty and jealousy can enhance sexual incentives.

Although *Exiles* seems to have fallen off the theatrical map yet again, there's no doubt that it lives on in countless later plays up to and even beyond Peter Nichol's *Passion Play* or Tom Stoppard's *The Real Thing*. As early as 1925, a New York critic noted of it, "*Exiles* is an Ibsen play but for Ibsen's symbols and solutions Joyce substitutes doubts and irresolutions that are typically modern…all the action is psychological and cerebral and the people of the play are exiled from happiness by all their own doubts."

CALENDAR

- All Broadway theatres close throughout February to save coal for the war effort
- Lady Gregory and WB Yeats take charge of the Dublin Abbey Theatre
- In October the 'flu epidemic closes hundreds of theatres across America. Variety reports that the list of entertainers killed by it is at least double those who have died in the war
- Will Rogers says in the *Ziegfeld Follies of 1918*, "England should give Ireland Home Rule but reserve the motion picture rights"
- Creation of Warner Brothers Pictures by Polish immigrant brothers Harry, Albert, Jack and Sam Warner
- Mary Pickford and Charlie Chaplin become first moviestars with $1,000,000 contracts
- Florenz Ziegfeld launches campaign against "unscrupulous brokers and ticket touts"
- In the Court, Carrie Arnstein sues Fanny Brice for alienation of the affections of her husband, Nick
- Federal Government refuses to allow special railway rates for vaudeville artistes
- Establishment of standard Actors' Equity contracts
- With the ending of the War, Variety notes "Weary nation demands happiness and gaiety"; it also notes, however, that the 10% war tax imposed by the Senate on all theatre tickets will not now be lifted
- First George Kaufman comedy *Someone in the House*, stars Lynn Fontanne but due to the 'flu epidemic Kaufman suggests changing the title to *No-one in the House*
- Walter Hampden hailed as greatest American Hamlet since Edwin Booth

BIRTHS Broadway musical star **Robert Preston** **Arthur Laurents** Playwright and director American actress **Beatrice Straight** **Alan Jay Lerner** Lyricist Choreographer **Jerome Rabinowitz,** later **Jerome Robbins**

DEATHS French composer **Claude Debussy** **Edmund Rostand** French writer American Dancer **Vernon Castle** killed in wartime plane crash **Sir George Alexander** former member of Irving's Lyceum Company

NOTABLE PREMIERES Puccini's **IL TRITTICO** Sigmund Romberg's **THE PASSING SHOW** on Broadway

MUSICAL NOTES First recording made of **TIGER RAG** Rachmaninov arrives in the US penniless, having had all his money and property confiscated by the Soviets Fritz Kreisler cancels all engagements sensing deep anti-German feelings

HIT SONGS How I Hate to Get Up in the Morning Mademoiselle From Armentieres A Good Man is Hard to Find After You've Gone Till We Meet Again Oh, Oh, Oh, It's a Lovely War

Heartbreak House

Completed in 1919, Bernard Shaw's *Heartbreak House* which he described as "a fantasia in the Russian manner on English themes", premiered on Broadway in 1920 and in Britain a year later at the Royal Court in London with Shaw himself directing a cast led by Edith Evans.

Since then, of all Shaw's plays, this is the one that has perhaps given the most work to the greatest number of stars. Over the last 80 years it has been played by Cedric Hardwicke, Robert Donat, Deborah Kerr, Roger Livesay, Michael Denison, Dulcie Gray, Judy Campbell, John Clements, Colin Blakeley, Eileen Atkins, Paul Scofield, Vanessa Redgrave, Anna Massey, Anthony Quayle, Rex Harrison and Diana Rigg.

As that roll call might suggest, there are several great roles here but whether or not this is a great play has always been a matter of some debate. Shaw himself always called this his King Lear and certainly in Captain Shotover you can find traces of a mad old man being betrayed by his daughters.

The play is set over a weekend at the family home *Heartbreak House*, in which uninvited guests – among them Shotovers' daughters, a burglar and a millionaire – arrive to form various misalliances, all of which ends in an air-raid. The house is much like the one where Shaw often stayed with Virginia Woolf, and while the plot barely exists, the passion is unmistakable.

The real comparison is to Chekhov's *The Cherry Orchard*. Once again we are in a country house where a leisured world is coming to an abrupt end as the country is overtaken not, in this case, by communist revolution but by a world war. For us, this has however always been a vaguely unsatisfactory play. The cleansing power of holocausts is much akin to the theory that earthquakes do wonders for a bad back and there is often in the first two acts an air of claustrophobic interminability. Shaw's are cut-out characters, infinitely more fragile than the ideas they are on-stage to represent. To drift, Shaw tells us, is the ultimate crime and the Zeppelin has come presumably to punish those who are fiddling while the home fires burn. Paradoxically, the ones who are killed by it are the only ones who did actually have some idea of what they were supposed to be doing with their lives but, then again, that's death for you.

Of all the Shotovers we ever saw, even including Scofield, far and away the best was Rex Harrison who in 1983, after years abroad, came back to the English theatre and his rightful Shavian territory. Sure, he was a little hesitant on the longer speeches, and there were moments when he appeared to be neither coming nor going but merely hovering like some benign Prospero over a British Isle that is still full of noises but somehow no longer very magical.

Yet all of that is a perfect role description of Shotover himself, and when Harrison got himself into the great speech about England ("The Captain is his bunk, drinking bottled ditchwater and the crew is gambling in the forecastle. She will strike and sink and split. Do you think the laws of God will be suspended in favour of England merely because you were born in it?") it was to be reminded with a sudden shock of what an extraordinary talent we have allowed to disappear over the Atlantic for more than 40 years.

But the problem with *Heartbreak House* is that although Shaw seems to have thought he was writing the English *Cherry Orchard*, what he has really come up with is an Edwardian *Hay Fever* in which the true star, apart from Shotover, is the house itself, one where hearts and nations can be broken with equal ease while the inhabitants debate the virtue of selling their souls to the devil in Zanzibar.

This has always been a rambling structure, apparently run up over a wet weekend by an unholy alliance of Ben Travers and Turgenev yet it remains high on the list of frequent Shaw revivals not only for the manic intensity of most of the characters but also for the curious sense we get that even after almost a century we are still watching a work in progress.

One of the other great moments in a random and rambling script is when Shotover tells his son-in-law

Hector to learn his business as an Englishman. "And what," asks Hector, "might my business as an Englishman actually be?" The old sea dog has an immediate reply, "Navigation: learn it and live or leave it and be damned."

For those of us who have never been devoted to the play, the American critic John Mason Brown sums up, "Although genius sails proudly upon the wind-tossed oceans of speech in *Heartbreak House*, it sails on a vessel which is covered with barnacles, burdened with a poorly packed cargo, steered in a haphazard manner, and manned by an unruly crew." Brown was writing of the Mercury Theatre revival in 1938 with Orson Welles as Shotover.

CALENDAR

• Eugene O'Neill wins Pulitzer Prize for *Beyond the Horizon*

• Oscar Hammerstein II's first play, *The Light*, closes after three nights in Springfield, Mass. Forever afterwards he calls it *The Light That Failed*

• In this year, Oscar also writes two songs with Richard Rodgers for a college revue, prefiguring the partnership they revived some years later for *Oklahoma!* in 1943

• Helen Keller and her teacher Annie Sullivan play the Palace Theatre in New York on a bill headed by Sophie Tucker. Variety notes "Miss Keller, who can neither hear nor speak, does an uplifting turn but it is all a bit grisly, especially when she tries to talk"

• Nicky Arnstein, Fanny Brice's husband, imprisoned on a charge of masterminding the plot to steal $5,000,000 in Wall St bonds. Fanny reacts "Nicky couldn't mastermind an electric bulb into its socket"

• The last theatrical boarding house on Broadway is torn down to make room for Loewe's State Cinema

• Four of the best-known names in pictures (Mary Pickford, Douglas Fairbanks, Charlie Chaplin, and director DW Griffiths) team up to form their own studio, known as United Artists

• In Philadelphia, opening of the Dunbar Theatre, first legitimate playhouse to be devoted to black productions for black audiences

• American actress Laurette Taylor is pelted with coins when she opens *One Night in Rome* at London's Garrick Theatre

BIRTHS	American actress **Celeste Holm**
	German-American actress **Uta Hagen**
	Molly Picon leading actress of the New York Yiddish theatre
	Joe Masteroff author of **CABARET**
	Liberace American piano entertainer
DEATHS	**Andrew Carnegie** builder of Carnegie Hall
	Opera singer **Adelina Patti**
	Sir Charles Wyndham actor/theatre manager
NOTABLE PREMIERES	**LA, LA, LUCILLE**, George Gershwin's first full-length musical described by the NY Times as "the incarnation of jazz"
	Diaghilev's Ballets Russes premieres **LA BOUTIQUE FANTASQUE**, a new ballet with music by Rossini and choreography by Massine
	Thomas Dixon, Ku Klux Klan supporter, responds to the victory of Lenin in Russia with **THE RED DAWN**, a play that imagines a Soviet state established on an island just off the coast of California
MUSICAL NOTES	First performance of Elgar's **CELLO CONCERTO**
HIT SONGS	**Don't Dilly-dally on the Way**
	I'm Forever Blowing Bubbles
	Dardanella

The Skin Game

When John Galsworthy died in 1933, loaded with honours including the Nobel Prize for Literature, he left 21 full-length plays and few would have guessed that they were almost all to vanish, leaving only the epic television series of his *Forsyte Saga* novels to ensure his immortality. True, none of the plays are exactly classics, but they are all decent, humane and often gripping.

The Skin Game, which had its premiere in 1920 at St Martin's Theatre and three major revivals before 1935, tells the story of a dispute between two families for a piece of land each is determined to wrest from the other. On the one side are the old-English Hillcrists, landed gentry but now too feeble to preserve their own heritage. On the other side are the Hornblowers, nouveau riches, brash and mercenary, determined to pay the going rate for their place in the sun but enraged by the boorish snobbery of the old squirearchy.

The irony is that the Hillcrists who think they are fighting for the integrity of their England only win through by resorting to the kind of blackmail apparently more characteristic of the Hornblowers. It is a neat twist and the only reason that *The Skin Game* has vanished from the standard repertoire (shamefully the National Theatre has never produced a Galsworthy) is that the class issues it debates were totally outdated by the end of World War Two.

Galsworthy matters because before Somerset Maugham he was the first to hold what Alfred Doolittle in *Pygmalion* calls "middle-class morality" up to microscopic inspection. By the end of *The Skin Game* one woman has lost her unborn baby, another is left a widow, a third is made destitute, and a fourth starves to death, all because of a class system that was not of their making and is often beyond their comprehension.

It was ten years earlier, in *Justice* that Galsworthy had the great triumph, almost unknown to any playwright, of getting prison conditions improved for solitary confinement and, although it cannot be said of *The Skin Game* that it had any similar success in shifting Anglo-Saxon attitudes, Galsworthy remains interesting as a dyed-in-the-wool conservative, increasingly drawn to radical liberal causes. We ignore him at our peril because what he has to tell us about the changing character of the England through which he lived and worked is often more interesting than the insights of more overtly political and fashionable writers.

During the 1920s, Galsworthy wrote a dozen plays, many based on the pride-and-prejudice themes of *The Skin Game* . "All life is a struggle," as Hillcrist tells his daughter, "between people at different stages of development, in different positions, with different amounts of social influence and property. The only thing to do is to have rules of the game and to keep them." But in the closing lines of the play we meet a much wearier and more cynical man, "What is it that gets loose when you begin a fight, and makes you what you think you are not? What blinding evil? Begin as you may, it ends in this skin game…when we began this fight we had clean hands – are they clean now? What is gentility worth if it cannot stand the fire?"

**St Martin's Theatre
in 1920**

CALENDAR

- Mary Pickford finally marries her longterm co-star, business partner and lover, Douglas Fairbanks
- Broadway debut of Frederic March
- Equity members vote for a closed shop
- *Irene* becomes longest-running musical with takings of $900,000 a year
- Yiddish theatre doyen Jacob Adler makes farewell tour as Shylock in *The Merchant of Venice* Although the rest of the cast perform in English, he performs in Yiddish
- Unsuccessful vaudeville comic Walter Winchell writes first Broadway gossip column
- The going rate for screen rights to hit Broadway plays now rises to $100,000
- Silent film star Roscoe "Fatty" Arbuckle arrested on charges of rape and murder
- Charlie Chaplin's wife divorces him on grounds that the name Chaplin "gets on my nerves"
- Edith Wharton awarded Pulitzer Prize for *The Age of Innocence*
- Rudolf Valentino breaks all New York box-office records with his film *Four Horsemen of the Apocalypse*
- Invention of the first portable gramophone
- Author Arthur Conan Doyle of Sherlock Holmes fame unwisely authenticates photographs of fairies at the bottom of a garden in Yorkshire
- In Chelmsford, home of the Marconi Company, opera singer Nellie Melba becomes the first professional performer to be paid to sing on the radio. She received £1000 to sing "Home Sweet Home" on the first advertised wireless broadcast

BIRTHS American composer/lyricist **Bob Merrill Ralph Meeker** American character actor American producer **Alexander Cohen Edward Montgomery Clift** American actor

DEATHS American critic and playwright **William Dean Howells** American actor **James O'Neill**

NOTABLE PREMIERES Provincetown Players bring to New York Eugene O'Neill's drama THE EMPEROR JONES At London's Lyric Hammersmith Nigel Playfair opens a revival of THE BEGGAR'S OPERA by John Gay Marilyn Miller opens in Jerome Kern's SALLY where she sings LOOK FOR THE SILVER LINING Josie Collins opens at Daly's as A SOUTHERN MAID with interpolated songs by Ivor Novello Noël Coward plays the juvenile lead in his own first London comedy I'LL LEAVE IT TO YOU. It closes in five weeks

MUSICAL NOTES Al Jolson writes the Republican campaign song MR HARDING, YOU ARE THE MAN FOR US American premiere of Elgar's ENIGMA VARIATIONS New York Symphony becomes first American orchestra to tour Europe Sibelius' FINLANDIA receives American premiere

HIT SONGS Wyoming Lullaby Avalon Apple Blossom Time Who Ate Napoleons with Josephine when Bonaparte Was Away?

The Circle

William Somerset Maugham (1874-1965), as previously noted, is now chiefly remembered for his short stories and novels. Yet, although his plays have now fallen into theatrical disrepair, it is still important to remember that he was one of the most prolific and successful dramatists of the early century.

Plays like *Lady Frederick*, *Our Betters*, *The Constant Wife*, *The Sacred Flame* and *For Services Rendered* all achieved long London runs, many of them under the management of Gladys Cooper at The Playhouse where, for fifteen years, Maugham was effectively the house dramatist.

The Letter, written for Gladys Cooper, became a triumphant movie first for Jeanne Eagels in 1929 and then again for Bette Davis in 1940, while his short story *Rain* became a vehicle for Gloria Swanson in 1928, Joan Crawford in 1932 and Rita Hayworth in 1953. The actress Sada Thompson, who was born in 1929 and probably named for the leading character Sadie Thompson, later played in an American television version.

In 1908, Maugham had had four hit plays simultaneously in the West End, a feat only matched in later years by Alan Ayckbourn and Noël Coward. His importance is essentially as the bridge from Pinero and Wilde to Coward and Rattigan.

The Haymarket in 1921

The Circle (most recently revived by Rex Harrison on both sides of the Atlantic in the early 1990s) has a double timeframe: a priggish young MP is embarrassed by a reunion between his parents thirty years after his mother has run off with her lover. They all find themselves, including the lover, together for a weekend houseparty at which it becomes clear that the MP's young wife is about to desert him precisely as his mother deserted his father all those years ago.

As a dramatist, Maugham was to become thoroughly chilly. He was always at least as cynical as his leading characters, "I wanted money," he once wrote, "and I wanted fame, so I reflected on the qualities which managers wanted in a play. Sometimes a comedy, for the public wished to laugh; sometimes a drama, for the public liked a thrill; always a little sentiment, for the public liked to feel good; and of course always a happy ending." It was essentially a formula that Maugham invented, not just for himself, but for the playwrights of his time.

Surprisingly, *The Circle* was booed from the gallery on its first night, perhaps because its dramatist had already begun to cut a little too close to the bone. Soon however it became clear that this was to be one of his most successful and revivable dramas – it was twice filmed, in 1925 and in 1930 – but by then Maugham had decided to abandon the theatre altogether.

Writing of Noël Coward (who was to 'out' him savagely in his last play *Song at Twilight* shortly after Maugham's death), Willie had said, "For us English dramatists, the younger generation has assumed the brisk but determined form of Mr. Coward. He knocked at our door with impatient knuckles and then he rattled the handle and then he burst in. After a moment's stupor, we older playwrights welcomed him and retired, with what dignity we could muster, to the shelf which, with a sprightly gesture, he had indicated as our proper place."

Maugham is now very often dismissed, and quite wrongly, as little more than a cynical hack but for a long time he alone seemed to hold the prescription for getting a West End audience up to the intellectual speed of the fringe followers of Ibsen and Shaw. He was unashamedly commercial, but he also had a lot to tell us about the society of his time, one still caught between the end of World War One and the coming of a new world.

Intriguingly, it was only after Coward had written his patriotic epic *Cavalcade* that Maugham bade farewell to the theatre with *For Services Rendered*, a furious counterblast to the 'English virtues' that Coward had been upholding. He may have been by his own definition one of the 'older playwrights' blown away by Coward, but Maugham's last play came as a sharp reminder that the older master still had all his own teeth.

CALENDAR

• Opening of Sardi's restaurant on West 44th St in the theatre district; Vincent Sardi is head waiter, his wife the cook

• Florenz Ziegfeld bans all his contract artists from appearing on radio or making gramophone records

• *Anna Christie* wins Pulitzer Prize for Eugene O'Neill, despite widespread criticism that he has "sold out" by giving it a "happy" ending

• Opening of Lindy's Restaurant, immortalised by Damon Runyon in many of his stories

• Irving Berlin appears in his own Music Box Revue of 1921

• Actress Katharine Cornell marries director Guthrie McClintic at the start of one of the longest theatrical partnerships in American stage history

• Gerald du Maurier opens 400-performance run as the detective Bulldog Drummond

• Robert Atkins, later to found Open Air Theatre in Regent's Park, London, directs ambitious Shakespeare cycle at the Old Vic – by 1923, all 37 plays in the canon will have been performed

• Founding of the Sheffield Repertory Theatre

BIRTHS British actor/playwright **Peter Ustinov**

Yossel Papirofsky later producer and founder of NY's Public Theater, Joseph Papp

Richard Adler American composer of PAJAMA GAME and DAMN YANKEES

Carol Channing American actress

DEATHS Italian tenor **Enrico Caruso**

French farceur **Georges Feydeau**

Sir John Hare one of the first actor-knights, managed both the Royal Court and the Garrick Theatres after starting out with the Bancrofts

NOTABLE PREMIERES Eugene O'Neill premieres ANNA CHRISTIE

LILIOM, the Molnar play on which Rodgers and Hammerstein based CAROUSEL

Henry Ainley stars in Lord Dunsany's IF, early forerunner of the JB Priestley "time" plays

Foundation of THE CO-OPTIMISTS, long-running West End concert party which established stardom of Stanley Holloway among many others

MUSICAL NOTES KATYA KABANOVA by Leos Janacek

British Musicians' Union founded

Prokoviev's THE LOVE OF THREE ORANGES

Sibelius' FIFTH SYMPHONY premieres in London

Founding of Salzburg Music Festival

HIT SONGS Kitten on the Keys

The Fishermen of England

Three O'clock in the Morning

Six Characters in Search of an Author

In February of this year, Pirandello's classic has a one-night London premiere given by the Stage Society – the play cannot be performed in public because it is still banned by the Lord Chamberlain. The morning after its Rome premiere on May 10th 1921, the critic Adriano Tilgher wrote that the evening "really was a battle for all of us, for the author, the public and also for the critics."

Six Characters in Search of an Author is Pirandello's attempt to break down the barriers between playwright, actors and audience by blurring the lines between the performers and the characters they play. Set in a theatre rehearsal room, as a company of actors rehearse a new play, six people – Father, Mother, Step-daughter, Son, and two small, non-speaking Children – interrupt the rehearsal and demand that their story be told instead.

This story, mainly told through the Father and Step-daughter, indicates Pirandello's interest in the way the same situation can be seen by different people, and the ability of drama to illustrate truth better than documentary evidence which can be skewed by choosing one point of view or another. It also examines, from the inside, the process of play-making.

The family explain that Mother has gone to live with another man and borne him children, though whether because of Father's cruelty or because of his love for her is never clarified. Step-daughter regards Father as a debauched old man who has incestuously bought her sexual favours while Mother tries unsuccessfully to win over her Son who feels abandoned by her. While they are occupied in accusing each other of causing the rifts between them, the little girl drowns, the little boy shoots himself, and the Step-daughter flees, leaving the rest of the family locked together in hopelessness.

But it is not the misery of the interlopers' family disasters that raise this play to the level of a classic; it is the skill with which Pirandello breaks down the protective

barriers behind which most playwrights hide. His characters, both the 'real' actors and the plot characters are, after all, all actors, while the 'playwright' has written not only the play we are watching but also the 'play' they are supposed to be rehearsing, as well as the story the characters tell the actors. There is nowhere here for any of them to hide – not behind fiction nor drama nor reality – but a totally exposed exploration of the shifting face of truth.

No wonder the critics of the early twenties, in Italy, in England, in Germany, found it so confusing although, to their credit, they recognised Pirandello's achievement for the breakthrough that it was. "From today we can say that Pirandello is most certainly among

Sir Ralph Richardson in the Mayfair Theatre's opening production in 1963

the leading creators of a new spiritual environment, one of the most deserving precursors of tomorrow's genius, if tomorrow ever comes." And "It was a success imposed by a minority on a bewildered, confused public who were basically trying hard to understand." And "It is neither a play-within-a-play nor yet a play in the making. Rather it is a trial – possibly an indictment – of the modern theatre." And "It clearly required considerable cleverness and Signor Pirandello has shown himself to be endowed with a quite enormous amount of ingenuity."

The most striking element of his work is his love of argument and several critics have referred to him as the dramatist of the question mark. His starting point is always a situation rather than a thesis, and his characters are allowed to explain themselves in often long, always closely reasoned speeches, even when they are insane or pretending to be insane, which allow them to find their own moral or spiritual centre. The audience is allowed merely to eavesdrop on these arguments, never taking sides, until the end when Pirandello invariably leaves us without resolution but still asking many questions for which there are no answers or rather, too many answers.

Luigi Pirandello was an established novelist and short story writer before he began his career as a dramatist. An unhappy childhood gave way to an early marriage to a mentally ill wife he adored and for whom he cared until her death in 1918 when he applied his preoccupation with mental illness in a practical and humorous way to his writing. Later, in 1924, he opened his own theatre and travelled with his own company all over America and Europe, where his plays were performed in Italian with simultaneous translation, often with Pirandello himself giving little 'explanatory' speeches during the act breaks.

His plays, particularly *Six Characters* and *Henry IV*, have never been out of the standard repertoire since their premieres in the early 1920s, although their staging difficulties mean they are almost always undertaken by major companies. Important productions include one by Tyrone Guthrie in New York in 1955 and Michael Rudman's National Theatre staging in 1987.

CALENDAR

• British Broadcasting Company (it was not to become a Corporation for some time) is founded with John Reith as General Manager: first broadcast on station 2LO is on November 14th and includes commercials

• In Hollywood, founding of first Producers' and Distributors' Organisation "to regulate film content and defend the film industry"

• Publication in Paris of James Joyce's *Ulysses*

• Lillian Gish stars in DW Griffith's *Orphans of the Storm*

• The newly-formed Theatre Guild buys American rights in all the plays of George Bernard Shaw

• Variety complains that because of the new and more restrained style of modern acting "Audiences in galleries are utterly unable to hear the mutterings and whisperings on stage"

• Broadway debut of Stella Adler, daughter of Jacob and sister of Luther, first family of Yiddish theatre

• Marriage of Alfred Lunt and Lynn Fontanne

• A Rochester, NY, judge censures Rose Hovick for allowing her 1-year old daughter onto the stage in defiance of the Society for the Prevention of Cruelty to Children. Rose agrees to tone down June's songs and hire her a tutor; the child was June Havoc and Rose is to become the subject of Jule Styne and Stephen Sondheim's 1959 musical *Gypsy*

• Classical Russian actress of the Moscow Art Theatre, Eugenie Leontovich, makes her Broadway debut in *The Russian Revue*

• In London Lord Cromer becomes the Lord Chamberlain, an official position as stage censor which he will hold until 1938 despite frequent calls for abolition. In this year he bans *The Queen's Minister* because it shows Queen Victoria and Lord Melbourne on stage

BIRTHS **Ethel Gumm** later Judy Garland
British classical actor **Paul Scofield**
British actress **Margaret Leighton**
James Nederlander theatre owner
Richard Kiley Broadway actor
Irish actress and director **Siobhan McKenna**
Barbara Bel Geddes American actress, daughter of stage designer Norman Bel Geddes

DEATHS **Marie Lloyd** British music hall star
Comedian-composer **Bert Williams**

NOTABLE PREMIERES **ABIE'S IRISH ROSE** opens record-breaking 2327 performance run on Broadway

John Barrymore opens in the longest-running Broadway **HAMLET** to date – 101 performances

Bernard Shaw's **BACK TO METHUSELAH** in Birmingham, London and New York

John Galsworthy's **LOYALTIES** opens in London and New York

THE LAST WALTZ by Oscar Strauss, first German operetta to succeed in London since outbreak of World War One in 1914

MUSICAL NOTES Vaughan Williams premieres his 3rd **PASTORAL SYMPHONY**

Ravel's **SONATA FOR VIOLIN AND CELLO**

Hindemith's first performance of his opera **ST SUSANNA**

Lehar operetta **FRASQUITA**

HIT SONGS **Limehouse Blues**

I Wish I Could Shimmy Like My Sister Kate

Chicago

Anna Christie

The first great American playwright was born Eugene Gladstone O'Neill in 1888 in New York City. With his mother and older brother, his childhood was spent on the road while his father James (later immortalised in *Long Day's Journey Into Night*) barnstormed the country as *The Count of Monte Cristo*.

James O'Neill was, from all accounts, a fine actor who got trapped by this one role. He saw himself as a classical star who had been sidelined by his own success and his drinking was legendary. His wife Mary, Eugene's mother, became, as does the mother in *Long Day's Journey*, a drug addict, often incoherent and unable to take care of herself or her family. Every member of the family, including O'Neill himself, became either a drug addict or an alcoholic and, fine actor that he was, James' drinking was what most often turned him back to *The Count*, not the success of his classical roles which foundered on his unreliability. The inability of the family to live either with or without one another tortured Eugene all his life.

He did, however, get into Princeton, only to drop out after a year and work in a mail-order catalogue house before spending time prospecting for gold in Honduras. An attack of malaria forced him back to the United States where he joined a theatrical touring company as assistant manager, made a disastrous early marriage and then fled to sea, where he signed on as a seaman on the voyages to South America and South Africa which were to give him the background to all his early work, climaxing in *Anna Christie* where the sea is a crucial image. He gave up sailing to accept a small role in his father's company (since a cut version of *Monte Cristo* was now being performed on vaudeville bills). At this point he tried to commit suicide, having been caught in bed with a prostitute in a failed attempt to create evidence for his first divorce. This was followed by the onset of tuberculosis – he entered a sanatorium and it was there that he began to write plays. His professional career began as the house dramatist of the Provincetown Players in 1916.

Heavily influenced by Ibsen, *Anna Christie* is in effect O'Neill's *Lady from the Sea*. It is set partly in a sailor's saloon where O'Neill always claimed he had himself slept under a whisky barrel. It tells of a young woman who returns to her old seaman father on the brutal NY dockside of 1921, having been away earning her living as a prostitute. She meets and falls in love with the survivor of a shipwreck and her sordid past is finally 'purified' by the sea itself.

It is, essentially, a play about "dat ole devil sea" (as the old sailor constantly repeats) and it speaks vividly and powerfully of the influence of the sea on three very different people – Anna herself, her father, Chris Christopherson, and her lover, Mat Burke. Suitably enough, the play moves in great waves of emotion, from Anna's initial despair, to her elation at reuniting with her much loved father, to her fear that her new lover would discover her wicked past, to her anger with her father's Old Country beliefs.

Its first title was *Chris Christopherson* and the first Anna, in Philadelphia, was Lynn Fontanne. O'Neill, however, then withdrew the play for revisions and it eventually opened in New York and later London with Pauline Lord in the title role and the performance of her career. Later Annas have included Ingrid Bergman, June Havoc, Celeste Holm, Jill Bennett, Liv Ullmann and Natasha Richardson, while the musical version, *New Girl In Town* (1957), starred Gwen Verdon. It ran a full season on Broadway and won the Tony Award for its star.

Between 1915 and 1945 O'Neill was the only American dramatist to achieve international world-class stature; yet there was always a feeling of not-for-profit inaccessibility, and it wasn't really until the celebrated London and Broadway revival of 1993 (Natasha Richardson, Liam Neeson, and Rip Torn as the old seadog) that younger critics really came to terms with this early masterpiece. As Frank Rich noted in the *NY Times*, "Of course O'Neill did not believe that the sea and the fog either cause or cure man's ills. What O'Neill did believe, as Anna puts it, is that 'we're all poor nuts, and things happen, and we just get mixed in wrong'."

When O'Neill won the Nobel Prize in 1936, it was in fact for Literature and there are those who believe that he would always rather have had his plays published than produced. His relationship with the live theatre, starting from his uneasy and unhappy memories of his father's touring company, was always hostile, yet although he never had the intellect of Shaw or even perhaps the poetry of O'Casey, they were his only real rivals. Eugene O'Neill was quite simply the greatest American dramatist of the first half of the century.

CALENDAR

• John Barrymore's *Hamlet* now taking $30,000 a week on Broadway

• Moscow Art Theatre open triumphant first season on Broadway including *Three Sisters*, *The Cherry Orchard* and *The Lower Depths*

• Alfred Lunt and Lynn Fontanne make their Broadway debuts with Laurette Taylor in the long-running *Sweet Nell of Old Drury*

• In Paris, the International Congress of Dancing Masters condemns the foxtrot and the tango

• Paul Robeson has controversial Broadway hit with *All God's Chillun Got Wings*, the story of a black man in love with a white woman

• First show to introduce nudity to Broadway, *Artists and Models* has, according to Variety, attracted long queues of rather elderly men

• Actor Walter Hampden starts longest-ever run of *Cyrano De Bergerac*

• John Barrymore quits Broadway for Hollywood where he seduces the 17-year-old Mary Astor

BIRTHS

Franco Zeffirelli
Italian stage, opera, and screen director

Richard Attenborough
British stage and screen actor/director

Greek/Italian operatic soprano **Maria Callas**

Marcel Marceau French mime

Jewish-American actor **Herschel Bernardi**

Vivian Stapleton later Vivian Blaine

DEATHS

Herbert Standing British actor who founded a dynasty including Sir Guy and John Standing

Sarah Bernhardt greatest French actress of all time. All Paris comes to a halt for her cortege

NOTABLE PREMIERES

Bernard Shaw's SAINT JOAN opens first on Broadway with Winifred Lenihan and then a few weeks later in London with Sybil Thorndike

Frederick Lonsdale's AREN'T WE ALL?, long-running country-house comedy opens in London and New York

Sean O'Casey's THE SHADOW OF A GUNMAN has world premiere at the Abbey Theatre, Dublin

Fred and Adele Astaire open in London in George Gershwin's STOP FLIRTING

MUSICAL NOTES

Darius Millhaud's CREATION DU MONDE

Manuel de Falla's MASTER PEDROS

William Walton's FAÇADE

Robert Mayer founds his children's concerts

HIT SONGS

Parisian Pierrot

Who's Sorry Now?

Farewell Blues

Juno and the Paycock

Sarah Allgood as the original Juno, a part she played on and off for fifteen years

Writing in 1986, the critic Simon Trussler noted, "Sean O'Casey has not been kindly dealt with by the theatre of his native Ireland or his adopted England. His reputation failed to survive the acclaim which greeted his earliest plays, while the critics were never easy with his shift from heightened naturalism to his own highly personal but gregariously generous form of celebratory theatre. He simply could not win. While the Catholic Right condemned him, the Progressives bemoaned his truth to his own vision."

Happily, in the last fifteen years, a lot has changed. In Britain both the National Theatre and the RSC have rediscovered a writer whose work for a very long time only survived in London thanks to Bernard Miles at the Mermaid, while in America the critic Brooks Atkinson, always his greatest supporter, managed to sustain his reputation and thereby interest a younger generation in the work.

Now, of course, that we have had the whole rebirth of Irish drama from Brian Friel to Conor McPherson, O'Casey is bound to seem somewhat dated, given that his Troubles were those of 1916. But, as was proved at the beginning of 2000 by a highly acclaimed new opera based on *The Silver Tassie*, O'Casey lives. Of all his plays, *Juno and the Paycock*, first performed on March 3rd 1924, with Barry Fitzgerald as Boyle, Sara Allgood as Juno and FJ McCormick as Joxer, this is perhaps the most quintessentially characteristic. When it first opened, Yeats told Lady Gregory, the founding patron of the Abbey, that it reminded him of a novel by Dostoevsky, "The trouble is, Willy," she retorted, "that you have never read a novel by Dostoevsky." In fact, although O'Casey himself called it a tragedy, we are often here dealing with a black and bleak comedy.

The story, set in contemporary Dublin, is of the Boyle family – 'Captain' Jack, his wife Juno, and their two children, living in a squalid tenement. The strutting Captain is the Paycock (peacock) of the title, and his hard-drinking sidekick is Joxer Daly. The false report of an inheritance leads them into still worse trouble; the daughter is left pregnant and the son executed for having betrayed the Republican cause. The Captain (and Joxer) react to these reversals with their usual drunken self-pity and, at the last, Juno and their daughter leave him and Dublin in the hope of a new and better life elsewhere.

The Sunday Times critic James Agate once famously described *Juno* as "as much a great tragedy as is *Macbeth*, except this tragedy takes place in the family of the Porter." But there is in fact a great deal more to it than that. Laurence Olivier, directing a National Theatre revival in 1966, noted that the play was closer to Osborne than to Chekhov, "It deals in eternals and there isn't a single character who has not made a turning-point mistake in his or her life…its switchback ride between hilarity and extreme pathos reminds me of an Irish hooley – in the middle of all the fun, somebody gets up and sings a nostalgic song and there is a sudden switch from hilarity to sadness and back again. In that sense, *Juno* is a hooley."

Benedict Nightingale, reviewing a later revival, thought that "Only O'Casey, for whom pain and foible, comedy and tragedy were inseparable, could have composed a play of such bitter hilarity and then left it to lurch and cackle round our skulls."

Sean O'Casey was born in the slums of Dublin in 1880, the son of a father who died when he was six and a mother whose refusal to give in to her circumstances was to characterise Juno and indeed many of his other female characters. Eight of his twelve brothers and sisters failed to survive infancy, and he himself had permanently poor eyesight which kept him out of school.

Largely self-educated, he became a secretary of the 'Irish Citizen Army' in 1913 but was then rounded up by the British too soon to take an active part in the Troubles. He soon came to believe that it was more important to fight Capitalism than the British, and for that reason he was never really adopted by any rebel group, unless of course you count the Abbey Theatre where all three of his major plays were premiered.

But as early as 1926, after a falling-out with the management, he exiled himself first to London and then to Devon, where he lived until his death in 1964. It was as much to do with bad luck as with bad theatrical management that Ireland's two greatest 20th century poetic dramatists, O'Casey and Samuel Beckett, chose to spend more than half their lives abroad.

In recent years it has been the Abbey's own production of *Juno and the Paycock*, directed by Joe Dowling, which has triumphed around the world and it is generally accepted that nothing O'Casey wrote in subsequent exile ever lived up to it.

Years later, O'Casey himself was asked what *Juno* was really about. "It is," he said, "a play about the calamitous Civil War in Ireland, when brother went to war with brother over nothing more than a few insignificant words in a Treaty with England."

CALENDAR

• George Gershwin chooses *Tell Me More* as the new title of his latest musical, the original being too uncommercial. It had been *My Fair Lady*

• Shubert Vaudeville circuit censors the following terms: 'A sock in the puss', 'ladies of the evening', 'hell', 'damn', 'God', 'cock-eyed liar', 'son-of-a-gun', and 'son of a Pollack'

• Dublin's Abbey Theatre becomes the first anywhere in the British Isles to receive a state subsidy from the Irish Free State

• Eugene O'Neill brings his Provincetown Players to New York to premiere Strindberg's *The Spook (Ghost) Sonata*

• A broadcast from New Jersey is heard a record 9000 miles away in Tokyo. Meanwhile, in Britain, the BBC's decision to start broadcasting plays and even musicals comes under threat from West End managements, terrified of losing their live audiences

BIRTHS   Lyricist/composer **Sheldon Harnick**
Colleen Dewhurst American actress
Wolf Mankowitz British author and playwright
Playwright and epic screenwriter **Robert Bolt**
English comedian **Tony Hancock**
American playwright and civil rights activist **James Baldwin**
Betty Perske later film actress Lauren Bacall

DEATHS   Italian opera composer **Giacomo Puccini**
Eleanora Duse great Italian actress
William Archer whose translations of Ibsen were instrumental in launching modern theatre

NOTABLE PREMIERES   Walter Huston opens in O'Neill's DESIRE UNDER THE ELMS at the Greenwich Village Theatre
I'LL SAY SHE IS, the first ostensibly "straight" play to star Herbert, Leonard, Julius, and Arthur Marx
Cole Porter contributes to the GREENWICH VILLAGE FOLLIES OF 1924
Noël Coward stars, directs, and helps to design THE VORTEX, his own play about drugs (probably a code for homosexuality) and mother-love.

MUSICAL NOTES   George Gershwin's RHAPSODY IN BLUE
Leos Janacek's THE CUNNING LITTLE VIXEN
Romberg's operetta THE STUDENT PRINCE

HIT SONGS   It Had to Be You
Fascinating Rhythm
All Alone

Hay Fever

Born just before Christmas 1899, hence the 'Noël', Coward was a boy actor by the age of ten, had made his first silent movie, Griffith's *Hearts of the World* with Lillian and Dorothy Gish by the time he was 16, and by the time he was 21 he had his first, albeit short-lived, play in the West End.

By 1925, he had also established himself as the writer of revue songs and sketches for Gertrude Lawrence and Beatrice Lillie, and in 1924, made his name as the actor, author, director, and partial designer of *The Vortex*, a play about drug-taking (in fact, homosexuality) and maternal obsession, long before even alcoholism was an acceptable stage subject.

This year's *Hay Fever* was to launch his career as a comic playwright. He had the idea for it back in 1921 when, on his first impoverished and unsuccessful visit to America, he had been taken by his childhood friend Lynn Fontanne to a Sunday evening up on Riverside Drive in New York, where the Broadway star Laurette Taylor and her playwright husband Hartley Manners would give nightmarish dinner parties involving the playing of elaborate word games which usually ended in tears.

Back in London, Noël wrote the play in three days as a vehicle for the Grande Dame of her time, Marie Tempest. She, however, speedily declined the work of a still unknown dramatist and it wasn't until 1925, by which time Noël had *The Vortex*, *London Calling* and *Fallen Angels* all playing in the West End, that her agent asked Noël to resubmit *Hay Fever*. "But," he replied, "she didn't care for it three years ago". "I think," said the agent, "you will find that she cares for it very much now." And, with Noël directing, the play opened in the West End in June of this year.

Since then, it has been the mistake of countless amateur dramatic societies and innumerable local theatres to assume that, because *Hay Fever* is a comedy with relatively few characters in one set, it must therefore also be easy to perform. Coward himself, as usual, knew better: "*Hay Fever* is far and away one of the most difficult plays to stage that I have ever

Edith Evans as Judith Bliss in 1964

encountered, but its technical symmetry always appealed to me, and although I wrote the whole thing in less than three days, I enjoyed directing and watching it very much indeed."

So did most of the critics, though already the words "flippant" and "trivial" were recurring with alarming frequency in their Coward reviews, as though somehow other stage comedies of this period were deeper and imbued with all kinds of significance denied by Coward to his audiences. It was as though the brittle, sometimes flash nature of his writing often distracted from the contrast between what his characters said and what they actually meant. Years later, when I was writing his first biography in 1968, both Harold Pinter and John Osborne told me it was Noël who first alerted them to the possibility that an audience could hear something other than what was being spoken on stage.

As John Russell Taylor was to put it: "Coward's comic creations do live as people, and their lives go on behind and under and around what they are saying; the text provides only the faintest guidelines as to what is really happening between people in his plays."

James Agate for *The Sunday Times* was considerably less ecstatic: "There is neither health nor cleanliness about any of Mr Coward's characters, who remain the same vicious babies sprawling upon the floor of their unwholesome creche…Mr Coward is rumoured to write his plays in a flowered dressing-gown and before breakfast; what I want to know is what kind of work he intends to do after breakfast, when he is clothed and in his right mind."

Nevertheless *Hay Fever* was to run on this triumphant first outing for more than a year, though on the Broadway where Laurette Taylor had first inspired it the comedy survived for less than six weeks. It remained frequently in revival in Britain however, and in 1964 Noël was invited by Laurence Olivier and Kenneth Tynan to direct it at the new National Theatre (Old Vic) where he duly became the first dramatist to direct his own work.

The cast of that revival (Edith Evans, Maggie Smith, Derek Jacobi, Lynn Redgrave, Robert Stephens) could, as Noël noted, "have read the Albanian telephone directory with equal success"; but this was the production which spearheaded what Noël himself called "Dad's Renaissance", and turned him almost overnight from an unfashionable tax exile to the grand old man of British theatre.

Major revivals since then have included London stagings with Celia Johnson (1968), Penelope Keith (1983) and Maria Aitken (1992). In 1985, Rosemary Harris brought it back to Broadway in triumph and in the year of Noël's centenary, 1999, Geraldine McEwan briefly starred at the Savoy in a radical reworking of the play by Declan Donnellan which, although it attracted one or two good reviews, seemed to me a travesty of the original.

CALENDAR

• F Scott Fitzgerald publishes *The Great Gatsby* which became a play as early as 1926, a film with Alan Ladd in 1949 and with Robert Redford in 1976, and in 1999, an opera for the Met in New York

• State of Tennessee outlaws the teachings of Darwin on human evolution, later famous trial and play/film *Inherit the Wind*. The prosecuting attorney, William Jennings Bryan, died later this year

• Posthumous publication of Kafka's *The Trial*

• PG Wodehouse publishes *Carry On Jeeves*, later play, film, musical and television series

• Virginia Woolf publishes *Mrs Dalloway*, later acclaimed play and film

• *Porgy*, the novel on which *Porgy and Bess* was based, is published by DuBose Heyward

BIRTHS
American musical star **Elaine Stritch**
Hal Holbrook American actor
New York Magazine drama critic **John Simon**
Peter Sellers British comic actor
American film director **Sam Peckinpah**
Richard Walter Jenkins, later Welsh actor, **Richard Burton**
Peter Brook British director
British actress long resident in America **Angela Lansbury**

DEATHS
American artist **John Singer Sargent**, "the Van Dyck of our age" as Rodin called him
British publisher **Sir Edward Hulton**

NOTABLE PREMIERES
James Joyce's EXILES opens in New York
In the West End Tallulah Bankhead stars in Michael Arlen's controversial THE GREEN HAT
Gladys Cooper opens in Lonsdale's THE LAST OF MRS CHEYNEY, a two-year run at the St James's
George Jessel opens as THE JAZZ SINGER (by Sam Raphaelson), later to become the first talking picture with Al Jolson
West End opening of NO, NO, NANETTE!, long-running American musical

MUSICAL NOTES
Aaron Copland's 1ST (ORGAN) SYMPHONY premiered by Kousevitsky
Alban Berg's opera WOZZECK

HIT SONGS
Tea For Two
Show Me the Way to Go Home
Always
Manhattan

On Approval

Written and premiered on Broadway this year and first staged in the West End in 1927, *On Approval* could be seen as forerunner of the *Private Lives* which, three years later, established the star partnership in adult life of Noël Coward and Gertrude Lawrence.

Here as there, we have an ill-assorted quartet of lovers unable to live apart or together. The rich young Helen has fallen in love with the conceited and penniless Duke of Bristol; meanwhile his friend, Richard, has for twenty years been in love with a bad-tempered, wealthy widow but is too shy to propose.

All four seek refuge in the widow's Scottish country house and after a predictably terrible weekend, the two couples re-align themselves with one of them beating a hasty retreat, leaving the other marooned by the weather and their own ill-temper.

But Frederick Lonsdale as a playwright matters for much more than just his direct and indirect influence on Coward. He was, to some extent, the bridge between the Edwardian and the post-World War One British stage comedy just as his favourite actor, Sir Gerald du Maurier, was the bridge from the barnstorming Victorian Shakespeareans to the new world of understated modern acting in street clothes with cigarette holders.

Born in 1881, Leonard Frederick Lonsdale made his name in the West End by providing the books for countless, mindless musicals (*The King of Cadonia*, *The Balkan Princess*, *The Lady of the Rose*, and, most famously, *The Maid of The Mountains*.)

It came therefore as a considerable shock to critics when, in 1923, Lonsdale had his first great comedy hit, *Aren't we All?*, which was effectively a Wildean 'woman with a past' drama, updated as a light comedy for the age of the flapper. Two years later came an even greater success, *The Last of Mrs Cheyney*, which once again gave us a shady lady – in this case she is an ex-Australian jewel thief who wins the hearts and minds, such as they were, of yet another country-house party.

What was new in *On Approval* was the deep unpleasantness of at least two of its four characters.

This was, as John Russell Taylor has noted, the culmination of the Lonsdalian comedy of rudeness. The refinements of insult and recrimination indulged in by the widow and the Duke are calculated to show that rudeness itself can be funny, but although he was to go on writing until 1950 he never again scored a comparable success, having been rapidly overtaken in the very early 1930s, first by Coward and then, in his more serious mood, by the likes of Emlyn Williams and Terence Rattigan.

It was once said of Lonsdale that he had written of every peer save Southend. Though his women characters often came originally from the wrong side of the tracks, his men were always titled and his wit was almost always of the Earl-and-girl variety.

For this reason, he is now much less often revived than Wilde or Coward, who stood as the two bookends of his playwriting. Most of Lonsdale's plots are both chauvinist and class-based, which has made them 'incorrect' for far too long. By contrast, his near-contemporary Ben Travers was able to enjoy a considerable late-life revival in the 1980s when he was in his 90s and his farces happily suffered no such latter-day constraints.

The loss of Lonsdale has been our loss too, however. If an audience could simply allow for the social mores that he was reflecting and indeed satirising, without making modern moral value judgments, they would rediscover an intensely bright and brittle writer who, through most of the 1920s, kept the flag of high comedy flying.

With Gladys Cooper, and her great partner Gerald du Maurier, Lonsdale formed part of a unique three-cornered West End alliance which may have been rooted more in *The Tatler* and *Country Life* than *The Stage*, but was subtly professional for all that. Among their greatest friends was PG Wodehouse; all but du Maurier had graduated to high comedy from musicals, and all agreed and believed that the name of the game was always to be sheer entertainment, specifically designed to amuse and titillate wealthy upper-class

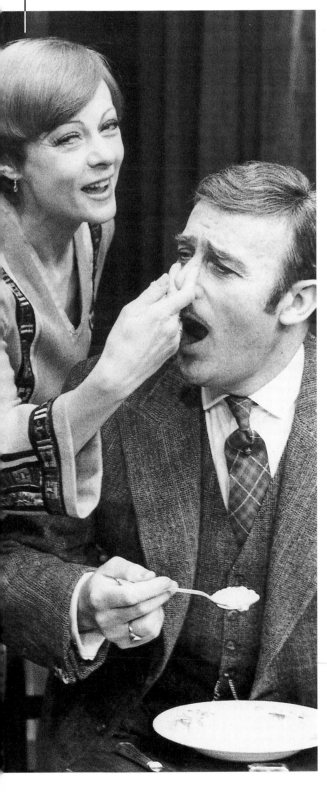

audiences whom they cultivated to the exclusion of nearly all others. Indeed, for some time, they all refused to play Monday nights in the West End on the grounds that nobody who was anybody returned to town from their country houses until Tuesday.

In recent years, Lonsdale revivals have been as hard to find as debutantes or tea-dances. There was, however, a surprisingly successful Joan Collins *The Last of Mrs Cheyney* at Chichester and, in 1984, Rex Harrison and Claudette Colbert opened in an American touring revival of *Aren't We All?* which subsequently played Broadway, the West End, and most of Australia.

The play had not been seen in London since the year of Lonsdale's death, 1954, when it provoked a barrage of abuse from Kenneth Tynan and others complaining about clapped-out drawing room comedies from the Cowardly 1920s.

Yet Lonsdale was a meticulous master craftsman, both in his timing and in the way he constructed characters for certain known players, much after the fashion in which a great tailor still constructs a suit.

CALENDAR

• Tallulah Bankhead takes London by storm in Sidney Howard's Pulitzer Prize-winning *They Knew What They Wanted*

• The Yiddish Art Theatre opens in New York

• Critic John Mason Brown notes the opening in New York of four experimental 'art theatres' where 'the price of one dollar a ticket is no more unusual than the plays that are performed there'

• Lord Chamberlain licences Shaw's *Mrs Warren's Profession* for public performance in the West End only 33 years after it was written

• In the midst of the Irish Troubles, O'Casey *Juno and the Paycock* and his *Shadow of a Gunman* achieve long London runs

BIRTHS　German actor **Klaus Kinski**
British playwriting twins **Peter** and **Anthony Shaffer**
American actor **Fritz Weaver**
Norma Jean Baker later American film star Marilyn Monroe
Gwenyth Evelyn Verdon later Broadway dancer and choreographer Gwen Verdon
American actress **Patricia Neal**

DEATHS　Italian-born American silent film star **Rudolph Valentino** aged 31 suddenly of a ruptured appendix and gastric ulcer
Sir Squire Bancroft one of the last great Victorian actor-managers
Hungarian-born escapologist **Harry Houdini**

NOTABLE PREMIERES　**GENTLEMEN PREFER BLONDES** in New York
Mae West opens in her own play **SEX** on Broadway and is imprisoned for ten days on obscenity charges
Edith Evans opens long London run as Rebecca West in Ibsen's **ROSMERSHOLM**
Noël Coward and subsequently John Gielgud star with Edna Best in Coward's **THE CONSTANT NYMPH**
Sean O'Casey's **THE PLOUGH AND THE STARS** provokes audience riot in Dublin

MUSICAL NOTES　Kodaly's opera **HARY JANOS**
Jelly Roll Morton forms his band, the **RED HOT PEPPERS** and they make first jazz recordings for Victor

HIT SONGS　Bye Bye Blackbird
Someone to Watch Over Me
Do, Do, Do
Clap Yo' Hands

Thark

To the astonishment of critics and audiences alike, the major new West End comedy hit of 1975 was an elegantly risqué bedroom farce by a sprightly young playwright of 89. His name was Ben Travers, and although many were amazed to find that he was still alive, considering that his last major hit had been *Banana Ridge* in 1939, we should not have been as amazed as we were. For although he is still ignored by many theatre reference books, Travers was not only the greatest British farceur of all time (his only ever rival being Feydeau in France), but he was also the founder of an entire school of Aldwych farces which kept London laughing from 1925 until the coming of World War Two.

Ben was, to the theatre, precisely what his contemporary and friend PG Wodehouse was to the comic novel. Both men were expert builders of complex plots which then, like houses of cards, fell unremittingly apart, to the joy of their beholders and the utter confusion of their participants.

Of all the Aldwych farces, this year's *Thark* is perhaps the perfect exemplar. It concerns an aristocrat with a roving eye who picks up a shopgirl and takes her to his country house unaware that his wife is there, and that the house has in fact been sold. Somewhere in Act Two, shotgun at the ready, Sir Hector is also having to deal with a sinister butler called D'eath and a prying Fleet Street reporter. From this wonderful chaos, a happy and romantic ending for all is finally extracted – but not before some of the greatest scenes of farce in all world theatre.

Travers' direct heirs in Britain were, of course, Brian Rix and then Ray Cooney, but although they both had many long-running and hugely profitable hits at the Whitehall and elsewhere, and although they too managed for some time to form resident companies of expert farce players, there is still no doubt that the golden period of British farce was in Ben's late 1920s.

Born in 1886, Travers came from a long line of surgeons, and before he could make any kind of a living as a playwright he took a number of jobs at home and abroad, developing as he did so what was to become his lifelong passion for cricket. He was briefly a publisher and a pilot in the first World War before deciding that what he really wanted most was to be a comic novelist. Three of his great farces, *Rookery Nook*, *A Cuckoo in the Nest*, and *Mischief*, all appeared first as Wodehousian comic novels and it was only really with their disappointing sales that he began to wonder about the possibility of turning them into plays.

At this point, Ben had the great good fortune to meet Tom Walls, a legendary comic actor and passionate race-goer who, with Ben's help, was now able to take over the Aldwych Theatre. There, Ben was to deliver, at the rate of one a year, his four great classics.

His first triumph of *A Cuckoo in the Nest* (1925), was followed by *Rookery Nook* (1926), *Thark* (1927) and *Plunder* (1928). All in all, there would be nine Aldwych farces, and all were written not only for the blustering Tom Walls but also the silly-ass Ralph Lynn and the put-upon grotesque Robertson Hare whose "Oh, calamity!" became one of the first great catchphrases of the century.

There was an absolute formula to Ben's writing and a remorseless, if eccentric kind of logic. Each play would start with somebody outlining a singularly daft plan of action, which would then be followed through relentlessly until, in Act Three, the resulting mass confusion of people and purpose usually had to be resolved by the sudden discovery of some old secret or new character. The timetable was always laid down by Walls and strictly obeyed: they would start rehearsing a new farce every August, play it to capacity through April, set it before primitive film cameras in May, and be free by the beginning of June for Tom to start the flat-racing season where, as an owner and punter, he was always happiest.

Walls often did his own directing, but the miracle of the Aldwych farces was the clockwork

Ralph Lynn and Tom Walls at The Aldwych in 1927

precision of the way he played off Hare and Lynn, each in the same character from plot to plot but increasingly manic as the years went by.

Essentially, the Aldwych farces were what Britain had instead of the Marx Brothers. Travers has never been treated to the respect accorded by the French to Feydeau but, for more than 90 years, he remained wonderfully unembittered. And, of course, very rich. Whenever he sensed that theatrical fashion was against him, he would simply turn out another filmscript or another comic novel. His renaissance, like that of Noël Coward, started at the National Theatre when in 1976 the director Michael Blakemore revived *Plunder*. Ben was then already celebrating his 90th birthday, and watching him raise a glass of illicit champagne from his seat in the stalls to the cast of his 50-year old farce, it was at last evident that our then greatest living comic dramatist had finally come into his own. And not before time.

At this point it became clear that Travers belonged, with Alan Ayckbourn and Noël Coward, to that unique trio of comic dramatists who, unrivalled in their chosen field, had kept British audiences falling about the aisles for the best part of the 20th century – so neatly timed, moreover, that Travers looked after the 1920s, Coward coped with the 1930s and 1940s, and Ayckbourn had become mirth-maker to the 1970s. In the 1950s, we don't seem to have laughed a lot.

In the early 1970s Robert Morley triumphantly revived *Banana Ridge*, and *Thark* became a short-lived but, in my view, enchanting musical called *Popkiss* with Daniel Massey, John Standing and a young Patricia Hodge; it was also due to come into the Savoy from the Lyric Hammersmith in a 1980s revival led by Griff Rhys-Jones when, in a calamity that Robertson Hare and Ben himself would have been the first to recognise, the theatre burned to the ground just before opening night.

CALENDAR

• NY Governer Al Smith signs controversial "padlock" bill allowing police to padlock theatres judged to be staging "dirty" plays

• Alfred Lunt and Lynn Fontanne now earning $1000 a week plus 5% of the box-office

• Monty Woolley resigns as Yale drama professor to go on the stage

• Shuberts ban critic Walter Winchell from all their theatres after hostile reviews; Winchell replies, "If I can't go to their openings, I'll just wait three days and go to their closings"

• Eddie Cantor becomes a blackface star in *Ziegfeld Follies of 1927* which also stars Claire Luce riding on a live ostrich. Cantor closes the show in mid-season, claiming exhaustion and low pay

• In London, French President walks out of *The Garden of Eden*, when Tallulah Bankhead appears on-stage in her underclothes

BIRTHS American playwright **Neil Simon**
Critics **Kenneth Tynan, Clive Barnes, Robert Brustein**
American show dancer and choreographer **Bob Fosse**
American singer/actress **Barbara Cook**

DEATHS Avant garde dancer **Isadora Duncan** killed in the South of France when her scarf becomes entangled with the wheel of the car she is driving and strangles her, shouting to her friends as she went, "Adieu, mes amis, je vais à la gloire"
Florence Mills early black comedienne

NOTABLE PREMIERES **STRIKE UP THE BAND**, Gershwin's anti-war musical, flops on tour
SHOW BOAT by Kern and Hammerstein II, the first through-sung musical opens on Broadway
Rodgers and Hart's **A CONNECTICUT YANKEE AT THE COURT OF KING ARTHUR**
Noël Coward is spat at in the street after catastrophic first night of his **SIROCCO** starring Ivor Novello

MUSICAL NOTES Igor Stravinsky's oratorio **OEDIPUS REX**, libretto by Jean Cocteau
Duke Ellington takes up residency at the Harlem's Cotton Club and becomes famous through his regular broadcasts

HIT SONGS **Among My Souvenirs**
Ain't She Sweet
Sometimes I'm Happy
St James Infirmary Blues

Show Boat

Despite the coming of talking pictures and the imminent Wall St Crash, it is some indication of the health of Broadway that when *Show Boat* first opened on December 27th 1927, there were eight other premieres that night along the Great White Way. Very few critics therefore attended the opening of what is quite unarguably the first great American musical and the one that was to set the standards and define the territory for at least half a century.

Presented by Florenz Ziegfeld at his own new theatre, *Show Boat* had a book and lyrics by Oscar Hammerstein II, based on the best-selling stories by Edna Ferber, and music by Jerome Kern. Unique in many ways, *Show Boat* was in fact the first musical to deal with racial issues. One of its plotlines tells of Miss Julie, a light-skinned black singer passing for white who is drummed out of the Mississippi entertainment steamer when she is found out and finishes up as a drunk in a tavern. Another is about Magnolia, innocent daughter of the *Show Boat*'s owners, who falls in love with a riverboat gambler, Gaylord Ravenal, and leaves with him for a marriage of feast and famine, coming full circle when their daughter becomes a Broadway star.

Hammerstein's brilliance was to take Ferber's loosely connected stories and to build a solid theatrical skeleton on which Kern could hang his all-time classic melodies in songs – "Only Make Believe", "Can't Help Loving Dat Man", "Ol' Man River" – that Hammerstein's lyrics made simultaneously integral to the show and able to stand on their own. Coming as he did from theatrical royalty – his grandfather Oscar had built the Metropolitan Opera, his father William was a producer and manager as was his Uncle Arthur who produced his early attempts at play-and-musical book-writing – Oscar II became convinced that, contrary to prevailing theatrical wisdom, audiences did in fact follow the plots in the musical and that, accordingly, they did matter. For the rest of his life – with Jerome Kern, with Otto Harbach, with Richard Rodgers – he built a firm plot with characters to believe in and ideas which drive them for all his musicals.

He was the first to deal in a mainstream Broadway musical with race (*Show Boat*), first to deal with religion (*Sound of Music*), feminism (*King and I*), poverty and crime (*Carousel*), sexual obsession (*Oklahoma!*), and war (*South Pacific*). His characters were not always young and beautiful but they were never ridiculous because they were middle-aged and older. Cap'n Andy in *Show Boat* and Aunt Ellie in *Oklahoma!* are fully written, fully realised people with

Drury Lane in 1928

opinions and feelings, while Emil in *South Pacific* is the hero, despite being an older man and a foreigner.

But Oscar was wise enough to work with the most melodic of composers who cloaked his radical ideas in accessible songs and to adapt his musicals from first-class plays and books. Edna Ferber's *Show Boat* started life as a serial in a woman's magazine before being published as a novel. Although initially unenthusiastic, she agreed to let the young Oscar Hammerstein and his older, more confident partner try to musicalise her loosely connected stories of life aboard a Mississippi riverboat, plying its theatrical trade in every port along the river.

Despite the fact that Hammerstein had never written a book musical by himself before, he and Kern were so sure of their radical show and how it should be staged that they did it themselves, not even bothering to enlist an experienced director. "What," Oscar asked Jerry while they were casting, "if the soprano can't sing the songs?" "Then," replied Kern with typical terseness, "we'll find one who can."

Ziegfeld as producer may not have understood the seriousness of the text behind the lovely songs but he certainly knew about how to mount a lavish production. The sweep and scope of the score and story was matched by his largesse in scenery and costumes, chorus and principals. There were 36 white chorus girls, 16 white chorus boys, 16 black male singers, 16 black female singers and twelve black female dancers.

They hired the tiny Helen Morgan for Miss Julie (and had to get her out of jail four days into the run when the speakeasy where she was singing after the performance was raided), and Norma Terris for Magnolia, but Joe, whose "Ol' Man River" most people associate for ever with Paul Robeson, was in fact played in the original company by Jules Bledsoe. Robeson had been signed to originate the role but the score took so long to write that he had another commitment and didn't join *Show Boat* until its London opening in May this year, at Drury Lane, where

it played 350 performances with Cedric Hardwicke as Cap'n Andy.

On opening night the audience sat stunned, hardly applauding, rarely laughing. By the first interval, Hammerstein and Kern were depressed and Ziegfeld was hysterical but they needn't have worried. The few critics who were in the audience were ecstatic and the rest quickly beat a path to the door of the Ziegfeld Theatre, "*Show Boat* has many of the finer attributes of musical comedy, operetta, even of revue, with a definite suggestion of legitimate drama" while another critic, Alan Dale, raved, "It never falls into the customary mawkish channels that mistake bathos for pathos." It was an immediate smash and ran for more than 570 performances.

The entire American musical theatre output now divides into two periods – before and after *Show Boat*.

CALENDAR

• American Equity suspends Jeanne Eagels for 18 months for "persistant alcoholism leading to sudden closing of shows"

• Directors Harold Clurman and Lee Strasberg gather a group of out-of-work actors for experimental theatre work

• Lynn Fontanne, starring in Eugene O'Neill's 9-Act *Strange Interlude* in her last appearance without her husband Alfred Lunt, is told by Lunt that if the play had one more Act he would sue for desertion

• Peggy Ashcroft, John Gielgud, Laurence Olivier, Donald Wolfit and Ralph Richardson all now playing minor roles in the West End

• James Cagney makes Broadway debut as a hoofer in *The Grand Street Follies*

• Edward Gordon Craig designs his first American production, an off-Broadway *Macbeth*

BIRTHS

Edward Albee American playwright

American childstar and subsequent Ambassador of the US **Shirley Temple**

Canadian actor **Peter Donat**, nephew of Robert

English born child star and prolific actor/photographer **Roddy McDowall**

DEATHS

Ellen Terry legendary classical actress and longtime partner of Henry Irving

Nora Bayes American classical actress

Playwright **Avery Hopwood**

NOTABLE PREMIERES

In Berlin Bertolt Brecht and Kurt Weill's THE THREEPENNY OPERA

JOURNEY'S END, RC Sheriff's classic all-male drama of life in the trenches of WW1

Jessie Matthews and Sonny Hale sing "A Room with a View" in Noël Coward's revue THIS YEAR OF GRACE

All black cast of BLACKBIRDS OF 1928 includes Bill "Bojangles" Robinson

Paul Robeson is suspended from Equity for refusing to leave the London production of SHOW BOAT

MACHINAL, Sophie Treadwell's existential drama

MUSICAL NOTES

Maurice Ravel's BOLERO

George Gershwin's AN AMERICAN IN PARIS

HIT SONGS

A Room with a View

I Can't Give You Anything but Love, Baby

Ol' Man River

Sonny Boy

There's a Rainbow Round My Shoulder

Rope

Patrick Hamilton (1904-1962) made his name at the age of 24 with this, his first play. Ten years later he was to score again with a 'Victorian' melodrama *Gaslight*. Both plays enjoyed long London and New York runs and both were subsequently filmed more than once.

Yet Hamilton regarded himself essentially as a novelist (*The Midnight Bell*, *Hangover Square* and *The West Pier*) and when he died a chronic alcoholic at the age of 58 he was already all but forgotten. As with his contemporary, Rodney Ackland, it took a concerted campaign of revival and biography to bring them both back to some kind of public awareness during the 1990s.

Like the infinitely more prolific and commercial Norman Collins, Hamilton was the chronicler in fiction of the mean streets of London between the wars. His novels were of seedy urban life, the rootless world of short-stay boarding houses, pubs, Lyons Corner Houses, and people living on pavements, a far more familiar sight now than it was 60 years ago.

Born in Brighton, Hamilton had early theatrical connections in that his sister married Sutton Vane, author of the successful *Outward Bound*. As early as his 17th birthday he was on the road, playing a series of bizarre roles including that of a comic clergyman and a gigantic negro in tours of *The Squaw Man*, a melodrama set in the Wild West and the seedy life of touring melodrama immediately appealed to him.

From there, he went into weekly rep, playing in everything from *The Count of Monte Cristo* to *The Monster*. First and foremost though, he still wanted to be a novelist and, aware that he was in any case never going to make it as an actor, he trained instead as a shorthand typist and went to work in the City.

He had already published several minor novels when he began to write on scraps of paper in pubs and Lyons Corner Houses, the stage thriller that was to make his name. Later, he would oddly always claim that *Rope* had no connection to the real life trial to which it has such an obvious resemblance.

In 1924 19-year old Nathan Leopold and 18-year old Richard Loeb, friends, lovers and students at the University of Chicago, obsessed with the 'Superman' theory of Nietzsche, decided to commit a perfect murder. On May 21st 1924, they kidnapped and killed the young Bobbie Franks, attempting then to extract a ransom from his wealthy parents. The murder was in fact far from perfect. Leopold's spectacles and his typewriter were quickly traced but after a famous courtroom

Ernest Milton and Brian Aherne at the Ambassador's Theatre in 1929

It is arguable that not since Noël Coward's *The Vortex* five years earlier had any young English playwright made a comparable overnight success. For the first and almost the last time in his life Hamilton had fame and money and the taste of genuine success.

Sadly, it was not to last. Hamilton's depressive nature, his closeted sexuality, his general inclination to tear defeat from the jaws of victory, and above all his increasing dependence on alcohol, meant that only once more, for a brief period surrounding the premiere of *Gaslight* in 1938, was he in any sense to enjoy public acclaim or private happiness.

CALENDAR

• Joan Crawford, 23, marries 19-year old Douglas Fairbanks, Jr
• 30 years after his death, the ban on Oscar Wilde's *Salome* is lifted by the Lord Chamberlain
• Opening of the first Malvern Festival with Bernard Shaw, its patron, promising to write new plays for it
• Broadway critic Burns Mantle reports the worst Broadway season in living memory with 50 fewer productions opening than in the previous season
• In London, actors vote in favour of a formalised Equity association
• Actress Helen Hayes marries playwright Charles MacArthur and goes to the promiscuous Tallulah Bankhead for contraceptive advice
• During preview of *Show Girl*, dancer/singer Ruby Keeler forgets her lines. From the audience, her new husband, Al Jolson stands up and sings her next song to remind her
• Variety describes a "dark epidemic" when the talent drain of artistes to Hollywood makes room in New York for several black shows

defence by Clarence Darrow they were spared the electric chair and sentenced instead to life imprisonment.

Hamilton's genius was to make the murder still more macabre. In *Rope*, the killers invite their victim's parents to dinner, solemnly serving them a three-course meal off the trunk that contains their son's body. When the play opened its long London run in March of this year, critics instantly recognised that here was something very new indeed – in fact, the first psychological stage thriller.

BIRTHS

British playwright **John Osborne**
Audrey Hepburn Hollywood star
Belgian theatre singer **Jacques Brel**
Brian Friel Irish playwright
Seymour Kaufman later American theatre composer, Cy Coleman
British classical actress **Joan Plowright**

DEATHS

Serge Diaghilev Russian impresario and founder of the Balles Russes de Monte Carlo
Lillie Langtry mistress of King Edward VII, who made her stage debut with the Bancrofts in 1881

NOTABLE PREMIERES

Bernard Shaw's **THE APPLE CART**, a political extravaganza, opens year-long run in London with Edith Evans and Cedric Hardwicke
HOT CHOCOLATES, an all-black revue which contains a new song by Fats Waller, played and sung by the young Louis Armstrong: **AIN'T MISBEHAVIN'**
Cole Porter has hits simultaneously on Broadway (**FIFTY MILLION FRENCHMEN**) and in the West End (**WAKE UP AND DREAM**)
Laurence Olivier makes Broadway debut in **MURDER ON THE 2ND FLOOR**

MUSICAL NOTES

Hindemith's opera **NEWS OF THE DAY**
Constant Lambert's **RIO GRANDE**

HIT SONGS

Tiptoe Through the Tulips
Stardust
Button Up Your Overcoat
Ain't Misbehavin'
I'll See You Again

Private Lives

The play that more than any other represents Noël Coward's greatest claim to theatrical permanence is on one level the lightest of his light comedies. *Private Lives* has a symmetry and durability that have assured it near-constant production in one language or another from the time of its first production in 1930 to the present day, arguably the best light comedy of appalling manners to have been written in England in the first half of the 20th century.

Despite the critics' predictions, at its opening at the Phoenix Theatre on 24th September 1930, that it would survive only as long as Gertrude Lawrence and Noël Coward starred in it, *Private Lives* has far outlived its original production, one which Noël himself directed, becoming instead a copper-bottomed sure-fire hit wherever it plays, sometime solely responsible for restoring the fortunes of impoverished theatres who have made a last-ditch effort by putting it on.

Its very frothiness belies its serious subject – that of a couple who can neither live together nor apart – and the success of the entire venture rests on how well the two leading actors can play the emotions that lurk just below the lines on the page. The dialogue itself is crisp, minimalist, and intended more to mask than to expose the essence of the play.

Amanda and Elyot are rich thirtysomethings, divorced from one another and just re-married to other partners. They meet, by accident, on adjoining terraces of a hotel in Deauville where both have gone to begin their second honeymoons. Within seconds of meeting, it becomes clear that they have both made mistakes in choosing their new spouses, indeed, that they are still in love and should never have divorced. In this, the second most famous balcony scene in all dramatic literature, Coward provides the audience with the conundrum common to nearly all his plays and, of course, also to his life; that of the impossibility of living with another human being, an impossibility second only to that of living without one.

The roots of *Private Lives* are in a quite different Coward play; Noël had originally planned his operetta *Bitter Sweet* for his childhood friend Gertrude Lawrence but, as it developed, it became clear that the score was too difficult for her to sing. Having promised her a play, he had to write it and, after wrestling with many different themes and periods, one sleepless night in a hotel bedroom in Tokyo, as he wrote in his diary, "as soon as I switched out the lights, Gertie appeared in a white Molyneux dress on a terrace in the South of France (sic) and refused to go away until 4am by which time *Private Lives*, title and all, had constructed itself." He wrote the play in four days and "It came easily, and with the exception of a few 'blood and tears' moments, I enjoyed writing it."

His own judgment is still the one that counts, "I thought it a shrewd and witty comedy, well constructed on the whole but psychologically unstable; however its entertainment value seemed obvious enough, and its acting opportunities for Gertie and me admirable." But his delight in acting in it did not obscure his awareness of its technical problems, "There is a well-written love scene in Act One, and a certain amount of sound sex psychology underlying the quarrel scenes in Act Two. As a complete play it leaves a lot to be desired…to begin with, there is no further plot and no further action after Act One, with the exception of the rough-and-tumble at the curtain of Act Two. Taken all in all *Private Lives* was more tricky and full of pitfalls than anything I ever attempted as an actor. But fortunately for me I had the inestimable advantage of playing it with Gertrude Lawrence and so three quarters of the battle was won before the curtain went up."

Noël's valet, secretary, manager, friend, and posthumous biographer, Cole Lesley, described them on stage together in *Private Lives*, "Gertie and Noël looked so beautiful together standing in the moonlight that no one who saw them can ever forget; and they played the balcony scene so magically, lightly, tenderly that one was for those fleeting moments brought near to tears by the underlying vulnerability, the evanescence of their love." Noël said later, "Sometimes I would look across the stage at Gertie and she would simply take my breath away."

The critics didn't entirely see it that way. They called it "brittle", "tenuous" and "thin", and Allardyce Nicholl wrote that it was "an amusing play, no doubt,

yet hardly moving further below the surface than a paper boat in a bathtub and, like the paper boat, ever in imminent danger of becoming a shapeless, sodden mess." The *Daily Telegraph* worried that, "They smash gramophone records over each other's heads and roll on the floor still thumping, kicking, possibly biting. Do people of apparent breeding really do these things?" For some years no actors dared risk comparison with Noël and Gertie but once revivals began, one followed hard on the other. Noël himself didn't help it along by declaring, "The part was written for Gertie and, as I conceived and wrote it, I can say with authority that no other actress in the world ever could or ever will come within a mile of her performance of it."

In 1999, the year of Coward's centennial, *Private Lives* was the Royal National Theatre's flagship production. "Legitimate at last," Noël might have said of this worthy but slightly dull Juliet Stevenson/Anton Lesser revival, "won't Mother be pleased?"

CALENDAR

• John Gielgud moves his triumphant *Hamlet* from the Old Vic to the Queens Theatre, Shaftesbury Ave. In the cast are Donald Wolfit and Martita Hunt. In this same year, Gielgud plays Marc Antony in *Julius Caesar*, Orlando in *As You Like It*, *Macbeth*, Antony in *Antony and Cleopatra*, and John Worthing in *The Importance of Being Earnest*. He is just 26

• There are several other Hamlets in London this year, those of Henry Ainley, Esme Percy, Gerald Lawrence, and the German, Alexander Moissi

• Paul Robeson's first London *Othello* – Peggy Ashcroft is Desdemona, Sybil Thorndike is Amelia and Ralph Richardson is Roderigo

• Broadway debut of Jessica Tandy

• Tennessee Williams writes first play *Beauty is the Word* while student at University of Missouri

BIRTHS **Harold Pinter** British playwright and actor

American composer/lyricist **Stephen Sondheim**

British director, founder of the Royal Shakespeare Company **Peter Hall**

American playwright **Albert Ramsdell (AR) Gurney**

DEATHS **DH Lawrence** playwright/novelist

Early English musical star **Marie Studholm**

Broadway producer **David Belasco** who leaves, among much else, a large library of pornography

NOTABLE PREMIERES **THE BARRETTS OF WIMPOLE ST**, long-running drama about the romance between poets Robert Browning and Elizabeth Barrett

Jessie Matthews and Sonnie Hale dance on the ceiling in Rodgers and Hart's **EVER GREEN**

Charles Laughton as the Chicago gangster in Edgar Wallace's **ON THE SPOT**

MUSICAL NOTES Stravinsky's **SYMPHONY OF PSALMS**

Kurt Weill's opera **THE RISE AND FALL OF THE CITY OF MAHAGONNY** opens in Berlin

Conductor Adrian Boult becomes the BBC's first Music Director

HIT SONGS On the Sunny Side of the Street

The King's Horses

Embraceable You

Biding My Time

But Not For Me

Of Thee I Sing

The first musical ever to win the Pulitzer Prize for Drama was also the first hit to use political satire in any serious way. The Gershwin brothers had now been working together for more than ten years and they had already collaborated with George Kaufman on *Strike Up the Band*, which had not been an entirely happy experience. In 1927, just before the Depression, a bitter satirical spoof on war, big business and politics proved too much for the public to take and it had closed during out-of-town tryouts. But in 1930, when Kaufman's book had been replaced by a far sweeter one by Maury Ryskind (a regular Marx Brothers writer) about battles over chocolate, the show did finally make it to Broadway where it survived 190 performances.

Inspired by that success, the Gershwins now brought Kaufman and Ryskind together for *Of Thee I Sing*, although ironically only they and Ira won the Pulitzer, not George. It wasn't until *Oklahoma!*, twelve years later, that the Pulitzer committee agreed to recognise a composer.

Kaufman and Ryskind wrote the book for *Of Thee I Sing* in just 17 days and it didn't take the Gershwins much longer to complete the score which then became the longest running book musical of the entire 1930s – 441 performances.

The story told of the Presidential campaign for John P Wintergreen of the "National Party". His problem is the absence of any kind of a platform and his party is less than popular in the polls, having just sold Rhode Island to a private company. Eventually, it is decided that the only hope for an election victory is to run Wintergreen on the Love ticket "the only one everybody is interested in and that doesn't matter a damn." It is decided that the Party will sponsor an Atlantic City beauty contest and that Wintergreen will marry the winner. Unfortunately, he has just proposed marriage to his secretary, Mary Turner, and she replaces the winner, one Diana Devereaux, who duly charges the President Elect with breach of promise. By the end of the show, Wintergreen is threatened with impeachment and only rescued by the arrival of twins, delivered by Mary in the nick of time.

What is interesting about the success that the Gershwins had with *Of Thee I Sing*, their greatest to date, was that it opened in the midst of the worst Depression the country had ever known and yet audiences were won over by its sheer good-natured, brilliance. As the *New York Times* wrote, "*Of Thee I Sing* is gold-flecked with virtuoso cleverness in all its departments and a caustic courage in its tune and talk. Yet it remains all the while somehow warm-hearted and

George Gershwin

gallant, free from any savagery or crankiness. We first-nighters were in at the liberation of musical comedy from the usual twaddle and treacle."

Although *Of Thee I Sing* was to disappear for almost half a century, overtaken by the greater historical impact of *Porgy and Bess* only four years later, when it re-emerged in concert performances we suddenly realised what we had been missing. The book may be softened by the charm and ingenuousness of John and Mary and their hopelessly befuddled Vice President Alexander Throttlebottom; the show is actually a savage parody of the ineffectuality and insularity of the current Herbert Hoover Administration. More importantly still, this was the first score in which the Gershwins set entire scenes to music, thereby creating a modern comic opera in a popular idiom. Not only the title song but also numbers like "Who Cares", "Love is Sweeping the Country" and "A Kiss for Cinderella", are among the most lyrical and enchanting that even the Gershwins ever wrote.

Of Thee I Sing is the bridge from *Show Boat* to *Porgy and Bess* but it is also the first book show of intelligence and rapier wit. In that sense, it points forward to Sondheim as well as back to its most obvious inspiration, the political satires of Ira's beloved Gilbert and Sullivan.

From the very opening couplet, "He's the man the people choose; loves the Irish and the Jews," audiences knew that lyrically *Of Thee I Sing* was to be way ahead of anything they had ever heard before and when it won its Pulitzer Prize a few months later, one of the judges noted that the show "so revolutionises the concept of musical comedy that the award is given in hope as well as in hooray."

So confident was George that *Of Thee I Sing* would be a hit that he insisted on lending his brother Ira $2500 so he could invest in the show – an investment which paid Ira back 500%. It was George Jean Nathan who first recognised the show as "a

landmark in American satirical musical comedy… whether it is satire, wit, doggerel or fantasy, Mr Gershwin pours music out in full measure and many voices – he has not only ideas but enthusiasm. This is the best topical travesty our musical stage has ever created – it has the depth of artistry and the glow and pathos of comedy."

And as George himself said, "This was one of those rare shows in which everything clicked and I am more proud of it than of anything else I have ever written."

CALENDAR

• When Charlie Chaplin visits his native England on holiday he is mobbed by rapturous fans
• At the Old Vic, Gielgud plays *King Lear*, Benedick in *Much Ado About Nothing*, and Inigo Jollifant in *The Good Companions*. He also plays Malvolio in *Twelfth Night* to the Toby Belch of Ralph Richardson at the start of a lifelong professional partnership
• Jack Buchanan and Elsie Randolph start their 30s partnership with *Stand Up and Sing* in the West End
• First TV broadcasts in the USA
• In Britain, first televised Derby
• Lillian Baylis of the Old Vic reopens Sadlers Wells as home for opera and ballet. Ninette de Valois' company, the Vic-Wells, later to become the Royal Ballet, transfers to the Wells as first resident ballet
• Bob Hope makes Palace debut in New York, as supporting act to Bea Lillie
• Roosevelt amends obscenity laws which now will hold responsible only playwrights and producers and not the cast or crew
• Final edition of *Ziegfeld's Follies*
• Founding of radical Group Theatre

Dangerous Corner

John Boynton Priestley (1894-1984) has fallen into the traditional limbo which seems to follow the death of most major writers. When his reputation eventually comes back, the chances are that he will be recalled as a novelist and historian rather than as a playwright. And yet, from his first adaptation of his own *The Good Companions* in 1931 through to 1955, he was to write more than 20 plays, among them the 1945 *An Inspector Calls* which throughout the 1990s had a long and triumphant West End revival in a radical new staging by Stephen Daldry.

This was the last in a sequence of "time" plays which started with *Dangerous Corner* (1932) and continued through *Time and the Conways* to *I Have Been Here Before* (both 1937). In all of these he drew on the philosophers Dunne and Ouspensky who had come up with revolutionary new theories about the nature of time itself. These Priestley plays were all an attempt to revitalise the old drawing-room drama by creating an alternative timeframe in which something strange and intangible would invade the cosy realism of the old form.

Sometimes, it was a "dangerous corner" in conversation which is crashed the first time but safely passes the second. Sometimes, it is the feeling that some things that happen for the first time seem to be happening again, and of course it is in *An Inspector Calls* that somebody from another world entirely brings home truths to those in the home who simply cannot bear to hear them.

In *Dangerous Corner*, an elegant family gathering is brought up against the reality of a suicide. After much discussion and revelation, it turns out to have been no suicide at all – the man was accidentally shot when, drug-crazed, he attempts to rape his mistress and they struggle with a gun. This last revelation leads to another death in the family but the play ends as it began, only this time the conversation takes a different turn and no revelations ensue.

Priestley's writing was the first serious attempt to deal with the problem of realism in 1930s theatre. Alongside his (equally now neglected) contemporary Emlyn Williams, he tried to take the conventional whodunit and give it a new psychological twist.

But Priestley's most successful play was the 1938 traditional North Country farce *When We are*

Flora Robson, William Fox, Richard Bird and Marie Ney at the Lyric in 1932

Married and one of his most interesting was the totally expressionistic *Johnson Over Jordan* which starred his lifelong friend and leading man, Ralph Richardson. His post-war plays were much less successful and often had to be financed from his earnings as a novelist. Yet he remained essentially a man of the theatre, was a familiar pipe-smoking radio and television pundit in the years surrounding World War Two and was also first President of the International Television Institute.

Apart from Shakespeare, he was the only British dramatist whose work was regularly performed in the Soviet Union in the 1930s and 1940s and, while his books were reasonably traditional, his plays tried with some success to push back the barriers of what an audience would accept. Priestley at his best always challenged their intelligence and their imagination at a time when precious few other writers were daring to do so.

His problem was twofold – critics distrusted his great commercial success as a novelist and found it hard to focus on a dramatist who delivered everything from music-hall nostalgia to time-shifting fantasy, overtly political diatribes and farce.

Jack Priestley was a jack of all literary and dramatic trades and many of his plays were simply ahead of their time. In playing with the nature of time itself he foreshadowed by twenty or thirty years the whole range of Hollywood science-fiction but characteristically he was never really interested in movies despite the fact that in a long and prolific career, he wrote screenplays for Gracie Fields (*Let The People Sing*) and a savage memoir of unhappiness in Hollywood (*Midnight on the Desert*).

CALENDAR

• The British actors union, Equity votes to operate a closed shop as of the beginning of next year

• Publication to great acclaim of Aldous Huxley's futuristic novel *Brave New World*, later play and film. Rebecca West describes it as "one of the half-dozen most important books published since the War"

• Opening of the new Shakespeare Memorial Theatre, following the fire which burned it to the ground

• John Galsworthy wins the Nobel Prize for Literature

• Laurel and Hardy embark upon a nationwide tour of Britain and receive rapturous receptions wherever they go

• Publications of Graham Greene's thriller *Stamboul Train*; Evelyn Waugh's satire *Black Mischief*

• Compton Mackenzie's war memoir, *Greek Memories* is suppressed under the Official Secrets Act for revealing the name of the head of the British Secret Service

• Lillian Gish stars in *Camille* at the re-opening of the restored Central City Opera House in Colorado

• In America, founding by the playwright and director, Rachel Crothers of the Stage Relief Fund. It has raised $58,000 to provide support for 6000 out of work actors

• The cinema has a new star in 4-year old Shirley Temple, later US Ambassador Shirley Temple Black The curly-headed tot stars in *Red Haired Alibi*

• A campaign is launched by the Broadway Association to clean up the garishness of Times Square

BIRTHS

Actress and moviestar **Elizabeth Taylor**

British farce writer **Ray Cooney**

Mary Francis Reynolds, later American singer/dancer/actress Debbie Reynolds

British playwright **Arnold Wesker**

Peter O'Toole, Irish stage and screen star

South African playwright **Athol Fugard**

DEATHS

Florenz Ziegfeld, creator of the FOLLIES and father of spectacular variety shows on Broadway

American "March King" **John Philip Sousa**

NOTABLE PREMIERES

WORDS AND MUSIC, Noël Coward revue at the Adelphi in which the songs "Mad Dogs and Englishmen" and "Mad About the Boy" made their first appearance

Kern and Hammerstein's MUSIC IN THE AIR starring Walter Slezak opens at the Alvin

John Gielgud directs Jean Forbes-Robertson and Robert Harris in STRANGE ORCHESTRA by Rodney Ackland at the St Martin's Theatre

MUSICAL NOTES

Gershwin's CUBAN OVERTURE makes its first appearance

Louis Armstrong, American trumpeter, makes his UK debut at the London Palladium

HIT SONGS

Brother, Can You Spare a Dime?

I'm Getting Sentimental Over You

The Sun Has Got His Hat On

Love is the Sweetest Thing

42nd Street

A Sleeping Clergyman

In the long list of 'lost playwrights' of the mid-20th century, James Bridie stands out as one of the most quirkily interesting. Though influenced by Ibsen and Shaw, he comes from no known playwriting tradition and he left behind him few disciples; yet for 20 years, from his first great 1930 hit *The Anatomist* through *Mr Bolfry* to one of his last, *Daphne Laureola* (one of Edith Evans greatest West End and Broadway hits in 1949), Bridie was one of the most prolific and successful of all Scots dramatists, having really come second in that league only to JM Barrie.

Quite apart from his importance as an often experimental and groundbreaking dramatist, Bridie was for many years the most important theatrical force in Scotland, encouraging and often producing younger dramatists. Still largely unknown in America, and never interested in the movies that might have made his fame international, Bridie, the son of an engineer, was born Osborne Henry Mavor in 1888. Like W Somerset Maugham, he qualified as a doctor and is perhaps now most notably recalled as the co-founder in 1943 of the original Glasgow Citizens Theatre. A puritan academic, it is unlikely that he would entirely have approved of what is now known as the Glasgow Citz, but the enduring success of that radical theatre in the Gorbals undoubtedly owes a great deal to his pioneering work. He was the first Scots writer to adopt the 'Play of Ideas', and in 1950 he was also the founder of the College of Drama in the Royal Scottish Academy of Music. He was also the dramatist and occasional producer who came closest to establishing the long-held but apparently impossible dream of a truly self-standing Scottish National Theatre.

Many of Bridie's plays seem now to suffer from very loose construction and feeble endings but as he himself once noted, "Only God can write last acts, and even He seldom does."

After *The Anatomist* came *Tobias and the Angel* (1931) and *Jonah and the Whale* (1932) both, as those titles would suggest, variations on familiar biblical themes; but *A Sleeping Clergyman* came as something of a surprise.

Until now, Bridie had written alternately about God and Science. This time, in adapting the parable of the Wheat and the Tares, he tried to combine his two themes. "I showed," he wrote later, "a wild horse after three incarnations finally harnessing itself to the world for the world's sake. God, who sets the whole play going, then takes his ease in an armchair for the rest of the evening. The odd quality of my play was apparent in rehearsal where even the electricians, stagehands, wardrobe ladies and charwomen seemed to find it interesting. I am even told that some of them wept."

The first scene of the play has a drunken blackguardly tubercular genius dying in filthy Glasgow lodgings in 1867, as his landlady starts one of the most dramatic speeches in any play of its time, "Out you go tomorrow morning. And you'll pay for the carpet, and the clock you broke, and the holes in the mantelshelf which you burned with your pipe, and the anti-macassar that you tore. Oh yes, you'll pay. And you needna pretend to be asleep. You know as well as I do...as I do...Jesus, Mary and Joseph, he is dead."

As all too often, Bridie never quite managed to live up to that splendidly melodramatic beginning, but he was nothing if not aware of the importance of sheer theatricality. He was also more than a little prophetic. His anti-fascist play *The King of Nowhere* seen at the Old Vic five years later, starred the young Olivier as a dangerously mad actor who escapes from an asylum to lead a threatening new political party.

Bridie also often made tremendous demands on his stage management; for *Jonah and the Whale* Jonah himself had to be seen sitting cross-legged in the belly of the whale on-stage while in a remarkable pre-cursor of stereophonic sound, Bridie asked for twelve loudspeakers around the auditorium. The stage direction for all this reads, "The audience is to be deafened by the bellowing noise and hypnotised by a small, impassive, red-lit figure on the stage."

Robert Donat at the Piccadilly in 1933

Of all the actors associated with Bridie, it was to be his great friend Alastair Sim, in a revival of *The Anatomist*, who best represented the mix of traditional schoolmaster and manic inventor that often summarised Bridie's style. Bridie wrote a play almost every year right up to his death in 1951 and his son, Ronald Mavor, also became a playwright, now best known for his 1973 *A Private Matter* which deals with an author writing a biography against the wishes of his subject's

family. This production was also one of the very first ever to feature full male nudity on-stage, something of which the playwright's father would probably have disapproved.

The way in which Bridie has now virtually disappeared from the English stage, while still frequently revived in Scotland, unfairly suggests that he was only a local dramatist. In fact, he was one of the very first writers to try to harness science, radical religion, and other relatively new 20th century intellectual concepts to the older traditions of drama.

His 1949 play *John Knox*, in some ways a re-write of *The Anatomist*, actually uses the alienation technique of Brecht long before any other British playwright was prepared to adopt it. And if you could imagine Bernard Shaw re-writing the novels of John Buchan, you could get some idea of what James Bridie was all about. Sometimes his dialogue almost seems to need sub-titles for non-Scots, and that too may be why his place in world theatre is so diminished today. But if ever a playwright was ripe for rediscovery it is Bridie.

CALENDAR

• Bertolt Brecht flees Germany and begins a self-imposed exile, while celebrated writer Heinrich Mann leaves the Prussian Academy of Arts

• The new Shakespeare Memorial Theatre in Stratford-upon-Avon attracts almost 134,000 spectators for its first continuous spring and summer season

• The Legitimate Theatre Code is signed by President Roosevelt and guarantees a minimum wage for actors of between $40 to $50 a week

• The film *King Kong* premieres in New York and demonstrates all the latest special-effects technology

BIRTHS **Daniel Massey** English actor

English playwright **Michael Frayn**

Joe Orton English playwright

English mezzo-soprano **Dame Janet Baker**

DEATHS British playwright **John Galsworthy**

English actress **Cicely Richards**

Joseph Urban Austrian-born set designer, who designed the sets for the Ziegfeld Follies

NOTABLE PREMIERES Wendy Hiller stars in LOVE ON THE DOLE by Walter Greenwood

Noël Coward's DESIGN FOR LIVING opens at The Barrymore on Broadway and stars Lynn Fontanne and Alfred Lunt

Elisabeth Bergner, already a film star, takes London by storm in Margaret Kennedy's drama ESCAPE ME NEVER

Charles Laughton makes his classical name in MEASURE FOR MEASURE at the Old Vic

W Somerset Maugham's SHEPPY opens at Wyndham's Theatre

MUSICAL NOTES Duke Ellington's orchestra make their first appearance in the UK

Kurt Weill's THE SEVEN DEADLY SINS (cantata)

THE THREEPENNY OPERA is not well received by the critics when it opens at the Empire, New York

HIT SONGS Smoke Gets in Your Eyes

Stormy Weather

Who's Afraid of the Big Bad Wolf

I've Told Every Little Star

Murder in the Cathedral

Of all the fashions, passions and trends in 20th century English-speaking theatre, perhaps the most curious was that of verse drama. It appeared to come out of nowhere in the mid-1930s and by the mid-1950s was utterly unsustainable. It produced only two playwrights of note – Christopher Fry and TS Eliot – and although it could be argued that their influence on prose dramatists was considerable, they left, after a short period of critical and public acclaim, no real heirs of any kind.

In 1934, TS Eliot began to write the play which a year later was to make his name as a dramatist and to launch the entire movement of poetic drama. It is, though, arguable, that long before this he had already been a playwright-in-waiting.

Thomas Stearns Eliot was born in St Louis, Missouri in 1888. Early in World War One he came to live in England, working first in a bank and then as one of the founders of the publishing house of Faber & Faber. He also founded and edited a magazine of poetry called Criterion, became a British subject and in 1927 joined the Church of England. He died in 1965, one of the most honoured and successful of all 20th century poets, and ironically is now best recalled as the original author of *Cats*.

As early as 1920, he had published an essay called *The Possibility of Poetic Drama* and from then on his poems virtually all contained a strong element of the dramatic; but only in 1934 did he write his first play *The Rock*, a prose pageant about the building of a church and, later in the same year, he began to write the play which became his first great pre-war triumph.

Murder in the Cathedral, too, it could be argued, really has the church as its star, and it was indeed first staged only 50 yards away from the actual spot where Thomas à Becket was assassinated in the year 1170. The play was originally meant just as a fund-raiser for Canterbury Cathedral, and Eliot himself had real doubts about its ever reaching a wider audience. He wrote at the time that in his view, "verse might be suitable for a historical play on a religious subject, written specifically for those serious people who go to festivals and therefore expect to have to put up with poetry."

What in fact happened was that *Murder in the Cathedral* broke through to a whole other audience around the world, who suddenly found in this chronicle of Becket's torture of mind and agony of spirit a kind of intellectual thriller to which they could easily relate.

Not until the early 1960s, with the London premieres of Anouilh's *Becket* and Bolt's *A Man for all Seasons*, was there to be a religious drama of such worldwide appeal and the fact that it was in verse made Eliot's play all the more remarkable. *The Times* hailed it as "the one great play by a contemporary dramatist now to be seen in England," and when it opened on Broadway a few months later, Brooks Atkinson added, "For exaltation, earthly terror and spiritual submission this is theatre restored to the highest…it testifies eloquently to the compelling power of poetry…a fervent and moving drama with moments of majestic beauty."

Since this first production, *Murder in the Cathedral* has more often been staged in churches than in theatres. It was immediately recognised as a timely warning of what would happen if Hitler were allowed to dominate the religion as well as the politics of Europe and at its heart is the constant agony of a man who has to choose between being a martyr and a saint or a real political force in a corrupt land.

Just as Bernard Shaw in the *Saint Joan* he had written a decade earlier concluded that she was a lot more useful dead than alive, so Eliot suggests that we might prefer any modern Becket to be safely sanctified rather than around to ask all the awkward questions. At the end of the play, Becket really chooses death as the only way he can severely damage the King who has turned against him.

Triumph in adversity is what *Murder in the Cathedral* is really all about, and although Eliot was to achieve later successes with *The Family Reunion* (1939) and above all *The Cocktail Party* (1950), his plays

The RSC production in 1993

became increasingly vulnerable to Tynan's famous jibe that he was just "Pinero on stilts". Nevertheless, without Eliot, without *Murder in the Cathedral*, there might well have been no such thing as verse drama.

It took an Anglo-American poet to try something so far outside the norm of mid-20th century playwriting in either of his countries that nearly 40 years after his death we know he mattered, but cannot agree precisely why or what the legacy. Perhaps in the end it is that he made poetry accessible to thousands of theatregoers who had never met a poet; in a sense of course, and from way beyond the grave, that is what Eliot is still doing "now and forever" with the musical *Cats*.

CALENDAR

- Robert Graves publishes *I, Claudius*, later aborted film and award-winning BBC Television series
- First showing of Leni Riefenstahl's seminal Nazi political film, *Triumph of the Will*
- Playwright Elmer Rice denounces critics as "stupid, jaded, illiterate, drunkards". This diatribe was given, coincidentally we are sure, just after his play *We The People* had been unfavourably reviewed
- First Oscar for Best Film Song goes to "The Continental" from the Astaire/Rodgers vehicle *The Gay Divorcee*
- Henry Fonda make his Broadway debut in the first-ever *New Faces*
- Katherine Cornell completes 16,000-mile American tour playing 75 cities to half a million theatregoers. Orson Welles, 18, plays small roles
- Roosevelt's "New Deal" includes, for the first time, Government aid for unemployed actors

BIRTHS British playwright **Alan Bennett**
British actor **Alan Bates**
Shirley MacLean Beatty later American stage and screen star, Shirley MacLaine, sister of Warren Beatty

DEATHS Actor/Manager **Gerald du Maurier**
British playwright **Sir Arthur Wing Pinero**

NOTABLE PREMIERES JB Priestley's **EDEN END**
Broadway premiere of **ANYTHING GOES**
TOBACCO ROAD, an adaptation of the Erskine Caldwell novel begins record-breaking Broadway run of 3182 performances
THE GOLDEN TOY, based on an old Indian legend, with dances by Ninette de Valois, opens at the Coliseum

MUSICAL NOTES Hindemith's opera **MATHIS DER MALER** completed but banned in Germany by the new Nazi regime
Steppan Grapelli forms the **QUINTETTE DU HOT CLUB DE FRANCE** in Paris
Shostakovich's opera **LADY MACBETH OF MINSK**
John Christie founds the Glyndebourne Opera at his home in Sussex, England
Rachmaninov's virtuoso piano piece, **RHAPSODY ON A THEME OF PAGANINI**
American opera **FOUR SAINTS IN THREE ACTS**
American violinist Yehudi Menuhin makes first world tour

HIT SONGS Mad Dogs and Englishmen
Isle of Capri
I Only Have Eyes for You
You're the Top

Waiting for Lefty

Clifford Odets in 1935

In the American theatre, 1935 was undoubtedly the year of Clifford Odets, in that it saw the New York premieres of no less than four of his plays: the one that made his name, *Waiting for Lefty*, swiftly followed by *Awake and Sing*, *Till the Day I Die* and *Paradise Lost*.

All were written for, and first staged by, the Group Theatre, a co-operative of writers, directors and actors which, from 1931 until the coming of World War Two, was unquestionably the centre of socialist and crusading, reformist drama in the United States.

Though he lived on until 1963, latterly writing many Hollywood screenplays, Odets never really managed to sustain or repeat his mid-Thirties triumphs; an unhappy and sometimes alcoholic private life, combined with the hysterical anti-Communist witch-hunts of the 1950s, meant that he fell rapidly from grace after the war, and as yet he has never been granted the posthumous rediscovery that is undoubtedly his due on both sides of the Atlantic. Odets was overtaken, only a decade or so after his initial triumphs, by Arthur Miller who undoubtedly owed him a certain debt, and he has never yet been restored to the pantheon, despite several individual attempts on both sides of the Atlantic to revisit his best scripts.

Odets himself, like many of his central characters, was perpetually torn and finally destroyed by an inability to equate the desire for fame and success and prosperity with his originally more radical beliefs about social and political crusades; in his own character, reputation and work, he was one of the first to personify the everlasting struggle between the 'legitimate' low-budget drama of the stage and the lure of Hollywood gold. Worse still, he began to accept at face value, towards the end of a distinguished writing career, the glib criticism that he had indeed 'sold out' and would never recover his artistic soul.

Clifford Odets was born in 1906 to a poor Jewish working-class family in Philadelphia, but their fortunes improved and by the time he was a teenager they were living a somewhat better life in New York. It was there that Odets started out as an actor in 1924, working often in church basements with small local community groups dedicated to experimental and socialist-worker dramas. He was also an early radio announcer and sound-effects expert, but it was as a charter member of the Group Theatre in 1931 that he found his true home. To his frustration, however, the Group rejected all his early plays and only wished to use Odets as an actor; but then, in 1935, a project fell apart in rehearsal and *Waiting for Lefty* was hastily accepted to fill the gap.

Neither the Group nor Odets were prepared for its overnight success, the first they had which was able to break through into mainstream Broadway from its small-stage and almost club-theatre origins. The play, written in six short scenes, was inspired by the 1934 New York cab drivers' strike, and follows the lives of some of the strikers as they try to decide how best to deal with management and their own domestic lives as they wait for their leader Lefty, who never arrives because, as we discover only at the end, he has already been killed by management thugs.

It is arguable that without *Waiting For Lefty* there might have been no *On the Waterfront* twenty years later, and that in this one brief, didactic drama Odets gave birth to the mid-century American theatre of protest and social conscience, the theatre that was at this very moment becoming known in Europe as 'agitprop'.

Of Odets' three other 1935 plays, *Awake and Sing* was a curious tragicomedy set in the Bronx where he had grown up, but influenced this time by the Irish family dramas of Sean O'Casey; *Paradise Lost* was another domestic drama about a father going bankrupt, and *Till the Day I Die* was the tragedy of a German communist committing suicide rather than betray comrades to the Nazis, this last a frightening foreshadowing of the McCarthy years to come.

But although most of them transferred to Broadway, none of these plays achieved real commercial success, and Odets was easily tempted to move out to California in search of Hollywood gold. Because he

was immediately accused of betraying his theatre colleagues by deserting them, Odets made sure that his first major Hollywood work was *Golden Boy*, written as a play in 1937 and filmed in 1939 with William Holden and Barbara Stanwyck. This was a modern boxing-ring *Faust* in which, through the central character of a young Italian-American prize-fighter, Odets attempted to debate and exorcise his own demons.

In Hollywood, (where he married Luise Rainer and had tempestuous affairs with Fay Wray and Frances Farmer) Odets, like so many other East Coast writers of the time, had rapidly to give up on idealism of any kind, although in such major post-war play and film scripts as *Sweet Smell of Success* (1957), *The Big Knife* (1949) and *The Country Girl* (1954, originally known on stage in Britain as *Winter Journey*) his vitriolic self-hatred, his rage at the sell-out that he and so many of his dramatist contemporaries had chosen in going for the movies and an apparently softer Hollywood option, gave his work a kind of bitter energy which is elsewhere really only evident in Arthur Miller. "Odets," one critic viciously asked, "Where is thy sting?"

CALENDAR

• Humphrey Bogart lands his first major Broadway role as a gangster in Robert E Sherwood's *The Petrified Forest*

• John Gielgud directs *Romeo and Juliet*, alternating the role of Romeo with Laurence Olivier

• New York Drama Critics Circle is founded

• In Britain, the foundation stone for a National Theatre is laid in London's Cromwell Road and it will take another 40 years before it was built on another site

• Composer Kurt Weill, escaping from the Nazi threat in his native Germany, arrives in the United States via London

BIRTHS American writer/director **Woody Allen**

Diahann Carroll American actress/singer

Julia Wells, later British actress singer

Julie Andrews

Judd Hirsch American actor

American actor **Richard Chamberlain**

Lee Remick American actress

DEATHS British actress **Dame Madge Kendal**

American theatrical manager

William A Brady

NOTABLE PREMIERES PORGY & BESS, George and Ira Gershwin's folk opera set in the Deep South, based on a novel by DuBose Heywood, with an all-black cast opens in New York to mixed reviews

TOVARICH, Robert E Sherwood adapts Jacques Deval's play about Russian émigrés at the Lyric, Shaftesbury Ave

Emlyn Williams' thriller NIGHT MUST FALL, opens in the West End starring the author with May Whitty and Angela Baddeley

Ivor Novello's first musical GLAMOUROUS NIGHT opens at the Theatre Royal, Drury Lane, the start of a glittering career in that theatre

MUSICAL NOTES ROMEO AND JULIET, Ashton's ballet set to the music of the suite by Prokoviev

Formation of the Benny Goodman Orchestra

HIT SONGS Blue Moon

Red Sails in the Sunset

Cheek to Cheek

French Without Tears

It would be hard to think of any 20th century dramatist, with the possible exception of Noël Coward, whose career peaked so early, slumped so badly on his death, and came back a decade or so afterwards in such posthumous triumph. What makes Rattigan (1911-1977) so perennially interesting is the way that his plays, while appearing to be written for the middle-aged, middle-class, Home Counties matinée theatregoer whom he himself once christened "Aunt Edna" are, when you look at them more closely, for the most part dramas of extraordinary depth and sexual pain.

True, this cannot really be claimed of his first great hit, the *French Without Tears* which came almost out of nowhere. Rattigan was 25, the Harrow and Oxford-educated son of a diplomat, who had thus far only achieved a couple of short-lived flops and even those in collaboration with other authors. This, his first solo effort, was the lightest of light comedies and ran a record-breaking 1039 performances.

Although its plot owes a certain amount to Coward, whom Rattigan always acknowledged as his Master, *French Without Tears* is in fact even lighter than anything Noël would have written at the time. It has virtually no plot of any kind – four young men are staying at a small language school on the French Riviera, where they are joined by the sister of one of them and a local French girl – and that is really that. Yet for three entire acts, Rattigan brilliantly conjures enough elegant dialogue and romantic misunderstanding to make his first play one of the great stylish comic triumphs of the British theatre between the wars.

The tone of *French Without Tears* is set early on by one of the recalcitrant male pupils, translating "She has ideas above her station" as "Elle a des idées au dessus de sa gare". But, just as in Coward's *Private Lives*, written six years earlier, the rest of the comedy then runs like indestructible clockwork to its inevitably happy ending. Again as in *Private Lives*, there are no obvious jokes as such; the humour comes entirely out of character and situation.

For nearly a decade after *French Without Tears*, Rattigan's hit seemed like a one-off. Although he wrote a number of other interesting plays, only *While the Sun Shines* (1943) and then of

Kay Hammond and Roland Culver at the Criterion in 1936

course *The Winslow Boy* (1946) began to suggest that he was a playwright in it for the long haul.

It was, as so often, Kenneth Tynan who got Rattigan bang to rights. "He is," wrote Tynan, "the Formosa of our theatre – geographically occupied by the old conservative guard, but temperamentally inclined toward the progressive rebels."

Ironically, Tynan himself and his fellow critics of 1956 did a great deal to destroy Rattigan in their eagerness to acclaim the new writers of the Royal Court. At that time, it wasn't enough for Osborne to succeed; Rattigan had to be seen to fail. Thirty years later, when his work began to come back into fashion, it was clear that yet again like Coward, Terry had a lot more to offer than escapist entertainment.

His own childhood was lonely and not helped by his father's frequent infidelity towards a beloved but frigid mother. Rattigan was also, of course, a lifelong if always firmly closeted homosexual, and all through his work from now on could be traced themes of sexual and parental despair. Several plays are about troubled relationships between fathers and sons while others, most notably *Separate Tables* (1954) and *Ross* (1960), have clear homosexual undertones. Mother-figures and older women falling in love with younger men (sometimes even leading to murder, as in the 1977 *Cause Celebre*) are also a persistent Rattigan concern.

What perhaps most matters about him is that, at precisely the mid-century moment when the England that he loved and lost was going through a peculiar social and sexual crisis of identity, Rattigan was there to report from personal experience and professional observation on precisely what it meant to be middle-class and English at time when suddenly most if not all of the old certainties were suddenly being blitzed for the first time since the Twenties.

In one sense, his plays are the well-made bridge from the new realism of Galsworthy to the literary sexuality of Simon Gray. On the one hand, Rattigan was never as archaic as his critics suggested;

but on the other hand, nor was he ever really able to come out of the closet to which his upbringing and conditioning had consigned him.

Rattigan was almost the last dramatist ever proudly to declare that he was a craftsman rather than an artist, and that he preferred characters to ideas. Sadly, he was so often taken at his own valuation that even when he became one of the very few playwrights ever to be knighted, there was still a feeling that he somehow was not 'serious' enough to deserve the honour. Intriguingly, one of his greatest post-war hits, *The Winslow Boy* (based on the true story of the child wrongly dismissed for petty theft from the Royal Naval Academy) was in 1999 re-filmed by the American dramatist David Mamet. If, at the time of Rattigan's death you had forecast that one of the most radical and scatological of all American playwrights was going to find in Rattigan a truth and a timeless emotional power, even he would not have believed it.

CALENDAR

• Broadway critic Percy Hammond, reviewing a new musical, "I find that I have knocked everything but the knees of the chorus girls, and there God has anticipated me"
• Broadway debut of Van Johnson
• Playwright Maxwell Anderson wins first-ever Critics' Circle Award for *Winterset*
• Publication of Margaret Mitchell's *Gone With The Wind*, later classic film and catastrophic stage musical
• Several Broadway theatres install air-conditioning
• BBC adds sound to television pictures from its new studio at Alexandra Palace

BIRTHS **Albert Finney** British actor
British actress and politician **Glenda Jackson**
Vaclav Havel Czech playwright and politician

DEATHS American musicals star **Marilyn Miller**
Maksim Gorky Russian dramatist
Italian dramatist **Luigi Pirandello**
Spanish playwright **Federico Garcia Lorca**, executed during the Spanish Civil War

NOTABLE PREMIERES Rodgers & Hart's new musical **ON YOUR TOES** stars Russian ballerina Tamara Geva and Ray Bolger
Alfred Lunt and Lynn Fontanne co-star in Robert Sherwood's Pulitzer Prize-winning **IDIOT'S DELIGHT**
Cole Porter's **RED HOT AND BLUE** stars Ethel Merman, Jimmy Durante and Bob Hope
Ralph Richardson and Laurence Olivier co-star for the first time in a short-lived farce by JB Priestley called **BEES ON THE BOAT DECK**
Robert Morley opens at the Gate as **OSCAR WILDE** in a new play by Leslie and Sewell Stokes which, because of its homosexual theme, was only licensed by the Lord Chamberlain for club performances

MUSICAL NOTES Stalin closes **LADY MACBETH OF MINSK** by Shostakovich and bans Rachmaninov in the USSR

HIT SONGS DeLovely
The Way You Look Tonight
When I'm Cleaning Windows
There's a Small Hotel
I've Got You Under My Skin

Amphitryon 38

Even the title nowadays needs some explaining. This was the 38th time that the French playwright Jean Giraudoux had attempted to retell for a modern audience the classical legend of Jupiter's love for Alkmena, but this was the one where he finally ceased to be an academic French playwright only known locally and, (thanks to a characteristically witty adaptation by another long-lost dramatist, the American SN Behrman), achieved a considerable Broadway and West End hit in which Alfred Lunt and Lynn Fontanne confirmed their joint reputations.

Hippolyte Jean Giraudoux (1882-1944) had originally made his name as a novelist with *Seigfried at la Limousin* (1921), which won the Prix Goncourt and also became in Paris his first hit play when he was already 45. But soon after that, the *New York Times* was already noting that "He is the most original figure in French literature for many a day...he has a rich imagination, and a great talent for poetic fantasy in realistic settings."

Giraudoux's two enduring hits are *Ondine* (1939) and *The Madwoman of Chaillot* (1943), but it was here in *Amphitryon 38* that he first established his academic, poetic talent, one that undoubtedly made him one of the three or four most important French dramatists of the 20th century, although he now proves curiously hard to revive, at least abroad.

Amphitryon 38 also established Giraudoux's partnership with the great French actor Louis Jouvet, and his next success *La Guerre de Troie N'aura pas Lieu* (later translated by Christopher Fry for Michael Redgrave as *Tiger at the Gates*) had an especial topicality in that its Paris and London premieres came on either side of World War Two: the play is about a war on the point of being averted when it breaks out only because of lies and misunderstandings on either side.

Shortly before his death in the closing months of the Occupation, Giraudoux, in a rare burst of activity, wrote three plays (*Madwoman of Chaillot*, *Pour Lucrece*

'The Lunts' in the first Broadway production

and *L'Apollo de Bellac*), all of which, posthumously staged by Jouvet, ensured his immediately post-war reputation. Audrey Hepburn had her only Broadway triumph as his *Ondine* in 1951, and a decade later it was again a considerable success for Leslie Caron and the director Peter Hall at the very birth of the Royal Shakespeare Company.

Elsewhere however, Giraudoux's plays have fared much less well away from his native land; an ambitious revival by Laurence Olivier's National Theatre company of *Amphitryon* with Christopher Plummer was a considerable failure in 1971, and before that Vivien Leigh made her last London stage appearance in another translation by Christopher Fry, *Duel of Angels*. This too flopped in 1958, despite a cast also headed by Claire Bloom, while on Broadway a Jerry Herman musical of *Chaillot*, retitled *Dear World*, was one of his rare failures in 1969, and the Bryan Forbes non-musical film of

Chaillot (also 1969) fared little better, despite a castlist headed by Katharine Hepburn, Danny Kaye, Yul Brynner, Edith Evans, Charles Boyer, Paul Henreid, Margaret Leighton and Giuliette Masina.

If that amazing international role-call of stars could do little to get Giraudoux back to a world audience, it is not entirely surprising that he has now fallen very far down the revivals list. All the same, we suspect that we haven't heard the last of him; there is something about his mixing of the classic and the poetic, the ancient and the modern, the austere and the achingly romantic, which transcends time and place. Poised somewhere halfway from Saint-Exupery to JM Barrie, Giraudoux is a curiously haunting writer, and he has one more claim to permanence in the history of the French theatre; when he and Jouvet were at the height of their stage fame, they took on a young secretarial assistant by the name of Jean Anouilh.

CALENDAR

• Billy Butlin opens first commercial British holiday camp

• Auden and Isherwood publish their modernist poetic drama *The Ascent of F6*, always a greater success on page than stage

• First publication of John Steinbeck's *Of Mice and Men*, later play and film

• Old Vic season dominated by Laurence Olivier (Hamlet, Henry V and Macbeth) and Vivien Leigh (Ophelia and Titania). They take the *Hamlet* back to its original setting at Elsinore Castle in Denmark

• Peggy Ashcroft makes Broadway debut with Burgess Meredith and Hume Cronyn in Maxwell Anderson's *High Tor*

• Thornton Wilder's *Our Town* beats Steinbeck's *Of Mice and Men* to Pulitzer Prize for drama

• Cole Porter thrown from horse in Central Park which caused lifelong agony, leading to more than 20 operations and eventually to amputation of his legs

• Tallulah Bankhead opens on Broadway as Cleopatra, and abruptly closes after appalling reviews. The New York Times calls her, "Queen of the Nil" and the Post notes, "Last night she barged down the aisle and sank"

• Rachel Crothers' *Susan and God*, with Gertrude Lawrence, becomes the first American play to be partially televised.

• American actor Osgood Perkins dies suddenly in Washington during the pre-Broadway of *Susan and God*. His 5-year old son demands to lead the funeral procession – his name is Antony Perkins

• Eva Le Gallienne opens in summer stock as Hamlet. The NY Times finds her "shrill and unmanly of voice and pathetically ineffectual in those moments which call for vigorous assault"

BIRTHS

British Actress **Vanessa Redgrave**

American actor **Dustin Hoffman**

Thomas Straussler, later playwright Sir Tom Stoppard

British actor **Tom Courtenay**

Welsh stage and screen actor **Anthony Hopkins**

DEATHS

Scots playwright **JM Barrie**

American composer **George Gershwin**

Lilian Baylis, long-time director of the Old Vic and Sadlers Wells, following a traffic accident

NOTABLE PREMIERES

In Germany, Hitler launches a full-scale attack on modern drama, music and art, describing it as "a decadent by-product of Bolshevik Jewish corruption"

GEORGE AND MARGARET, Gerald Savory's long-running London comedy in which neither title character ever appears

Noël Gay's ME AND MY GIRL, the "Lambeth Walk" musical which ran on into World War Two and was then triumphantly revived in London and New York with a new book in the 1980s

MUSICAL NOTES

Aaron Copland's THE SECOND HURRICANE

Toscanini signs with NBC Radio to conduct the orchestra they have created for him.

HIT SONGS

Whistle While You Work

The Lady is a Tramp

My Funny Valentine

September in the Rain

Thanks for the Memory

Our Town

The years have not been kind to Thornton Wilder and, at the turn of the 21st Century, he would be lucky to get into the second half of any top ten listing of major American dramatists. And yet there was a time when this three-time Pulitzer Prize-winner would have been acclaimed as the greatest playwright of his generation and his one true masterpiece *Our Town* (1938) is still the most frequently performed community play in the whole of the United States.

Yet no Wilder has to date been performed by the National Theatre or by the RSC and if, at the time of this writing, you had to establish his claim to international fame it would only really be as the author of *The Matchmaker* (1938, itself based on an Austrian original) which later became Jerry Herman's musical *Hello, Dolly!*

One reason why Wilder's fame has proved harder to sustain than, say, that of O'Neill or Miller or Williams is that he came from a very strong literary background and neither followed nor introduced any mainstream line of drama. His first Pulitzer was in fact for a novel, *The Bridge of San Luis Rey*, which he later adapted for stage and screen. He made his Broadway name adapting European classics like Ibsen's *A Doll's House* for the American actress Katherine Cornell.

Though born in 1906 in Madison, Wisconsin, Wilder spent much of his childhood in the Far East where his father worked as both a diplomat and a newspaper editor. He began as a schoolmaster in Rome before completing a Master's degree in French at Princeton although, as early as 1915, he began writing short dramatic sketches, nearly all based on the Bible or lives of the great composers.

In 1931 he published a collection of one-act plays including *The Long Christmas Dinner* and *Pulman Car Hiawatha* but it wasn't until the opening of *Our Town* in this year that he felt confident enough to give up a teaching job at the University of Chicago and become a full-time writer.

The reason that *Our Town* became an instant classic constantly in revival is that it is, in effect, a community play. It tells the story of the mythical Grover's Corners, a small New Hampshire town during the first 14 years of the 20th Century. The narrator is a Stage Manager who introduces us to the loveable inhabitants of the town as they go about their daily lives. Across three acts, we follow them as they get born, go to school, find jobs, get married and sometimes killed, and we finish up in the cemetery where all come back to life for one last chat about the meaning of life and love.

More cynical European audiences have always had trouble with Wilder's undeniable and even schmaltzy folksiness, but *Our Town* would not have survived this long in constant revival were it not that below the apparently soap-operatic events of Grover's Corners that Wilder traces so lovingly, and with such detailed observation, there is also something both mythic and eternal in Wilder's realisation that to some extent or other, we all live and die in our own Grover's Corners.

From his opening chat to the audience ("Nice town, y'know what I mean?") to his very last line ("There go the stars doing their old criss-cross journeys in the sky…11 o'clock in Grover's Corners. You get a good rest too. Good night.") there is a sense that Wilder has written the most American play of all time. You could argue that a few years later Dylan Thomas was to find the inspiration for his very similar *Under Milk Wood* in Wilder's highly theatrical and poetic mixture of the eternal and the folksy.

In this same year, Wilder also wrote *The Merchant of Yonkers* which (as first *The Matchmaker* and then *Hello, Dolly!*) gave both Ruth Gordon and then Carol Channing their signature roles.

During the War, however, his *The Skin of our Teeth* was a very much more experimental and courageous mixture of slapstick and fantasy which gave (on Broadway) Tallulah Bankhead and (in London) Vivien Leigh one of their greatest roles as the time-travelling Sabina. When, in 1955, America was asked to

send a major play to the Paris Festival of that year it was *The Skin of our Teeth* they chose, now with Mary Martin and Helen Hayes in the leading roles. This play ran into considerable trouble, however, when James Joyce scholars remarked that its characters, philosophy and language were thinly disguised borrowings from *Finnegan's Wake*.

By now, although his old friend Alexander Woollcott was still standing by him ("*The Skin of our Teeth* is a classic of cosmic and cock-eyed proportions") the general critical consensus, even in America, had sharply turned against Wilder, "He is," said the *NY Times*, "now using the theatre as a medium to distract attention from the fact that he has nothing left to say of any interest."

After the War, John Gielgud had a rare failure as Julius Caesar in Wilder's adaptation of his own novel *The Ides of March* while his 1955 *A Life in the Sun* was so unenthusiastically reviewed at the Edinburgh Festival that it never reached London or New York.

Undaunted, Wilder took to writing librettos for obscure German operas and a marathon cycle of 14 one-act plays devoted to the seven ages of man and the seven deadly sins. This was never completed and Wilder spent much of his later life playing the Stage Manager in local community revivals of his one unchallenged original hit.

Since his death in 1975, his career has begun the long, slow process of rehabilitation but it is still as an academic that he is chiefly studied. On the other hand, of course, as long as anyone revives *Our Town* (and they do, they do) his place in world theatre is uniquely secure.

CALENDAR

• Queen Mary, now Queen Mother, lays cornerstone for National Theatre in the Cromwell Rd. The stone is moved three more times before finally coming to rest on the South Bank where the theatre was built more than thirty years later. In this year, however, Edwin Lutyens designed and published his model for the National, one that was never built

• The BBC begins broadcasting Spelling Bee, the first game show

• New York World's Fair gives employment to many American entertainers

• Peggy Ashcroft, Gwen Ffrangcon-Davies and Carol Goodner triumph as Chekhov's *Three Sisters*

BIRTHS	British playwright **Caryl Churchill**
	Derek Jacobi British actor
	American playwright **John Guare**
DEATHS	Russian actor **Konstantin Stanislavsky**
	Czech playwright **Karel Capek**
NOTABLE PREMIERES	The last Rodgers and Hart triumph, **THE BOYS FROM SYRACUSE**, a musical adaptation of Shakespeare's **A COMEDY OF ERRORS**, has choreography by George Balanchine, and a cast including Burl Ives and Eddie Albert
	Katharine Hepburn in Philip Barry's **THE PHILADELPHIA STORY**
MUSICAL NOTES	Benny Goodman's first Carnegie Hall concert
	Samuel Barber's **ADAGIO FOR STRINGS**
HIT SONGS	Jeepers Creepers
	My Heart Belongs to Daddy

The Little Foxes

Although her career as a playwright was to go wrong after the war, there can be no doubt that in the 1930s not only was Lillian Hellman (1904-1984) among the most successful of all American playwrights but also one of the very few women to make it to the top.

By 1939 she had already made her name as the author of *The Children's Hour*, the first major play to deal with lesbianism. Her *Days to Come* (1936) was a quick flop about the effects of a strike on a mid-Western family but in 1939 she achieved her masterpiece.

The title of *The Little Foxes* is taken from the Song of Solomon "they are the little foxes that spoil the vines" and it tells the story of a family in Alabama at the turn of the century who are so caught up in their own greed that murder becomes the only practical outcome. Virtually the entire cast of Hellman's melodrama are meretricious, unscrupulous and manic of temper but it was the sense of a relentless, ruthless updated Greek tragedy which gave *The Little Foxes* its undeniable power.

The unforgettable moment in *The Little Foxes* is the scene in the last act where the matriarch Regina watches her invalid husband dying at her feet after she has graciously declined to hand him the pills that might have saved his life. But nearly all the characters here are larger and more venal than life and their vicious in-fighting nowadays suggests nothing more than a turn-of-the-century version of "Dallas" or "Dynasty".

One reason perhaps why Hellman no longer has the stature that was undoubtedly hers during World War Two is that her plays seldom have very much in common although her *Another Part of the Forest* (1946) was a "prequel" to *The Little Foxes* set against the same family background twenty years earlier. She never wrote the third play that was intended to make up the trilogy. If there is a theme running through all her work it is simply that of individual evil. She was among the first to write psychological studies of people so brutal that they kill all the love around them and if she now seems unduly melodramatic it is worth remembering that all

**Charles Dingle and Tallulah
Bankhead at the Piccadilly in 1942**

her writing stems from a strict moral code – the evil characters invariably come to terrible ends and it is not entirely her fault if, as usual, the devil has all the best lines.

Hellman was born into a Jewish family in New Orleans. Her father was a travelling salesman who, by the time she was 18, could afford to send her to University in New York. Emerging from college in the late 1920s, she went into publishing as a reader, reviewer and wrote some early short stories. But her sights were already set on Broadway where she first worked as a playreader for the producer Herman Shumlin who later presented most of her plays.

In 1930, with most of her work still in the future, she went out to Hollywood as a script reader and there fell in love with the crime writer Dashiell Hammett, author of *The Maltese Falcon* and *The Thin Man*. Though they never married, Hammett was the love of Hellman's life and it was while with him that she wrote *Watch on the Rhine* (1941), the best ever American anti-Nazi play and one which, just months before Pearl Harbour, tried to express the urgency with which America had to enter the war.

Though born in the Deep South, Hellman's plays do not ever really have a strong sense of location. What she always did best was to indicate the various human characteristics which can destroy love and lives and her own sympathy is always with the victimised whether one single member of a family or an entire race.

After the war, her best play was *Toys in the Attic* (1960) which dealt with two spinster sisters and their deranged sister-in-law in another bitter (and this time incestuous) family tragedy. In later years, Hellman spread her literary net widely with journalism, essays, novels and even a libretto for Leonard Bernstein's musical adaptation of Voltaire's *Candide*. She was in honourable company – later librettists for this same work included Hugh Wheeler and Stephen Sondheim, Dorothy Parker and most recently, John Wells.

Towards the end of her life she was caught up in a prolonged but unresolved battle with the novelist Mary McCarthy ("Everything she says is a lie, including *and* and *but*"), over a long magazine piece about a Jewish refugee, subsequently filmed as *Julia* (1977) with Vanessa Redgrave and Jane Fonda, which purported to be reportage but which, according to McCarthy, several times crossed the border between truth and fiction.

There are many who believe that her best play was one of her few real disasters – *The Autumn Garden* set in a summer resort in 1949, is in one sense her *Heartbreak House*, an extended family aware that somehow life has passed them by. But what matters most about Hellman are her sulphurous scenes, her specialisation in hate, frustration, helpless rage, and inarticulate loathing and above all her realisation that love only exists through the ache of its absence.

CALENDAR

• With the Lyceum due for demolition, John Gielgud closes his *Hamlet*, taking it, like Olivier the previous year, to Elsinore

• The Royal Opera House at Covent Garden has become, for the duration of the War, a dance hall

• Following a negative NY Times review by Brooks Atkinson for the black actress Ethel Waters in *Mamba's Daughters* on Broadway, Oscar Hammerstein II, Judith Anderson and Tallulah Bankhead write a letter of protest whereupon Atkinson goes back to the play and finds her wonderful, noting that he was feeling "under the weather" when he wrote his original notice

• Only months away from his death, John Barrymore, now a hopeless alcoholic, returns briefly to Broadway

• Immediately after the Declaration of War on September 3, all London theatres close for two weeks. Some then reopen, often starting performances at 5pm so audiences can get safely home before nightfall

BIRTHS
British classical actor and gay rights activist **Sir Ian McKellen**
American dancer/director **Tommy Tune**
Lily Tomlin American comedienne
Broadway singer/actor **Len Cariou**

DEATHS
Irish poet, patriot, playwright and politician, **William Butler Yeats**, co-founder of the Abbey Theatre in Dublin and the Irish National Theatre
German dramatist **Ernst Toller**

NOTABLE PREMIERES
At the Martin Beck on Broadway, THE DEVIL AND DANIEL WEBSTER
Paul Muni, Ute Hagen, Jose Ferrer and Karl Malden star in Broadway premiere of Maxwell Anderson's KEY LARGO, later classic Humphrey Bogart film
Peter Pears stars in ON THE FRONTIER, an anti-war play written by Auden and Isherwood with music by Benjamin Britten
TS Eliot's THE FAMILY REUNION brings Aeschylus into a contemporary setting. Michael Redgrave leads the cast
First play to deal exclusively with the coming of World War Two is the anonymously written ANSCHLUSS

MUSICAL NOTES
Leopold Stokowsky, long chafing against the traditional arrangement of the orchestra, re-arranges them for a concert series and causes a scandal in the classical music world

HIT SONGS
South of the Border
Over the Rainbow
We're Going to Hang Out the Washing on the Siegfried Line

The Corn is Green

Although it had first reached the West End in the closing months of 1938 with Sybil Thorndike in the lead, it wasn't until Ethel Barrymore opened the Broadway staging of *The Corn is Green* in 1940 that Emlyn Williams could truly be said to have achieved world status as a dramatist.

He is yet another mid-century British playwright (in fact highly Welsh) whose plays seem to have fallen into disuse, but at least he lives on as an actor in countless movies, while as a director he was one of the very first to recognise the talent of a later Welsh classical and modern star, Richard Burton, who with Anthony Hopkins was his only real heir.

The Corn is Green is in fact a very lightly disguised account of Williams' own early years, largely spent as they were in a small Welsh village where a crusading English schoolteacher (Miss Moffat in the play, Miss Cooke in real life) discovers the unusual talent of the young George Emlyn and gets him, against all local odds, into Oxford University on a scholarship.

What makes the play something more, though, than early chapters of Emlyn's autobiography (which he was anyway to write in two volumes with considerable success in later years) is that it touches with great warmth and sympathy on the world from which, thanks to his teacher, he narrowly escaped. As one of the characters in *The Corn is Green* points out, "Round here, children are only children until they are twelve; then they are sent away over the hills to the mines, and in one week they are old men".

There are also some early glimpses of feminism in the defiance of Miss Moffat to behave as small-community schoolmarms were then expected to be, and as Richard Findlater noted, the enduring strength of the play "lies in Williams' creation of the two central characters, the teacher and the pupil, who, intensely linked as they are, never seem to speak the same language; theirs is a relationship full of frustration, humiliation and devotion treated with unsentimental candour; yet it is a relationship which salvages and remakes a human life in the nick of time".

Since *The Corn is Green*, many other plays (not least *The Miracle Worker* about the deaf-and-dumb Helen Keller) have taken up and onwards the theme of the odd-couple teacher and pupil. But Williams did it first and best, though this was precisely because the rest of his work was varied, and indeed he only occasionally went back for inspiration to the Wales he left for Oxford in 1924.

Emlyn first made his name as a writer with two melodramas (*A Murder Has Been Arranged* in 1930 and *Night Must Fall* in 1935) and his interest in the psychology of murder was lifelong; one of his last publications was a detailed non-fiction account of the Moors Murders of the 1960s.

The son of a stoker and a barmaid who ran the local village pub, Emlyn grew up speaking at first only Welsh, but by the time he got into Oxford he was already fascinated with the possibilities of theatre. Like Noël Coward (who, with John Gielgud, was soon to become a lifelong friend; although Williams was married for almost all of his adult life and had two sons, he was also a lifelong homosexual) Williams wrote, directed and starred in his first West End play in 1931. His early failures, both written in the mid-1930s for Gielgud, were the unfortunately-titled *He Was Born Gay* (about the 'lost' Louis XVII) and *Spring 1600* (about Shakespeare's leading man Richard Burbage) but unlike many dramatists of his era he was always able to get work as an actor in movies when the plays which were his first love went wrong.

His later plays were never to achieve the worldwide stage and screen success of his two 1930s hits (*The Corn is Green* and *Night Must Fall*), but many would repay revival now. *The Light of Heart* (1940) is the account of an alcoholic actor making a comeback as King Lear, a play amazingly close in character and theme to Clifford Odets' 1949 *The Country Girl*; *The Morning Star* (1941) was about England's resistance to the

Sybil Thorndi
and Eml
Williams at t
Duchess in 19

Luftwaffe and made a star on Broadway of Gregory Peck; and after the war *Accolade* (1950) was an intriguingly early account of a public figure having his knighthood threatened by revelations of his sexuality, while *Someone Waiting* (1953) was a return to Emlyn's old fascination with the stage thriller.

Like many other actors (and Gielgud again), when Williams felt the Royal Court revolution of the 1950s to have gone against his generation of dramatists, he turned to the safety of the one-man show, and spent many of his later years touring with celebrations of (most successfully) Charles Dickens, Dylan Thomas and Saki. There was also the disappointment of a failed Broadway attempt to make over *The Corn is Green* as a vehicle for Bette Davis, and the tragedy of his wife's death by accidental suffocation.

But Williams remained at work to the last; he had been a notable Iago, Shylock and Angelo at Stratford-upon-Avon, and directed for London both Lillian Hellman's British hits, *Watch on the Rhine* and *The Little Foxes* (both 1942). His major movies included *The Citadel*, *They Drive By Night*, *Jamaica Inn*, *The Stars Look Down*, *Major Barbara*, *The Deep Blue Sea* and his own *The Last Days of Dolwyn* which he also directed. Prolific, hardworking and versatile, Emlyn Williams was a stage and screen craftsman of considerable energy and talent; he died in 1987 at the age of 83, curiously unhonoured even in Wales, having recently re-adapted his *The Corn is Green* as an American television vehicle for Katharine Hepburn.

CALENDAR

• Ingrid Bergman plays Julie in Molnar's *Liliom* in New York

• Bombs close the Shaftesbury Theatre and the Queen's, on Shaftesbury Avenue. *Rebecca*, with Celia Johnson and Margaret Rutherford, is forced to close

• Sunday performances begin on Broadway

• At The Gate, in Dublin, Maxwell Anderson's *The Masque of Kings* launches their fourteenth season

• At Stratford, a notice in the theatre reads "By order of the Police, persons can under no circumstances be admitted to performances at the theatre unless they have their gas masks"

BIRTHS   British stage and screen star **John Hurt**
Trevor Nunn   British director
American playwright   **David Rabe**
American dancer   **Donna McKechnie**

DEATHS   American novelist, playwright and poet
DuBose Heyward, whose novel became the ground-breaking folk opera PORGY AND BESS
Aubrey Hammond   British designer
Great British actress **Mrs Patrick (Beatrice) Campbell**

NOTABLE PREMIERES   At the Saville Theatre, UP AND DOING is a revue starring Cyril Ritchard, Binnie Hale, Stanley Holloway, Graham Payn and Leslie Henson.
Max Wall stars in a musical by Frank Eyton and Noël Gay called PRESENT ARMS at the Prince of Wales Theatre
MY SISTER EILEEN, based on Ruth McKenna's stories opens on Broadway and in the West End
A rare 'book' musical with an all-black cast CABIN IN THE SKY opens on Broadway, starring Ethel Waters and Dooley Wilson
Cole Porter's musical PANAMA HATTIE
Edith Evans, Alec Guinness and Peggy Ashcroft star in Clemence Dane's COUSIN MURIEL, at the Globe

MUSICAL NOTES   Michael Tippett's oratorio A CHILD OF OUR TIME
Agnes de Mille's ballet RODEO, to a score by Aaron Copland

HIT SONGS   Taking a Chance on Love
How High the Moon?
You Are My Sunshine
When You Wish Upon a Star

The Man Who Came to Dinner

Although this was an immediate critical and popular success when it first opened on Broadway in 1938, and was subsequently to enjoy a long life on the road and as a Hollywood movie, it was somewhat unexpectedly in the West End from December 1941 that it was to have its longest unbroken run, stretching well into late 1943.

Together and apart, George S Kaufman and Moss Hart were unquestionably the most successful team of writer-directors in the whole 20th-century history of Broadway. Kaufman, the elder of the two, was born in 1889 and as early as 1921 had his first Broadway hit with *Dulcy*. Through the rest of the 1920s he wrote and usually directed at least one play a year, as well as being called in as director, play-doctor or co-author to rescue countless other dramas, comedies and musicals on their way into Broadway.

In that sense he was the first-ever play-doctor, a role he was to share in later years with George Abbott and the young Neil Simon. Kaufman also in the 1920s collaborated with Edna Ferber and Ring Lardner, wrote the book for several Marx Brothers comedy-musicals on Broadway and later in Hollywood but only ever achieved one solo hit as a dramatist, the 1925 *Butter and Egg Man*.

And then, in 1930, he was joined by the 26-year-old Moss Hart and over the following ten years they achieved four of the greatest comic hits in the whole history of Broadway: *Once in a Lifetime*, *You Can't Take it With You*, *The Man Who Came to Dinner* and

Monty Woolley in an American production at the Savoy in 1941

George Washington Slept Here. They also wrote the rather less successful *Merrily We Roll Along*, which forty years later became a Stephen Sondheim musical.

But Hart always maintained a separate theatre life, writing the books for such musicals as *Face the Music Jubilee* and the revolutionary *Lady in the Dark* (with Ira Gershwin and Kurt Weill). His solo plays included *Christopher Blake* and *Light Up the Sky*, and before his death in 1961 he had two major Broadway hits as a director (*My Fair Lady* and *Camelot*); Hart also wrote the screenplay for the 1954 Judy Garland film *A Star is Born*.

But of all their individual and partnership scripts, it is *The Man Who Came to Dinner* which remains the most frequently revived. The play had its start in a casual remark made to George by his wife Beatrice; the critic and broadcaster Alexander Woollcott had been to spend a weekend in the country with them, one which he spent complaining about their house, their food, their guest bedroom and their choice of other weekend guests. As he was leaving on the Monday morning, the Kaufmans breathed a sigh of relief and began to speculate on how terrible it might have been had Aleck been forced to stay with them for any longer.

From that fragile notion grew a classic farce in which Whiteside/Woollcott, arriving to lecture in a small Midwestern town, accidentally breaks a limb on his hosts' doorstep and is forced to billet himself on them for a long Christmas vacation. By the end of it, he has filled their unsuspecting household with Harpo Marx, Noël Coward, Gertrude Lawrence (or reasonable facsimiles thereof) plus several dozen penguins, choirboys and a full-size Egyptian Mummy case.

He has also reorganised the love lives of his hosts' two children, discovered that one of their aunts is the Lizzie Borden who once axed her parents to death, and starts to depart only once again to trip over the doorstep.

The Kaufman-Hart partnership ended amicably early in World War Two, and while Hart occupied himself mainly with musicals, Kaufman also directed one more classic, *Guys and Dolls*, as well as writing the book for *Silk Stockings* (an adaptation of Garbo's *Ninotchka*) and his last stage and screen hit, *The Solid Gold Cadillac* in 1953.

He was also a considerable impromptu wit; "watching your performance from rear of stalls" he once cabled an unfortunate actor, "wish you were here". On another occasion he was introduced by one of his many former mistresses to her new husband, a cotton millionaire; "them that plants it" murmured Kaufman, "is soon forgotten". In gala bad taste, he also noted of a Spanish hotel fire in which many guests were burned to death "Never put all your Basques in one Exit". And finally, going backstage after a bad Boston preview of a play he had written and was now directing, his way was barred by an unusually officious stage manager who asked him "Are you with this show?" "Well", said Kaufman thoughtfully, "let's just say I'm not entirely against it".

CALENDAR

• More than half the shows currently playing on Broadway have been sold to Hollywood, except for *Pal Joey* because of its dubious moral content

• Newspaper tycoon William Randolph Hearst bans his theatre critics from mentioning the name of producer and director Orson Welles in their reviews of his production of *Native Son*. The feud is the result of Hearst's correct assumption that the leading character in Welles' film *Citizen Kane* is based on himself

• *Native Son*'s programmes are now distributed after the show rather than before, because, during the blackouts which end every scene, the audiences had been striking matches in order to read, thus causing a fire hazard

• A circus acrobat and clown making his New York stage debut in *Twelfth Night* will soon change his name to Yul Brynner

BIRTHS   American playwright **Tom Eyen**
Susannah York British actress
British actress **Sarah Miles**

DEATHS   Broadway producer **Sam Harris**.
Helen Morgan Torch singer and star of *Show Boat*, at the age of 41

NOTABLE PREMIERES   LADY IN THE DARK music by Kurt Weill, lyrics by Ira Gershwin, book by Moss Hart, opens starring Gertrude Lawrence
18 year old Carol Channing, in her first professional appearance, steals the show in Marc Blitzstein's experimental opera, NO FOR AN ANSWER
Boris Karloff stars in ARSENIC AND OLD LACE, a comedy by Joseph Kesselring
Cole Porter's LET'S FACE IT! opens on Broadway with Danny Kaye in his first starring role alongside Eve Arden, Vivian Vance and Nanette Fabray
Noël Coward's BLITHE SPIRIT opens on Broadway, starring Peggy Wood, Clifton Webb and Mildred Natwick
Bertold Brecht's MOTHER COURAGE AND HER CHILDREN

MUSICAL NOTES   Shostakovitch's 7TH SYMPHONY, 'The Leningrad', smuggled out of Russia on microfilm
The New Opera of New York, forerunner to the New York City Opera, is formed

HIT SONGS   Bewitched, Bothered and Bewildered
Boogie-Woogie Bugle Boy
White Cliffs of Dover
Blues in the Night
Waltzing Matilda

Antigone

With Paris under Nazi occupation, Anouilh's variation on the Sophocles original could not in fact be performed until 1944, but this was the year he first published it in France, in a collection of what he called "Pieces Noires" ('Dark Plays') which also included his other Greek variation, *Eurydice*, as well as his only real pre-war hit; the 1937 *Le Voyager Sans Bagage* (Traveller Without Luggage).

Born in 1910, Jean Anouilh has a thinly-disputed claim to being the greatest French playwright of his century. His work can mainly be divided into classical adaptations, usually with a dark heart, and apparently fluffy country-house comedies, often concerned with aristocrats and actresses, though these also tend to be dark-hearted and fundamentally, if not tragic, then at least elegantly sad about the human condition and its various compromises and betrayals.

Anouilh was brought up in Bordeaux, the son of a successful tailor and a mother who played a violin in the resident orchestra of the local Casino. He was sent to Paris as a teenager to study Law, but with showbusiness already in his maternal background he soon found work, (after a brief spell as an early advertising copywriter), as secretary to Louis Jouvet, the leading French actor of his day and, more significantly still for Anouilh, one who was already in theatrical management with the playwright Jean Giraudoux.

From them both in their different lines of work, Anouilh learnt his craft as a dramatist; throughout the early 1930s he stayed with their management until in 1934 he achieved financial independence by selling to MGM in Hollywood an unsuccessful playscript about an imprisoned businessman. From then on he became a full-time dramatist, writing at least one play a year almost up to his death in 1987 at the age of seventy-seven.

Anouilh's prolific output, his strong sense of stage-management and his versatility ensured him sustained commercial success over half a century, though now it is only perhaps *Ring Round the Moon* (which in

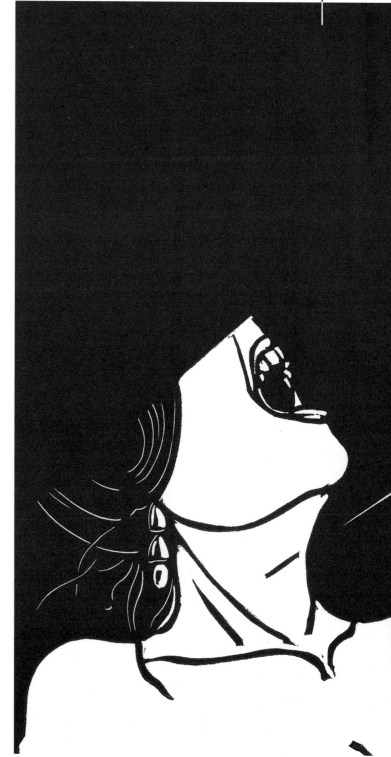

the early 1950s established Paul Scofield as something lighter than a Shakespearean) and *Becket* (which in the early 1960s gave magnificent roles to Laurence Olivier, Anthony Quinn, Christopher Plummer and, on film, Peter O'Toole and Richard Burton) that can be utterly sure of everlasting revival.

Those two plays reflect the best of either side of Anouilh's playwriting character; he was the dramatist of elegantly escapist "Pieces Roses" usually about the corruption of a young and innocent girl, and also the chronicler of fiercely religious studies of the church in crisis. *Antigone* became a considerable success in the last year before the Liberation of Paris, not least because Anouilh had refocused the story so that Antigone herself ("What a person can do, a person ought to do") is the personification of a nation having to make the grim choice between practical compromise and unyielding idealism.

After the war, Anouilh added three more personal genres to his "Pieces Roses" and "Pieces Noires"; these were the "Pieces Brillantes", "Grincantes" and "Costumees" ('brilliant', 'grating' and 'period'), achieving local and sometimes international hits in all three. Plays like *Dinner with the Family*, *Ring Round the Moon*, *The Rehearsal* and *Colombe* all seemed to define him in translation early in the 1950s as the Marivaux-like creator of backstage or country-house comedies with a dark heart. Not entirely coincidentally did Stephen Sondheim consider *Ring Round the Moon* as the basis for his *A Little Night Music*; only Anouilh's refusal to release the rights turned him toward Ingmar Bergman's *Smiles of a Summer Night*, another country-house comedy which goes very bleak by nightfall.

But then, later in the 1950s, came *Waltz of the Toreadors* and *Poor Bitos* and *The Fighting Cock*, all of which gave great leading roles in London to actors like Donald Pleasance and Hugh Griffith and Rex Harrison, but none of which proved to have long commercial lives in translation. It wasn't until 1959 with *Becket Ou l'Honneur de Dieu* that Anouilh achieved his last worldwide stage and screen hit, though another

'costume' piece, this one about Saint Joan (*The Lark*) ran respectably on both sides of the Atlantic a few years earlier.

In the 1970s Rex Harrison tried another Anouilh, *The Fighting Cock* in America, and at Chichester John Clements had a considerable success with one of his very last plays, *Dear Antoine*; both were wistfully romantic, stylish comedies about people in elegant retreat from a world they no longer understood or much cared for, and it would be hard not to see in them some sort of late-life autobiography for Anouilh himself. The theatre of the 1960s, 1970s and 1980s was no longer of much interest to him, and when he wrote it was usually a black, bleak comedy about disintegration and death.

Yet Anouilh left behind him a body of work unrivalled in 20th-century French theatre; an infinitely private man, perhaps the last major dramatist who managed to live and die without ever broadcasting or giving a major interview to any journalist, he will be remembered above all for his plays of conscience (*Antigone*, *The Lark*, *Becket*) where an ordinary man or woman is suddenly forced to make an extraordinary and usually already doomed stand in the name of what is right.

CALENDAR

• The Stage Door Canteen, set up by theatre professionals to entertain servicemen passing through New York, opens in the basement of the 44th St Theatre

• The Liverpool Playhouse, having ceased production temporarily because of the war, is leased to the Old Vic Company whose historic theatre in London has been bombed. The Old Vic will not return to the Vic until 1946

• Dublin's Abbey Theatre begins producing plays in Gaelic for the first time

• Broadway is feeling the effects of the war in Europe – actors and materials are in short supply – and as a result the NY Critics do not give a Drama Critics' Circle Award this year; nor is there a Drama Pulitzer

• Playwright William Saroyan renames the Belasco on Broadway the Saroyan Theatre

• With the war now worldwide for the first time, theatres on Broadway and in the West End specialise in musicals, variety shows, light comedies, revues and classic revivals. New drama is to be in very short supply until 1945

BIRTHS English stage and screen actor **Michael York** **Barbra Streisand** American actress/singer Israeli pianist/conductor **Daniel Barenboim** British actor **Michael Crawford**

DEATHS American actor **John Barrymore**, while rehearsing a radio ROMEO AND JULIET **Tom Irving** English actor who was a member of Sir Henry Irving's company from 1889

NOTABLE PREMIERES On Broadway, THE SKIN OF OUR TEETH, Thornton Wilder's fantasy saga proves controversial with audiences Jack Hulbert opens with Cicely Courtneidge and Nora Swinburne in a new musical, FULL SWING, at the Palace Theatre in the West End

MUSICAL NOTES Shostakovich's 7TH SYMPHONY, 'Leningrad', having been smuggled out of St Petersburg, is now performed in New York with Toscanini conducting

HIT SONGS As Time Goes By White Christmas We'll Meet Again

Oklahoma!

It was the poet Carl Sandburg who got it right: "*Oklahoma!*," he said, "smells of new-mown hay on barn dance floors." In the history of 20th century stage musicals, I would suggest that only *Show Boat* and *Porgy and Bess* (before *Oklahoma!*) and *West Side Story* and *Les Miserables* (after it), did as much to change the whole look and sound and shape and sense of the genre.

But *Oklahoma!* did not have an easy birth, and it was the impresario Mike Todd, seeing the show during its New Haven tryout (where the title was changed to *Oklahoma!* from *Away We Go*), who best summed up the early feeling in the business about its chances. His comment was simply "no girls, no gags, no chance" and by that he was merely echoing the conventional wisdom of an age in which chorus lines of showgirls and star comedians were reckoned essential to any kind of musical comedy.

True, there had three years earlier been *Pal Joey*, but this dark, plot-led show was regarded as a one-off and it had the advantage of the usual Manhattan setting. What first frightened insiders about *Oklahoma!* was that it was about the birth of a state from which no songs had yet emerged.

Originally, this was not to have been a Rodgers and Hammerstein show at all. The Theatre Guild, which owned the rights to Lynn Rigg's play *Green Grow The Lilacs* and were now in the kind of deep financial trouble from which they thought that only a hit musical could save them, had brought it to Richard Rodgers and his partner, Lorenz Hart, despite their misgivings about Hart's physical and mental condition. But Hart, quite apart from his ill-health, shared the conventional wisdom that the idea was a non-starter for a musical, at any rate one in his old 1930s urban, wisecracking tradition, and it was then, with some reservation, that Rodgers turned to Oscar Hammerstein. The two men had known each other since college days and written one or two songs together, but Hammerstein, after some early Broadway hits, not least *The Desert Song*, and

Show Boat, had recently gone through a succession of Broadway flops and was now considered a brave choice. What mattered, though, was that he (like Rodgers but precious few others), loved the idea and saw that, for the first time, there was a chance of getting the Broadway musical away from its old pre-war obsessions with lavish sets and stand-up comics and endlessly incestuous backstage plots.

So from its very beginnings, *Oklahoma!* was radical and revolutionary, despite its outward appearance of old-fashioned rural values. The curtain first went up not on the usual line of leggy dancers, but on an almost bare stage occupied only by one old lady churning butter in the sunrise. The first lines of the show (and one of its greatest songs, "Oh, What A

The "Dream Ballet" from Oklahoma! in 1994

Beautiful Morning") are in fact sung offstage, and from that unusual beginning, almost nothing that happens in *Oklahoma!* resembles anything that had ever happened in musicals before. Speciality numbers were forbidden, as was anything which did not advance the plot; there were no stars to demand 'special material' or showcase songs, and even the great title number was originally conceived as a quiet duet for the two leading lovers.

Even the backstage team was highly odd – again because the usual Broadway regulars of the time were all keeping well clear of what they thought might be a flop. Thus the director was Rouben Mamoulian, who spent virtually all the rest of a long career in movies, and the choreographer was Agnes de Mille, a dancer with only one choreographic hit to her name – a ballet set in the West with a Copeland score called *Rodeo.*

It could be argued that other Rodgers-Hammerstein scores, notably *Carousel* and *South Pacific* were more thoughtful, intelligent and intriguing, but never again were they to capture so perfectly the mood of a nation in transition – its hopes, its aspirations, and its fears at the height of World War Two. *Oklahoma!* remains the closest America has ever come to a national anthem. It is also unique in that, from the very first night, even those critics (and they still exist) deeply opposed to the idea of musicals, recognised exactly what was going on here. In nearly sixty years, no major production of *Oklahoma!* has ever had a bad review anywhere in the world. And it was Richard Rodgers himself who summarised, very simply, what it was all about, "When a show works perfectly, it's because all the individual parts complement each other and fit together…in a great musical, the orchestrations sound the way the costumes look. That's what made *Oklahoma!* work…it was a show created by many, that gave the impression of having been created by just one."

CALENDAR

• Rita Hayworth apparently engaged to Victor Mature, marries Orson Welles
• In Scotland, playwright James Bridie forms a new repertory company which will achieve fame as the Glasgow Citizens Theatre
• Playwright Eugene O'Neill's teenage daughter, Oona, marries Charlie Chaplin, many years her senior; the playwright, appalled, will never see or speak to her again

BIRTHS

Ben Kingsley British actor

American playwright **Sam Shepard**

Michael Bennett Choreographer and director

Andrei Serban Czech-born stage and opera director

DEATHS

American lyricist **Lorenz Hart**

Revolutionary Austrian director **Max Reinhardt**

French playwright **Jean Giraudoux**

NOTABLE PREMIERES

Cole Porter's SOMETHING FOR THE BOYS, starring Ethel Merman with book by Herbert and Dorothy Fields, opens at the Alvin in New York

TOMORROW THE WORLD opens at the Ethel Barrymore theatre

In New York, LOVERS AND FRIENDS, by Dodie Smith, describes the lives and loves of a couple played by Raymond Massey and Katherine Cornell.

Noël Coward stars in his latest play, the semi-autobiographical PRESENT LAUGHTER, which also opens in the autumn on Broadway

Ivor Novello has a rare flop – largely due to the fact that he wasn't in it – with his latest musical, ARC DE TRIOMPHE

MUSICAL NOTES

Bartok's CONCERTO FOR ORCHESTRA

William Schuman's SYMPHONY FOR STRINGS

Copeland's FANFARE FOR THE COMMON MAN

HIT SONGS

You'll Never Know

Oh What a Beautiful Morning

GI Jive

The Surrey With a Fringe on Top

The Life of Galileo

One of the most influential figures in all of world theatre was born Eugen Berthold Friedrich Brecht at Augsberg in Germany on February 10th 1898. The son of a Catholic mother and a Protestant travelling-salesman father, he grew up with a deep loathing of his middle-class background, and after studying medicine and science at university he was briefly called up at the end of World War One to serve as a medical orderly.

He wrote his first play, *Baal*, at the age of twenty during the Bavarian rebellion of 1918; within the next two years he had experienced the birth of an illegitimate son, joined the Communist party, become the theatre critic of their newspaper, and most importantly met the dramatist Lion Feuchtwanger who, recognising a fellow-rebel, gave him a series of masterclasses on the technique of playwriting.

By 1922 he had married the actress Marianne Zoff with whom he had his first daughter, and had begun to work the cafes of Munich, reading aloud his own ballads while accompanying himself on the banjo. By now he was also publishing critically-acclaimed short stories, but it was when he moved to Berlin in 1924 to join Max Reinhardt's Deutsches Theater that his full-time theatre life began. Also with the Reinhardt company at that time were the playwright Carl

Michael Gambon in the title role at the RNT in 1980

Zuckmayer, best-known for the satirical *The Captain from Köpenick*, and the equally radical epic director Erwin Piscator with whom Brecht immediately went to work on *The Good Soldier Schweik*.

He also directed his historical drama *Edward II*, but it wasn't until two crucial meetings in 1927 that Brecht really came into his own. The first was with the communist actress Helene Weigel, for whom he left his first wife and to whom he was to remain married for the rest of his life, and the second was with the composer Kurt Weill.

Together, Brecht and Weill immediately went to work on *Die Dreigroschenoper*, an updating of the world's first-ever musical, John Gay's *Beggar's Opera*. This, largely because of Lotte Lenya (now married to Weill) and its *Mack the Knife* showstopper, was to triumph all over the world for the next seventy years. But with the rise of the Nazis, their subsequent and openly pro-communist work was frequently either banned altogether or interrupted by gangs of marauding pro-Nazis, and the morning after the Reichstag fire in February 1933 Brecht and Weill and their families all fled to Paris, where their last collaboration was on *The Seven Deadly Sins*.

By the end of that year Weill had moved on to America and Brecht settled as an exile in Denmark; he too was later to move to America, and only returned to run the Berliner Ensemble in East Germany with his wife in 1948; Weill never returned to Europe.

It was during Brecht's Scandinavian exile, (he and Weigel fled on to Sweden and Finland, staying just ahead of the invading Germans until they finally got an American entry visa in 1941) that many of his best plays were at least started, among them *The Life of Galileo* which he began to write in 1938. Given the world situation of that time, it is not hard to find, in the story of the medieval astronomer who was forced to save himself from prison and torture by publicly recanting his own discovery that the earth is but one of many planets, some kind of metaphor for those still trying to decide what kind of peace they should make, if any, with Hitler, Mussolini and/or Stalin.

But the issues of personal and political compromise which dominate *Galileo* were by no means over; Brecht wrote his last play (*Days of the Commune*) in 1949, and thereafter spent his time running his Berliner Ensemble.

CALENDAR

• New York gets tough on overcharging ticket agencies as license commissioner Paul Moss suspends the Levlang theatre ticket agency
• Impresario Billy Rose takes over the Ziegfeld theatre which has been a cinema since Ziegfeld's death
• After years of decline, Broadway is booming and there is a shortage of available theatres
• *Trio*, a play about lesbianism, runs into opposition from Lee Shubert who declines to make the Cort Theatre available, on moral grounds. It opens at the Belasco but is rapidly closed by New York City licence commissioner Paul Moss on the advice of twenty priests, only one of whom has seen the play
• David Merrick co-produces *Bright Boy*, his first Broadway show
• The actor Sydney Blackmer closes *Pretty Little Parlor* and steps into *Chicken Every Sunday* two days later, thus becoming the first actor to perform two lead roles on Broadway in one week
• On his *Othello* tour, Paul Robeson instructs theatres to reserve good seats in all locations for black theatre-goers to ensure that they will not be either segregated into a single area, or relegated to the worst seats. He specifies that he would leave the stage immediately if he noticed a pattern of segregation in the audience

BIRTHS **Stockard Channing** American actress

American actress **Geraldine Chaplin**

British actress **Jacqueline Bisset**

Tim Rice British lyricist

British set designer **John Napier**

DEATHS American band leader **Glenn Miller**'s plane mysteriously disappears en route to France from England.

NOTABLE PREMIERES Montgomery Clift appears in New York with Cornelia Otis Skinner and Dennis King in Lillian Hellman's THE SEARCHING WIND

Ruth Gordon's autobiographical farce, OVER 21, opens at the Music Box and deals with a soldier and his writer wife

Mike Todd's extravagant production of MEXICAN HAYRIDE is dismissed by its composer, Cole Porter, whose judgement is "It stinks"

The American Negro Theatre produces ANNA LUCASTA which is subsequently filmed, starring Eartha Kitt and Sammy Davis Jr

Every major New York actor turns down the leading role in Mary Chase's HARVEY. It becomes an instant hit when it opens at the 48th Street theatre

MUSICAL NOTES Stravinsky's SONATA FOR TWO PIANOS

Bartok's SONATA FOR UNACCOMPANIED VIOLIN

HIT SONGS Maizy Doats

Don't Fence Me In

Accentuate the Positive

Perchance to Dream

In the century which roughly separates Gilbert and Sullivan from Rice and Lloyd Webber, there were several stage West End musical writers of note, from Vivian Ellis and Noël Gay through to Julian Slade and David Heneker, and some indeed who reached Broadway long before *Jesus Christ Superstar*, among them Sandy Wilson, Lionel Bart, Antony Newley and Leslie Bricusse.

But only two were ever capable of filling Drury Lane; both were also actors from a very early age with dominant mothers, both were gay and both became film stars. They were also lifelong if wary friends, colleagues and rivals; one of course was Noël Coward and the other Ivor Novello who in this year had one of his greatest hits.

Like Noël again, Ivor was an astute reflector of the changing mood of his nation, and equally adept at raising the national spirit in time of crisis. As early as 1914 when he was barely twenty-one, he made his name with one of the greatest of all World War One songs, "Keep The Home Fires Burning", and then again in World War Two his *The Dancing Years* was uniquely a romantic musical with an anti-Nazi theme, one moreover which had opened six months before the outbreak of war and was the first popular hit to have Nazis as on-stage villains, some thirty years before *The Sound of Music*.

And now, as World War Two came to its end, Ivor sensed another change in the national mood; the desire now was for peace, domesticity and a return to an older, more romantic England far removed from the last six years of food shortages, blackouts and air-raids, and at the London Hippodrome in *Perchance to Dream* Novello delivered all of that in a score where songs like "We'll Gather Lilacs" and "Love Is My Reason" took the mood back to what Ivor always did best – a love story in a romantic setting.

The storyline was in a sense similar to that of Alan J Lerner's *On a Clear Day You Can See Forever*

written twenty years later; both musicals dealt with love connecting across the centuries. In *Perchance to Dream*, we go from Regency highwaymen to modern times; the show ran 1022 performances prior to long tours of Britain and South Africa and was still on the road when Novello left it for his last large-scale musical *King's Rhapsody*, which he died performing at the Palace theatre in 1951.

The casting featured Ivor's usual semi-permanent company (his lifelong lover Robert Andrews, Olive Gilbert, Roma Beaumont, Muriel Barron) plus on this occasion Margaret Rutherford, replaced in South Africa by another Novello regular, Zena Dare.

Ivor Novello, Muriel Barron and others at the London Hippodrome in 1945

This was also his first new score since a vindictive magistrate in 1944 had sent Ivor to prison for a month on a charge of conspiring to break wartime petrol rationing. Many believe that Novello never entirely recovered from the shock of this experience, and that his early death at 58 six years later was at least partially caused by it; on the other hand, the love of his audiences (far greater for Ivor in person than ever it was for Noël) seemed to increase after his jail-term and certainly had no lasting effect at the box-office.

Although he is now chiefly recalled as the composer and star of a sequence of long-running British stage musicals (none of which ever made it to Broadway, so essentially local were they in spirit), Novello's career was in fact considerably more intriguing. He had started out as one of the very first silent screen stars of the early

Perhaps because, unlike Coward, he was a better composer than he was a playwright – his plays, with the exception of *Proscenium* and *I Lived With You* (the latter turned into one of Novello's few successful talking films) are hopelessly dated and lacking both Coward's wit and are no longer bolstered by Novello's extraordinary stage presence and charm.

CALENDAR

• Times Square is not as bright as usual on account of a midnight curfew for the duration of the war but in May, VE Day celebrations begin with a two-day street and theatre party all over Broadway as the curfew is lifted

• A new agreement between theatre owners and stagehands, providing them with a 15% pay raise, avoids a strike

• Actors Equity wastes a good deal of time and energy trying to expel members who attend meetings at which communist sentiments are expressed

• At Stratford-upon-Avon, actor/director Robert Atkins hands over control of the company to Barry Jackson, also director of the prestigious nearby Birmingham Rep

• Major Maurice Evans, after long wartime tour, brings his *GI Hamlet* to the Columbus Circle Theatre in New York. Cuts in the interest of retaining troop attention include two scenes: the burial of Ophelia and the gravediggers in the final act

1920s: he worked for the legendary American director DW Griffith, he was the star of Hitchcock's first hit *The Lodger* and he also filmed two of Coward's early plays. Early in the 1930s he went as a screenwriter to Hollywood and worked on the first *Tarzan* movie; he also played in his own dramas on Broadway and for many years he was London's most bankable matinee idol, usually starring in plays that he had written, and which he would then turn into screenplays, starring in the film versions as well.

It was always said at the time that Noël envied Ivor's looks while Ivor envied Noël's wit, but there were many seasons in which Novello was clearly the greater star of the two. Why then, as Coward after a brief posthumous slump has come back into constant revival at home and abroad, is Novello now so neglected?

BIRTHS American actor and director **John Lithgow** **Bette Midler** American singer and actress American playwright **August Wilson**

DEATHS Composer **Jerome Kern**, in New York for a revival of SHOW BOAT, collapses on a New York street and is taken to a public hospital until he can be identified via the ASCAP (American Society of Composers) card in his pocket. Pulitzer Prize-winning American dramatist **Hatcher Hughes**

NOTABLE PREMIERES Laurette Taylor stages a dramatic comeback from alcoholic obscurity as Amanda, the mother in Tennessee Williams' THE GLASS MENAGERIE SIGH NO MORE, Noël Coward's only post-war revue, runs barely four months despite a cast headed by Joyce Grenfell and Cyril Ritchard On Broadway BILLION DOLLAR BABY has a book by Comden and Green, music by Morton Gould and choreography by Jerome Robbins

MUSICAL NOTES Schoenberg's PRELUDE TO A GENESIS SUITE Hindemith's PIANO CONCERTO Stravinsky's SYMPHONY IN THREE MOVEMENTS William Schuman becomes President of Juilliard Lucia Chase and Oliver Smith become co-directors of Ballet Theatre, later American Ballet Theatre

HIT SONGS Autumn Serenade On the Atchison, Topeka and the Sante Fe It Might as Well Be Spring June is Bustin' Out All Over Dig You Later a Hubba Hubba Hubba My Guy's Come Back

All My Sons

All My Sons didn't actually reach Broadway until the middle of January 1947, but the word from the rehearsal rooms in late 1946 was already predicting the arrival of a major new dramatist. Many of us have always believed that Arthur Miller (born 1915) is the greatest of all American playwrights of the 20th century, although clearly a strong case can also be made for Eugene O'Neill and Tennessee Williams. But what sets Miller ahead even of them is that he alone was always prepared to take on America itself – he has always been the historian and keeper of the moral conscience of a nation undergoing massive changes, and if you truly want to understand America in the 20th century then Miller is your best guide and guardian.

At the time of *All My Sons*, he was already 32. A child of the Depression which effectively ruined his family, he took menial jobs (including that of carpentry, his lifelong occupation when he wasn't writing stage or screenplays) to put himself through college as a journalism major at Ann Arbor; he was then an early writer for the Federal Theatre Project just before the war, and a radio scriptwriter. Rejected for military service because of a football injury, he worked on an award-winning documentary about the front-line reporter Ernie Pyle, and had his first success in 1945 with a novel about anti-Semitism, *Focus*. By now, he had written nine plays but only one (*The Man Who Had All The Luck*, 1944) ever made it to Broadway and then only for four days, although there was at least one encouraging review suggesting that, whatever the shortcomings of this play, he should keep writing.

All that was to change, however, with the success of *All My Sons*. It tells of Joe Keller, an aircraft-parts manufacturer who, committed to windfall profits in the war, allows defective machinery to be fitted to American Air Force planes where they result in fatal crashes. Rather than go to jail himself, he allows his partner to take the blame. It subsequently emerges that his son, thought killed in the war, has in fact committed suicide in shame at the discovery of his father's sin. The play ends with Joe also committing suicide.

Told against the single setting of an ordinary middle-class American home, this was the first of Miller's many parables about the corrupting and ultimately fatal power of greed. It was a drama of force and passion, all the more terrible and brilliant at a time when the American theatre was coming, very gently, back to life in the ongoing euphoria of peace.

Miller was the first to suggest that the American dream, for which so many thousands had fought an overseas war, was already in real danger of turning into a nightmare. The story of a monstrous scandal in which 21 army pilots died because of Joe's greed was a high-voltage, engrossing drama which owed a considerable debt to Ibsen, the 19th century playwright whom Miller has always reflected.

In *All My Sons* for the first time, Miller contrasts the privacy of an apparently happy nuclear family with the public community which it has somehow appallingly failed. The constant theme in this and later work is that people cannot just walk away from the consequences of what they have done and that, if they try, it is nearly always their families who suffer most.

This one play shot Miller into the top ranks of great American dramatists, and he was to stay there for the next half-century. Unusually, the overnight reviews recognised this at once. Miller was acclaimed out of

James Hazeldine and Catherine McCormack in the RNT's 2000 revival

holding up a mirror to the American people, one they seldom really wanted to look into for fear of what they would learn about themselves and their nation in the second half of the 20th century.

Two years after *All My Sons* came Miller's greatest hit, *Death of a Salesman* (1949), another scorching drama of personal and national failure – Willy Loman goes out there "on a smile and a shoeshine", the symbol of the post-war American achiever who is, in fact, dead behind the eyes and for whom, in the end, as for Joe Keller, the only way out is suicide. Both Joe and Willy kill themselves because, while apparently sticking to the rules of social and commercial morality, they have in fact affronted moral decency and they are still close enough to their original belief in themselves to know how far they have strayed.

All My Sons is a Greek tragedy contained within the fences of an archetypal mid-Western backyard. It is *Our Town* rewritten in acid and poison and blood, and once again it is a play about one lone individual holding up a mirror to his neighbours, a mirror which has to be smashed if the neighbourhood is to survive. If only for the moment when Joe, all too late, accepts the parental responsibility of the title, it is possible to argue that, alongside *Death of a Salesman*, this, rather than Theodore Dreiser's, is the real American Tragedy.

nowhere as not just promising but already arrived, a judgement justified by subsequent history. True, the public came to him more slowly, as if always aware that he was going to tell them something about themselves that they didn't really want to hear.

Unlike O'Neill or Williams whose plays were essentially private works of memory, Miller (in his life as well as his dramas) was always plugged into the heart, conscience and mind of post-war America. His experience up against the McCarthy Committee led him to a play about witch-hunting (*The Crucible*), and his marriage to one of the great American icons, Marilyn Monroe, provided the raw material for both his moviescript for her (*The Misfits*) and a play, *After the Fall*, which was a not entirely successful attempt to exorcise his own personal and political demons during the 1950s. Here as elsewhere, Miller was forever

CALENDAR

• Both John Gielgud and Donald Wolfit tour British theatre companies across America, noting gratefully that food, still heavily rationed in Britain, is plentiful there
• Paul Scofield and Peter Brook make their debuts at the Shakespeare Memorial Theatre in Stratford
• At the Old Vic, Laurence Olivier stages and plays King Lear; Ralph Richardson triumphs as *Cyrano de Bergerac* in a revival directed by Tyrone Guthrie.

BIRTHS **Liza Minnelli** Broadway and Hollywood star
American actress **Candice Bergen**
American screen actress **Sally Field**
British producer **Sir Cameron Mackintosh**
American producer **Lynne Meadow**

DEATHS German Expressionist playwright **Gerhart Hauptmann**
British playwright, stage director and academic **Harley Granville Barker**

NOTABLE PREMIERES Disastrous Orson Welles/Mike Todd stage musical of AROUND THE WORLD IN EIGHTY DAYS becomes known as 'Wellesapoppin'
EG Marshall and James Barton open on Broadway in O'Neill's THE ICEMAN COMETH
Judy Holliday opens 1600-performance run of Garson Kanin's BORN YESTERDAY which she also films
Irving Berlin's ANNIE GET YOUR GUN opens on Broadway with Ethel Merman as the sharp-shooting Annie Oakley
In London, Alec Guinness and Ralph Richardson open in JB Priestley's classic about a family implicated in the death of a shopgirl, AN INSPECTOR CALLS

MUSICAL NOTES Leonard Bernstein becomes Director of the Symphony Programmes at New York's City Center

HIT SONGS Doin' What Comes Natur'lly
Come Rain or Come Shine
Zip-a-Dee-Do-Dah
There's No Business Like Show Business

A Streetcar Named Desire

Within a few months of the end of World War Two, America already had its two greatest playwrights of the second half of the century and they were as strongly contrasted as the plays they wrote: Arthur Miller, Ibsenite, rigorous, the keeper and rabbi of America's moral conscience, and Tennessee Williams, the Deep Southern boy who was all emotion and sloppy heart where Miller was the chilly intellectual head.

Thomas Lanier Williams (1911-1983), was born in Columbus, Mississippi, the son of a travelling shoe salesman and his wife, the daughter of an Episcopalian minister. After what he called "a lonely and miserable" childhood in St Louis, where he was bullied at school for his short stature and delicate constitution, he set out to be a writer and, by the time he was taken out of the University of Missouri in 1932 when the family money ran out, he had already published a number of short stories. Five years later, he was at the University of Iowa, supported by his grandparents, studying to be a playwright with a professor who regularly marked his work down. The following year, in 1938, hearing that a lobotomy had been performed on his beloved but troubled sister Rose, he cut off all connection with his family and went to New York, where in 1940 he won $100 prize for drama and aroused the interest of the legendary agent, Audrey Wood.

The title *A Streetcar Named Desire* refers to a now long-defunct tramline in New Orleans, where three of the stops on the route were named Cemeteries, Elysian Fields and, finally, a housing estate called Desire. Blanche DuBois, the central figure of the drama, makes that journey metaphorically as well as literally, when, destitute, she lands on her earthier younger sister, Stella, happily and recently married to a highly sexual rough diamond called Stanley Kowalski and living with him in the close quarters of the Desire tenements. Blanche's aristocratic, fragile and cultured spirit collapses under the violent impact of a brother-in-law who rapes both her body and her mind.

Although *Streetcar* was to win Williams the Pulitzer and provide career-defining roles for Jessica Tandy (the first Broadway Blanche) and Vivien Leigh (in London and on film) and Marlon Brando (Stanley on Broadway and film), it did not open to universally good reviews. George Jean Nathan felt that "Mr Williams seems to labor under the misapprehension that theatrical sensationalism and dramatic truth are much the same thing", while Howard Barnes complained that "at the end, Blanche goes off like a frightened child...her world ends not with a bang but with a whimper. We leave the play depressed, not exalted as after tragic surge. The play deals with sexual abnormality, harlotry, perversion, venality, rape and lunacy...while unpleasant, it is never disgusting, yet never rises to be enlightening. Williams has insisted on making a tragedy out of a cartoon."

In many ways, *Streetcar* was ahead of its time, in the way it really introduced the contemporary notion of psychological drama. We experience Blanche's solitary agony and her terrible descent into madness as though we are seeing into her mind, just as that mind fragments. For those who always had to depend, like Blanche, "upon the kindness of strangers", the play holds a terrible truth and it could be argued that in her own subsequent collapse into a kind of madness, Vivien Leigh was, for the whole of the rest of her life, to live out Blanche's nightmares. On stage and screen, the play made a star of Marlon Brando and effectively therefore introduced the style of Method acting which he came to embody. Although he and Vivien were to leave their fingerprints all over *Streetcar* for many years to come, since their time it has been possible to re-consider the play as something more than just the clash of two cultures.

Streetcar defines the modern American theatre, and its ultimate message about the fragility of the blasted soul was never to be overtaken. The wrought-iron

Vivien Leigh at
the Aldwych in
1949

screens of the Tennessee Williams South may always have seemed dreadfully overwrought but, carrying on from Eugene O'Neill, he became the theatrical voice of the dispossessed and the mentally unstable.

If Arthur Miller speaks for the American city, the educated and Northern morals of the urban dwellers, then Tennessee Williams speaks for the fragility of the overheated swamp country of the Deep South, with its sexual violence, its traditional divisions and its political ambiguities. To that extent it could even be argued that a hundred years later, Williams for the South and Miller for the North were still fighting the Civil War.

CALENDAR

• Both *Oklahoma!* and *Annie Get Your Gun* arrive in London

• Julie Andrews makes her stage debut in the Hippodrome revue, *Starlight Roof*

• 24-year old Peter Brook's production of *Romeo and Juliet* is a highlight of the Stratford summer season

• On Broadway, *Life With Father* reaches a record-breaking 4000 consecutive performances

• Eugene O'Neill refuses to make any of the cuts in *The Iceman Cometh* demanded by the Boston censor

• Two Hollywood stars return to the stage this year in Los Angeles Charles Laughton plays *The Life of Galileo* and on Broadway James Stewart takes over in *Harvey*

• Elia Kazan, Martin Ritt, and Cheryl Crawford found the Actors Studio, home of the Method School of acting

• 300 Broadway and Hollywood writers, directors, and actors are now on the blacklist of alleged Communist sympathisers

BIRTHS   American stage and screen star **Glenn Close**
David Hare   British playwright
Broadway star **Betty Buckley**
David Mamet   American playwright

DEATHS   British theatre critic **James Agate**
American composer and singer **Bert Kalmar**
Irish actor **FJ McCormick**, one of the
founding players of Dublin's Abbey Theatre
Opera star **Grace Moore**

NOTABLE   Charles Laughton directs and stars in Brecht's
PREMIERES   **THE LIFE OF GALILEO**
FINIAN'S RAINBOW, Yip Harburg's satirical
musical fantasy, triumphs on Broadway but flops in
the West End
BRIGADOON, Lerner and Loewe's first hit musical,
runs two years in New York and London
Kurt Weill's musical **STREET SCENE**, based on the
1929 play by Elmer Rice opens on Broadway
Robert Morley and Peggy Ashcroft open two-year
West End run of his own play, **EDWARD, MY SON**
AE Matthews opens in **THE CHILTERN
HUNDREDS**, first of many long-running West End
comedies by William Douglas Home
Jean-Paul Sartre's existentialist **NO EXIT** opens on
Broadway

MUSICAL   Bernstein's **THE AGE OF ANXIETY**
NOTES   Babbitt's **THREE COMPOSITIONS FOR PIANO**
ALBERT HERRING, Benjamin Britten's opera

HIT SONGS   Almost Like Being in Love
Papa, Won't You Dance With Me
How Are Things in Gloccamora

The Lady's Not For Burning

It would be hard to find any playwright, anywhere in the world, whose work was more highly praised in the 1940s, more roundly condemned in the 1950s and who, well into his nineties at the time of this writing, remained so cheerfully and resolutely unaffected by either success or failure.

This may well have something to do with his devout religious belief. He was born Christopher Harris in 1907, the son of an architect turned Church of England lay preacher, and a mother whose name he took after the death of his father, that of her famous Quaker family.

Fry's God lives in all his plays, and one of his most powerful, *A Sleep of Prisoners* (1951), was specifically written for performance in church using biblical tales, as dreamed by modern prisoners of war, to advocate Fry's crusading pacifism and his everlasting belief in the possibility of spiritual revival. As he wrote in that play, "the human heart can go to the lengths of God."

Fry started out in 1926 as a teacher, but a year later he joined the Bath Repertory Company as an actor. Within another year, he had returned to teaching; but in the end the stage won out over the classroom, and by 1934 he was running a local theatre in Tunbridge Wells.

Somewhat surprisingly, his first West End work was as a composer and lyricist for intimate revues; but in 1937 he wrote *The Boy with a Cart*, a pageant to celebrate the 50th anniversary of a church near the home in Sussex where he has always lived. By 1939 he had written three other amateur church pageants and become resident director of the Oxford Playhouse. As a conscientious objector, he was assigned to wartime bomb-clearance but then, in 1946, came his first verse drama, *A Phoenix Too Frequent*, and the invitation to become resident dramatist at the then-private Arts Theatre Club in the West End. There followed two religious dramas, *The Firstborn*, and *Thor, With Angels* (both 1948).

Less than a year later came *The Lady's Not For Burning*, Fry's first full-length verse play, a comic treatment of a witch-hunt in a small English town during the Middle Ages. In a curious way, this could be seen as an immediate forerunner of Arthur Miller's *The Crucible*, but Fry, working in an infinitely lighter vein, was really concerned with a much more local response to the gloom and the austerity of post-war Britain. "When you think of *The Lady*," wrote Fry several years later, "think in terms of light, of inconstant April sunshine, of sunset and twilight and full moon; think of human intelligences in a dance together."

From the first stage direction, informing us that we are in the house of Hebble Tyson, the Mayor of Cool Clary in 1400, "either more or less exactly", it is clear that we are about to enter a whole new world. Love, we are told, is "an April anarchy" and characters are, "in their usual April fit of exasperating nonsense." Of the two central characters, the disillusioned soldier Thomas Mendip tells us that it is time for God "to end the deadly human anecdote with a cosmic yawn of boredom", and that he himself wants nothing more than to be hanged as soon as possible. The other leading character announces at her arrival on-stage, "I am Jennet Jourdemayne and I believe in the human mind." The irony of the play is, of course, that Mendip, who craves death, is doomed to live while Jenny, who aches for life, is fated to die. The principal conflict of the play is therefore between the death wish and the life force. Its last line, "May God have mercy on our souls," as Benedict Nightingale has written, means that "body has been infused with soul, matter with spirit, defeatism with hope, winter with spring, the ordinary with the miraculous; all has been made whole by the power of love, and the perplexing kindness of God."

But by the late 1950s, Fry was being dismissed by many critics including Denis Donoghue, "Fry's philosophy is naïve, his verse is the wanton prancing of words, his plays are marked by mere whimsy and spurious joviality, and he himself is guilty of a verbal flippancy that points to a really fundamental triviality." Yet ten years earlier, *The Lady's Not For Burning* had

Eliot Bakeham, Richard Leech, Harcourt Williams and John Gielgud at the Globe in 1949

become the hottest ticket in town. John Gielgud directed and starred in the transfer to the West End, where it ran at the Globe for almost a year with an amazing cast led by Claire Bloom, Pamela Brown, Peter Bull, Richard Burton (in his first West End appearance) and Richard Leech. Gielgud played this medieval frolic with a lyrical sense of beauty and wit, and it could be argued that this was the first post-war 'snob' hit – a play you really had to see, even if you didn't entirely understand it.

Though they met with varying fortunes, all Fry's plays were essentially comedies which, he claimed, provided the escape from despair into faith. Clearly, Fry owed a considerable debt to the infinitely more solemn TS Eliot, but poetic drama was to have a very short commercial life and by the early 1950s Fry was already in Rome writing the screenplay for *Ben Hur* and advising on other Hollywood biblical epics. One of his last plays, *Curtmantle*, about Thomas à Becket and Henry II, suffered from comparison with Anouilh's *Becket* and for the next 40 years Fry was to live in a kind of gentle twilight, translating Anouilh, writing poems and memoirs and organising church pageants in his beloved English countryside.

CALENDAR

• South African writer Alan Paton publishes his novel, *Cry The Beloved Country*, later a movie and, next year, as *Lost in the Stars*, a Kurt Weill musical
• *Oklahoma!* closes on Broadway after 2248 performances, a record which would not be broken for more than 20 years
• ASCAP strikes for better radio and recording terms for its composers and songwriters
• Producer Cheryl Crawford asks Arthur Miller. "Who on earth would pay good money to see a play about an unhappy travelling salesman?"

BIRTHS Russian ballet star **Mikhail Baryshnikov** **Andrew Lloyd Webber** British composer British stage and screen star **Jeremy Irons**

DEATHS Austrian operetta composer **Franz Lehár** Veteran Broadway critic **Burns Mantle** Broadway producer, playwright and songwriter **Earl Carroll** in a Pennsylvania plane crash

NOTABLE PREMIERES Henry Fonda opens 1100-performance run as MR ROBERTS in Josh Logan's play. Tyrone Power takes it to London where it runs for 200 performances. **SUMMER AND SMOKE**, Tennessee Williams play about a repressed woman in love, starts brief Broadway and West End life Frank Loesser's musical **WHERE'S CHARLEY** has choreography by Balanchine and runs two Broadway years with Ray Bolger in one of his keynote performances **KISS ME KATE**, Cole Porter's most successful Broadway musical opens two-year Broadway run Gertrude Lawrence opens in her only post-war London appearance in Daphne du Maurier's only play **SEPTEMBER TIDE**

MUSICAL NOTES First television music specials include Toscanini with the NBC Symphony and Eugene Ormandy with the Philadelphia Orchestra Ferruccio Burco, aged 9, makes his Carnegie Hall debut conducting Wagner and Beethoven

HIT SONGS Buttons and Bows It's a Most Unusual Day A, You're Adorable On a Slow Boat to China

Lost in the Stars

When the opera composer Kurt Weill, forced out of his native Germany by Hitler, first arrived in America his only important international hit was *Die Dreigroschenoper* (*The Threepenny Opera*), written with the equally serious avant-garde playwright, Bertolt Brecht. Weill died at the age of only 50, during the run of his last major musical, *Lost in the Stars*, and he had been on Broadway for only fifteen years; but his work during that time marked a total break with the music he had written before his arrival in the new world.

Kurt Julian Weill, was born in Dessau on March 2nd 1900. He began as a conductor and repetiteur in his local theatre, but by 1922 his first stage work, a children's piece called *Zaubernacht*, was staged in Berlin. Three years later he was writing one-act operas with the playwright Georg Kaiser, but it wasn't until he turned to the world of musical comedy in 1928 that he made his name with a musical, written with Brecht, the music deliberately contemporary and jazzy. Songs like "Mack the Knife" and "The Moritat" made him famous overnight and although the second Brecht-Weill collaboration *Happy End* featured the "Bilbao" song and "Surabaya Johnny" its lack of plot meant that the show folded in chaos after only three performances.

Then, in 1930 and again with Brecht, came *The Rise and Fall of the City of Mahagonny* but with the rise of the Nazis in 1933 Weill and his wife Lotte Lenya joined the mass exodus of Jewish writers and artists from Germany, abruptly ending, in his early 30s all connection with the German theatre and, indeed, with Brecht.

After brief stays in Paris and London (where he wrote the music for two more unsuccessful scores), Weill settled in America and became almost overnight a totally different man and writer. By now, more American than most Americans, his first Broadway musical was the 1936 *Johnny Johnson*, an anti-war parable briefly produced by the Group Theatre and then, in 1938, with the playwright Maxwell Anderson, he wrote *Knickerbocker Holiday* which contained the Walter Huston classic "September Song".

It was three years later, in 1941, that Weill achieved the only Broadway success which could be said to have measured up to that of his *Threepenny Opera*. *Lady in the Dark* was an extraordinary extravaganza which brought together the lyricist Ira Gershwin (still recovering from the early death of his brother George), the playwright and director Moss Hart (who had just ended his triumphant Broadway partnership with George S Kaufman), the English star Gertrude Lawrence (who had just ended her partnership with Noël Coward) and an up-and-coming young comic called Danny Kaye.

Because of Moss Hart's new-found interest in psychiatry, this was the story of a glossy magazine editor (loosely based on the young Diana Vreeland, also immortalised in the Fred Astaire musical *Funny Face*) who, under hypnosis, tries to work out which of three very different suitors would be her best bet for marriage. With its vast dream sequences and its extended opera-style 'scenas', *Lady in the Dark* was the first Broadway 'theme' musical pointing the way forward to Stephen Sondheim. It would be hard to imagine a more 'New York'- style show, or one more up-to-date, glossy, or American. Weill revelled in the very idea that he, a serious German composer, should be asked to compose it and rose magnificently to the substance and style, suiting his music to the colouration of the Broadway post-war interests and fitting perfectly into the keys and limited ranges of Gertie Lawrence and Danny Kaye, neither of them great singers. It managed to be both a critical and popular success on stage, though the subsequent Ginger Rogers movie was something of a travesty. Nevertheless, songs like "My Ship" and "Jenny" and "Girl of the Moment" made Weill the hot new Broadway composer, the most gleefully 'American' of his time, incorporating the musical history of ragtime, modern jazz, the edginess of 'cool' and the rigorous austerity of opera.

His subsequent show *One Touch of Venus* (1943), written with Ogden Nash and SJ Perelman, was equally successful not least because it established the stardom of Mary Martin, directed by Elia Kazan and choreographed by Agnes de Mille.

**Kurt Weill
c1949**

But then, in 1945, came a major disaster. *The Firebrand of Florence*, again written with Ira Gershwin, was a weird period piece about the sculptor Benvenuto Cellini which ran less than six weeks. Undeterred, Weill then composed the score for a musical version of Elmer Rice's award-winning drama *Street Scene*. The intention here was to write a Broadway opera in the tradition of *Porgy and Bess*, and though it did not originally achieve the success of *Lady in the Dark* or *One Touch of Venus*, *Street Scene* was to become one of the very first Broadway musicals to cross over into the repertoire of opera houses in Britain and America, thereby posthumously vindicating Weill's belief that there were only two kinds of music – good and bad – and that the lines which divided different kinds of musical theatre were false and destructive.

CALENDAR

• Variety advises young playwrights to start writing for television where the opportunities for production are "much greater than those on Broadway"

• Tony Awards go to TS Eliot for *The Cocktail Party* and Ezio Pinza and Mary Martin for their roles in *South Pacific*

• Founding of the off-Broadway Theatre League which achieves Equity agreement that non-union members may work there so long as they represent less than half the cast

• Broadway ticket prices now reach $7 at weekends

• Tallulah Bankhead threatens to run as Democratic Vice-president on the Republican ticket; her slogan will be "Tallulah for Vice"

• Gwen Verdon and Bob Fosse make Broadway debuts in two short-lived musicals

BIRTHS

Mary-Louise, later Meryl **Streep**, American stage and screen actress

American playwright **Christopher Durang**

Gregory Mosher American stage director

Broadway musicals star **Patti Lupone**

DEATHS

American character actor **Wallace Beery**

British radio and stage comedian **Tommy Handley**

American stage and screen tap dancer **Bill "Bojangles" Robinson**

NOTABLE PREMIERES

Arthur Miller's DEATH OF A SALESMAN wins the Pulitzer Prize, the Drama Critic's Circle Award and a run of 750 performances

SOUTH PACIFIC, Rodgers and Hammerstein's adaptation of James Michener stories runs nearly 2000 performances on Broadway and the same again at the Theatre Royal, Drury Lane

Carol Channing becomes a star in her signature role as the diamond-digging Lorelei Lee in GENTLEMEN PREFER BLONDES.

At the Old Vic, Laurence Olivier plays his first RICHARD III with Vivien Leigh as Lady Anne

The two Hermiones – Gingold and Baddeley – co-star in long-running revival of Noël Coward's FALLEN ANGELS

MUSICAL NOTES

Sadler's Wells makes first visit to the New York Metropolitan Opera House with SWAN LAKE and SLEEPING BEAUTY

HIT SONGS

Diamonds Are a Girl's Best Friend

Some Enchanted Evening

Mona Lisa

Rudolph, the Red-Nosed Reindeer

Come Back Little Sheba

Though, tragically, he took his own life at the age of 60 in 1973, convinced that his playwriting career had ended in failure, William Inge had three great Broadway and Hollywood hits – *Come Back Little Sheba* (1950), *Picnic* (1953), and *Bus Stop* (1955) – all of which told the tales of lonely, sexually obsessed mid-Westerners struggling towards some glimpse of happiness.

William Motter Inge was born in Independence, Kansas in 1913, the youngest of five children of a small-town travelling salesman and his wife, a descendant of theatre folk. Like the little boy in *The Dark at The Top of The Stairs* he tried to escape reality by collecting film-star photographs. He was educated at the University of Kansas before finding work as a schoolteacher and then a local actor. In 1943 he became the drama critic of the *St Louis Star-Times* and four years later sent his first play *Farther Off From Heaven* (rewritten ten years later as *The Dark at The Top of The Stairs*) to Tennessee Williams, whom he had met as an interviewer who in turn recommended it to Margo Jones for her Dallas theatre.

The play never reached Broadway but three years later Inge scored a success with his second *Come Back Little Sheba* which recounted the unhappy marriage of an alcoholic and his frowsy day-dreaming wife. With Shirley Booth and Sidney Blackmer this became an overnight hit encouraging critics to write of a major new talent.

In 1953, Inge was to win both the Pulitzer and the New York Drama Critics Circle Awards with his *Picnic* in which a handsome, cocksure vagrant awakens the sexual frustrations of some small-town Kansas women. Expanded from an early Inge sketch about five frustrated women on a Kansas porch, this was also the story of a lonely schoolteacher and an eager young girl and was the play in which Paul Newman made his name. As the *New York Times* reported, "Taking a group of commonplace people in a small Kansas town on a hot

William
Inge
c1950

Labor Day, Inge has made a rich and fundamental play out of them that is tremendously moving."

Two more hits quickly followed: *Bus Stop* was about the unlikely odd-couple romance of a bar-room singer and a love-sick cowboy stranded by a storm and *The Dark at The Top of The Stairs* was about an unhappy Oklahoma family in which a boy commits suicide and a son can never come to terms with his jealousy at seeing his parents together in the warm light at the top of the stairs.

Richard Watts, writing for the *NY Post*, thought the latter "a moving and perceptive drama which again indicates Inge's unique ability to probe sympathetically into tortured souls under a façade of frequently humorous brightness." A very strong cast, led by Teresa Wright, Pat Hingle, and Eileen Heckart ensured a long Broadway run.

All Inge's four major hits were subsequently filmed: *Come Back Little Sheba* won a 1952 Oscar for Shirley Booth, now partnered by Burt Lancaster; *Picnic* in 1955 starred William Holden, Kim Novak, Rosalind Russell and Susan Strasberg and *Bus Stop*, filmed in 1956, starred Marilyn Monroe and Don Murray, while *Dark at the Top of the Stairs* starred Robert Preston, Dorothy McGuire and Angela Lansbury in 1960.

But that, amazingly, was it. The run of hits which had started for Inge in 1950 ended just as abruptly and unexpectedly with that decade, although he was, in 1961 to have one final triumph. He won an Oscar for writing the screenplay *Splendor in the Grass*, directed by Elia Kazan with Natalie Wood and Warren Beatty, but then, although throughout the 1960s he wrote another six plays, all of them opened to poor reviews and many never even reached Broadway.

Critics began to feel that even in so short a time as ten years, Inge had written himself out and that all his later work was merely a retread of something he had done better before. Though he constantly reworked his scripts they all seemed to be psychological studies of the same confused family and his almost obsessive interest in the domestic problems of lower middle-class Americans began to seem trite and repetitive.

The loss of love, the loss of innocence and the loss of energy which he was always writing about became now autobiographical. Privately, Inge had not dealt well with his sudden success and even less well with habitual failure. No playwright of the Broadway 1950s rose higher to fall further, and by the time he killed himself in 1973 it seemed already almost an anti-climax.

His last play *The Last Pad* (1970) told of three men on Death Row and survived only very briefly way off-Broadway. By that time, haunted by alcohol, clinical depression and the loss of his reputation, Inge himself was already under sentence of death and he has never yet enjoyed the rediscovery that most playwrights of his era have been able, if only posthumously, to enjoy.

CALENDAR

• The Old Vic, which lost its roof in the bombing of 1941, finally reopens with Peggy Ashcroft in *Twelfth Night*

• Sir Laurence Olivier and Sir Ralph Richardson are both fired as directors of the Old Vic company on the grounds that they have too many other commitments. The theatre is now taken over by Tyrone Guthrie

• Menotti's *The Consul* wins the Pulitzer for best musical

• At Stratford-upon-Avon, season highlights include Gielgud's *King Lear* and *Much Ado About Nothing* and Peter Brook's *Measure For Measure* starring Paul Scofield

• Opening of Arena Stage in Washington DC

• First late-night television talk show, Broadway Open House, starts with Maurey Amsterdam

• Paul Draper is fired from the Ed Sullivan Show because of Communist accusations, the first major public indication of the blacklist

• Senator Joseph McCarthy publishes *Red Channels*, "the Report of Communist Influence in Radio and TV", as CBS requires that all its employees sign a new loyalty oath. Among those listed in Red Channels are Leonard Bernstein, Lee J Cobb, Gypsy Rose Lee, Burgess Meredith, Arthur Miller, Zero Mostel, Pete Seeger, and Orson Welles

BIRTHS British stage and screen actress **Julie Walters** **William Hurt** American character actor American playwright **Wendy Wasserstein**

DEATHS Scots music-hall star singer **Sir Harry Lauder** **Kurt Weill** German-born composer Russian ballet star **Vaslav Nijinsky** Irish playwright **George Bernard Shaw** **Pauline Lord** British actress Irish actress and founder member of the Abbey Theatre, Dublin **Sara Allgood**

NOTABLE PREMIERES Alec Guinness, Irene Worth and Cathleen Nesbitt open on Broadway in TS Eliot's mystical THE COCKTAIL PARTY. Ethel Merman opens in Irving Berlin's CALL ME MADAM Uta Hagen and Paul Kelly open in the Clifford Odets play THE COUNTRY GIRL Frank Loesser's GUYS AND DOLLS opens 1200-performance run. Brian Rix opens nearly two decades of farces at the Whitehall Theatre with RELUCTANT HEROES

MUSICAL NOTES DON QUIXOTE, ballet by Ninette de Valois In Louisville Kentucky Martha Graham dances a new work, JUDITH, to music by William Schuman Sir Thomas Beecham triumphantly tours the USA with the Royal Philharmonic

HIT SONGS Autumn Leaves A Bushel and a Peck La Vie en Rose My Heart Cries for You

A Penny for A Song

Although there were encouraging signs, at the turn of this new century, that he was beginning to be rediscovered, and not before time, John Whiting remains, with Christopher Fry and Rodney Ackland but precious few others, one of the most important and unduly neglected British playwrights of the immediately post-war years.

Had he not died of cancer at the early age of 45, Whiting would undoubtedly have delivered on the promise that he was always showing; indeed his last play, *The Devils* (1961), is one of the most important of its decade, and in the fallen priest, Grandier, there is the archetypal Whiting hero, well described by Eric Salmon as "a self-immolating romantic in search of the absolute".

One of the reasons that Whiting never in his lifetime achieved the success that was his due lay simply in timing; he came immediately after the short-lived fashion for the poetic drama of Eliot and Fry, but only just before the revolution at the Royal Court, and he belonged to neither movement. Not only was Whiting always a loner and an outsider to both the old and the new theatrical establishments of the 1950s, he was also a dramatist who wrote all kinds of different dramas, fantasies and histories. Hard to define, sometimes hard to like, his plays nevertheless live longer in the memory than many more immediately successful works.

Shortly before his death Whiting, who was also for many years a drama critic on intellectual magazines, wrote a tough response to Tynan who in a characteristically flamboyant column had proclaimed that drama was dead in the theatre. "I am," replied Whiting, "one of that disappearing species, a private individual; but the tragedy of men is that they are men, and when there is food and drink, houses and clothing, health, security and sanity for all, we will still be scared to death of death. The germ of tragedy will always be there".

Whiting was born in 1917, the son of a soldier turned lawyer; thinking at first that he wanted to be an actor, he trained at Royal Academy of Dramatic Arts but spent much of the war in the Royal Artillery, which ill-health forced him to leave in 1944.

He returned to acting in regional repertory companies, but increasingly realised that he really wanted to be a dramatist. Two early, sardonic comedies (*No More A-Roving* and *Conditions of Agreement*) failed to get produced in his lifetime, but then in 1951 came both *Saint's Day* and *A Penny for A Song*, the two plays that made his name, albeit against considerable critical opposition.

Saint's Day was a violent, allegorical drama about a reclusive old poet convinced that his villagers are trying to kill him; by the end of what is supposed to be a day of celebration, a dog and several characters are dead, and Whiting has for the first time made his point about the alienation and self-destruction of the artist in society.

What is intriguing about *Saint's Day* (which won a Festival of Britain playwriting award judged by, among other notables, Christopher Fry), is how quickly its cause was taken up by the acting profession, who instantly recognised in Whiting a writer unafraid of the theatrically flamboyant at a time when drama was already in danger of greying up around the edges. In response to its initially hostile reviews, Peggy Ashcroft, Tyrone Guthrie, Peter Brook and John Gielgud all wrote to *The Times* praising the play's passion, unbroken tension, and finding it "moving, beautiful and fascinating".

As if aware, though, that if he was to succeed as a dramatist he would have to move on to something at least vaguely more commercial, Whiting's second play of this year was a weird and wonderful comic fantasy.

A Penny for A Song, later transformed into an opera by Sir Richard Rodney Bennett, is set in Dorset during the Napoleonic wars, at a time when the Emperor himself was thought to be building a channel tunnel through which to invade England in disguise. In readiness, a Dad's Army of characteristic Whiting eccentrics goes into action, an action which climaxes

Brian Cox with the RSC at the Barbican in 1986

with one of them trapped down a well in a hot-air balloon while another spends the entire play on lookout duty, equally trapped high in a tree and wearing a saucepan on his head by way of protection from flying objects.

Whiting was ultimately destroyed as a dramatist because he refused to believe that the Royal Court was the only way forward for British contemporary drama or that a classless, narrowly political theatre was necessarily better than one which dealt with a much wider social tapestry and the possibilities of magic. Had he been born French, or a few years earlier, he would not have had a problem; you have only to look towards Anouilh and Giraudoux to see where Whiting was really coming from. As it was, he left his work ticking away like a time-bomb.

At the time of his early death in 1963, Whiting was working on a new play and also a translation of the dramatist he in the end most resembled, Jean Anouilh. He would perhaps at any time have been an isolated figure in the theatre, since he wanted primarily neither to entertain nor to uplift an audience but simply to pose them a number of unanswerable questions about life and death.

CALENDAR

• The House Un-American Activities Committee names Jose Ferrer, Judy Holliday, and Abe Burroughs as members of Communist front groups
• Alec Guinness, due on Broadway next year with a modern-dress *Hamlet*, has been savaged by the critics at its London opening
• Jose Ferrer becomes the first actor to win a Tony and an Oscar for the same role, *Cyrano*
• Variety reports that Richard Rodgers and Oscar Hammerstein are considering adapting Shaw's *Pygmalion* as a musical
• The Ziegfeld Theatre hosts Laurence Olivier and Vivien Leigh in Shakespeare's *Antony and Cleopatra*

BIRTHS

Treat Williams American classical stage actor

American stage actress **Judith Ivey**

DEATHS

American comedienne and star of Ziegfeld Follies, **Fanny Brice**

British musical director, composer and critic **Constant Lambert**

English actor-manager **Cyril Maude**, for many years president of RADA

Composer, actor-manager and silent screen star **Ivor Novello**

NOTABLE PREMIERES

Maureen Stapleton and Eli Wallach open on Broadway in Tennessee Williams' **THE ROSE TATTOO**

Gertrude Lawrence and Yul Brynner star in Rodgers and Hammerstein's **THE KING AND I**

Opening on Broadway of the Lerner & Loewe musical about a California goldrush, **PAINT YOUR WAGON**

Frith Banbury directs Edith Evans, Sybil Thorndike and Wendy Hiller in NC Hunter's **WATERS OF THE MOON**

Peter Ustinov stars in his own **THE LOVE OF FOUR COLONELS**

MUSICAL NOTES

Igor Stravinsky's opera **THE RAKE'S PROGRESS**

Benjamin Britten's opera, **BILLY BUDD**

HIT SONGS

Shall We Dance?

The Little White Cloud that Cried

Hello Young Lovers

In the Cool, Cool, Cool of the Evening

Unforgettable

The Pink Room

It could be said of last year's playwright, John Whiting, that if he has still not been adequately rediscovered on stage, he has at least now made it into all the mid-century theatre histories. Rodney Ackland, his near-contemporary, is still however missing from almost all the reference books, despite a triumphant National Theatre revival of his *Absolute Hell* (his revised version of *The Pink Room*) with Judi Dench who had first played the role on television in 1991, a few months before Ackland died.

He was born, as his only chronicler Charles Duff relates, Norman Ackland Bernstein in 1908, the son of a Jewish businessman and a mother (Ada Rodney, from whom he took his Christian name) who had been Principal Boy in pantomime. When Rodney was six, the family fortune abruptly disintegrated as his father was declared bankrupt, and the rest of his youth was spent in drastically straitened circumstances while his mother sold stockings door to door.

Like Whiting, Ackland started out as an actor, having won a scholarship to Elsie Fogerty's drama school; he played some leading roles on regional tours and in repertory theatres, notably Young Woodley, but rapidly found himself drawn to the new world of talking pictures. Then however, seeing the 1926 Komisarjevsky *Three Sisters* with John Gielgud, he turned to playwriting and, still only 21, he had his first drama, *Improper People*, briefly staged at the Arts; it was, he said, "a play about two young lovers and a suicide pact, and my aim was to tell the truth about living without money in the suburbs, a subject on which I felt I could speak with authority".

In rapid succession Ackland then wrote two more plays (*Marion-Ella* and *Dance with No Music* (both 1929), the first about schizophrenia and the second about an actress in seaside repertory), but it was his fourth, *Strange Orchestra* (1931) that first brought him to the attention of the director Frith Banbury, who was to champion his work for the rest of his life alongside that of such other Banbury discoveries as the playwrights NC Hunter and Robert Bolt.

A year later, it was John Gielgud who directed *Strange Orchestra* for the West End, the first contemporary play he had ever undertaken; Gielgud found the characters enthralling, as he later wrote: "They are uncertain of their jobs, they quarrel, make love, engage in scenes of hysteria, behave abominably to one another, perform deeds of unselfish heroism, and dance to the gramophone".

Ackland was already halfway from Coward to Rattigan, and setting up as the chronicler of a new London Bohemia, one which clearly came as something of a shock to the veteran Mrs Patrick Campbell, when she was asked by Gielgud to consider the leading role: "Who," she enquired imperiously, "are all these extraordinary people? Where do they live? Does Gladys Cooper know them?"

In the end, her role was played by Laura Cowie, and though the play was not a commercial success it did draw a rave review in *The Sunday Times* from the most influential critic of the day, James Agate: "*Strange Orchestra* is as much superior to the ordinary stuff of our theatre as tattered silk is to unbleached calico".

Ackland himself acted in his next two plays, *Birthday Party* (1934) about the appalling Moorehouse-Reese family, and the semi-autobiographical *After October* (1936).

Later came what many consider to be his best play, *The Dark River*, the one that in 1984 brought him back into favour with a revival at the Orange Tree in Richmond (where Ackland now lived in retirement and ill health) by Sam Walters, who along with the *Spectator* critic Hilary Spurling had long been proclaiming his virtues to a heedless world. Peggy Ashcroft played the lead in the first production as the mother of an irritable family living on a backwater of the Thames and signally failing to come to terms with a rapidly-advancing crisis in Europe.

But none of these plays achieved real commercial success, despite Agate's persistent support, and when even he finally turned against him, he was turned into the ugly old lesbian critic in *The Pink Room*.

**Judi Dench as Christine
at the RNT in 1995**

It was left to Hilary Spurling to write his best obituary: "Ackland was Chekhovian in the sense that, virtually alone among the playwrights of his generation, he saw no reason why contemporary intellectual, political, social and sexual undercurrents should not be dealt with on the stage as freely as by any of the other arts. In the context of the well-made West End play between the wars, this was a revolutionary proposition. When the theatre set itself to hold a glamorous and reassuring mirror up to nature, Ackland produced a bright, clear, unflattering glass in which audiences saw their world reflected too clearly for comfort...but Ackland remains the only serious playwright whose work will bear comparison, in point of imaginative strength and emotional delicacy, with the novelists and poets (Powell, Waugh, Greene, Spender, Auden) this country produced between the wars".

CALENDAR

• Carol Channing gives her 1000th performance as Lorelei Lee in *Gentlemen Prefer Blondes*
• Elia Kazan names names to the House Un-American Activities Committee including Clifford Odets and Morris Carnovsky
• In Washington DC the National Theatre, boycotted by Equity because of a segregationalist policy, is taken over by a Broadway production company, who re-open it with non-segregated seating
• Playwright Lillian Hellman, summoned to appear before the HUAC, says "I cannot and will not cut my conscience to fit this year's fashions"; she agrees to testify about her own political activities, but not those of others

BIRTHS Broadway actress **Christine Baranski**
American playwright, actor and monologist
Eric Bogosian

DEATHS **Gertrude Lawrence**, of cancer, at the tragically early age of 54
Hattie McDaniel Black stage and screen star

NOTABLE PREMIERES Christopher Fry's **VENUS OBSERVED** stars Rex Harrison and Lilli Palmer and is directed by Laurence Olivier on Broadway
NEW FACES OF 1952 discovers Eartha Kitt and Carol Lawrence
DIAL M FOR MURDER, Frederick Knott's thriller, stars Maurice Evans and is an immediate hit
Tom Ewell opens on Broadway in George Axelrod's **THE SEVEN YEAR ITCH**
Terence Rattigan's **THE DEEP BLUE SEA** stars Peggy Ashcroft
Agatha Christie's thriller **THE MOUSETRAP** opens starring Richard Attenborough and his wife Sheila Sim. It will become the longest–running play in all theatre history

MUSICAL NOTES Louis Armstrong tours Europe with his All Stars and becomes an international ambassador of jazz
At the Royal Opera House, Covent Garden, an unknown Greek soprano sings a rarely performed Bel Canto opera, Bellini's **NORMA**. The singer is called Maria Callas

HIT SONGS Anywhere I Wander
Pretend
Your Cheatin' Heart
I Saw Mommy Kissing Santa Claus
Singin' in the Rain

A Day by The Sea

In the brief, four-year hiatus between the collapse of poetic drama in 1952 and the coming of the Royal Court in 1956, two genres dominated the West End theatre. One was that old standby the thriller: nobody could have guessed that *The Mousetrap*, now completing its first year, was in fact to complete at least half a century of unbroken performances, but the form was successful enough for even such 'highbrow' playwrights as Emlyn Williams to write them regularly – *Someone Waiting*, about a man hanged for a murder he did not commit, was his entry for this year.

The other genre was neatly defined as 'English Chekhov', and the two leading exponents of this had two of their greatest successes opening within a month of each other at the very end of 1953 – Wynyard Browne's *A Question of Fact* (admittedly, like the Emlyn Williams, more of a cultured whodunnit than his usual conversation piece) and NC Hunter's *A Day By The Sea*.

1953 had been a year of considerable turmoil both onstage and backstage around the West End; the summer of the Coronation had also been the summer of Gielgud's knighthood and subsequent arrest for homosexual soliciting, and the theatre generally seemed on the brink of some sort of revolution which nobody could yet define. As a result, it fled back into what it knew and loved, and in this category both Hunter and Browne were perfect casting.

They had a great deal in common, not least the admiration of the director Frith Banbury and the producer Hugh Beaumont of HM Tennent, who both ensured that their plays were immensely starrily cast and handsomely mounted for the then all-powerful matinee audiences taking tea in the interval at the Theatre Royal Haymarket or, at the very least, the Savoy.

Norman Hunter had started out as a schoolmaster, much like the Robert Bolt whom Banbury was later to discover, and had written nine unsuccessful plays and several novels before the drama that made his name in 1951, *Waters of the Moon*. As Charles Duff (the only notable chronicler of them both, as he is of

Rodney Ackland in this same theatrically under-researched period) has written, this is a deliberately Chekhovian piece set in what would now be called a country-house hotel; as a forerunner of Rattigan's *Separate Tables* (also set in an English hotel), *Waters of the Moon* also concerns a class struggle between wealthy interlopers and the resident poor, and at certain moments

the plot is virtually identical to that of *The Cherry Orchard*, and an amazingly starry Haymarket cast was led by Edith Evans, Sybil Thorndike, Wendy Hiller and Kathleen Harrison.

Two years later, Hunter followed this with an even starrier vehicle: *A Day By The Sea* again featured Dame Sybil Thorndike, this time with Sir John Gielgud (who also directed, since Banbury was engaged on the new Wynyard Browne), Sir Ralph Richardson, Sir Lewis Casson and Irene Worth.

"Hunter has a way of presenting life naturally," noted *Theatre World*, 'as though it were a quiet, slow-moving

Lockwood West, Ralph Richardson, Frederick Piper, Sybil Thorndike, Megs Jenkins, John Gielgud, Irene Worth and Lewis Cusson at the Haymarket in 1953

river' and sure enough here again was a conversation-piece about a Dorset family to whom very little happened very slowly.

There was however considerably more drama backstage, as the pre-London opening at Liverpool came only five days after the arrest of Sir John Gielgud for homosexual soliciting in Chelsea; although she was

not due on stage for several minutes, Dame Sybil pre-empted any possible audience reaction to Sir John's first solo appearance on stage in act one by, to his surprise, taking a chair downstage and sitting on it, staring like a stern schoolmistress into the stalls ready to silence with a stare any unfortunate comments. None came, and Sir John's career was saved overnight; by the time they reached London, there were the usual stage-door queues for his autograph. Like *Waters of the Moon* it ran over a year at the Haymarket, though unlike it *A Day by the Sea* has never had a major revival, not least perhaps because it needs a cast of the kind of stardom which has simply been unavailable ever since.

Neither Hunter nor Browne, who went on writing less and less successful plays until they were totally overtaken and expelled even from the West End by the Royal Court writers a decade or so later, ever feature in such reliable guides as Benedict Nightingale's *50 Modern British Plays*. They have been as effectively 'disappeared' as any Soviet writer under Stalin, and yet no understanding of Britain in the 1950s can really be complete without them. Their director Frith Banbury summed up their work as "quiet plays from quiet men" and that perhaps is all that in the end needs to be said; yet in such plays as Hunter's *A Day by the Sea* and Browne's *Holly and the Ivy* can be found a whole lost English way of life – genteel certainly, representative only of precisely the middle classes who most often

went to see such plays, but for all that as socially and historically interesting as the best of the Chekhov they so wanted to emulate. Their only real rivals were two near-contemporary female dramatists, Dodie Smith and Enid Bagnold, who also wrote primarily of the family-that "dear octopus from whose tentacles we never really escape, nor ever really wish to".

CALENDAR

• Birth of the Goon Show, one of the most popular of all radio shows, which combined the talents of Harry Secombe, Michael Bentine, Peter Sellers, and scriptwriter/performer Spike Milligan
• It's a busy year for Shakespeare: Richard Burton is in *Henry V* at the Old Vic, and the Hollywood movie of *Julius Caesar* stars John Gielgud, James Mason and Marlon Brando
• A device is invented for moving curtains and scenery with an electrically controlled winch.
• The Theatre Royal, Stratford East, becomes the home of Joan Littlewood's Theatre Workshop, which she described as "A British People's Theatre"
• More than 300,000 tickets are sold at London's Old Vic during this Coronation season
• The Shakespeare Festival at Stratford Ontario, Canada, inspired by the dream of a Canadian journalist, and directed by Tyrone Guthrie, opens its doors for a five-week season which, due to its popularity, has to be extended for another week
• British and American Equity negotiate to ease restrictions on exchanges between their country's theatres. They fail to reach agreement

BIRTHS American actor **John Malkovich**

Amy Irving American actress

DEATHS American playwright **Eugene O'Neill**

NOTABLE PREMIERES Arthur Miller's drama **THE CRUCIBLE**, ostensibly about the Salem witch trials of 1692, is in fact equally about the current political witchhunts in Washington DC

William Inge's **PICNIC** stars Ralph Meeker, Kim Stanley and Paul Newman in Josh Logan's production

With music by Leonard Bernstein, lyrics by Betty Comden and Adolph Green and a book (based on Ruth McKenny's stories **MY SISTER EILEEN**) by Joseph Fields and Jerome Chodorov became the hit musical **WONDERFUL TOWN**. It was a success in both New York and London

A new musical, **KISMET**, uses the music of Borodin with lyrics by Robert Wright and George Forrest and a book by Luther Davis and Charles Lederer

AIRS ON A SHOESTRING, a revue with material by Flanders and Swann featured Denis Quilley and Max Adrian

MUSICAL NOTES The New York City Ballet, with the arrival of Jerome Robbins, mounts a record-breaking 12 new productions

An innovative new choreographer, Alwin Nikolais, makes his signature work **MASKS, PROPS** and **MOBILES**

HIT SONGS Baubles Bangles and Beads

Stranger in Paradise

The Boy Friend

If, in the four decades that separated World War Two from the coming of *Les Miserables*, there was any one 'annus mirabilis' for the British stage musical, then it was undoubtedly 1954 which saw, within six months, the West End openings of both Julian Slade's *Salad Days* and Sandy Wilson's *The Boy Friend*; and if the Wilson has edged slightly ahead in the nostalgia stakes, despite the fact that the Slade had an initially longer run, it is simply because *The Boy Friend* made it to Broadway and the cinema screen, albeit not happily, where *Salad Days* proved untranslatable into any other idiom. For both scores, a kind of two-piano simplicity was the key, and both started out very small indeed; *The Boy Friend* came out of the Players Theatre, a Victorian music-hall club underneath the arches of Charing Cross, and was ultimately responsible for making stars of both Julie Andrews (in the first Broadway staging) and Twiggy (on film).

Its genius was in the way that Sandy Wilson celebrates rather than parodies the musical comedies of his early youth; like Rattigan's *French Without Tears* (also set in a south of France finishing school for young English ladies) *The Boy Friend* is a perfect miniature period piece, and its score has such hauntingly romantic hits as "A Room in Bloomsbury" as well as the splendidly comic "Never Too Late To Fall In Love". Hearing it on the first night at Wyndhams, (where it was to stay for two thousand performances), Noël Coward told Wilson "There are only three good lyricists left – you, me and Cole".

Precisely because *The Boy Friend* was a tribute to an already lost world, witty, elegant, charming and nostalgic, and as its composer/lyricist noted '"a loving salute to those far-off days of the cloche hat and the short skirt, a valentine card from one post-war era to another", it showed the one way in which the West End could still challenge the invasion of the Broadway big-band shows. Small was indeed beautiful, and *The Boy Friend* only ran into any kind of trouble when (in the original Broadway version, and later in the Cameron

Mackintosh revival and a catastrophic Ken Russell movie), subsequent directors tried to make it bigger and broader, succeeding only in blowing the little treasure up to the point of explosion. When it left the relatively sheltered confines of the Players and Wyndhams, Sandy Wilson's score was to lose a great deal of its charm.

Like *The Fantasticks* in America, another product of this era which thrived in direct competition to the big-band shows on Broadway and is at the time of this 2000 writing still the longest-surviving New York musical after forty or so years, *The Boy Friend* came out of nowhere and had very little in common with any other musical of its period. But six months after it first transferred to Wyndhams, it was joined in the West End by another small-scale classic, this one written originally for the Bristol Old Vic.

Salad Days by Julian Slade is simply the tale of two nostalgic young college graduates coming out of college into a supposedly real world and finding instead a tramp with a magic piano capable of making all who hear it break into dance routines. The West End opening prompted Ivor Brown of the *Observer* to note that "while jet planes crash the sound barrier, a piano tinkles and we suddenly take this to be the music of the spheres", though for the *Evening Standard* Milton Shulman had his reservations: "Those best qualified to enjoy this show would be an aunt, uncle or some other fond relative of members of the cast".

Nevertheless, *Salad Days* was to remain at the Vaudeville for five and a half years, outlasting and overtaking *Chu Chin Chow* and *My Fair Lady* and *The Boy Friend* to become the longest-running musical in the history of the British theatre, until, a decade later, its record was in turn overtaken by the run of Lionel Bart's *Oliver*.

But these shows were the exception to a largely American rule; though they wrote many other scores, neither Slade nor Wilson managed ever to repeat the triumph of these first two musicals, and their longevity did nothing to halt the Broadway invasion. *Salad Days* was never seen abroad or on screen, and because both

The Players Theatre in 1953

were financed on a shoestring by often grudging managements who never really thought they could succeed commercially, they lacked the professional back-up to ensure their ultimate survival. At this time in the mid-1950s, there was as yet no sign of a management like that of Cameron Mackintosh which, thirty years later, would turn the strictly local stage musical into a worldwide industry; and at a time when the general feeling along Shaftesbury Avenue was that the homegrown stage score was effectively dead in the water, nobody really knew how to handle for the long-term these two uncharacteristic but undoubted hits.

Their success was simply due to the British public trying to spread the word that they could still remember a pre-Broadway world in which little local shows, stretching all the way back to those by PG Wodehouse and Jerome Kern after a previous world war, were even now always welcome.

CALENDAR

• As an early example of crossover, Gian Carlo Menotti's opera *The Saint of Liquor Street* wins a Pulitzer Prize for music and the Best Musical award from the New York Drama Critics Circle, but is not a hit at the Broadway Theatre, where it loses its entire investment

• Audrey Hepburn is awarded a Tony for *Ondine*, three days after she wins her Oscar for *Roman Holiday*

• When *Me and Juliet* closes in April, it marks the first time in eleven years that Broadway has no show by Rodgers and Hammerstein

• When heiress Gloria Vanderbilt makes her debut in a summerstock theatre the diamond tiara she is wearing is real, and it's hers

• Jo Papp's first season of free Shakespeare begins with a modern dress production of *As You Like It*

BIRTHS American actress **Kathleen Turner**

Harvey Fierstein American playwright/actor

DEATHS American actor **Lionel Barrymore**

Sydney Greenstreet American actor

British dramatist **Frederick Lonsdale**

Will Hay British stage and screen comedian

NOTABLE PREMIERES THE THREEPENNY OPERA starring Lotte Lenya, re-opens on Broadway

Jerome Moross and John Latouche's musical THE GOLDEN APPLE is a modernisation of The Odyssey and The Iliad

Oscar Wilde's LADY WINDERMERE'S FAN is adapted by Noël Coward as a musical, AFTER THE BALL

Terence Rattigan writes two one-act plays under the collective title SEPARATE TABLES, later a hit on Broadway

Paul Scofield and Mary Ure star in Jean Anouilh's TIME REMEMBERED

John Whiting's MARCHING SONG

MUSICAL NOTES Debut of young American pianist Andre Watts

Foundation of the Chicago Lyric Opera

Benjamin Britten's opera THE TURN OF THE SCREW

William Walton's opera TROILUS AND CRESSIDA

HIT SONGS Fly Me to the Moon

Shake, Rattle and Roll

Rock Around the Clock

Waiting for Godot

Sean O'Casey, who was to live on for ten more years after effectively handing on the torch of Greatest Living Irish Playwright to Samuel Beckett after the 1955 West End opening of *Waiting for Godot*, noted that it was "a rotting and remarkable play, with a lust for despair". Beckett himself always refused to add anything else by way of explanation, and if there is a secret key to *Godot*, then its creator took it with him to the grave in 1989.

Although it is not now for *Godot* alone that we remember Beckett, this was undoubtedly the play which first established him in world theatre and defined what we mean by 'Beckettian'. Its initial production in 1954 at the Arts Theatre was the first success for a young Peter Hall, and its transfer in 1955 to the West End could be said to have opened a new period in the history of theatre, one in which plays no longer had to be either 'well-made' or easily accessible.

Samuel Barclay Beckett was born (depending on which reference you choose to believe) on either Good Friday, April 13th, or May 13th 1906. The son of a successful surveyor, he grew up south of Dublin ("You might say I had a happy childhood in that my father did not beat me, nor did my mother run away from home") and at 13 he was sent to Portora Royal School in Enniskellan, where Oscar Wilde had also once been a pupil.

Graduating from Trinity, Dublin, in 1927 (where he was recalled as a cricketer, boxer, rugby and swimming star, though not as a writer) he moved to Paris in 1928, to become a teacher of English at the Ecole Normale. In Paris he met James Joyce, who had a profound influence on him, and there Beckett began to write his first short stories and poems..

He returned to Dublin in the early 1930s and taught French at Trinity before settling briefly in London. By 1937 however, he was permanently living in Paris, and by then (after 47 rejections) his first novel, *Murphy*, had found a London publisher. When the Germans invaded Paris in 1940 Beckett joined an Irish Red Cross medical unit, became active in the Resistance, lived in hiding and in 1945 was awarded both the Croix de Guerre and the Medaille de la Resistance for his courage.

His first play, *Waiting for Godot* was written in the winter of 1949-50, chiefly he said "as a relaxation, and to escape the awful prose I was writing at the time". The play was first produced on French radio in 1952, and in Paris and Germany a year later, but it wasn't until the Peter Hall staging reached the West End in 1955 that *Godot* really made its mark.

Timothy Bateson, Hugh Burden, Peter Bull and Peter Woodthorpe at the Arts Theatre in 1955

Early reviews were somewhat mixed, though the two most influential Sunday critics of their day, Harold Hobson and Kenneth Tynan, both came out in support, Hobson remarking that whoever Godot may have been meant to be, (Beckett always said that if he knew he would have said so in the play), the title emphasis should be on the act of waiting rather than the mysteriously missing Godot himself.

A few months later still, *Godot* had a catastrophic American premiere in Miami, though by the time it reached Broadway, with the veteran comic

Bert Lahr and a new director, the tide had turned in its favour. What seldom seems noticed is the possibility that the play is deeply rooted in Beckett's wartime years with the Resistance; an age of eternal waiting, with the sinister Pozzo as a Nazi official and a general air of foreboding and uncertainty.

Be that as it may, Beckett now turned his attention almost exclusively to the theatre, as if making up for lost time, writing more than thirty new plays over the next thirty years, some of them no longer than a few minutes and all minimalist in the extreme, some written for no more than a disembodied mouth. In 1969 he was awarded the Nobel Prize for Literature, and his reputation began to grow so fast around the time of his death that entire festivals of all his stage work have now been seen in Dublin, London and New York.

CALENDAR

• Herman Wouk writes *Marjorie Morningstar*, later adapted for film and stage

• The American Shakespeare Festival opens in Stratford, Connecticut with *Julius Caesar*

• Formation, in New York, of The League of Off Broadway Theatres and Producers to negotiate with the unions working off Broadway

• When *Peter Pan* closes on Broadway, Mary Martin and Cyril Ritchard perform in the television version which is watched by 70 million people, about half the population of the United States

• Establishment of the Obie awards for performances off Broadway, the first of which goes to Jason Robards for *The Iceman Cometh*

• The Tony Award ceremonies are televised for the first time

• Noël Coward goes to Las Vegas, playing two shows a night at The Desert Inn, where he earns between $30,000 and $40,000 a week

BIRTHS American musicals star **Peter Gallagher**

DEATHS South American singer/actress **Carmen Miranda**

English actor/producer **Maurice Browne**

John Golden American producer/playwright

British actress **Constance Collier**

NOTABLE PREMIERES Peggy Mount leads the cast of King and Cary's long-running domestic comedy SAILOR, BEWARE!

THE RELUCTANT DEBUTANTE by William Douglas Home stars Celia Johnson and Wilfred Hyde White

Orson Welles directs and stars in his own disastrous adaptation of MOBY DICK

Denis Quilley and Joan Heal star in Peter Mayer's adaptation of Louisa May Alcott's LITTLE WOMEN

Kim Stanley, Albert Salmi and Elaine Stritch premiere William Inge's BUS STOP Tennessee Williams' CAT ON A HOT TIN ROOF, starring Barbara Bel Geddes and Ben Gazzara, wins the Critics Circle Award for Best American play

Arthur Miller opens a double bill of A MEMORY OF TWO MONDAYS and A VIEW FROM THE BRIDGE

In New York Gladys Cooper, Siobhan McKenna and Betsy von Furstenburg run successfully in Enid Bagnold's play, THE CHALK GARDEN

MUSICAL NOTES At La Scala in Milan, PORGY AND BESS becomes the first American opera to be performed in Italy

HIT SONGS Cry Me a River

Love and Marriage

Love is a Many-Splendored Thing

Look Back In Anger

The easy shorthand view of Osborne and *Look Back in Anger* is that an angry young man out of nowhere sent a first play to the Royal Court which, when staged, changed overnight the history of the British theatre and gave it a future, while instantly killing off its past.

Kenneth Haigh and Mary Ure at the Royal Court in 1956

In fact, it was all a good deal more complex than that. John James Osborne (1929-1994) was not the rough working-class boy from the wrong side of the tracks, and *Look Back in Anger* had as one of its characters an old colonel drawn by its author with vastly more sympathy than he ever allows Jimmy Porter. "Angry young man" was a slogan dreamed up by a Royal Court publicist, unaware that it had first been used of Noël Coward at the time of *The Vortex* in 1924, and during the remaining forty years of Osborne's life, he was to move steadily so far to the right as to be almost out of sight, certainly of his original and more radical followers. This is not to suggest that he was not, at least for the first half of his career, a major playwright; merely that, after the initial Court 'revolution', he was lucky enough to have three great stars at the height of their powers, Laurence Olivier (for *The Entertainer*), Albert Finney (for *Luther*) and Nicol Williamson (for *Inadmissable Evidence*); subsequent and less starry or successful revivals of all three plays have suggested that their original strength had more than a little to do with their original casting.

John Osborne was born in London on December 12th 1929, the son of a commercial artist and a mother whom he spent several chapters of his memoirs describing as a she-devil incarnate; expelled from school, so he always said, for striking a headmaster who had objected to his mockery of the royal family, Osborne started out as a trade journalist on the paper *Gas World* but by 1948 had decided to try his luck as an actor in regional repertory. It was there that he started tentatively writing plays, at first in collaboration with Stella Linden and then Anthony Creighton, with whom he shared a houseboat on the Thames in Chelsea for several years.

After a brief spell as the manager of a seaside theatre, Osborne took up full-time playwriting, and (after many commercial producers had rejected it) his first solo full-length play, *Look Back in Anger*, found its way to the top of the pile on George Devine's desk at the Royal Court, which Devine had just taken over with a view to founding an English Stage Society devoted to new writers, a mission very similar to that with which George Bernard Shaw and Harley Granville Barker had first occupied the Court exactly half a century earlier.

But the early plays in Devine's first season had not been successes, and first indications were that *Look Back in Anger* was going also to fail; the overnight reviews were mixed at best, and it wasn't until Kenneth Tynan, then the most influential of all drama critics, wrote a column for the (Sunday) *Observer* remarking that he "could not love anyone who did not wish to see this play at once" that the tide abruptly was turned; the following morning, there was a queue stretching right across Sloane Square, such was the power of the *Observer* in these pre-Suez months.

But if there was nothing very new about the shape or form of *Look Back in Anger*, there was something radically different about its central character. It might be stretching a point to suggest that Jimmy Porter was England's answer to James Dean, but he was certainly the first ostensible anti-hero of the modern British theatre to be given his head, to be created as a neurotic, egotistical, overgrown teenager who only really lives to annoy himself and those who love him.

Osborne was married four times, more or less catastrophically; his second and fourth wives, the actresses Mary Ure and Jill Bennett, both committed suicide, two others (Pamela Lane and Penelope Gilliatt) divorced him, and he finally only found contentment in an irritable West Country semi-retirement when married to the *Observer* journalist Helen Dawson, who alone seemed to know how to manage and even love him. It was of Jill Bennett that John had written how much he would have liked to spit on her open grave, and yet in a curious way the more bitchily eccentric he became, the more recognisably old-English and even loveable he also seemed. One was only surprised not to find him propping up the bar of the Garrick Club, railing at the ways of a modern world which had somehow passed him by.

His greatest play was surely *The Entertainer*, which came barely a year after *Look Back in Anger*;

written again for the Court, but this time also for Olivier, this was a breathtaking obituary for the old England as personified by a music-hall comedian on his last, shaky legs, falling apart precisely as were the end-of-the-pier theatres he played ("Don't clap too loudly, lady, it's a very old building"). As the dead-behind-the-eyes Archie Rice, Olivier gave what many of us considered the performance of his career; but without him the play has never seemed quite so good, and that goes also for Osborne's next hit, *Luther* (1961), in which Albert Finney gave the first great performance of his career. Osborne was to go on writing for the next thirty years of his life, everything from polemical diaries to adaptations of Oscar Wilde; his tragedy like that of Maitland in his *Inadmissable Evidence* was that of a man whose fatal flaw was the inability to give, or sustain, or even receive the love that mattered so much to him.

CALENDAR

• English Stage Company (Artistic Directors, George Devine and Tony Richardson) opens residency at the Royal Court

• Brecht's Berliner Ensemble visits England for first London production of *The Threepenny Opera* led by Brecht's widow, actress Helene Weigel

• American playwright Arthur Miller marries Hollywood star Marilyn Monroe; a few weeks later, Miller is indicted for refusal to 'name names' to the House Un-American Affairs Committee

• Siobhan McKenna triumphs as Bernard Shaw's *Saint Joan*

• In Germany, seven stage productions of *The Diary of Anne Frank* open this year

• Nat King Cole is beaten up by six white men in racist attack on stage in Birmingham, Alabama

• West End stage stars Sybil Thorndike and Laurence Olivier join Marilyn Monroe in his film *The Prince and the Showgirl*

BIRTHS **Carrie Fisher** American actress/writer
Broadway actress **Cherry Jones**

DEATHS **Sir Alexander Korda** Hungarian producer
American playwright **Owen Davis**
Band leader **Tommy Dorsey**

NOTABLE
PREMIERES At the Royal Court, Angus Wilson's THE
MULBERRY BUSH and John Osborne's LOOK
BACK IN ANGER

West End premieres of Anouilh's WALTZ OF THE
TOREADORS and POOR BITOS

On Broadway, Alan Jay Lerner and Frederick
Loewe's MY FAIR LADY stars Rex Harrison, Julie
Andrews and Stanley Holloway

Leonard Bernstein's CANDIDE opens on Broadway

EG Marshall, Bert Lahr and Kurt Kasznar premiere
WAITING FOR GODOT on Broadway

Peter Ustinov writes and stars in his greatest stage
hit ROMANOff AND JULIET

First staging of Dylan Thomas' UNDER MILK
WOOD transfers from the Edinburgh Festival
directly to Broadway

MUSICAL
NOTES Galina Ulanova leads first triumphant Bolshoi tour
to Covent Garden

Benjamin Britten's PRINCE OF THE PAGODAS

Maria Callas sings NORMA in her Metropolitan
Opera debut

Jerome Robbins founds Ballet USA

HIT SONGS Heartbreak Hotel

Love Me Tender

Blueberry Hill

Que Sera Sera

I'll Be Home for Christmas

Hound Dog

West Side Story

Opening in New York only a few months after what might well be considered the greatest of all traditional post-war musicals, *My Fair Lady*, *West Side Story* brought about the same kind of revolution that was almost simultaneously happening on the British stage with the coming of John Osborne's *Look Back in Anger*.

As Keith Garebian has noted, *West Side Story* was a landmark musical. When it premiered on Broadway in 1957, it showed how dancing, singing, acting and design could merge into a single means of expression, a seamless unity. Whether it was a completely new vision as a 'concept' musical or the pinnacle of an already established tradition, it marked the most impressive body of choreography (Jerome Robbins) in a single show and it was acclaimed as

Leonard Bernstein's strongest work for the Broadway stage. There was no overture – and the setting was an urban underworld; the libretto was one of the shortest on Broadway record...and street brawls and double deaths suddenly became the very fibre of a Broadway musical...*West Side Story* represented a major departure."

In fact, the origins of *West Side Story* went all the way back to 1948, when Jerome Robbins had been given a copy of Shakespeare's *Romeo and Juliet* by his close friend, the actor Montgomery Clift who was thinking of starring in a revival. Robbins suddenly began to think of it as a musical; his first idea was that Bernstein should write both music and lyrics. The second idea was to offer the lyrics to Comden and Green (with whom they had both worked on *On the Town*) but as they were now otherwise occupied in Hollywood, the project lay fallow until the playwright Arthur Laurents, who had now come on board to write the book, happened to meet a young Stephen Sondheim at a cocktail party and, on the spur of the moment, asked him to meet Bernstein with a view to writing the lyrics.

Sondheim's original suggestion for the title *Shut Up and Dance* was rapidly rejected, as was the producer Cheryl Crawford's feeling that "we don't want to go down to the West Side and listen to the gangs". At this stage, the writers were still calling their show *East Side Story*, and Laurents was still thinking of the gangs as black versus white before they eventually settled on Puerto Rican immigrants. At this point, Crawford abandoned the project as unworkable, and a musical which had already been six years in the making looked abortive until a young Harold Prince (already the successful co-producer but not director of *The Pajama Game* and *Damn Yankees*) came on board.

As Kenneth Pearson then reported, "Suddenly, all the threads of the production came together like cars on an assembly line. Sondheim and Bernstein began working night and day, raiding Shakespeare and Arthur Laurents like an enemy patrol. A phrase like 'whistling down the river' would disappear from the book, only to reappear in the song, 'Something's Coming'".

Sondheim himself has always said that certain lyrics from his first great hit still come back to haunt him, notably the lovers' "today the world was just an address," and Maria, supposedly a naïve 17-year old Puerto Rican with English as her second language, singing, "It's alarming how charming I feel". What he doesn't say is that among his lyrics was one of the finest comic songs ever written for the musical theatre without a wasted word or emotion, "Gee, Officer Krupke". But, never satisfied, he also later wrote, "In terms of individual ingredients, the show has a lot of very severe flaws – purpleness and over-writing in my songs, and characters who are necessarily only one-dimensional."

That was not, however, the general critical consensus in 1957. *West Side Story* was instantly hailed as one of the crowning masterworks of the American musical. True, Sondheim came out very badly, with hardly a mention of his lyrics, which most critics seemed to assume were also by Bernstein or Laurents, and plans for it to be staged at the World's Fair in Brussels and the Soviet Union were abandoned when Washington decided that the show represented an "unsuitable picture of modern New York life."

Yet, by 1968, it was already in the repertoire of the Vienna Volksoper, and is now generally accepted as a classic of all time. Of the first London production in 1958, Kenneth Tynan wrote, "the score is smooth and savage as a cobra; it sounds as if Puccini and Stravinsky had gone on a roller-coaster ride into the precincts of modern jazz."

CALENDAR

• Tommy Steele, aged 20, becomes a star with "Rock With the Caveman"

• Samuel Beckett premieres *Endgame* in which two old people spend the evening of their days in dustbins. It is banned in England for blasphemy

• Three Greenwich Village theatres, Circle in the Square, Cherry Lane and Theatre de Lys form a co-operative to share costs

• Producer David Merrick now has four shows playing side by side on 45th St. They are: *Look Back In Anger*, *The Entertainer*, *Romanoff and Juliet* and the musical *Jamaica*

• In the West End, Vivien Leigh leads street demonstration protesting the demolition of the St James's Theatre

• Police fine Joan Littlewood £17 for "vulgar and not in good taste" changes to *You Won't Always Be On Top*

BIRTHS
American actress **Geena Davis**
John Turturro American actor
French star **Carole Bouquet**
American director **Ethan Coen**

DEATHS
Singer **Beniamino Gigli**
Hollywood comedian **Oliver Hardy**
Ezio Pinza Opera and Broadway star
Award-winning West End and Broadway playwright/director **John van Druten**

NOTABLE PREMIERES
Harold Pinter's THE ROOM, his first one-act play, staged by the Bristol Old Vic Drama School
Laurence Olivier opens in the West End and then on Broadway in one of his signature roles, as John Osborne's THE ENTERTAINER
Siobhan McKenna opens off-Broadway as HAMLET
Maureen Stapleton and Cliff Robertson open on Broadway in Tennessee Williams' ORPHEUS DESCENDING
Beatrice Lillie returns to Broadway in the last edition of the ZIEGFELD FOLLIES, a major flop
Zero Mostel and Uta Hagen open on Broadway in Brecht's GOOD WOMAN OF SETZUAN
Playwright Robert Bolt makes his name overnight with FLOWERING CHERRY about a man taking refuge in dreams and lies

MUSICAL NOTES
Creation of the Royal Ballet in London
Sir Adrian Boult and the BBC Symphony Orchestra perform premiere of Michael Tippett's 2nd Symphony

HIT SONGS
All Shook Up
Mary's Boy Child
Wake Up, Little Susie (banned in Boston)
Peggy Sue

The Birthday Party

Although his first full-length play, *The Birthday Party*, was a critical and commercial disaster which played only one week at the Lyric, Hammersmith in 1958, this, in retrospect and many subsequent successful revivals, can now be seen as the first to establish what we mean by 'Pinteresque'.

It tells the story of Stanley, apparently safe in a run-down seaside boarding house, suddenly confronted with the arrival of the mysterious and menacing hired killers, Goldberg and McCann.

Harold Pinter was born on October 10th 1930, in the East End of London, the only child of a Portuguese-Jewish immigrant family (da Pinta). Encouraged by an enthusiastic drama teacher, he began acting in school plays and went on to the Royal Academy of Dramatic Art. Dissatisfied with their methods, however, he left after a year, claiming a nervous breakdown. He then risked prison by refusing to do National Service on the grounds that he was a conscientious objector, and joined a series of regional repertory companies before signing up with the legendary Irish touring actor/manager Anew McMaster, the brother-in-law of Micheal MacLiammoir.

For the next ten years, Pinter acted under the stage name of David Baron; but from the age of 13 he had been writing poetry and, while working as an actor, he also began to write short sketches and the one-act play *The Room*, staged briefly at Bristol in 1957.

With the extreme hostility of the overnight reviews for *The Birthday Party*, Pinter had all but decided to give up play-writing when, on the Sunday morning after the play had closed at Hammersmith, he received a notice from Harold Hobson in the *Sunday Times*, encouraging him to persevere.

This he did, although it was not until 1960 with *The Caretaker* that he had his first real commercial as well as critical success. A bleak plot synopsis of *The Birthday Party* doesn't begin to convey the true menace of what was now to become exclusively Pinter's own territory. We never discover what Stanley has done to invite his two persecutors, nor do we ever discover what is really their agenda, but, as Benedict Nightingale has noted, "the vagueness of this increasingly odd and lengthy indictment of Stanley is obviously deliberate. *The Birthday Party* is about everyone's long-repressed guilt and unspoken fears, everyone's dim suspicion that one day his past may catch up with him and vengeance be exacted for what he has done or is thought by someone, somewhere to have done."

Pinter had grown up in a pre-war East London that was distinctly anti-Semitic, and some of that turns up in *The Birthday Party* but, as always with Pinter, any attempt to pin down or footnote his work too closely is immediately to lose something of its meaning. He is always unsettling, precisely because he is unspecific and yet all through his work, especially in the later years when he would write about the collapse of human rights around the world, there is the constant presence of menacing and demanding strangers suddenly appearing at the door.

Pinter's style, whether writing early comic sketches for intimate revues or such later classics as *The Collection, The Caretaker, The Homecoming, Betrayal,* and several screenplays, is minimalist. His characters

Nigel Terry and Timothy West at the Piccadilly in 1999

From the very beginning, as director and playwright, he formed a loosely-connected group of players who excelled at performing his apparently elliptical dialogue. His first wife, Vivian Merchant, who died from chronic alcoholism some years after their marriage ended, was one of his finest interpreters. Others from the time of *The Birthday Party* have included Donald Pleasance, Barry Foster, and, more recently, Lindsay Duncan, while his regular directors have included (onstage) Peter Hall and (on film) Joseph Losey.

Not only is Pinter still the most original British dramatist of his generation but in terms of the sheer spread of his work as playwright, screenwriter, actor, polemicist and political activist, he remains its most challenging and often unexpected creative force. All you really know about the next Pinter play is that it will be nothing like his last.

CALENDAR

• American producer Joseph Papp opens his first free Shakespeare season in Central Park with William Marshall as Othello

• Michael Benthall takes the Old Vic Company to the Broadway Theatre for six weeks: John Neville is Hamlet and Laurence Harvey is Henry V

• The Globe Theatre on West 46th St now renamed the Lunt-Fontanne

• In the NY Times list of the top ten plays of the Broadway season, two are by John Osborne – *Look Back In Anger* and *The Entertainer*

• Broadway producers raise statue in Times Square to George M Cohan; American Equity, recalling Cohan's opposition to the strike of 1919, refuses to contribute

• Cole Porter, following years of agony and 30 operations after falling under a horse, finally agrees to have his right leg amputated

say very little or sometimes nothing at all, while meaning a very great deal.

For many years, Pinter was widely regarded as bleak and unapproachable and yet his ten-year start as an actor, his comic writing, and some of his most recent work, notably *Celebration* (2000) in fact suggests a much funnier and even warmer writer than critics have usually allowed.

His writing, over more than forty years, has encompassed radio and television, journalism and poetry, and screenplays, and in almost all of that time, he has also appeared on stage and screen in his own work and as (usually menacing) characters in other peoples'.

BIRTHS American actress **Holly Hunter**

British actor **Daniel Day Lewis**

American actress and writer **Jamie Lee Curtis**, daughter of Janet Leigh and Tony Curtis

DEATHS British stage and screen actor **Robert Donat**

Broadway drama critic **George Jean Nathan**, champion of O'Neill and O'Casey

Revolutionary designer and producer **Norman Bel Geddes**

Stage and screen producer **Mike Todd** (in air crash)

NOTABLE PREMIERES Alfred Lunt and Lynn Fontanne have their last major success in Dürrenmatt's **THE VISIT**

On Broadway, Elaine Stritch stars in the musical **GOLDILOCKS**

In London, father and daughter, Michael and Vanessa Redgrave, star in NC Hunter's **A TOUCH OF THE SUN**

Robert Stephens plays the title role in **EPITAPH FOR GEORGE DILLON** by John Osborne and Anthony Creighton

John Gielgud directs a first play by Peter Shaffer, **FIVE FINGER EXERCISE**

At the Royal Court, Joan Plowright opens long run in Tony Richardson's first London production of Ionesco's **THE CHAIRS** and **THE LESSON**

British premiere of **ENDGAME**

MUSICAL NOTES The first Monterey Jazz Festival in California

American debut of Russian pianist Vladimir Ashkanazy

HIT SONGS Is That All There Is?

Bird Dog

Gigi

Roots

As he understandably spent almost the next half-century pointing out, few playwrights who achieve fame in the Royal Court revolution of the late 1950s have ever had quite so much trouble getting their subsequent work staged at home. Arnold Wesker (born 1932) has almost always been a prophet without much honour in his own country while being widely revived, premiered, and admired abroad.

Like the more fortunate Harold Pinter, he was born the son of an immigrant Jewish tailor in the East End of London but unlike Pinter, Wesker very often uses his own experience and background as the centre of his plays.

In *Roots*, the Norfolk girl, Beatie, has been a waitress in a local hotel just like Arnold's wife. In *Chicken Soup with Barley* (1958), the mother, like his own, is a communist. In *I'm Talking about Jerusalem* (1960), the two leading characters withdraw from London to Norfolk, as did Wesker's brother and sister, and *Chips with Everything* (1962) is based on Wesker's National Service in the RAF where he became a pastry cook. This experience also informs *The Kitchen* (1959) which was his first-written play two years earlier.

As was proved by a marvellously vital revival by Stephen Daldry at the Royal Court in the late 1990s, *The Kitchen* is, in many ways, Wesker's most vivid play, almost a documentary about a typical day in the lives of a large team of chefs, waiters and kitchen porters, all of whom we grow to know and love as they go about their frantic, babbling business.

Chips with Everything is also almost a documentary about the basic training of a group of widely-assorted RAF recruits, and although it is written with realism and socialist anger, in a curious way it is also a throwback to all those British war films about a cross-section of serving officers and men, usually trapped in some kind of lifeboat or submarine.

Patsy Byrne and Joan Plowright at the Belgrade Theatre, Coventry in 1959

But the Trilogy which starts with *Chicken Soup With Barley*, runs through *Roots*, and ends in *I'm Talking About Jerusalem*, all written and staged over a three-year period, still represents Wesker's greatest achievement. It opens in 1936, on the day of the East End battle against Mosley's Fascists and it ends 20 years later, just after the Soviet invasion of Hungary. As Tynan noted, "Wesker thinks internationally but feels domestically, and it is this combination of attributes that enables him to bring gigantic events and ordinary people into the same sharp focus...In *Roots*, Wesker has written the most affecting last act in contemporary English drama."

Roots was also, of course, the play which made a star of Joan Plowright as Beatie, and for a while Wesker enjoyed the kind of acclaim which was elsewhere achieved in this period only by John Osborne and Harold Pinter. Wesker himself, writing a programme note for the first time (1960) that the Trilogy was performed in its entirety, explained, "My people are not caricatures, they are real though fictional, and though the picture I have drawn of them is a harsh one, yet still my tone is not of disgust. I am at one with these people – it is only that I am annoyed with them and myself...*Chicken Soup With Barley* handles the Communist aspect. *Roots* handles the personal aspect, and *I'm Talking About Jerusalem* is a study in a William Morris kind of socialism. So these three plays are about three aspects of socialism, played through the lives of one Jewish family. These are not true life stories, they are distillations."

But like another almost exact contemporary, John Osborne, as early as the middle 1960s, less than a decade after he had first made his name, Wesker's work was already beginning to lose focus as well as popular or critical esteem. In his case, one problem would seem to be that when he ran out of autobiography, he could find nothing as powerful with which to replace it. At this time, much of Wesker's energy went into the founding of Centre 42, named after a resolution that had been passed by the Trades Union Congress in 1960,

committing the TUC to "developing art for the working-class public".

Sadly, the TUC was never willing to back this noble resolution with any kind of cash or practical help, and Wesker's subsequent disillusionment with the socialist movement is reflected in such later plays as *Their Very Own and Golden City* (1965), *The Four Seasons* (also 1965) and *The Old Ones* (1972).

His later work has been notably poetic but it too has almost always failed to find favour at home. Despite a triumphant revival at the National of *Chips With Everything* in the late 1990s, there has been no sustained attempt to bring back the rest of the Trilogy or to grant Wesker the honour at home that he has always been accorded abroad. It is as though the British simply don't wish to be reminded about the failure of true socialism, which has always been central to his writing.

CALENDAR

• Bernard Miles opens the Mermaid Theatre in London's Puddle Dock, the first new theatre in the City of London for 300 years

• Two British actors, David Niven and Wendy Hiller, win Oscars for film of Rattigan's *Separate Tables*

• Kenneth Tynan replaces the late Wolcott Gibbs as drama critic of the New Yorker

• Lloyd Richards becomes the first African-American to direct a Broadway show when he premieres Lorraine Hansberry's *A Raisin in the Sun*, the first Broadway play by a black woman

• Noël Coward, asked how he feels about turning 60 replies, "Well, at least I am younger than Marlene Dietrich"

• Peter Hall becomes director of the Stratford Memorial Theatre and forms there the Royal Shakespeare Company with a home also in London at the Aldwych Theatre

BIRTHS British actress **Emma Thompson**
American stage and screen actor
Matthew Modine

DEATHS American comedian **Lou Costello**
Mario Lanza American tenor
Veteran American actress **Ethel Barrymore**
British actress **Kay Kendall**

NOTABLE PREMIERES Geraldine Page, Paul Newman, Rip Torn, and Bruce Dern open in Tennessee Williams' SWEET BIRD OF YOUTH
Rodgers and Hammerstein's last score THE SOUND OF MUSIC opens on Broadway with Mary Martin and Theodore Bikel
Lou Jacobi, Gene Saks and Jack Gilford open year-long Broadway run of Anski's THE DYBBUK
In London, Michael Redgrave adapts and stars in Henry James' THE ASPERN PAPERS
Shelagh Delaney's A TASTE OF HONEY opens
At Stratford, Glen Byam Shaw, in his last season as Director, assembles an amazing company: Paul Robeson, Sam Wanamaker, Albert Finney and Mary Ure in Tony Richardson's OTHELLO; Edith Evans and Zoë Caldwell in Tyrone Guthrie's ALL'S WELL THAT ENDS WELL; Charles Laughton and Vanessa Redgrave in Peter Hall's A MIDSUMMER NIGHT'S DREAM; Olivier's CORIOLANUS; and Laughton's KING LEAR

MUSICAL NOTES British jazz saxophonist Ronnie Scott opens Soho club

HIT SONGS **Living Doll**
Travellin' Light
What a Difference a Day Makes
Do Re Mi

A Man for All Seasons

At the height of the Royal Court revolution, one playwright made his name in a totally different tradition and convention. Robert Bolt (1924-1995) was the son of a Manchester shopkeeper who became a village schoolteacher in Devon and then an English teacher at Millfield, Britain's then most expensive public school. Early in the 1950s, he began to write radio plays including an early version of the one that was to make his name, *A Man for All Seasons*, the story of Thomas More and his struggle with Henry VIII.

Although he always said that this play was intended to be 'Brechtian' (and it does indeed have the alienation effect of a scene-changing narrator, The Common Man), Bolt as both playwright and subsequently screenwriter was in fact an anachronistic throwback to a much earlier kind of writer – playwrights such as the 1930s' RC Sherriff or Clemence Dane or Gordon Daviot, all of whom were useful craftsmen, accustomed to turning historical events into rattling good plays or films.

What Bolt brought that was different was his post-war academic cynicism and revisionism. In his scripts, the hitherto simple historical division between the good and the bad becomes infinitely more complex – Bolt's history is no longer about heroes or villains, but about famous people who were always a bit of both.

It was the director Frith Banbury, having already discovered such 'English Chekhov' writers as NC Hunter and Wynyard Browne, who first found Bolt for the theatre when the author, in 1957, sent him a play called *Flowering Cherry*. Unlike most of Bolt's later work this was pure fiction, the story of an insurance man (Jim Cherry) who, fired from his job, lives instead a fantasy life dreaming of an orchard in his native Somerset.

Thanks to Banbury's production, one which starred Ralph Richardson and Celia Johnson at the Haymarket, this was a huge success and even drew comparisons with Arthur Miller's *Death of A Salesman*

although, as Tynan noted, "the analogy will not hold… Miller the sociologist attributes Willy Loman's downfall to social forces outside himself. Bolt the psychologist looks inside Jim Cherry for the seeds of his failure and somehow never manages to find them."

But the *Guardian* hailed, "this fine, sad play" as the best from any English playwright since *Look Back In Anger* and its triumph meant that Bolt was able to attract Michael and his daughter Vanessa Redgrave to his next, *The Tiger and the Horse* (1959). But the senior Redgrave's prior commitment to *The Aspern Papers* meant a delay of 18 months, and in the meantime Bolt went back to his old radio play about Thomas More, turning it into one of the greatest stage and screen hits of this entire decade. Paul Scofield played it for many months in the West End and on Broadway, and won his only leading-actor Oscar for the Fred Zinneman movie in 1966, one which also led Bolt into a long-term partnership with the film director David Lean (*Lawrence of Arabia*, *Dr Zhivago*, *Ryan's Daughter*) as well as a less successful stint as a film director himself (*Lady Caroline Lamb*).

The central argument of *A Man For All Seasons* is not in fact so very far removed from TS Eliot's *Murder*

The other major turning point in Bolt's life had come in 1961, when Lean had brought him in to improve the dialogue for the *Lawrence of Arabia* that he had already begun to shoot in Jordan with Peter O'Toole and Alec Guinness. Those seven weeks on that film extended to more than a decade as Bolt and Lean went on to *Dr Zhivago* (for which they both won Oscars) and then a catastrophic *Mutiny on the Bounty* re-make with Marlon Brando. This gave Bolt his first heart attack, followed by a stroke which left him partially paralysed, and only at the end of his life did he find a kind of peace and tranquillity, reunited with his beloved Sarah Miles.

in the Cathedral almost a quarter of a century earlier. What shall it profit a man to gain the whole world and lose his own soul? The battle for secular supremacy between More and Henry VIII was, of course, very similar to that between Henry II and his Archbishop Thomas à Becket, but through Bolt's invention of The Common Man as stage-hand and storyteller, he was able to update the argument and give it a modern twist, so that we see the problem through the eyes of the 1960s rather than those of the 16th century.

If *A Man For All Seasons* was to be Bolt's signature play, it was followed by a couple of disappointments. Despite the Redgraves, father and daughter, *The Tiger and the Horse* did not really work and nor did *Gentle Jack* (1963), a weird throwback to the whimsical fantasies of JM Barrie, which failed despite the unusual star casting of Edith Evans and Kenneth Williams.

Not surprisingly, Bolt then returned to what he did best; in 1970 at Chichester and then in the West End, *Vivat! Vivat! Regina!* again dealt with a famous historical struggle, this time that of Mary, Queen of Scots and Elizabeth I.

CALENDAR

• Vivien Leigh finally divorces Laurence Olivier
• Peter Hall's first full season as Director of the RSC Peggy Ashcroft and Peter O'Toole open in *The Taming of the Shrew*, and Hall directs his famous sand-pit *Troilus and Cressida*
• At the Old Vic, Franco Zeffirelli makes his London reputation with a ravishing *Romeo and Juliet* starring newcomers John Stride and Judi Dench
• Young Brooklyn singer Barbra Streisand wins talent contest in Greenwich Village club
• British stars Richard Burton (*Camelot*), Elizabeth Seal (*Irma la Douce*) and Joan Plowright (*A Taste of Honey*) all win Tony Awards
• Because of increased competition from television and off-Broadway, many Broadway theatres introduce twofers – two tickets for the price of one early in the week.
• Brendan Behan, though never exactly sober, becomes a New York television star on the Jack Paar Show while selling his *The Hostage*
• Rex Harrison goes to the Royal Court in a Centenary revival of Chekhov's *Platonov*

BIRTHS
Italian-born actress **Greta Scaatchi**
British actor **Kenneth Branagh**

DEATHS
Lyricist **Oscar Hammerstein II**
Opera star **Jussi Bjoerling**
American actress **Margaret Sullavan**
American opera star **Lawrence Tibbett**
Bobby Clark Broadway vaudevillian
Veteran British actress **Lillah McCarthy**

NOTABLE PREMIERES
Four young Oxford and Cambridge graduates, Alan Bennett, Peter Cook, Jonathan Miller and Dudley Moore open Edinburgh Festival revue **BEYOND THE FRINGE**
Lionel Bart's **OLIVER** becomes first major local musical hit since the days of Coward and Novello
Albert Finney stars on stage as **BILLY LIAR**
Donald Pleasance, Alan Bates and Peter Woodthorpe star in world premiere of Harold Pinter's **THE CARETAKER**
Olivier stars in Ionesco's **RHINOCEROS**, directed by Orson Welles
After a brief German premiere, Edward Albee's first play **THE ZOO STORY** has its first American performance at the Provincetown Playhouse
Zia Moyheddin and Gladys Cooper star in long-running West End staging of EM Forster's **A PASSAGE TO INDIA**

MUSICAL NOTES
Arthur Bliss' **TOBIAS AND THE ANGEL**
Henze's opera **THE PRINCE OF HAMBURG**

HIT SONGS
Cathy's Clown
Three Steps to Heaven
The Shadow of Your Smile
Je ne Regrette Rien
Yellow Polka Dot Bikini

The American Dream

The American Dream was the first of Edward Albee's one-act plays to win real critical acclaim, albeit not universal, when it ran this year off-Broadway in Alan Schneider's production for 370 performances. Albee had already written The Zoo Story, and was to go on to write such landmark plays of the American theatre as Who's Afraid of Virginia Woolf (1962), A Delicate Balance (1968), and Three Tall Women (1991).

But for effectively thirty years after A Delicate Balance, he was all but ignored by the American theatrical establishment, and his plays only found favour, if at all, overseas. Yet in his writing, as in his teaching,

Albee has always remained alone and apart, apparently unaffected by the changing whims and fashions of theatrical criticism and secure in the knowledge that one day his work would find its true audience.

Edward Albee was always a loner, not least because he was abandoned by his natural parents two weeks after his birth in Washington DC on March 12th 1928. By happy chance, he was adopted and given his name by a family who had become millionaires as the owners of a profitable chain of vaudeville theatres, so very early in life Albee was able to meet Thornton Wilder and WH Auden, both of whom suggested to him

From the Royal Court productio of 1961

that his initial desire to be a poet was, on the evidence of what he showed them, a little unwise, and that he might like to turn to playwriting instead. Albee's background, his childhood as an outsider amid great wealth, and his early meetings with great mentors, all bring instantly to mind the early years of another great Broadway writer and near-contemporary, Stephen Sondheim. The men even for a while looked and sounded alike, and if anyone were ever rash enough or brave enough to turn an Albee play into a musical, then that writer would have to be Sondheim, the other great craggy giant of the New York theatre who has always made it clear that what matters is the work, not the immediate reception of it.

Shortly before his 30th birthday, Albee decided that his future lay in playwriting, and a year later his first play, the one-act *Zoo Story*, was accepted not at home but by the prestigious Schiller Theatre in West Berlin. Following its success there, it opened early in 1960 off-Broadway on a double bill with Samuel Beckett's *Krapps's Last Tape*. Reviews and early houses were not good, but an impassioned endorsement from Tennessee Williams turned them around, and the two plays went on to a run of 19 months.

In April, 1960, Albee's second one-acter *The Death of Bessie Smith* again had its world premiere in Berlin, and was not to reach off-Broadway for another year. Set in Memphis in 1937, it concerned the death in a car crash of the great black blues singer, although she is not a character in the play. Instead, the leading figure is a viciously racist white nurse, the first of Albee's many characterisations of malicious and compulsive women.

In all his early one-acters, his recurrent theme was the need to distinguish reality from illusion, and to try to sustain a humane vision in rapidly deteriorating human and physical environments. But it wasn't until 1963, when his first full-length play *Who's Afraid of Virginia Woolf* ran for nearly two years in New York and then repeated its success in London and around the world before becoming the best of all the Richard Burton-Elizabeth Taylor films, winning countless stage and screen awards, that Albee really came into his own.

Albee's greatest talents include waspish dialogue, an almost Pinteresque ability to suggest the unmentionable menace lurking just beyond the footlights, and perhaps above all, the ability to elevate one apparently insignificant episode into the basis for an entire drama. He is a minimalist whose work reaches out toward the universal. Like Sondheim, Albee lives on the borderline where the American Dream is always threatening to become a nightmare and, as Albee himself once said about his ability to live and write in a world of his own, "I never wrote *Catcher in the Rye*; I simply lived it."

CALENDAR

- Robert Bolt and Paul Scofield scoop Tony Awards for *A Man For All Seasons*
- Writing a series of articles in the London Sunday Times, Noël Coward accuses young British playwrights of focusing only on tramps and prostitution, indulging in vulgarity, and assuming that only the working class can be interesting on stage
- John Osborne sues Mary Ure for divorce, citing Robert Shaw. Osborne is, however, already living with English film critic and novelist Penelope Gilliatt, who first introduced Ure to Shaw
- Vivien Leigh and Robert Helpmann lead marathon Old Vic tour of Australia and South America
- British Prime Minister Harold Macmillan goes to the theatre to see himself viciously parodied by Peter Cook in *Beyond The Fringe*

BIRTHS

German actress **Nastassja Kinski**

American actress **Elizabeth McGovern**

DEATHS

American actress **Grace George**

American playwright/producer **George S Kaufman**

Celebrated Broadway and Hollywood comic **Chico Marx**

Producer and playwright **Sir Barry Jackson**

Veteran British actress **Violent Kemble**

English music-hall and movie star **George Formby**

NOTABLE PREMIERES

Broadway premiere of **SUBWAYS ARE FOR SLEEPING** written by Jule Styne, Betty Comden and Adolph Green

COME BLOW YOUR HORN, Neil Simon's first full-length Broadway play, runs 700 performances

Dorothy Tutin, Max Adrian, Diana Rigg, and Roy Dotrice open triumphant London run for the RSC of John Whiting's **THE DEVILS**

Anthony Newley and Leslie Bricusse write their first musical **STOP THE WORLD – I WANT TO GET OFF**

Albert Finney opens long London and subsequently Broadway run as John Osborne's **LUTHER**, directed by Tony Richardson

MUSICAL NOTES

British cellist Jaqueline du Pré makes her London solo debut aged 16

HIT SONGS

Moon River

Exodus

Wooden Heart

Happy Birthday Sweet Sixteen

Walking Back to Happiness

The Pope's Wedding

The first of Bond's plays to be seen on stage was given a production without décor in London this year. In some ways, this is the countryside cousin to *Saved*, the play with which Bond hit the headlines three years later because of a violent scene in which a baby is stoned to death in a city park.

The Pope's Wedding is set in East Anglia, where the local labourers appear to be as violent and as nihilistic as the town-dwellers of *Saved*. The story is simply of a young man, obsessively trying to form a relationship with a local hermit who he eventually kills, and the title is just a pointer to the unlikeliness of any good human relationships ever being possible.

Edward Bond was born in North London in 1934. He was the son of a workman who had moved into the capital from East Anglia in search of employment. During the War, Bond was evacuated to Cornwall and it was there, he said later, that he began to grow up. He left school at 15 and after several dead-end jobs, heavily influenced by a visit to *Macbeth*, began to write plays. "Again and again," writes Benedict Nightingale, "Bond looks with embarrassing directness at cruelty and pain, and asks us, in a manner analogous to those advertisements which depict starving children in India, how we can bear to go on living in a world which allows such things."

In the forty years which separated John Osborne from the tragically short-lived Sarah Kane, no play at the Royal Court (or for that matter anywhere in London) caused the shock-horror of Bond's 1965 *Saved*. Although its notoriety depended on the baby-stoning,

The Royal Court in 1984

the entire play, in its violence and the inarticulate quality of its characters, seemed to symbolise a new, no-hope England from which there was no escape but death. Yet Bond, like his East Anglian characters, has always been an outsider. Several eminent reference books still refuse even to acknowledge his existence, despite the fact that his later work has been broad enough to encompass the surrealism of *Early Morning* and the well-made lyricism of *The Sea*, given an impressive revival on the Minerva stage at Chichester in the summer of 2000.

Like John Arden, another Royal Court dramatist whose work seemed to disappear from view in the 1980s, Bond often wrote for Left-wing fringe companies as well as the mainstream National Theatre. His style, as Christopher Innes has noted, covers virtually the whole of the modern stage spectrum, "the surreal fantasy, Brechtian parables, stripped-down realism, Shakespearean revisionism, or Restoration parody, the historical epic and even opera librettos – all are interchangeable moulds for his political message." That message essentially concerns the way in which bleak concrete housing estates breed little but violence, and the fact that people (not so much living on as trying to exist below the poverty line) are not likely to fill their minds with noble thoughts or generous gestures.

In one of Bond's most interesting period plays, *Bingo* (1974), Shakespeare himself appears, not as the greatest of all playwrights, but as a rapacious local landlord, while the inequalities of the 19th century are traced in *The Fool* (1976) through the life of the mad poet John Clare.

Almost half Bond's major plays have either a poet or a playwright at their centre and just as a very different playwright of this era, Peter Shaffer, often uses two alter egos in his plays to symbolise the head and the heart, so, in nearly all Bond's plays, there are twin heroes, one the anti-type of the other. But where many of the plays of Osborne's contemporaries grew darker as the years went by, Bond's, in a curious way, seem to get more cheerful, even if they do increasingly rely on

an escape from the real present to the mythical past. In *Bingo*, he has Shakespeare driven to suicide by the realisation that his plays have failed to do any specific good for his own time and place, while John Clare, in Bond's next play *The Fool* is driven to madness by his refusal to compromise with the social and political rules of his time.

When, during the 1970s and 1980s, the Right-wing triumphalism of Prime Minister Margaret Thatcher seemed to silence contemporary playwrights, Bond took to advocating political violence against a class society. But by now, his plays no longer had much influence and were often even having a hard time finding theatres.

Latterly, politics and polemics seem to have overtaken playwriting in Bond's priorities, but that could also have been said of Bernard Shaw and interestingly (like Shaw) Bond writes very long prefaces to his plays, as if already aware that they will live on the page rather than the stage.

CALENDAR

• In New York *My Fair Lady* closes after 2717 performances, making it the longest-running musical ever

• At Stratford, Peter Brook's new staging of *King Lear* with Paul Scofield and Alec McCowen is likened by critics to *Waiting for Godot*

• *Beyond The Fringe* star Peter Cook saves the satirical magazine Private Eye from bankruptcy; in America, he also saves David Frost from drowning

• Laurence Olivier announced as first director of the Chichester Festival

• Hume Cronyn, Jessica Tandy, Zoe Caldwell and George Grizzard lead the company for the opening season of the Guthrie Theatre in Minneapolis

• Directors Peter Brook and Michel Saint-Denis join Peter Hall as directors of the new RSC

BIRTHS American actor **Matthew Broderick**

DEATHS American comic actor **Ernie Kovacs**
British actor **Charles Laughton**
John Christie Founder of the Glyndebourne Opera
Veteran American comic **Victor Moore**

NOTABLE PREMIERES The first hit musical for which Stephen Sondheim writes music and lyrics stars Zero Mostel and triumphs on Broadway after a rocky road tour. It is A FUNNY THING HAPPENED ON THE WAY TO THE FORUM
Uta Hagen and George Grizzard star in Edward Albee's first Broadway hit WHO'S AFRAID OF VIRGINIA WOOLF
Harold Pinter has first off-Broadway hit with THE DUMB WAITER and THE COLLECTION in a double-bill
Arnold Wesker's CHIPS WITH EVERYTHING transfers from the Royal Court to the West End for nearly a year
Playwright Peter Shaffer has double bill THE PRIVATE EAR and THE PUBLIC EYE for a long run in London with Maggie Smith and Kenneth Williams

MUSICAL NOTES Debut of The American Symphony at Carnegie Hall, Leopold Stokowsky conducting
Nureyev makes American debut in DON QUIXOTE at the Chicago Opera Ballet

HIT SONGS The Days of Wine and Roses
I Left My Heart in San Francisco
Walk On By
What Kind of Fool Am I?
As Long as He Needs Me

The Workhouse Donkey

In his preface to *The Workhouse Donkey*, the playwright John Arden states, "Our theatre must grant pride of place to noise, disorder, drunkenness, lasciviousness, nudity, generosity, corruption, fertility and ease." And that is probably as good a credo from Arden as we are ever going to get.

The Workhouse Donkey is the story of a police chief who falls disastrously in love with the daughter of one of the more corrupt officials in a town he is trying to purify, according to its own rigid statutes. The play is about the struggle in local politics between Puritanism and license, order and anarchy, and it ends (characteristically of Arden) with total failure on all sides.

John Arden was born in 1930 in Barnsley, educated privately and at Cambridge, and started out as an architect. In 1957, with a grant from the Royal Court (where he was the first writer to earn a Sunday night production-without-décor), he turned to playwriting, and one of his greatest successes there was *Serjeant Musgrave's Dance* (1959). This was a play about a 19th century soldier who, obsessed by Old Testament justice and military discipline, arrives to execute 25 apparently innocent people in a town from which one of their number has been involved in the killing abroad of five natives, in revenge for the murder of one soldier on foreign service. The idea is to bring home to the town the cost of colonialism by visiting retribution on the colonisers.

It is only the women in the play who point out the ludicrous nature of all this loss of life, and they are dismissed as "crooked, dirty, idle, untidy anarchists". As so often in his later work, Arden sets up two extremes while acknowledging that a state of confusion somewhere between the two is what will probably last.

Although the initial reviews were generally confused and uncomprehending, in many early revivals *Serjeant Musgrave's Dance* rapidly grew in stature. Arden often said that among the playwrights he most admired were Lorca and John Whiting, and he often referred back to traditional ballads and mummer's plays,

the kind of primeval street theatre where a Turkish knight would kill Saint George only to find an interfering doctor raising him from the dead again.

The Chichester revival of 1963

Of all the Royal Court playwrights of his radical and revolutionary generation, Arden is the one who covered more of the waterfront (often writing with his wife, Margaretta D'Arcy) than any of the others, although eventually both husband and wife fell out violently with their managements at the RSC and the Court, so that for the last thirty years they have really only worked as novelists and with small, non-professional and usually Marxist groups of often strolling players.

Arden could easily be compared to Brecht, in that both are preoccupied with contemporary social or moral problems but use major stories from history to illuminate them, but that's about where the comparison ends. Arden is simply unclassifiable; he often writes in rhyming verse, based one of his three major hits, *Armstrong's Last Goodnight* (1965), on an old Scottish ballad, and wrote in the same year a pageant to celebrate the 750th anniversary of Magna Carta. He and his wife also wrote a musical about Nelson – *The Hero Rises Up* (1968), and an unwieldy epic based on Arthurian legends – *The Island of the Mighty* (1972).

If *Serjeant Musgrave's Dance* was about the inextricability of pacifism and violence, then his greatest hit *Armstrong's Last Goodnight* (Chichester and National Theatre) is about a duel in the middle of the 16th century between a suave diplomat and a buccaneering Borders chieftain, oddly akin to Shaffer's nearly simultaneous *The Royal Hunt of the Sun*. But unlike Shaffer, a master of construction and careful period detail, Arden even at his best is wild and woolly, confrontational and endlessly verbose.

In the view of the critic Irving Wardle, "The objection to Arden is that he is a cold writer, that he adopts comic forms without displaying much personal sense of fun, and that, for all his apparent concern with structure, audiences often get lost inside his plays. None of these objections diminishes his importance. He occupies a unique place on the post-war English scene, as a major dramatist pledged to the idea of community theatre and as an artist whose imagination operates in harmony with his social purpose."

For all that, the bitter realist truth is that in the forty years or so since he first made his name, Arden has never had a commercial hit nor made any kind of reputation outside fringe or subsidised or academic theatre, and that he remains yet another of the late-1950s generation of Royal Court dramatists who all seem to have done their best work within a decade of discovery, and who never managed to cross the barriers to major West End or Broadway runs. On the other hand, Arden would be the first to declare that such a crossover was never part of his game-plan. The truth about most of his initial and revolutionary Court generation is that they were not the Angry Young Men of Osborne's army, but the Outsiders of Colin Wilson's.

CALENDAR

• Laurence Olivier, while still running Chichester Festival, also establishes the first ever British National Theatre Company at the Old and later Young Vic
• Opening of the Traverse Theatre in Edinburgh, soon to become Scotland's most radical playhouse
• Elia Kazan and Robert Whitehead set up the Repertory Theater of Lincoln Center
• Barbra Streisand, singing at a gala for JFK asks him for an autograph and is surprised to read what he writes – "Fuck You, The President"
• Young playwright Sam Shepard is working by day as a horse-dung remover at the Santa Anita Racetrack and writing at night
• Coleen Dewhurst is playing *Cleopatra* for $100 a week in Central Park. Elizabeth Taylor is playing her in the movie for $1,000,000 in Rome
• All Broadway theatres go dark from Friday, November 22nd, when President Kennedy is assassinated, and stay dark until the following Tuesday

BIRTHS British actress **Natasha Richardson**, daughter of Tony Richardson and Vanessa Redgrave

DEATHS French poet and playwright **Jean Cocteau**
Dick Powell Broadway and Hollywood star
American actor **Monty Woolley**
Max Miller British music hall comedian
French singer **Edith Piaf**
Clifford Odets American playwright
British playwright **John Whiting** of cancer

NOTABLE PREMIERES Joan Littlewood triumphs at Stratford East with Charles Chilton's bitter anthology of songs from 1914-18 OH, WHAT A LOVELY WAR!
At Stratford upon Avon, Peter Hall and John Barton establish their epic cycle of Shakespeare's history plays, THE WARS OF THE ROSES
Peter O'Toole opens the National Theatre at the Old Vic as HAMLET
Neil Simon establishes his reputation with BAREFOOT IN THE PARK
John Neville and Glenda Jackson star in Bill Naughton's second hit of this year ALFIE
THE REPRESENTATIVE Rolf Hochhuth's hit about the alleged indifference of Pope Pius XII to Jewish suffering under the Nazis opens in London

MUSICAL NOTES Pavarotti's Covent Garden debut in LA BOHEME
American debut of violinist Itschak Perlman

HIT SONGS I Want to Hold Your Hand
24 Hours from Tulsa
Summer Holiday
The Times they Are A-Changing
Puff, the Magic Dragon
Sweets for My Sweet

The Royal Hunt of the Sun

Although his work has never been as critically fashionable as the plays that came out of the Royal Court, or the London fringe, or the Irish movement, it is arguable that Peter Shaffer (born 1926, twin of *Sleuth* playwright Anthony) has been one of the most consistently successful British dramatists of the second half of the 20th century.

From *Five Finger Excercise* (1958), through *The Royal Hunt of the Sun* (1964), *Black Comedy* (1965) and *Equus* (1973) to *Amadeus* (1979) and *Lettice and Lovage* (1987) his plays have (with the exception of a very few flops) run consistently well on both sides of the Atlantic.

But of all his plays, undoubtedly the most epic was *The Royal Hunt of the Sun* which first opened at Chichester and went on to the West End and Broadway before being filmed in 1969 with Robert Shaw and Christopher Plummer. As in almost all his major plays, Shaffer sets up two equal protagonists – the carefree romantic pitched against the more sombre and solo man of intellect. Usually, of course, they are the two opposing sides of the same character. In this play, the romantic is the Inca King-God, the Son of the Sun Atahuallpa, while his counterpart is the dedicated Spanish adventurer, Francisco Pizarro, who sets out with a tiny army to conquer 16th century Peru.

As so often in Shaffer, the two apparent opposites get locked into an uneasy kind of embrace, and when Atahuallpa is killed by his own men Pizarro, totally broken-hearted, awaits the miracle of a resurrection that never comes.

Peter Shaffer was born in Liverpool in 1926 and during the war was, like his twin, a Bevin Boy, working in the Welsh mines. Their family was, however, well endowed with property, notably in Kensington, London, and after college he started to work right away as a television writer whose first two plays were *The Salt Land*, a classical tragedy set in modern Israel, and *Balance of Terror*, a modern espionage thriller.

Although the play now seems a rather slight psychological drama about the effect on a prosperous upper middle-class family when the arrival of a young German tutor destroys their tranquil world, there is no doubt that at the time this seemed a remarkable updating of Rattigan, bringing issues of homosexuality and psychology far more into the open than had ever been done before.

But if *Five Finger Excercise* owed a filial debt to Rattigan, it owed an even greater one to Robert Bolt because here, as in Bolt's *Flowering Cherry* of the previous year, the real issue is the way in which each member of the family has a private dream which gets shattered when they try through the outsider to make it a reality. Years later, Shaffer himself was to describe it as, "semi-autobiographical and deliberately well-made, a latter-day version of the story of the Passion."

But as if to signal that he had no real interest in remaining under the shadow of Rattigan or Bolt, Peter Shaffer's next hit was a double bill, *The Private Ear* and *The Public Eye* (London 1962, Broadway 1963) which established the stardom of Maggie Smith in two very different comedies, in both of which she was partnered by Kenneth Williams. Further proof of Shaffer's remarkable versatility also came in 1963 when he wrote for Joan Littlewood at Stratford East *The Merry Roosters* pantomime.

But it was the following year, with *The Royal Hunt of the Sun* that Shaffer really marked out his historical territory and by now there was simply nobody else in his particular league.

An inquiry into the very existence of God (and whose God is He, anyway?) is pursued through Shaffer's next great hit, *Equus*, while *Amadeus* further develops this symbiotic relationship where Mozart is now the mad but godly youth, and court composer Salieri the older and wiser alter ego whose terrible fate it is to deny his genius and so to deny God.

As if aware that he had always given this double-act to only one sex, Shaffer's next great hit

Lettice and Lovage allowed Maggie Smith and Margaret Tyzack to take on the roles of the romantic and the realist. But this constant pairing of opposites went disastrously wrong in *Yonadab* (1986), a biblical account of two opposing half-brothers, Amnon and Absalom, which like the 1970 *The Battle of Shrivings* flopped horrendously. Since *Lettice and Lovage* his only other major work has been *The Gift of the Gorgon* (1992), the updating of a Greek tragedy which starred Judi Dench and Michael Pennington.

As his most consistent director Peter Hall has noted, no Shaffer play is ever merely written but constantly re-written. They are all works in progress, and when *Amadeus* came back to London and New York in 1999 with David Suchet as Salieri, Shaffer was still making major changes right up to opening night. In that sense, he remains the most meticulous craftsman of his generation.

CALENDAR

• Impresario Peter Daubeny establishes his first World Theatre Season at the Aldwych

• Stratford-upon-Avon governors support Peter Hall when attacked for allowing his new RSC to produce Peter Daubeny's foreign plays and Peter Brook's 'Theatre of Cruelty'

• House of Commons committee supports Sunday opening for theatres. Almost 40 years later this has still not become a widespread practice

• Joan Littlewood, citing exhaustion and a desire to live in France, quits her company at the Theatre Royal, Stratford East

• At the Royal Court, John Osborne and Nicol Williamson star in a rare revival of Ben Travers' 1920s farce *A Cuckoo in the Nest*

• In Hollywood, Sidney Poitier becomes first black actor to win the Oscar (for *Lillies of the Field*)

DEATHS Broadway and Hollywood comic **Harpo Marx**
Brendan Behan Irish playwright
Irish playwright **Sean O'Casey**
Cole Porter American lyricist/composer

NOTABLE PREMIERES At New York's Lincoln Centre, Arthur Miller's semi-autobiographical account of his life with Marilyn Monroe AFTER THE FALL. Jason Robards never leaves the stage in more than three hours but he later attacks the play as "pretentious, ponderous, and tasteless"

Carol Channing starts a near-lifelong run on Broadway of Jerry Herman's HELLO, DOLLY!

Barbra Streisand opens 1400-performance run of FUNNY GIRL by Bob Merrill and Jule Styne

Stephen Sondheim's ANYONE CAN WHISTLE (book by Arthur Laurents) stars Angela Lansbury

Zero Mostel opens 3000-performance Broadway run of Joseph Stein, Jerry Bock and Sheldon Harnick's FIDDLER ON THE ROOF

THE PERSECUTION AND ASSASSINATION OF MARAT AS PERFORMED BY THE INMATES OF THE ASYLUM OF CHARENTON UNDER THE DIRECTION OF THE MARQUIS DE SADE, possibly the longest title of any stage play this century, opens in London

MUSICAL NOTES Debut of pianist John Ogden
Founding of The Harkness Ballet

HIT SONGS Downtown
Walk On By
House of the Rising Sun
Anyone Who Had a Heart
Baby Love

Loot

Ironically, Joe Orton is probably more famous worldwide for the manner of his death than for anything he achieved in an all-too-brief lifetime. In a scene worthy of any of his own black comedies, he was brutally clubbed to death in Islington in 1967 by his long-term but envious lover Kenneth Halliwell, who then committed suicide.

His plays, from *Entertaining Mr Sloane* (1964) to *What the Butler Saw* (first staged 1969), were universally greeted at first with fear and loathing, only to be rediscovered a very few years later as comic masterpieces.

Joe Orton was born in Leicester in 1933, the son of an inarticulate gardener and a socially ambitious mother. His life is best told in the *New Yorker* critic John Lahr's definitive biography *Prick Up Your Ears*, and it was for many years Lahr, working with Orton's letters and diaries, who fought to have his work taken more seriously than the tabloid headlines of his 'shocking' life and death.

Like many young playwrights of his generation, Orton was virtually adopted in private and in public by the agent Margaret (Peggy) Ramsay who almost single-handedly forced a still very conventional West End to accept the anarchy of an entire generation of new playwrights with Joe Orton at the forefront.

By the time of his first stage success, when he was just 30, Orton had already become a figure of scandal and concern and even served a very brief prison sentence for, amazingly, the sin of stealing and defacing library books. Influenced by a mother who was always desperately trying to improve the family's social standing, his plays, not unnaturally, focus on the striking contrasts between genteel pretentiousness and the awful truth. In *Entertaining Mr Sloane*, a brother and sister both lust after their lodger, the eponymous Mr Sloane, even after he has kicked their father to death.

Loot, in the following year, with a title deliberately echoing that of the great farce-master Ben Travers' *Plunder*, is again about the uprooting of traditional pretension as a corrupt police chief ensures that the only law-abiding character in the whole black comedy is also the only one who will be arrested and subsequently murdered.

What Orton had realised, way ahead of his audiences, was that there was something horribly hilarious in the contemporary collapse of all the old police-station values. Indeed, when Truscott, the corrupt copper, handcuffs his victims with the cry, "You're fucking nicked, my old beauty," these were the actual words of the notorious real-life Inspector Challenor who, a few months before *Loot* first opened, had been suspended for planting evidence on suspects.

Time and again, the dialogue of *Loot* suggests nothing so much as Oscar Wilde on speed: "Complete extinction has done nothing to silence her slanderous tongue." Later in the play there is an exchange which perfectly summarises a new blend of lethal hilarity of which Orton was the first and perhaps last master: "Have you never heard of Truscott of the Yard, the man who tracked down the limbless girl killer, or was that sensation before your time?" "But who would kill a limbless girl?" "She was the killer." "But how did she do it if she was limbless?" "I am not prepared to answer that question to anyone outside the profession. We don't want a carbon-copy murder on our hands, now, do we?"

Loot best summarises the abrupt turnaround in Orton's critical fortunes. The first 1965 production closed on the road, but a year later it won the *Evening Standard* Award for the best play of the year. Similarly, the opening in 1969 of *What the Butler Saw* was comparable to the Dublin riots of the 1920s over Sean O'Casey, and one actor in the original cast recalled, "On stage we had a guilty sense of exhilaration in fighting an audience who really wanted to jump up on stage and kill us all."

Orton was always ahead of his time, not just in his writing but also in his determination to lead, as openly as possible, a promiscuous and often violent gay life which, in the end, was also to be the death of him.

Michael Bates and Sheila Ballantyne at the Criterion in 1965

But by and large, the difference between having a major Orton flop or a major Orton hit (there was very little in between) came down to the director. In one of the oldest and wisest clichés in the theatre, comedy is a very serious business, and Orton only really works when his scripts are played absolutely seriously, at which point, like those of Travers and Feydeau, they become totally hilarious.

Orton's genius also lay in his wondrous ability simultaneously to celebrate and parody the conventional theatrical forms within which he always worked. Thus *What The Butler Saw* has a traditional farce set, but a character arriving on-stage for the first time immediately asks, "Why are there so many doors? Was this house designed by a lunatic?" Among the tantalising projects left unfinished when Orton was murdered at the age of 34, was a filmscript for the Beatles and a television series to be called *The Seven Deadly Virtues*.

CALENDAR

• British singer Adam Faith cancels South African concert tour after being refused permission to play to multi-racial audiences
• On British television, Coronation Street tops the ratings, as it will for the next half-century or so
• In British television, opening of BBC 2, the first network to go into colour which is inaugurated with *The Forsyte Saga* and *Late Night Lineup*, a talk show which runs for nearly 10 years, seven nights a week, with Joan Bakewell, Tony Bilbow, Michael Dean and Sheridan Morley
• Mary Whitehouse founds her campaign against "offensive and immoral" broadcasting
• Jenny Lee, widow of Aneurin Bevan, becomes Britain's first Minister of the Arts and is instrumental in the building of the National Theatre, the Barbican, and many other new playhouses around the country

• Founding by André Gregry of the Philadelphia Theatre of Living Arts
• Pulitzer Prize for Drama and the Best Play Tony to Frank D Gilroy's *The Subject Was Roses*
• Founding in the United States of the National Council for the Arts, which subsequently became the National Endowment for the Arts and the National Endowment for the Humanities

DEATHS American poet and playwright **TS Eliot**
English-born comic **Stanley Jefferson**, later Stan Laurel
William Somerset Maugham; on his 91st birthday, a few weeks ago, he said, "Death is the final freedom, I fly to it as to a lover."

NOTABLE PREMIERES Walter Matthau and Art Carney open long Broadway run in Neil Simon's THE ODD COUPLE. DO I HEAR A WALTZ is a short-lived Broadway musical, the only one written by Richard Rodgers and Stephen Sondheim
Liza Minnelli opens on Broadway in Kander and Ebb's short-lived FLORA, THE RED MENACE
In London and later in New York, Peter Hall for the RSC directs Harold Pinter's sinister THE HOMECOMING

MUSICAL NOTES The start of the great ballet partnership of Margot Fonteyn and Rudolf Nureyev begins at the Royal Ballet

HIT SONGS California Girls
Help
Mr Tambourine Man

Rosencrantz and Guildenstern are Dead

If you had to name the three most critically and commercially successful of all British playwrights of the second half of the 20th century, it wouldn't take you long to come up with (in alphabetical order) Sir Alan Ayckbourn, Harold Pinter, and Sir Tom Stoppard; their only other connection is perhaps that none of them ever attended university.

But, of course, Stoppard is only English by the choice of his mother. He was born Tomas Straussler in 1937 in Zlin, Czechoslovakia but as an infant he was taken by his parents (his father was a doctor) to Singapore, where the father was killed by the invading Japanese. His family was then evacuated to India, where his mother re-married a British soldier named Stoppard and by 1947 Tom, aged ten, was being educated in a small village school near Wargrave in Berkshire.

Professionally he started out as a journalist on a local Bristol paper and Stoppard has always said that what turned him from journalism to playwriting was the triumph of *Look Back in Anger* in 1956: "The theatre was suddenly the only place to be; it was receiving disproportionate attention."

His first play *A Walk on the Water*, later re-christened *Enter a Free Man*, did not achieve production until 1968 and then only because of his amazing triumph in the previous year. What happened then was that he

Adrian Scarborough and Simon Russell Beale at the RNT in 1995

had written a play called *Rosencrantz and Guildenstern are Dead* about the lives and confusions of two minor characters in *Hamlet*. Though this has seldom been noticed, and Stoppard may well have been totally unaware of it, the idea had in fact been tried before by no less a writer than WS Gilbert who, in the 1880s, came up with a brief verse drama about these two characters.

With Olivier's cautious approval, Tynan commissioned a professional production which opened at the Old Vic in the following April.

From its lengthy opening word game, *Rosencrantz and Gildenstern* was the play which was to mark out Stoppard's personal and unique territory: a lexicographer's interest in language, a philosopher's interest in the obscure workings of the human mind, a journalist's interest in reflecting and reporting events which are usually misunderstood, uncontrollable, and shrouded in a perpetual fog of mystery.

A paradox like this has always been at the heart of Stoppard's writing, and although early critics were eager to compare Rosencrantz and Guildenstern to the tramps in *Waiting for Godot*, Vladimir and Estragon, there is really no sense in which this can be made to hold good.

Stoppard's next major hit, *Jumpers* (1972), would focus on a professor of philosophy, a tortoise, and a chanteuse, not to mention several gymnasts, one of whom is shot dead as he starts to form a human pyramid. At the centre of this play is also a character having a nervous breakdown because she has suddenly realised that with men now walking on the moon, we are no longer at the centre of God's universe.

Then again, *Travesties* (1974) brings together James Joyce, Lenin, and the absurdist philosopher Tristan Tzara, in an amateur dramatic performance of *The Importance of Being Earnest* in Zurich in 1917 which, amazingly and very typically of Stoppard, actually happened.

Of his other plays, many have been one-acters (one double-bill *Dirty Linen* and *New-Found-Land*)

ran three years in the West End, while *Every Good Boy Deserves Favour* was a successful attempt to write (with André Previn) an entire play for a symphony orchestra.

In more recent years, apart from several radio and television plays as well as a number of adaptations and screenplays, Stoppard's major stage successes have ranged from the journalistic *Night and Day* (1978) through the scientific *Hapgood* (1988), an immensely complex espionage thriller, and *Arcadia* (1993), a country house romance set in two different timeframes, to *Indian Ink*, a nostalgic account of the Raj, and, most recently, *The Invention of Love* (1998), a touchingly wry story of the Oxford life and love of the academic and poet AE Housman. These plays, and many others, had essentially only one thing in common – the wayward genius and meticulous craftsmanship of Sir Tom Stoppard himself.

CALENDAR

• At the Royal Court, the English Stage Company is served 18 summonses as a result of Edward Bond's controversial *Saved*, which has ignored all the changes demanded by the Lord Chamberlain

• In Dublin, the Irish President Eamonn de Valera opens the newly completed Abbey Theatre on the site of the one damaged by fire in 1951

• Joe Papp's New York Shakespeare Festival buys the Astor Library which it will convert into the Public Theatre

• Edward Albee tells a radio interviewer that the only time he has ever been unhappy with an actor was with John Gielgud in *Tiny Alice*

• In the chorus of *Fiddler on the Roof* is a young Bette Midler, while in the company of the Lincoln Center Repertory is a young Frank Langella

DEATHS American actor **Montgomery Clift**
Lenny Bruce Radical American comedian
Sophie Tucker American singer
British actor/director **George Devine**, founding father of the English Stage Company at the Royal Court
Revolutionary designer, director, writer and actor, **Edward Gordon Craig**, son of Ellen Terry and uncle of John Gielgud
Veteran English music-hall star **Ada Reeve**

NOTABLE PREMIERES After its London flop, Brian Friel's PHILADELPHIA, HERE I COME! opens on Broadway
On Broadway, Joel Grey, Lotte Lenya and Jill Haworth open Kander and Ebb's musical CABARET based on Christopher Isherwood's BERLIN STORIES
Noël Coward makes his farewell stage appearance in the West End run of SUITE IN THREE KEYS
Vanessa Redgrave opens Jay Presson Allen's adaptation of Muriel Spark's novel about the Scottish schoolmistress, THE PRIME OF MISS JEAN BRODIE
At the National Theatre, Albert Finney and Geraldine McEwan open Feydeau's A FLEA IN HER EAR as adapted by John Mortimer

MUSICAL NOTES John Lennon says that the Beatles are more popular than Jesus Christ; in response, their records are burned in the American Bible Belt

HIT SONGS Good Vibrations
Eleanor Rigby
Green, Green Grass of Home
Georgie Girl
Strangers in the Night

A Day in the Death of Joe Egg

The playwright Peter Richard Nichols makes surprisingly few appearances in the major academic textbooks about theatre towards the end of the 20th century, perhaps because he has always remained resolutely outside any of its mainstreams.

Born in 1927 and brought up in the West Country, he was called up into the army and served in the Far East, acting and singing alongside Kenneth Williams and several other subsequent showbiz stars in a series of eccentric army camp concert parties, all of which gave him the basis for *Privates On Parade* (1977).

Long before that, he had started out writing television plays and made his name in 1967 when the Australian actor turned director Michael Blakemore rescued his script for *A Day in the Death of Joe Egg* from a slush-pile at the Glasgow Citizens Theatre.

A Day in the Death of Joe Egg, which has always remained his greatest commercial hit, was a semi-autobiographical account of what it is like to be the parents of a brain-damaged child. In a mixture of fact and fantasy, love and hate, optimism and despair, the play traces the blackly comic reality of a family situation which had never been staged before, and it was the new production company formed by the actors Michael Medwin and Albert Finney who transferred *Joe Egg* to London, and then took it in equal triumph to Broadway before Alan Bates and Janet Suzman made the 1971 movie.

By this time, Nichols was luckily old enough and experienced enough not to be traumatised by the triumph of a first stage play, and almost immediately he began to write for the National Theatre *The National Health* which, long before Lindsay Anderson's movie *Britannia Hospital*, was the first script to see a bleak parallel between the collapse of Britain's National Health Service and the collapse of Britain itself.

By now, certain recurrent themes in Nichols' work were becoming faintly perceptible – the use of fantasy and flashback; the frequency of a middle-aged narrator looking back in astonishment and amusement rather than anger at his early life; and a devotion to the traditions of the music-hall entertainers of his youth.

In 1971, he wrote *Down Forget-Me-Not Lane*, another semi-autobiographical account, this time of his upbringing, and then, in 1974, with Albert Finney again starring, came the more conventional *Chez Nous* about

Zena Walker and Joe Melia at the Comedy in 1967

an expatriate marriage in crisis. In that same year, as if aware that there was a limit to the number of times he could dig dramatically back into his past, he also wrote (again for the National Theatre) *The Freeway*, a brave but doomed attempt to find another metaphor for Britain in the increasing number of its traffic-jammed flyovers and motorways.

Then, in 1977, came *Privates on Parade* which brilliantly counterpointed the cheesy cheerfulness of a derelict Far Eastern troop concert party with the reality of Britain's final and often disastrous attempts to maintain an empire overseas. On the face of it, this is a wonderfully comic musical which allowed Denis Quilley (on-stage and in the Michael Blakemore film) to impersonate everyone from Vera Lynn to Marlene Dietrich, but just below this greasepaint surface, as Nichols once remarked, is a very much darker play about the way that even survivors are destroyed by war.

After *Privates on Parade* came *Born in the Gardens* (1980) in which Beryl Reid played an eccentric old widow living with her middle-aged son, but it wasn't until 1981 with *Passion Play* that Nichols had another real hit. Revived in London early in 2000, this is the play about the doppelgangers; the two leading characters, again coming to the end of a middle-class, middle-aged marriage, are each played by two different actors, one of whom simply voices the hidden thoughts of the other.

CALENDAR

• In a decision which led to a major battle on the National Theatre Board, the Lord Chamberlain bans Rolf Hochhuth's *Soldiers* translated by his British champion Robert David MacDonald which attacks Winston Churchill for wartime murder
• The Shaw Festival at Niagara-on-the-Lake appoints actor Paxton Whitehead as artistic director
• *The Mousetrap* celebrates its 15th anniversary
• John Steinbeck's play *Of Mice and Men* is banned in the Soviet Union because he supports the war in Vietnam, which is no financial problem because the USSR never pays royalties on plays anyway
• Edward Albee is awarded the Pulitzer prize for *A Delicate Balance*

BIRTHS   American actress **Julia Roberts**

DEATHS   **Vivien Leigh** English actress
American playwright/director **Elmer Rice**
American playwright and poet **Langston Hughes**, one of the first to chronicle the black American experience
Basil Rathbone English actor
British playwright **Joe Orton**, at the age of 34

NOTABLE PREMIERES   Cartoonist Charles Schultz's comic-strip characters become a musical hit, YOU'RE A GOOD MAN, CHARLIE BROWN
Julie Styne/Comden and Green/Arthur Laurents' new musical HALLELUJAH, BABY! stars Leslie Uggams
Peter Ustinov's play about soldiers through many centuries THE UNKNOWN SOLDIER AND HIS WIFE stars Christopher Walken
George Tabori's THE NIGGER LOVERS runs for only 25 performances but is notable for the first starring role of a very young Morgan Freeman
Robert Morley in London enjoys a long run in Peter Ustinov's HALFWAY UP THE TREE
Alan Ayckbourn's domestic comedy, RELATIVELY SPEAKING stars Michael Hordern, Richard Briers and Celia Johnson

MUSICAL NOTES   Leonard Bernstein conducts 125th anniversary concert of the New York Philharmonic

HIT SONGS   Soul Man
Penny Lane
Can't Take My Eyes Off You
I'm a Believer
A Whiter Shade of Pale
Puppet on a String

Forty Years On

Most playwrights of the second half of the 20th century would claim to be in some way topical or relevant to the way we lived then; but only two major plays, in our view, can really be said to live on into the new millennium as mainstream reflections of Britain in a time of frequent social and political change. One of those is David Hare's 1978 *Plenty* ("Sold out: is that the phrase?") and the other is surely Alan Bennett's first play.

His subsequent fame as a television writer and the author of such National Theatre triumphs as *The Madness of George III* and *The Wind in the Willows*, not to mention a succession of West End hits (and occasional flops) over almost thirty years leading up to the 1999 *Lady in the Van* have tended to obscure his first great hit, but this is still the one which more than any other captures what was to become the hallmark of Bennett's writing, a kind of poisoned nostalgia in which the past is somehow at the same time both damaging and desirable, whether we like it or not.

Much of Bennett's later writing has had the one-to-one intimacy of his television *Talking Heads*, but *Forty Years On* wonderfully tackles the whole history of England from the 1920s into the 1960s, and though its frame is the relatively modest one of a school play, it is not entirely fanciful to consider this his *Cavalcade*. Just as Coward's 1930 epic took England from the Relief of Mafeking to the coming of the Jazz Age, so Bennett takes it on through World War Two and into the age of disillusion: "In our crass-builded, glass-bloated, green-belted world, Sunday is for washing the car, tinned peaches and carnation milk. A Sergeant's world it is now, the world of the lay-by and the civic improvement scheme. Country is park and shore is marina, spare time is leisure and more, year by year. We have become a battery people, a people of under-privileged hearts fed on pap in darkness, bred out of all taste and season to savour the shoddy splendours of the new civility."

Born on May 9th 1934 in Leeds, the son of a Co-op butcher and a sometimes depressive mother,

Emlyn Williams at the Apollo in 1968

Bennett's own brand of irritable self-deprecation has been so successful that he features in almost no academic studies of late 20th-century theatre, despite the fact that in our (admittedly not universally shared) view, *Forty Years On* is the greatest play ever written about post-war England in decline and disarray. It also happens to be the play that gave John Gielgud his first great role in post-war modern dress, and found him the courage to go on to David Storey's *Home* and Pinter's *No Man's Land* a few years later.

The play is set at Albion House, a metaphor for Little England itself and a somewhat rundown boys' preparatory school at which they are staging *Speak for England, Arthur*, a school play covering wars, literary gossip and reminiscences. Watched over, and performed in, by the reactionary headmaster and his more radical deputy, the play covers everyone from Hitler to Harold Nicolson, Virginia Woolf to Oscar Wilde, and although it is frequently dynamited from within by recalcitrant rugger-playing schoolboys and disaffected members of staff, it builds in its own lyrical, satirical way to a devastating obituary for the old values: "Who now sees death? We tidy the old into hospitals…desolation at fifteen storeys becomes a view…the crowd has found the door into the secret garden. Now they will tear up the flowers by the roots, strip the borders and strew them with paper and broken bottles."

After *Forty Years On* Bennett had another long-running West End hit with *Getting On* (1971), another murmur of unease about an increasingly plastic Britain and the shoddy splendours of the new civility, this one however undermined by its star Kenneth More's determination to play a bitter comedy for old-world charm.

Next came the 1973 *Habeas Corpus* in which Alec Guinness played a doctor for whom the human body had lost more than a little of its mysterious charm ("I've seen 25 thousand sets of private parts; a conscientious whore could not have seen more"). A prolonged dance of death which actually ended in one, *Habeas Corpus* had some great one-liners ("A passing-out parade at Sandhurst left him forever incapable of having children") and a vintage cast acting out scenes of Bennett's philosophic despair as if they were in a latter-day Ben Travers farce, which in one sense of course they were.

The Old Country (1977), which Alec Guinness played in London and Robert Morley in Australia, was Bennett's first spy play, an account of two disgruntled Burgess-and-Maclean characters living out an enforced exile in Russia after their defection from Britain; Bennett was to return to this theme in his brilliant real-life account of Burgess meeting the actress Coral Browne backstage in Moscow (*An Englishman Abroad*) and his near-real-life account of the Queen meeting Anthony Blunt (*A Question of Attribution*), which were eventually staged as the double-bill *Single Spies* in 1989.

CALENDAR

• David Merrick writes, in Esquire magazine, that the New York Times should toss that "fat limey posterior out in the street" – referring to the London-born New York Times drama critic Clive Barnes

• Theatre 69, formed expressly to produce serious new plays, loses £130,000 and gives up after two weeks

• For the first time, tickets for Broadway shows may be purchased through a centralised computer system

• The assassination of Dr Martin Luther King starts a series of riots, which seriously affect theatre box offices

• The New York State Human Rights Commission issues a statement that Broadway producers must begin to hire more black performers

• Peter Hall leaves the RSC. Its new artistic director will be Trevor Nunn, aged 28

• Long hoped-for abolition of the Lord Chamberlain's Office of Theatrical Censorship

DEATHS

Stage and television comedian **Tony Hancock**

Tallulah Bankhead Broadway actress

American producer **George White**

Howard Lindsay Broadway playwright

British actor-manager **Sir Donald Wolfit**

Finlay Currie Veteran Scottish actor

American actor **Bert Wheeler**

NOTABLE PREMIERES

Arthur Miller premieres THE PRICE, a family drama about two brothers and a second-hand furniture dealer

Three one-act plays by Neil Simon, all set in the same suite at a hotel in New York, PLAZA SUITE, stars Maureen Stapleton and George C Scott

Leonard Sillman's NEW FACES OF 1968 features two talented young performers – comic-singers Robert Klein and Madeleine Kahn

HAIR opens at the Public Theatre, New York

PROMISES, PROMISES is a Bacharach and David musical based on the 1960 Billy Wilder film, THE APARTMENT, by Neil Simon

CANTERBURY TALES, a musical adaptation of Chaucer, runs in London for more than 2000 performances

Tom Stoppard's THE REAL INSPECTOR HOUND is a short parody of an Agatha Christie murder mystery, featuring two derelict critics

MUSICAL NOTES

Harrison Birtwistle's opera, PUNCH AND JUDY

HIT SONGS

Wonderful World

Lady Madonna

I Heard it through the Grapevine

Son of a Preacher Man

Mrs Robinson

Christie in Love

Not to be confused with the contemporary but more brutalist Howard Barker, Howard Brenton was born in Portsmouth in 1942, the son of a policeman turned Methodist minister. Insofar as he comes from any group of late-century British dramatists, it is perhaps the one that Benedict Nightingale identifies as Theatre of Cataclysm, in which *The Times* critic also includes Barker, David Hare (who first staged Brenton's work and wrote several plays with him), Tony Bicat, Stephen Poliakoff and Snoo Wilson.

Though all these writers were later to go their separate ways, and could no longer be identified as any kind of a group, it is true that their early work shared the conviction that Britain was in deep and terminal decay, and that only acts of violence and social engineering could change an increasingly right-wing and some would say repressively Thatcherite Britain.

To this end, many of the group would turn popular heroes into villains and then reverse the process, making villains into heroes. Brenton, in first *Christie in Love* and then *The Churchill Play*, was especially adept at this. He wrote his first play while still at Cambridge in 1966, and three years later had written four others, one of which was given a Sunday-night reading at the Royal Court. But it was David Hare's decision to produce *Christie in Love* for his Portable Theatre Company in 1969 which first established Brenton. It relied on a simple role-reversal; Christie the mass-murderer was seen as an everyman figure, killing as an act of love, while the police and public on his trail were caricatured as puppets out of some deadly Punch and Judy show.

Another Brenton play of that year, *Revenge*, had a policeman and a master criminal played as two faces of the same actor, while England was seen as "one giant pinball table, with its casino towns, brothel villages, cities red with blood and pleasure; public life the turn of a card, the fall of a dice."

Two years later, Brenton's *Scott of the Antarctic* was predictably not the hero-figure of the John Mills

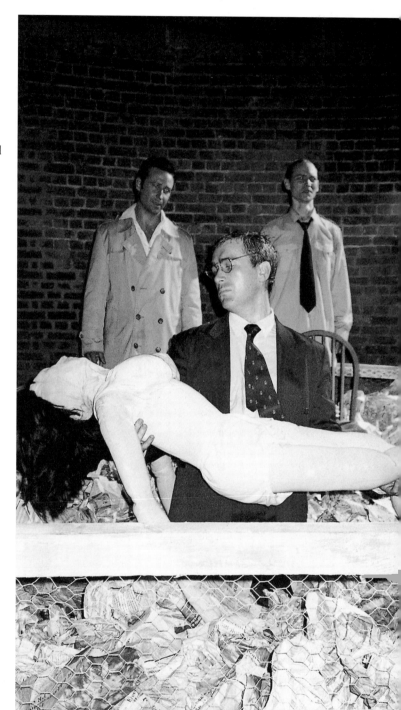

Scott Bushell, Jez Foster and Chris Routh in The Permanent Transients' production at the Roundhouse, London 2000

1948 movie, but instead an upper-class prat uttering platitudes as he fails to survive a ludicrous imperial adventure. Similarly, *Hitler Dances* (1972) set up Violette Szabo, the Second World War spy, not as the Virginia McKenna heroine of *Carve Her Name with Pride* (film, 1958), but instead as a bloodthirsty sexual predator. But it was with *Magnificence* at the Royal Court in 1973 that Brenton really made his name; the story of a squatter who turns terrorist after a bailiff's violence causes his young wife to miscarry. This was also a magnificent political tragedy about the ultimate inadequacy, futility and waste of current revolutionary thinking. Its climax was a bomb in an English country garden, where an old gay don (magically played by Robert Eddison) is mistakenly believed to be hanging on to some kind of age-old Tory power.

After *Brassneck* (political corruption in a Midlands town, written in collaboration with David Hare) and *Weapons of Happiness* (1976, the unsuccessful occupation of a potato-crisp factory), Brenton confounded those of us eager to classify him as a revolutionary activist with *Epsom Downs* (1977) a wide-ranging panoramic look at Derby Day on a British racecourse.

But it was a year later that Brenton hit the headlines as no other playwright since Joe Orton's murder a decade earlier. His play *The Romans in Britain* contained a scene featuring the homosexual rape of a druid, and because it was in the repertoire of the National Theatre, this proved too much for Mrs Mary Whitehouse, Britain's leading campaigner for sexual censorship on stage and screen. She and several supporters brought a private prosecution, and both Brenton and his director Michael Bogdanov came perilously close to prison before the case was ultimately thrown out of court, thereby fortuitously ending any serious attempt ever again to bring criminal charges against an artist in Great Britain.

Among Brenton's other work, *The Churchill Play* was about an Ireland reduced to totalitarianism, notably seen in a 1979 RSC revival; *Greenland* at the Royal Court in 1988 was a waspish attack on Swinging London which degenerated into a wild and woolly version of a futurist Utopia, and far and away his best and most successful play of recent years has been *Pravda* which he co-wrote for the National with David Hare in 1985, the Fleet Street play in which Anthony Hopkins gave one of his greatest and (to date) last stage performances.

This remains a savagely bitchy and wildly funny attack on newspaper moguls of the Rupert Murdoch/Robert Maxwell generation which not only created in the character of Lambert LeRoux one of the great villains of the 20th-century stage but also wickedly and wonderfully showed up the workers on the Street of Shame for the spineless sycophants many were.

Brenton's most recent plays have not echoed his earlier successes, but like many dramatists of his generation he has to some extent been wrong-footed by history; if the Thatcher years were disillusioning and depressing for Brenton's generation, the collapse in the 1990s of Communism and with it any real political alternative has left them with precious few political theories of left or right to celebrate or even recognise.

CALENDAR

- Debut of radical television series *Monty Python's Flying Circus*
- Samuel Beckett wins Nobel Prize for Literature
- British stage director John Schlesinger and British actress Maggie Smith both win Oscars
- The Tony and the Pulitzer Prize for Best Play go to Howard Sackler's *The Great White Hope*
- Police raid a gay bar in Greenwich Village, thereby starting the Stonewall demonstration
- Writers Norman Mailer and Jimmy Breslin run for Mayor and Deputy Mayor of New York. Their platform is to make their City the 51st State, thereby preventing the State Government levying city taxes
- America's La Mama Troupe come to London briefly in Last Chance Saloon
- At the National Theatre, Michael Blakemore directs Jim Dale in Peter Nichols' satire *The National Health*
- Opening in London of the Round House as a theatre
- David Mamet, future author of *Glengarry Glen Ross*, unable to find work as an actor, sells real estate
- In England, Laurence Olivier gets the first-ever peerage given to an actor, and Noël Coward also is knighted

DEATHS
Veteran English actor **Boris Karloff**
Judy Garland American film star and singer
Broadway composer **Frank Loesser**
Thelma Ritter American comedienne

NOTABLE PREMIERES
In Boston, world premiere of THE INDIAN WANTS THE BRONX by Israel Horowitz
On Broadway, the first nude revue transfer from London, Kenneth Tynan's OH! CALCUTTA
In her Broadway musical debut, Katharine Hepburn plays COCO in the musical by André Previn and Alan Jay Lerner
In London, Derek Godfrey opens as the mad aristocrat in Peter Barnes' THE RULING CLASS

MUSICAL NOTES
In the USA, nearly one million people attend the three-day Woodstock music and arts fair

HIT SONGS
Honky Tonk Woman
Sugar Baby
Hair

The Philanthropist

Christopher Hampton, born in 1946 and brought up for several years in Egypt where his father was with the Cable & Wireless company, is intriguingly a member of no definable generation or group of late-century British dramatists. Educated at Lancing College in a vintage intake which also included the lyricist Tim Rice and the dramatist David Hare, something perhaps about Hampton's early life abroad has stood him aside and apart, a commentator and a social reporter rather than an involved, polemical or overtly political writer. In that sense, you might have to go as far back as Rattigan to find an even distant influence, although looking ahead you could argue that Hampton paved the way for Simon Gray and perhaps even Ronald Harwood, both also his near-contemporaries.

Hampton's first hit came when he was 22, having just come down from Oxford and already a resident dramatist at the Court on the strength of his first play, *When Did You Last See My Mother?* His second, *Total Eclipse*, was an account of the early lives of Verlaine and Rimbaud, both seen as 'poets maudits', homosexual rebels cast out from respectable society.

Then came *The Philanthropist* (1970), loosely derived from Molière, but with a callously brilliant coup-de-theatre at the end of the first scene which makes the rest of a languidly brilliant conversation piece seem something of a dramatic anti-climax. This is where we first enter what was to become the Simon Gray territory of *Butley* and *Otherwise Engaged*; a world where the peaceful seclusion of academic life is contrasted with hints of an altogether more savage world just outside the college gardens.

As if to answer those who were already accusing him of a certain unworldliness, Hampton's next play was the 1973 *Savages*, in which Paul Scofield memorably played the ineffable English diplomat Alan West, who in keeping with his surname stood for the whole of the 'civilised' world up against a tribe of Brazilians fighting for their survival. At a time when hostages were to be much in the news, Hampton's

Shavian debate (involving diplomats and anthropologists) about the morality of capture became a passionate, angry, bitterly cynical and yet wholly workable play which cross-cut the murder of one western diplomat with the anonymity surrounding the slaughter of a hundred Brazilian Indians.

Then, in 1976, came the mildly disappointing *Treats*, an updated *Design for Living*, in which a woman and two men revolved through nine scenes of matching and mismatching in a kind of London *La Ronde*, but this was followed by two brilliant English adaptations (of Horváth's *Tales from the Vienna Woods* in 1977 and Laclos' *Les Liaisons Dangereuses* in 1987) which were to be among Hampton's greatest hits. The latter also became a successful movie (*Dangerous Liaisons*, 1988, Glenn Close and John Malkovich) and on stage as on screen, Hampton found something in the distant format of a courtly, albeit lecherous and treacherous, correspondence which totally suited his own distanced, cool style.

Then, in 1983, came Hampton's most ambitious play, *Tales From Hollywood*, an episodic, touching, brilliantly witty account of what happened to Brecht, the brothers Thomas and Heinrich Mann, Salka Viertel and Lion Feuchtwanger when on the run from Hitler they all finished up in California, all that is except the unfortunate Horváth because he was killed on the Champs Elysées by a falling tree in a thunderstorm on his way into exile.

As for the others, what Hampton found was something both comic and tragic in the way that, having escaped one totalitarian dictatorship in the nick of time, most of them rapidly ended up under the only faintly more benign one of the Warner Brothers. The shadows of Stoppard's *Travesties* and even *Dinner at Eight* were faintly discernible here, but Hampton agilely threaded together a series of disparate stories from the Hollywood hills to form the pattern of exile. The idea of a rueful Mann realising that "my entire American reputation stands on the legs of Marlene Dietrich", or a Tarzan hurtling through the trees to announce "Me Johnny Weissmuller, you Thomas Mann" was just brilliant, and this was perhaps the closest the theatre will ever come to the feeling of celluloid and literary decay that permeates Budd Schulberg's *The Disenchanted*.

Since then, Hampton's major original contribution to the National has been the 1991 *White Chameleon*, a touching if somewhat random account of his early life abroad, but he has also been occupied with a vast range of stage, television and movie adaptations, as well as his first musical, the book and lyrics (with Don Black) for Andrew Lloyd Webber's 1993 *Sunset Boulevard*, a version of the classic Billy Wilder movie from 1950 to which Hampton brought his characteristically stylish and somewhat acid vintage Hollywood knowledge.

During the late 1990s, Hampton went back to his earliest *Les Liaisons Dangereuses* tradition and found another French drama to translate. This one was *Art*, immensely profitable three-handed debate by Yasmina Reza about the meaning, if any, of modern art. Produced by Mrs Sean Connery, *Art* has become a long-running phenomenon in more than forty cities around the world and it looks as though Hampton will be Reza's translator of choice for any subsequent work, thereby ensuring him the kind of financial security that he, almost alone among modern dramatists, does not really need.

CALENDAR

• A court in Boston rules that *Hair* may only continue its run if they cut the nude scene
• Charles Gordone becomes the first black playwright to win Pulitzer Prize for Drama for his *No Place to be Somebody*
• Producer Kermit Bloomgarden writes a speech attacking the war in Vietnam and demanding a minute of silence for the four young students killed at Kent State

• At 72, Judith Anderson starts a national tour as *Hamlet*. Previous female Hamlets have included Sarah Bernhardt, Eva Le Gallienne and Siobhan McKenna
• On September 9, *Hello, Dolly!* overtakes *My Fair Lady* as the longest-running musical in Broadway history
• In Scotland, the Glasgow Citizens Theatre is taken over by a triumvirate of directors – Giles Havergal, playwright Robert David MacDonald and designer/director Philip Prowse

DEATHS Broadway composer **Ray Henderson**
Yiddish theatre comedian **Lenasha Skulnick**

NOTABLE PREMIERES Ethel Merman, in her final Broadway appearance, takes over the lead in HELLO, DOLLY!
John Gielgud and Ralph Richardson make their Royal Court debuts in David Storey's HOME
Robert Morley opens 900-performance run in Alan Ayckbourn's first hit, HOW THE OTHER HALF LOVES
At Stratford upon Avon, Peter Brook's celebrated 'white box' production of A MIDSUMMER NIGHT'S DREAM
In London, Dario Fo's ACCIDENTAL DEATH OF AN ANARCHIST

MUSICAL NOTES Philip Glass' MUSIC FOR CHANGING PARTS
Ulysses Kay's THE CAPITOLINE VENUS
Michael Tippett's opera THE KNOT GARDEN

HIT SONGS We've Only Just Begun
Let It Be
Bridge Over Troubled Water
Raindrops Keep Falling On My Head

Follies

"Every time Stephen Sondheim writes a new score," said the impresario Alexander Cohen, "Broadway gets rebuilt," and by that reckoning it had already been rebuilt some half a dozen times. *Follies* was however Sondheim's most ambitious and multi-layered score to date, and it all began with a *New York Times* photograph of Gloria Swanson standing in the rubble of the theatre in New York where she had started out as a dancer in the 1920s.

From that one photograph grew the idea for the story of a group of showgirls having what may well be their last reunion in their former home; Hal Prince and Michael Bennett started working on a Sondheim score of which even the title had many meanings and resonances. To American audiences, it meant of course the lavish pre-war revues of Ziegfeld; to English audiences (those of us at any rate lucky enough to see the original production) it meant a kind of grandeur, and

the French it meant simply lunacy. "Welcome," says the Ziegfeld figure as the show opens "to our first and last reunion; a final chance before my theatre comes down to stumble through a song or two and lie about ourselves a little."

At the time of *Follies*, Steve Sondheim was just forty and already the composer and/or lyricist of six major Broadway scores: *West Side Story* (with Leonard Bernstein), *Gypsy* (with Jule Styne), *Do I Hear A Waltz?* (with Richard Rodgers) and, alone, *A Funny Thing Happened On The Way To The Forum*, *Anyone Can Whistle* and *Company* which was also of course a reunion story, though this one set high amid the skyscrapers of Manhattan.

For *Follies*, Sondheim's score was a mixture of private-relationship songs and showbiz pastiche; within the course of this one show he manages to parody Irving Berlin ("Beautiful Girls"), Mistinguette ("Ah Paree"),

The Shaftesbury Theatre in 1987

American vaudeville ("Buddy's Blues") and de Sylva, Brown and Henderson ("Broadway Baby"). But there was more to *Follies* than conscious nostalgia; there was here a very real attempt to explore memory, to look through the distorting mirrors of time present and time past. The whole show was about illusion and reality, and Sondheim himself acknowledges the Pirandellian quality of the climax.

The casting of *Follies* was also a work of art: Ethel Barrymore's daughter, Gene Nelson, Alexis Smith, Yvonne de Carlo and Fifi d'Orsay from vintage Hollywood movies, Dorothy Collins who'd been a lead singer on the radio Hit Parade, Ethel Shutta who had once been Eddie Cantor's leading lady, and the Shakespearean Arnold Moss. Set on the bare stage of a Broadway theatre in demolition, the four principals were all victims of collapsing marriages and other midlife crises, but gradually we see them as they once were, with four younger figures stepping out of their shadows to relive in black and white their early meetings.

Follies reached Broadway on 4th April 1971 after an uneasy Boston tryout; as so often with middle-period Sondheim, the reviews were distinctly mixed. *Variety* thought it had "too many songs, too many leading players, too many scenes and the most bewildering plot-line in years", while the *New York Daily News* found it "brilliant and breathtaking; it is unlikely that the resources of the Broadway musical have ever been used to more cunning effect than in this richly imaginative score."

Of all the 'showbiz' songs of Sondheim, none is more resonant than "Broadway Baby" with its conclusion:

> "I should have gone to an acting school,
> That seems clear.
> Still someone said, 'She's sincere'
> So I'm here…
> First you're another
> Sloe-eyed vamp,
> Then someone's mother,
> Then you're camp…"

Follies won a total of eight Tony Awards, ran 520 performances on Broadway and lost its backers something in the region of six hundred thousand dollars, roughly a hundred thousand less than its total costs. It had been a phenomenally expensive musical to run but its importance was clear at least to a young student reviewer on the Harvard Crimson, later the *New York Times* critic Frank Rich: "*Follies* is a musical about the death of the musical; its creators are in essence presenting their own funeral." Except of course that over the next thirty years Sondheim was to go on to another dozen major scores, everything from *A Little Night Music* and *Pacific Overtures* through *Sweeney Todd* to *Sunday in the Park with George* and *Assassins* and *Passion*. Almost alone he got the Broadway musical through the second half of the 20th century and into the 21st, and in our view he is the only writer in that field who can seriously be compared to Edward Albee, Arthur Miller, Tennessee Williams and even Eugene O'Neill.

CALENDAR

• In Washington DC, the opening of the John F Kennedy Center for the Performing Arts

• Formation of the Black Theatre Alliance

• At the end of the Broadway season, only four shows have repaid their investment. There have been 56 productions, of which only 14 are new American plays

• Voices of protest are raised against various depictions of religious figures in Tim Rice and Andrew Lloyd Webber's new musical *Jesus Christ Superstar*

• At the Royal Court, opening of the eighty-seat Theatre Upstairs, for experimental productions

• *Fiddler on the Roof* overtakes *Hello Dolly!* to become Broadway's longest-running musical with its 2845th performance

DEATHS — Canadian born comedienne **Bebe Daniels**
Leland Hayward Broadway producer
British playwright **NC Hunter**
Tyrone Guthrie English producer/director
Broadway dancer **Ann Pennington**

NOTABLE PREMIERES — STICKS AND BONES, David Rabe's Vietnam–era fantasy, opens at the Public
A musical version of TWO GENTLEMEN OF VERONA opens on Broadway starring Raoul Julia with Stockard Channing in her Broadway debut
Edward Albee's ALL OVER is all over in 42 performances, despite a cast which includes Colleen Dewhurst and Jessica Tandy
GODSPELL, a rock musical by John-Michael Tebelak and Stephen Schwartz, is a big hit on Broadway
Andrew Lloyd Webber and Tim Rice bring their JESUS CHRIST SUPERSTAR to New York in a triumphant Tom O'Horgan staging
Triumphant premiere of Anthony Marriott and Alistair Foot's farce NO SEX PLEASE – WE'RE BRITISH
John Mortimer's A VOYAGE ROUND MY FATHER, has considerable success in the West End

MUSICAL NOTES — A young conductor, James Levine, makes his Metropolitan Opera debut

HIT SONGS — Brown Sugar
What's Going On
My Sweet Lord
Chirpy Chirpy Cheep Cheep
Rainy Days and Mondays
It's Too Late

Butley

Unlike his close friend, fellow-cricketer and frequent director, Harold Pinter, Simon Gray has in thirty years of British playwriting remained resolutely unfashionable among critics; he writes plays which nobody seems to like except the public, and has admirably refused to join any of the groups of writers who have dominated the London theatre in the fall-out from the Royal Court. If he has a social agenda, he keeps it pretty much to himself; like Christopher Hampton and Ronald Harwood but precious few others of their extended generation, he remains a craftsman who believes that each play should stand alone, unsupported by any wider theatrical movement or political philosophy; in that sense alone, these three are all the children of Rattigan.

Born Simon James Holliday Gray in October 1936, Gray was the only son of a middle-class doctor, and educated at Westminster and Cambridge. He started out as an English lecturer at the University of British Columbia, but since 1965 has been attached as a teacher to Queen Mary College at the University of London, the source perhaps of such 'academic' plays as *Butley* (1971) and *Otherwise Engaged* (1975).

But it was now, in 1972, that Gray first made his name internationally as a playwright with the Broadway premiere of *Butley*, played as in London by

Alan Bates at the Criterion in 1971

Alan Bates under the direction of Harold Pinter. Until that play, Gray's career had not been exactly triumphant; his first four plays, *Wise Child* and *Sleeping Dog* (1968), *Dutch Uncle* (1969) and *Spoiled* (1971) failed to find much favour with audiences or critics, though *Spoiled* was an intriguing perversion of *Tea and Sympathy* in which, this being a new era, it was the schoolmaster rather than his wife who falls in love with the winsome young male student.

This began the line of Gray's 'academic' plays, all of which resembled nothing so much as Rattigan's *The Browning Version* rewritten in acid and blood for a new generation who had fallen out of love with the image of the virtuous or misunderstood teacher. But it was with the 1971/2 *Butley* that Gray really brought this anti-elegy to its finest, thanks also to the virtuoso leading performance of Alan Bates.

Three years later, Alan Bates again starred for Harold Pinter in Gray's next hit, *Otherwise Engaged*, which was essentially *Butley* transferred to the world of publishing. Once again here was a man holed up in his own office, using it as a kind of literary womb and doing his best to repel all (lodger, brother, friend, wife) who, with very good reasons, try to invade it from the outside.

As if aware however that there was a limit to the creative life of the chronicler of 1970s urban, modern, semi-detached and otherwise-engaged London life, Gray in 1978 came up with *The Rear Column*, set in the Congo of 1887. Stanley (of Livingstone fame) has gone to rescue Emin Pasha from the clutches of the Mahdi, leaving a rear column to guard his supplies and bring up eventual reinforcements.

Though it ran healthily for months, *The Rear Column* was a mixed critical success, and Gray's 1979 *Close of Play*, though again directed by Harold Pinter and with a star National cast led by Michael Redgrave (in his last, virtually mute, stage appearance), was again something of a disappointment, an odd throwback to the 'English Chekhov' plays of NC Hunter and Wynyard Browne in the 1950s.

By now, Gray had started to write regularly for television and occasionally for the wide screen, though his own work was seldom to transfer; in the theatre, however, 1981 brought one of his best and most haunting plays, *Quartermaine's Terms*, the story of a group of latter-day misfits who have ended up teaching English to a bunch of increasingly recalcitrant foreigners at the Cull-Loomis School of English in Cambridge in the early 1960s.

In the 1990s came *Hidden Laughter*, *Old Flames* and his most recent play, the 1999 *Late Middle Classes* which was shamefully denied a London theatre after its critically-acclaimed Watford try-out. With Pinter again directing, this was a bittersweet obituary for the British class system in post-war meltdown, and a closet autobiography of sorts.

Gray has always been at his best as here, when like Rattigan he is chronicling the collapse of the old sexual and social certainties in plays about inner exile of the heart, frustration, duplicity and barely-suppressed passions.

CALENDAR

• On May 24, the NY Drama Critics Circle announce that they have miscounted the votes for Best Play and that the winning drama is Jason Miller's *That Championship Season*

• When *Older People* opens at the Public, the critic from Associated Press refuses to cover it, claiming that the opening night has been rescheduled too many times merely in order to accommodate the schedule of the New York Times critic

• In an upstairs room at the Bush pub in London's Shepherd's Bush Green, formation of a 'writers' theatre'. The first production is John Fowles' *The Collector*

• Opening on Manhattan's Upper East Side of the Manhattan Theatre Club

DEATHS

Broadway director **Margaret Webster**

Maurice Chevalier French born singer/actor

British Shakespearean actor **Robert Atkins**

British actress **Mary Ure**, by suicide

Bobby Howes British musicals star

British actress **Margaret Rutherford**

Miriam Hopkins American actress

British actor **Russell Thorndike**

NOTABLE PREMIERES

Barry Bostwick stars with Carole Demas in **GREASE** on Broadway

Tennessee Williams' **SMALL CRAFT WARNINGS** receives good reviews off-Broadway. Williams himself steps in for an absent actor and describes the experience as "excruciating"

Jack Albertson and Sam Levene star in Neil Simon's comedy **THE SUNSHINE BOYS** on Broadway

The Negro Ensemble Company premieres Joseph Walker's **THE RIVER NIGER** which transfers to Broadway and is one of the hits of the season

Diana Rigg and Michael Hordern star in the West End in Tom Stoppard's **JUMPERS**

Alan Ayckbourn's **TIME AND TIME AGAIN** comes into the West End starring Tom Courtenay and Cheryl Kennedy who are soon to marry.

MUSICAL NOTES

Impresario Sol Hurok's New York office is bombed in retaliation for his booking Russian artists to perform in the United States. His receptionist is killed

HIT SONGS

I'd Like to Teach the World to Sing

Lean on Me

Where is the Love

Puppy Love

American Pie

I Can See Clearly Now

The Changing Room

Born in 1933, the third son of a Yorkshire miner, David Malcolm Storey is one of the most intimately autobiographical playwrights and novelists of his North Country generation. He remains best known for three plays, *The Contractor* (1969), *The Changing Room* (1971) and *Home* (1970) which first brought Ralph Richardson and John Gielgud into their late-life 'brokers'men' partnership, one they continued with the West End and Broadway transfers of *Home*, and then five years later with Pinter's *No Man's Land*.

Stovey's first success was the 1960 novel *This Sporting Life* which, while never a play, became a triumphant Lindsay Anderson movie, one which won Oscar nominations for both Richard Harris and Rachel Roberts. The story of a tough miner who becomes a successful rugby player, but can never come to terms with the violence in his own character, it was followed by a second novel, *The Restoration of Arnold Middleton*, which did become a 1967 play for the Royal Court.

The original script which made Storey's name as a dramatist however was the 1969 *In Celebration*, the story of three middle-class sons going north to visit their parents, a Yorkshire miner and his wife. Here, directed as usual by Lindsay Anderson, Storey made his name as a latter-day DH Lawrence, concerned with the same broad issues of how to equate a miners past with the educational and intellectual self-improvement of his own children

In that same golden year, Storey also wrote *The Contractor*, a demonstration of tent construction which also managed to be an absorbing and dramatic account of the men doing their complicated job at a time when that was still a matter of posts and pulleys. Here as in the contemporary *In Celebration*, Storey's aim was to lay bare the bones of a family, in this case that of the wedding party for whom the tent is being constructed and also, of course, the 'family' of builders.

A year later came *Home*, set in what we eventually discover is some kind of mental institution; as the play opens, two men are sitting in a garden watching the clouds roll by. Their language, like that of the tramps in *Godot*, is a kind of verbal shorthand governed by rhythm and economy rather than instant understanding, and just below its surface lingers the faint idea that this clinic itself, just like the old music-hall theatre in Osborne's *The Entertainer*, could in reality be a metaphor for England itself in terminal decline and decay. In the rare presence (at any rate in modern dress) of Sir Ralph and Sir John, this accidental,

The Royal Court production in 1971

incidental duologue became almost comparable to a piece of classical music, and there was a rare chemistry about the partnership of Gielgud and Richardson, wonderfully orchestrated by their director Lindsay Anderson.

In 1971 came Storey's best-known play, *The Changing Room*, a return to the 'group drama' which had characterised such earlier scripts as *The Contractor*.

As its title would suggest, the entire play is set in the changing room of a rugby-league football club, dividing into three acts before, during and after the big match. A sort of still life with jokes, this was a wry, telescopic depiction of one close-knit northern community coming together every Saturday afternoon, but united only by the game they have chosen to play and replay in an almost holy ritual of sport.

With Anderson again orchestrating their fractured conversations, nothing much happens in *The Changing Room*; the players come together, change, go out on the field and come back. One gets injured, the rest carry on until the final whistle, change back into their civilian identities and go off home, retaining for the most part a cheerful insouciance about the game. Nobody questions the basic tenets of the sporting life; there are moments of nostalgia, unrest, even uneasiness but fundamentally we know they will all be back in the changing room next week, and the year after that. The play is a collective observation, rather than a comment, and like all good documentaries it leaves the audience to decide whether this is really the life.

Storey's later hits included the 1974 *Life Class* (again a group study, this time of art students, and again based on his own early apprenticeship at the Slade) and in 1980 *Early Days*, which reunited him with Ralph Richardson for a brief, infinitely resonant dramatic tone-poem about the old age and loneliness of

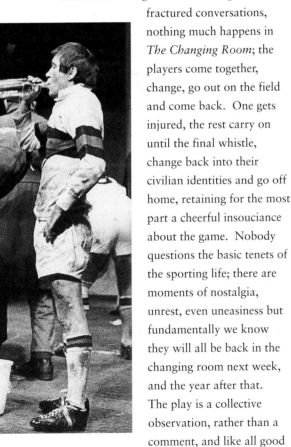

a dying politician. Storey's point here was that life does not always go on for good, but sometimes for bad to worse, and that the journey from birth to death can often narrow rather than broaden the mind.

Such other Storey plays as *Mother's Day* (1976) and *Sisters* (1978) met with neither critical nor popular success, and *The March on Russia* (1989) was a bleak National Theatre play about the collapse of idealist communism.

In the 1990s, Storey wrote two or three award-winning novels, notably *Pasmore* and *Radcliffe*, and several volumes of poetry, but seemed to be in a kind of voluntary exile from the theatre; one can only hope it will not be a permanent one.

CALENDAR

• Peter Hall is appointed next director of the National Theatre, over protests from Lord Olivier; Michael Blakemore and Kenneth Tynan are also in the running, as is Jonathan Miller

• British actress, later politician, Glenda Jackson wins first of her two Oscars for *A Touch of Class*

• London's New theatre is renamed The Albery, while on the site of the former Winter Garden Theatre, the New London opens its doors

• In Times Square, a new booth is set up at Broadway and 47th Street so that theatre-goers can buy same-day half-price tickets to Broadway and off-Broadway shows. By the end of next year, this ticket booth will be accounting for 4% of the total Broadway gross

• The League of New York Theatres, the producers' association, meets with the New York Times to ask for more extensive coverage of the Broadway scene

• Lillian Gish, George C Scott, Nicol Williamson, Julie Christie and Kathleen Nesbitt star in Mike Nichols' Broadway production of Chekhov's *Uncle Vanya*

DEATHS British actor, director, film star, composer, lyricist, novelist, painter and poet **Sir Noël Coward**

William Inge American playwright and poet

John Cranko British dancer/choreographer

British actor **Jack Hawkins**

Laurence Harvey Lithuanian-born actor

Max Adrian classical actor and musicals star

British West End theatre producer **Hugh ('Binkie') Beaumont**

NOTABLE PREMIERES Stephen Sondheim's **A LITTLE NIGHT MUSIC** stars Glynis Johns, Len Cariou and Hermione Gingold

Sam Shepard's **THE TRUTH OF CRIME** stars Timothy Sheldon and Spalding Grey off-Broadway

Debbie Reynolds plays **IRENE** in a reworking of an early musical about a fashion designer

On Broadway, with the movie book and lyrics by Alan J Lerner and the music by Frederick Lowe, **GIGI** becomes a stage musical

In London, Alec Guinness stars in Alan Bennett's **HABEAS CORPUS**

Alan Ayckbourn's **ABSURD PERSON SINGULAR** stars Sheila Hancock and Richard Briers in the West End, and Geraldine Page in New York.

At the Old Vic, Alec McCowen stars in Peter Shaffer's **EQUUS**

MUSICAL NOTES Britten's opera **DEATH IN VENICE**

Copeland's **NIGHT THOUGHTS**

HIT SONGS Killing Me Softly with his Song

Leader of the Gang

Goodbye Yellow Brick Road

Tie a Yellow Ribbon

Delta Dawn

The Norman Conquests

For the last thirty or so years, three writers have always headed the listings of the most-produced playwrights in Britain; William Shakespeare, Alan Ayckbourn and (perhaps more surprisingly), Willy Russell, whose *Educating Rita* and *Blood Brothers* are seldom off the stage.

As for Ayckbourn, the trajectory of his career has been much like that of his American alter ego, Neil Simon; both have graduated from early comedies and farces of considerable ingenuity to darker, more philosophic and sometimes autobiographical work; both have written the books for musicals, and both have real problems with audience and critical appreciation once they cross the Atlantic.

From 1964, when he was just 25, up to the present, Ayckbourn has never written less than one play a year, many of which have achieved long-play records in London and Scarborough and around the world. His

first, *Mr Whatnot*, was an unsuccessful mime about a manic piano-tuner; but in 1965 came *Relatively Speaking* an immensely adept four-handed farce built (as always were the best of Feydeau and Ben Travers) on one simple misunderstanding, in this case a young man mistaking his girlfriend's elderly lover for her father.

Then, in 1969, came *How the Other Half Loves* which Robert Morley played in the West End, Australia and on the road for almost three years; this was the first play to indicate Ayckbourn's considerable technical dexterity, centred as it is on a dinner party taking place simultaneously in two totally separate households. After such later hits as *Absurd Person Singular* and *Time and Time Again*, in 1974 he wrote (as usual first for Scarborough and only then for Greenwich and the West End) his most ambitious work to date, a sequence of three overlapping plays under the overall title *The Norman Conquests* and all concerned with the

Michael Gambon and Felicity Kendall in Round and Round the Garden at the Greenwich Theatre in 1974

events of one fraught weekend in the life of a suburban family as seen from the separate perspectives of different rooms in the same house. In this, his annus mirabilis, Ayckbourn also had *Confusions* and *Absurd Person Singular* (three couples falling apart on three consecutive Christmas Eves) running in the West End, but it was in many ways *The Norman Conquests* trilogy which established the stardom of Penelope Keith and Felicity Kendal, who later, joined by such other Ayckbourn regulars as Paul Eddington and Richard Briers, were to unite in *The Good Life*, a long-running BBC television sitcom which owed everything but its by-line to the conventions and characters that Alan had created on stage.

Later in the 1970s, Ayckbourn went on to a short-lived musical of *Jeeves* (written with Andrew Lloyd Webber and successfully revived on both sides of the Atlantic in 1997) and then the National Theatre triumph of *Bedroom Farce*, one of the very few of his comedies ever to have run lengthily on Broadway. It has been said that the more farcical Ayckbourn becomes, the more clearly one hears the underlying despair; yet at one point in the late 1970s he had five plays running simultaneously in London, thereby beating records set in the 1920s and 1930s by Somerset Maugham and Noël Coward.

His plays had always had a kind of darkness around their edges (envy in *Joking Apart*; bereavement in *Absent Friends*; class conflict in *Ten Times Table*) but now in these 1980s they grew progressively darker still, far removed from the original intention "to write plays which would make people laugh when their seaside holidays at Scarborough were spoiled by the rain."

Instead, in plays like *Way Upstream* (1982), *A Chorus of Disapproval* (1986) and *The Revengers Comedies* (1991) he continued to explore relationships in meltdown, often focussing on his characters' desires to escape to an altogether different dimension. This in turn led to a fascination with robots and alternative time-frames that in Hollywood might have made him a still richer writer, but Ayckbourn's loyalty has always

been to the live theatre, and in 1999 (National 2000) his *House* and *Garden* was a throwback to his 1970s time and puzzle-plays, this one taking place simultaneously on two separate stages in two separate theatres, one for the house and one for the garden.

His science-fiction future is similarly bleak and full of foreboding, in plays like *Henceforward* (1988) and *Comic Potential* (1999) where robots effectively invade humanity, but Ayckbourn's genius never allows him to forget that his first duty is to entertainment. Running a theatre, having regularly to attract and satisfy audiences with a vast range of work, may well be an unusual occupation for a playwright but it keeps him in close touch with his own public as well as those of others. Whereas most writers of his generation lead comparatively solitary lives, Ayckbourn's is largely spent in rehearsal rooms and theatre foyers; he is therefore more directly plugged into the daily and nightly life of the theatre than any other dramatist of his time.

CALENDAR

• In Boston, police arrest two actors in Terrence McNally's *Sweet Eros* for lewdness and fornication
• Peter Shaffer's *Equus* wins Tony and Critics Circle Best Play awards; the Pulitzer goes to Edward Albee for his very short-lived *Seascape*
• Before a performance of *Good Evening*, starring Peter Cook and Dudley Moore, Richard Nixon's resignation speech is shown to the audience on widescreen television
• Opening of Dan Crawford's King's Head in Islington, with the long-running *Kennedy's Children*
• At the Brooklyn Academy of Music for the RSC, Ian Richardson and Richard Pasco alternate Richard and Bolingbroke in *Richard II*

DEATHS

Broadway lyricist **Dorothy Fields**
Jack Benny American comic
Innovative Broadway choreographer **Jack Cole**
Billy DeWolfe American dancer and comic
Russian-born American impresario **Sol Hurok**

NOTABLE PREMIERES

Carol Channing opens on Broadway in the short-lived LORELEI
OVER HERE is a World War Two nostalgia musical starring the two surviving Andrews Sisters, Patty and Maxine, with three relative newcomers, John Travolta, Treat Williams, and Ann Reinking
Jim Dale becomes a Broadway star in the transfer from the Young Vic of Moliere's SCAPINO
On Broadway, Dustin Hoffman directs Murray Schisgal's short-lived farce ALL OVER TOWN
Opening in London and New York of MONTY PYTHON'S FIRST FAREWELL TOUR
Opening at the RSC and subsequently long-running in the West End and on Broadway, Tom Stoppard's TRAVESTIES about James Joyce, Lenin, and Tristan Tzara in the Zurich of 1917
Opening in London of Willy Russell's first long-running musical JOHN PAUL GEORGE RINGO... AND BERT

MUSICAL NOTES

Nationwide revival of interest in the ragtime compositions of Scott Joplin as a result of the soundtrack for the Paul Newman-Robert Redford movie THE STING
Swedish pop group ABBA win Eurovision Song Contest

HIT SONGS

The Entertainer
Seasons in the Sun
Please, Mr Postman
The Way We Were

Chicago

In the sixty years since *Oklahoma!*, the traditional Broadway musical has been dominated by just three great partnerships – first, Rodgers and Hammerstein; second, Lerner and Loewe; and third, Kander and Ebb, the team responsible not just for half a dozen of the most edgy, dark and innovative of all American musicals on stage and screen, but also for effectively creating and sustaining, as far as has been possible, the career of Liza Minnelli for whom they have been writing since the early 1960s.

Their first hit was, in fact, a single song, "My Coloring Book", taken up by Barbra Streisand, and their first joint musical was the 1965 *Flora, The Red Menace*, although Kander alone had briefly made a name among the critics, if not audiences, by scoring a play called *A Family Affair* by the brothers William and James Goldman.

They were also immensely prolific, and immediately after *Flora* they were to write the score for their first international hit with the stage and screen musical that is still the first we immediately associate with them. Unlike *Flora*, which had been based on a relatively unknown novel called *Love Is Just Around The Corner* by Lester Atwell, the new project, *Cabaret*, came as a readymade bookshop, stage and screen hit. The English novelist, Christopher Isherwood, had published in the late 1930s his Berlin Stories of the wayward English girl, Sally Bowles, in the Germany of the rising Nazis. These, in turn, had become in 1951 a considerable Broadway and West End success as John van Druten's play *I Am A Camera*, which had, in its turn, become a hit movie in 1955 with Julie Harris and Laurence Harvey.

What was new here was the first-ever attempt to 'translate' Brecht and Weill into an idiom that an all-American audience would be able to accept as something more than a translation. By focussing on the Isherwood role of the young writer at large in pre-war Berlin but now, for the first time, making him an American, Kander and Ebb were able to involve a local audience. In following his conventional odd-couple love affair with Jill Haworth's original Broadway Sally, they were also able to counterpoint a conventional musical romance with the much darker story of Lotte Lenya and Jack Gilford as the two old Berliners who have their lives destroyed by the coming of Hitler. By the end of the show, Sally and her young American have moved on and only the Master of Ceremonies is left to introduce a cabaret which has now grown unbearably dark.

By the time they came to the 1972 film directed by Bob Fosse, Kander and Ebb had cut some of their original stage score and written new songs for Liza; but the result, although less crisp and clear than the stage original, was perhaps the last truly commercial Hollywood musical until the coming of *Evita*, almost thirty years later.

After *Cabaret*, Kander and Ebb started to work on one of their rare flops, *The Happy Time* based on a Canadian play by the author of *The Rainmaker* Richard Nash, and in the same year, 1968, they had another disappointment with an ambitious but unwise attempt to turn the classic Cacoyannis movie *Zorba the Greek* into a Broadway musical which retained Anthony Quinn as Zorba, but somehow lost everything else along the way.

But then, in 1975, they came back to the Bob Fosse who had directed their Cabaret movie and also engineered a remarkable triple for Liza who in one single year, under his aegis, had won an unprecedented triple – a Tony, an Oscar and an Emmy.

Once again, they decided to rely on tried and trusted material. *Chicago* had started out in 1926 as a Broadway hit comedy, loosely based on the true story of the murderess Roxie Hart, who had escaped the electric chair to spend a lifetime touring in American vaudeville, thanks to the efforts of a crooked, money-grubbing lawyer and an American press which was (in these Al Capone years) desperate to make stars out of gangsters.

But what is truly revolutionary about Fosse's *Chicago* and the reason, perhaps, why it has never yet made it back to Hollywood, is that it is based on a succession of only loosely connected vaudeville acts on a black hole of a stage.

The Adelphi in 1997

Indeed, when it was reborn in the late 1990s as a New York concert performance intended to last only a couple of nights, the reason that it moved on unaltered to its longest-ever Broadway and West End runs was that it finally got stripped right down to a no-scenery, no-costume band show in which the orchestra, rather than the actors, was always at centre stage.

But if *Cabaret* and *Chicago* still represent the best of Kander and Ebb, several later scores suggest the on-going versatility of their work: *The Act* (1977) was an unsuccessful vehicle for Liza as a faded film-star on the comeback trail; *Woman of the Year* (1981) was a Broadway musical version of an old Katharine Hepburn movie rebuilt for Lauren Bacall; *The Rink* (1984) was, in our view, a brilliant and still very underrated book musical, written with the playwright Terrence McNally and set in Atlantic City, about a mother and daughter (originally Chita Rivera and Liza Minnelli) who run a seaside roller-skating rink; *Kiss of the Spider Woman* (1990), again written with McNally, was an adaptation of Manuel Puig's bleak yet loving novel and play and movie about two cell-sharing prisoners in South America.

Most recently, the short-lived Broadway *Steel Pier* (1998) was an interesting but doomed attempt to revisit the dance marathon territory of *They Shoot Horses, Don't They* and the greatest Kander and Ebb hit of the late 1990s was a wondrous anthology called *And The World Goes Round*, which included many of their greatest show songs but also such movie and cabaret hits as "New York, New York".

CALENDAR

• Maggie Smith and John Standing co-star on Broadway in long-running revival of Noël Coward's *Private Lives*, directed by John Gielgud

• At Stratford upon Avon, opening of the RSC's experimental space, The Other Place with a triumphant small-scale *Hamlet* directed by Buzz Goodbody, 28, who is found dead the following morning

• Starting in a derelict London cinema, Richard O'Brien's *The Rocky Horror Show* becomes a cult worldwide stage and screen hit

• At only five days notice, Liza Minnelli steps into *Chicago* for an indisposed Gwen Verdon

DEATHS American actress **Susan Hayward**
Josephine Baker of the Folies Bergère
Scottish actor **Thornton Wilder**
British playwright **RC Sherriff**

NOTABLE PREMIERES On Broadway, first of 1600 performances of all-black update of **THE WIZARD OF OZ** entitled **THE WIZ**
Michael Bennett's **A CHORUS LINE** wins the Tony and the Pulitzer with its record-breaking run at the Shubert on Broadway
On Broadway, Tovah Feldshuh opens six-month run in Isaac Bashevis Singer's **YENTL**
David Kernan opens British premiere of **A LITTLE NIGHT MUSIC** by Stephen Sondheim

MUSICAL NOTES Rudolf Nureyev makes his modern dance debut with Martha Graham's company

HIT SONGS Bohemian Rhapsody
Sailing

Sexual Perversity in Chicago

A vagrant is quietly begging on a Broadway sidewalk when a somewhat pompous passer-by reprimands him, "Neither a borrower nor a lender be – William Shakespeare". Quick as a flash, the beggar responds, "Fuck you – David Mamet."

Few playwrights, living or dead, get equal billing, even anecdotally, with William Shakespeare but this was the year when the newly discovered Chicago-born dramatist (and the one who was eventually to emerge as the leader of his generation) made his name in New York with the off-Broadway productions of no less than three early plays – *Sexual Perversity in Chicago*, *Duck Variations* and *American Buffalo*.

Mamet was already 29; brought up in the American Mid-West, he had first made his name locally in 1973 as the co-founder of the St Nicholas Theatre Company in a Chicago church hall, where he was playwright in residence (and from 1973-76, artistic director), and where he remained loosely, and sometimes unhappily, attached until 1988.

If Mamet, born in 1947, can be said to have a single theme as a dramatist, then that theme is undoubtedly the destruction of ordinary people by the greed of materialism or what he calls, "the American Dream gone bad."

His characters, often trapped in clichéd stereotypes, all seek power or money by bullying or manipulating others, even if this eventually destroys themselves in the process.

To that extent, Mamet is perhaps the natural heir to the Arthur Miller of *All My Sons* or *Death of a Salesman*; but writing thirty years later, his dialogue is

Glory Annen and Stephen Hoye at the Regent Theatre in 1977

totally different from the careful prose formulations of Miller or indeed any other of Mamet's predecessors in the age of the well-made play.

In sharp contrast, Mamet writes totally naturalistically, capturing the basic inarticulacy of his favourite characters in a frenetic, scatological, often blasphemous street-cred language which floods out of them with precious little time to pause for grammar or sometimes even coherence.

Even in 1975, this still came as something of a shock. The original Greenwich Village production of *American Buffalo* with Al Pacino (like Joe Mantegna and Bill Macy, one of Mamet's semi-permanent repertory company) amazed and sometimes appalled even off-Broadway audiences with its raging, frenzied account of two second-rate crooks shambolically trying to steal a coin collection.

Of the other two plays that were first seen in New York this year, *Duck Variations* was a rambling conversation between two old men, and *Sexual Perversity in Chicago* dealt with what was to become one of his regular themes – the last days of a failing or failed marriage.

Mamet is intriguing for many reasons, not least that whilst an innovative and cutting-edge contemporary, he is also a rare throw-back to the days when Chicago could genuinely challenge New York in its claim to be the heartland of the American theatre. To that extent, he is an heir to Ben Hecht and Charles MacArthur and such epic dramas as *The Front Page* and *Detective Story*, all of which came out of the Second City long before the war.

If we had to choose a single Mamet script above all the others, it would almost certainly be the Pulitzer Prize-winning *Glengarry Glen Ross* which Harold Pinter, hearing an outline, urged Mamet to write first for the National Theatre in 1983. Unusually, it did not reach Chicago until the following year, and Broadway a year after that.

From *Speed-The-Plow* (1988), a savage Hollywood satire, through *Oleanna* (1992), a perversion of the student/tutor relationship at a time of overblown political correctness, Mamet has seldom gone back over previous territory. He has somehow found the time to adapt all of Chekhov's major plays, an accomplishment only equalled by Michael Frayn in England, but a list of only his major movies which he has directed and/or written would again suggest amazing versatility: *The Postman Always Rings Twice* (1981); *The Verdict* (1982); *The Untouchables* (1985); *House of Games* (1987); *Homicide* (1990), *Glengarry Glen Ross* (1992) and in 1997, an amazing double – *The Edge* and *Wag The Dog*. There also followed *The Spanish Prisoner* (1998).

And all that, between running theatre companies in Chicago, writing roughly one new play a year and now directing much of his own work himself. Mamet is not yet sixty at the time of writing, and there is as yet no sign of any lessening of energy. In his American generation, perhaps only Sam Shepard has ever offered any kind of a challenge, but to rephrase Kenneth Tynan on Noël Coward, in a hundred years' time we shall know exactly what we mean by "a very David Mamet kind of character."

CALENDAR

• The American Bicentennial gives rise to massive national celebrations which, paradoxically, impact negatively on Broadway box-offices

• In the basement of a Chicago church, paying $10 a month rent, a group of Chicago actors form the Steppenwolf Company. In the next few years, it will launch the careers of John Malkovich, Gary Sinese, Joan Allen, among many others

• When his now ex-wife Gwen Verdon leaves *Chicago*, director Bob Fosse replaces her as Roxie Hart with his long-time lover, Ann Reinking

• Robert Morley, in his last West End appearance, opens a year-long run at the Savoy Theatre in Ben Travers' vintage farce *Banana Ridge*

DEATHS

Broadway choreographer **Busby Berkeley**

Agatha Christie British thriller writer

Legendary black actor/singer and political activist **Paul Robeson**

Broadway star **Rosalind Russell**

Jo Mielziner Broadway set designer

Kermit Bloomgarden Broadway producer

British actress **Dame Sybil Thorndike**

Dame Edith Evans British actress

Broadway columnist **Leonard Lyons**

Alistair Sim Eccentric British actor

NOTABLE PREMIERES

On Broadway, Tammy Grimes and George Grizzard open year-long run in three short plays by Neil Simon collectively known as CALIFORNIA SUITE

Playwright-director Mike Stott makes his name in London with FUNNY PECULIAR

Barry Humphries in drag opens the first of his triumphant Edna Everage solo shows HOUSEWIFE SUPERSTAR!

Opening in London of SIDE BY SIDE BY SONDHEIM, directed and narrated by Ned Sherrin

Penelope Keith opens two-year run in Michael Frayn's DONKEY'S YEARS

MUSICAL NOTES

Jamaican singer/songwriter Bob Marley makes reggae into mainstream cult

New York City Ballet opens George Balanchine's UNION JACK

Phillip Glass's EINSTEIN ON THE BEACH becomes a huge success

HIT SONGS

I Write the Songs

Fifty Ways to Leave Your Lover

Dancing Queen

Hotel California

The Kingfisher

Considering that his career was widely believed (at least by drama critics) to have been totally annihilated by the coming of the Royal Court revolution twenty years ago, it may seem a little late and indeed contrary to be coming around only now to the long playwriting career of William Douglas Home.

But theatre history is never as straightforward as it appears in reference books and in 1977 Douglas Home had no less than three new plays all in major West End premieres. Admittedly, of these three, only *The Kingfisher* became a hit but the other two – *In The Red*, a domestic comedy, and *Rolls Hyphen Royce*, an account of the private lives of the celebrated car manufacturers – give some indication of not only his versatility, but also his remarkable ability to survive in a theatrical world which nearly always found him either unfashionable or Neanderthal.

William Douglas Home was born in Edinburgh on June 3rd 1912, the younger brother of the future Conservative Prime Minister and Foreign Secretary, Alec Douglas Home, who became Baron Home of the Hirsel. Willie was educated in some style at Eton and New College, Oxford, where he took 'a Gentlemen's degree' in history. He then enrolled at the Royal Academy of Dramatic Art, in a late 1930s era when they were short of male students. But even Willie soon realised that he was never going to make it as an actor, and it was with a certain relief that he joined up to serve in the Royal Armoured Corps for the duration of World War Two.

But it was here, in 1944, that Douglas Home gave his greatest indication of an extraordinary moral

Alan Webb, Celia Johnson and Ralph Richardson at the Savoy in 1977

courage and a determination, whenever possible, to rebel against the grain of his undoubtedly upper-class upbringing. As a pilot, he was ordered to bomb Le Havre, where he knew that there were still more French civilians than German soldiers. The German general in charge of the port had requested permission to evacuate all civilians, but this had been refused (or at any rate, ignored) by the British Army, and Douglas Home knew that 12,000 civilians had already been killed in local air-raids. Determined that he at least would not be responsible for adding to what he saw as a needless slaughter of the innocents, he simply refused the command.

Eventually, the German general of Le Havre was immediately given permission to evacuate his civilians, and Douglas Home was sentenced to one year in prison with hard labour for disobeying a wartime command while in uniform.

That year in prison gave him his first great success as a dramatist. *Now Barabbas…*(the rest of the biblical quotation being, of course, "was a robber") was a contemporary prison play in which Willie wrote movingly and topically about the men with whom at close quarters he had just spent a year of his life. He wrote the play in ten days, as soon as he was released from prison in 1945, and although it was too dark to be a commercial success, it attracted some of the best reviews of his entire career.

But it was with his next play, *The Chiltern Hundreds* (also 1947) that he established his place as the most successful West End comic dramatist of the years immediately following the war. Like its sequel *The Manor of Northstead* (1954), this was a wry satire on the eccentricities of the British parliamentary system. By now, Douglas Home was starting to write regularly for such West End eccentrics as AE Matthews and David Tomlinson, and he would alternate upper-class social satire with curiously subversive and usually socialist dramas which regularly amazed those who recalled that his brother was to remain for most of his lifetime at the head of the conservative establishment.

In London as on Broadway, Douglas Home's greatest hit was the 1956 *The Reluctant Debutante* which made a star of Anna Massey and was, once again, a deceptively light comedy about love and loss among those for whom hunting, shooting and fishing on their own estates were still regular pursuits.

In 1974, as if to acknowledge that Douglas Home was not as frivolous as his critics suggested, Ralph Richardson and Peggy Ashcroft (later replaced by Celia Johnson) started a two-year run of a bitter little comedy about a discontented wife threatening to commit suicide if a motorway is driven through her estate. Originally entitled *Lady Boothroyd of the Bypass*, this became better known as *Lloyd George Knew My Father.*

Douglas Home's last plays included *The Dame of Sark*, about the Nazi occupation of the Channel Islands (again Celia Johnson, one of his most constant players, 1974) and, three years later, *The Kingfisher*, the story of a faithful butler saving a precarious upper-class marriage.

CALENDAR

• In New York, two homosexual men are diagnosed as having the rare Karposi's Sarcoma. They will become the first American victims of an illness that will decimate the theatre, opera, music and dance world over the next 20 years; it is to be known as AIDS

• Broadway actress Lindsay Crouse marries playwright David Mamet, thereby becoming the only actress to bear the names of three award-winning dramatists (Howard Lindsay, Russel Crouse, David Mamet)

• On the American road, *Oh, Calcutta!* has now played 119 cities, in 27 of which it has been taken to court for obscenity

• On Broadway, Walter Kerr becomes only the second drama critic to win a Pulitzer Prize

• Joseph Papp withdraws his New York Shakespeare Festival from Lincoln Center, citing "artistic differences"

• Critic John Simon is again banned from all Shubert Theatre and Alexander Cohen first nights for describing *The Shadow Box* as "a piece of shit"

• In London, opening of the National's third and last new stage, the Cottesloe, with Ken Campbell's eccentric science-fiction *Illuminatus*. This is quickly followed by Bill Bryden's epic staging of the York mystery plays, *The Passion*

DEATHS **Groucho Marx** Broadway comic

American crooner **Bing Crosby**

Legendary music hall and Hollywood comedian

Sir Charles (Charlie) Chaplin

Maria Callas Italian opera star

British playwright **Sir Terence Rattigan**

Alfred Lunt Legendary Broadway actor

NOTABLE On Broadway, Robert Duvall stars in David Mamet's
PREMIERES **AMERICAN BUFFALO**

Ned Sherrin, Julia Mackenzie, Millicent Martin and

David Kernan open long Broadway run and then

American tour of **SIDE BY SIDE BY SONDHEIM**

MUSICAL William Alwyn's opera **MISS JULIE**
NOTES First performances of the Sex Pistols

HIT SONGS **Knowing Me, Knowing You**

Mull of Kintire

Nobody Does it Better

Buried Child

David Mamet's only true rival among late 20th-century native American dramatists was born Samuel Shepard Rogers in Fort Sheridan, Illinois, on November 5th 1953. Educated in California, he briefly married O-Lan Johnson and has a daughter by the actress Jessica Lange, with whom he has had a long relationship.

His first jobs were as a stable-hand, orange-picker, sheep-shearer and car-wrecker, all in California. He was then briefly a touring actor, a waiter and musician in New York restaurants, and lived in London from 1971 to 1974 where many of his earliest plays were written.

But in spite of his prolific output (more than fifty plays and screenplays since the late 1960s), Shepard is still best known internationally for only five – *Curse of the Starving Class* (1977), *Buried Child* (1978), *True West* (1980), *Fool for Love* (1983), and *A Lie of The Mind* (1987).

Explaining what, if anything, these have in common, Shepard once said, "I'm interested in exploring playwriting through attitudes derived from music, painting, sculpture and film…I am pulled towards images that shine in the middle of junk and I have been influenced by Jackson Pollock, Little Richard, Cajun fiddlers, and the great American South West."

As the critic Ruby Cohn has noted, more than any other contemporary American dramatist, Shepard has woven into his own dramatic idiom the strands of a youth culture which thrives on drugs, rock music, astrology, science fiction, old movies, detective stories, cowboy films, and the racing of cars and horses and dogs. More than any other writer of his time, he also tries to get mythic dimensions into his drama.

His first real hit was *The Tooth of Crime* (1972) which, as he says, is really a synthesis of the slangs of rock, crime, astrology and sports. Soon afterwards, Shepard became more and more involved in his careers as a film actor and writer, but his claim to theatrical greatness lies in what he has always called his family trilogy – *Curse of the Starving Class*, *Buried Child* and *True West*.

In fact, of course, there is no continuity of characters here, nor any very obvious link. Nevertheless, like the plays of Eugene O'Neill, they do all dramatise a tragic America, beset by sin but always striving to reach out toward the mythic.

Curse of the Starving Class is vaguely akin to Mamet's *Glengarry Glen Ross*; not, of course, in its language or characterisation but in the idea that the greatest American sin is betrayal of the land to soulless speculators. *Buried Child* is about incest, cruelty and murder, while *True West* (the funniest of the three plays) is about the opposition of two brothers with very different lives and attitudes towards the Western ideal.

Fool for Love is also about a love-hate relationship between two characters, only in this case they are lovers as well as being half-siblings. Observed by an unseen (except of course by the audience) father, they veer from love to hate in a motel room which finally goes up in flames.

The last of these major plays, *A Lie of The Mind*, also contrasts the violence of the Old West with the tenderness of the New Woman, and the message here is that if America is to have any hope of a future, then it must abandon its violent past and move forward in utter gentleness.

Like no other dramatist of his generation or even century, Shepard has made the folklore of the American South West his own exclusive territory. His language is a mixture of rock'n'roll idiom and 'B' movie dialogue, and his characters are frequently farmers, devils, witch-doctors, rock stars, space-men, cowboys, gangsters, and all the other anti-heroes of American comic-book culture.

Though he may lack the intellectual and verbal intensity of a David Mamet, or indeed the more laid-back nostalgia of AR Gurney, there is a case to be made for Sam Shepard as the most theatrically powerful of current American dramatists. In his *Fool For Love*, two lovers, unable to live either together or apart, tear the living daylights out of each other both sexually and emotionally. If you could imagine Thornton Wilder's *Our Town* re-written as a case history of downtown Incestville, Nebraska, you would get some idea of a mythic study in impossible lust where the revelation of incest (which any lesser dramatist might have saved for a shocking final curtain) here informs and energises a truly shocking play. As in his screenplay of the same period, *Paris Texas*, Shepard seems keen to throw small people up against huge landscapes; and all the time American is out there in all its vast bland territory, just waiting to turn a domestic disaster into an epic tragedy.

What saves *Fool For Love* from being merely a bus-and-truck re-run of Albee's *Virginia Woolf* is Shepard's ability to give his desert rats an immediate but haunting pedigree. Marlboro Country is never going to look quite the same again.

Shepard may come out of O'Neill, but he comes by way of John Steinbeck and Tennessee Williams. His America is an acridly funny, suddenly tragic and ultimately screwed-up society of blue jeans and brain-rot where years of in-breeding have produced a community of mentally and physically damaged wrecks who are now even uncertain as to whether or not they might be their own children.

CALENDAR

• Elizabeth Taylor stars in catastrophic Hal Prince filming of Sondheim's Broadway and West End hit *A Little Night Music*
• Opening (with *Timon of Athens*) of the Oregon Shakespeare Festival
• Closing of the Brooklyn Academy of Music's theatre company after less than six months
• On Broadway, the Shubert Organization announces Ticketron, first computerised box-office system

• David Mamet goes home to become playwright-in-residence at Chicago's Goodman Theatre
• Planned Broadway revival of *King Lear*, starring Richard Burton and directed by Elia Kazan, is cancelled by producer Alexander Cohen when Burton refuses to play more than six performances a week
• The early departure of Jack Lemmon (from *Tribute*) and Henry Fonda (from *The First Monday in October*) underlines the problem of Broadway's increasing dependence on movie stars

DEATHS Anglo-Irish actor, director, designer, playwright **Micheal MacLiammoir**
British stage and screen star **Robert Shaw**
Broadway star and torch singer **Ruth Etting**
Broadway producer and famous proprietor of the Village Gate **Max Gordon**

NOTABLE PREMIERES In London, Elaine Paige opens in the title role of Rice and Lloyd Webber's West End musical EVITA
Tom Conti opens long London and Broadway run as the paralysed sculptor in Brian Clark's WHOSE LIFE IS IT ANYWAY?
Opening at the National Theatre of David Hare's play and later movie of post-war British disillusion, PLENTY

MUSICAL NOTES At Temple University, Philadelphia, American premiere of André Previn and Tom Stoppard's EVERY GOOD BOY DESERVES FAVOUR

HIT SONGS Summer Nights
You're the One that I Want
Rivers of Babylon
Stayin' Alive

Bent

In his own quietly modest way, Martin Sherman could claim to be one of the most truly international of all contemporary playwrights. He was born in Philadelphia on December 22nd 1938, of Russian-Jewish parentage and has lived most of his working life in England where his work has always been more readily acclaimed than elsewhere.

Though it was by no means his first, the play that really made his name was the 1979 *Bent* staged almost simultaneously in London and New York and at the time of this writing, the only one of all his plays to have been made (admittedly unsuccessfully) into a movie.

As the curtain first rose at the Royal Court on this chilling new play, we appeared to be in a flat owned or at least inhabited by a homosexual night-club dancer and his friend, Max. The time and place are left unspecified and for the first few minutes it looks as though we are in for a gay retread of *The Odd Couple*.

But then, it suddenly becomes all too clear: the year is 1934, the place Berlin, and it is the morning after Hitler's notorious homosexual purge in The Night of the Long Knives. Immediately, therefore, the two men have to go on the run, and much of the rest of the first act is taken up with the unacceptable face of *Cabaret* – night-club scenes from Berlin life intercut with indications that to be homosexual in that time and place was only fractionally easier than being Jewish.

For a while this remains a comedy, albeit a very black one. As one of the men says, "I know pain is very chic in Berlin right now, but I still don't care for it." By Act Two we are no longer in some German version of *Some Like It Hot*, we are instead in Dachau where to be homosexual is now actually worse than to be just Jewish. Max is now forced to beat his friend to death and has become a determined survivor in a camp built for the sole purpose of defeating survival. In the end, *Bent* is a play about coming out and admitting who you are even in the most hostile surroundings imaginable. This is *The Boys in the Band* rewritten in blood and death.

Tom Bell and Ian McKellen in the original production

Before *Bent*, Sherman had written no less than ten other plays, ranging from satirical soap operas through science fiction to a hippy whodunit (*Cracks*) so totally opaque that the identity of the killer is never revealed but the success of *Bent* brought Sherman to settle semi-permanently in England where his next play *Messiah* (1982) was a dark drama set in 17th century Poland dramatising the life of a courageous, resilient female Job in whose soul, as in the play itself, doubt, superstition and disillusionment battle against wit, kindness and faith.

As the critic Tish Dace has noted, *Messiah* is "a battle between religion and sexuality" but in Sherman's next play *When She Danced* (1985) it is the human spirit

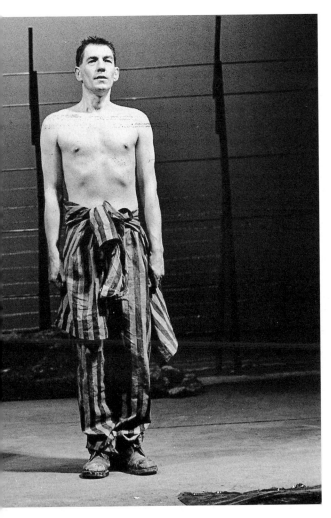

His next play, *A Madhouse in Goa* (1989) was in fact two short plays linked by at least one central figure – rather as though Terence Rattigan's *Separate Tables* had been re-written by an unholy alliance of Gore Vidal and Tennessee Williams.

We first meet a writer arriving on a great island after having chased his melancholy around Europe for several months. There he meets an older woman, not exactly Mrs Stone having her Roman Spring, but instead a kind of cultural Auntie Mame who carries around with her a little private bell for summoning waiters and is only finally dispossessed by an elaborate and (it has to be said) unbelievable blackmail plot designed to have her vacate her favourite terrace table so that it may be used by the King of Greece.

But this first play *A Table for a King*, then gives way to an infinitely chillier second on *Keeps Raining All The Time* in which we move forward a quarter of a century to 1990, by which time the young writer has become a brain-dead wreck living on a volcanic island and watching in angry silence as the world breaks up around him.

To move in one evening from a sunny, romantic terrace to an apocalypse of AIDS, terrorism, and death by cancer suggested, not for the first time, that Sherman is among the most ambitious as well as the most tricky, treacherous and intermittently manic of all his generation.

which triumphs over all odds. The true story is that of Isadora Duncan, an improvident but charismatic middle-aged dancer living in Paris with a young Russian husband whom she is unable to address except through an interpreter because they share no common tongue. In the West End Vanessa Redgrave (who had also appeared as Isadora in a somewhat overwrought Ken Russell movie) made this very much her own eccentric evening. But what had now become intriguing about Sherman was the way in which, without repeating himself, he was always managing to write about people who were outsiders because they are gay, or Jewish, or female, or foreign, or strangers in a strange land, or sometimes just strange.

CALENDAR

• Broadway choreographer and director Bob Fosse films a kind of auto-biography in *All That Jazz*

• Since *Grease* first opened on Broadway, Richard Burton and Elizabeth Taylor have divorced each other twice and there have been three American Presidents

• In New York, release of The Ethel Merman Disco Album in which she sings several of her old hits to a new beat

• Advice to a class of young dramatists from playwright Lanford Wilson, "Just type 'This is the next play by last year's Pulitzer Prizewinner' at the top of a blank sheet of paper, and try to write something under it"

• It now costs $1 million to stage a musical on Broadway, and half a million to stage a play there

• Director Harold Prince, defending Patti LuPone after a shaky tryout of *Evita*, says simply, "She is a fucking gem"

• With its 3243rd performance, *Grease* overtakes *Fiddler on the Roof* as Broadway's longest-running show to date

• For the first time, there are now on Broadway four times as many theatres dark as open

DEATHS Suicide of American actress **Jean Seberg** **Gracie Fields** British singer and actress Broadway composer **Richard Rodgers** **Leonide Massine** Russian-born ballet dancer and choreographer

NOTABLE PREMIERES Mickey Rooney and Ann Miller open 122-performance run in **SUGAR BABIES** The black anthology musical **ONE MO' TIME** opens 1400-performance run at the Village Gate At the NT in London Peter Hall directs **AMADEUS**

MUSICAL NOTES Moscow Philharmonic cancels American tour after defections of Bolshoi Ballet stars Alexander Godunov and Leonide and Valentina Koslov

HIT SONGS I Don't Like Mondays I Will Survive

The Dresser

Ronald Harwood was born Ronald Horwitz in Capetown, South Africa on November 9th 1934. In his late teens he left South Africa for London to study as an actor at the Royal Academy of Dramatic Art and, like two other contemporary playwrights, Alan Ayckbourn and Harold Pinter, he got his start carrying spears on long provincial tours behind the already-ageing Sir Donald Wolfit. Unlike them, however, he found in Wolfit the source of his greatest success as both a dramatist and biographer, for Wolfit is unmistakably the Sir and Harwood himself sometimes the dresser in the play of that title (1980).

For several years he went through the motions of denying that *The Dresser* was really based on his touring life with Wolfit, and there is some truth in the view that this could really be an archetypal story of any old barn-storming actor/manager crashing into the realistic and subdued reality of post-war British theatre.

Tom Courtenay in the original production

Not for nothing is the old ham about to go on stage as *King Lear*; for he too has been abandoned by his nearest and dearest, and thrown back on the sole company of his underprivileged and bullied dresser, who is of course also Fool to his Lear.

Harwood first made his name not as a playwright at all but as the screenwriter in 1970 of *One Day in the Life of Ivan Denisovitch*, the harrowing account of Solzhenitsyn's 1950s life in a Siberian labour camp. This first brought Harwood together with his most constant player, the actor Tom Courtenay; but as if, yet again, to establish his versatility, Harwood's first West End success came in 1974 when he wrote the book for the Johnny Mercer-André Previn musical of Priestley's *The Good Companions*.

Three years later, he went back to Manchester with another adaptation, this one of Evelyn Waugh's late novel *The Ordeal of Gilbert Pinfold* about the invalid author himself harassed on a cruise by the figments of his own imagination.

Although his second original play *A Family* closed quickly in 1978, it is important to recall that by the end of the 1970s Harwood had published six novels, most notably *The Girl in Melanie Klein*; an underrated collection of Hollywood stories (*One. Interior.Day.*); a biography of Wolfit; and no less than eight screenplays for movies ranging from *Private Potter* (1962) through *A High Wind in Jamaica* (1965) to *Cromwell* (1970). He had also written more than a dozen original radio and television plays.

The term 'workmanlike' may now have fallen from critical favour, but that is exactly what Harwood is; a craftsman first and foremost, a professional who can turn his typewriter to whatever project next comes towards him down the road. But this is never to underestimate the greatness and artistry of *The Dresser*. Playwrights from Chekhov, all the way through to Clifford Odets and Emlyn Williams had, of course, already written the one about the old actor nearly at the end of his days in states ranging from nostalgia through

alcoholism to penury. Reflections in a dressing room mirror have always had this Pirandellian fascination – if what the actor does for a living is by definition unreal, how real can the rest of his life hope to be?

In that sense, *The Dresser* is a tragedy, a long day's journey into would-be knight at the end of which we are left with a mixture of sadness and relief that the days of tacky Shakespearean touring have long gone.

The running joke here is that we are in the midst of a 1943 air-raid. The Luftwaffe are thus providing the sound effects for this *King Lear*, and Herr Hitler has left Sir with a company comprised solely of "old men, cripples, and nancy-boys" with which to carry the immortal words of the Bard out into the number three touring dates around England.

In the end, *The Dresser* is hugely entertaining ("Keep your teeth in and serve the playwright," instructs Sir) but a very schizoid play, reflecting in the end Harwood's own inability to decide whether it is his love or his hatred for the final generation of the great over-actors which should emerge strongest. For all that, *The Dresser* remains (alongside John Osborne's *The Entertainer*) the most quintessentially theatrical play written in the second half of the 20th century.

Like Simon Gray, whose career trajectory much resembles that of Harwood, he has been shamefully neglected by both the Royal National Theatre and the RSC. It is also arguable that their careers have been as badly bruised by the coming of the alternative, Fringe and Irish theatre of the 1990s as were those of Coward and Rattigan by the original Royal Court revolution of the 1950s. Unlike Gray, however, Harwood is fortunately always able to turn back to novels, short stories, screenplays, and lucrative American television adaptations of the classics.

CALENDAR

• Lillian Hellman sues Mary McCarthy for $3million after she has called Hellman "a dishonest writer" on television

• Alec Guinness wins Lifetime Achievement Oscar

• James Nederlander, talking about his Shubert rivals, Gerald Schoenfeld and Bernie Jacobs, "whereas I am in business to make a profit, for them it is all ego"

• Andrew Lloyd Webber, on his first meeting with producer Cameron Mackintosh, "for some reason, I thought he was going to be a wizened 62-year old Scot"

• With the publication of Richard Rodgers' will, a clause forbids anyone ever to alter or add to the lyrics of any of his songs

• Anna Strasberg resigns from the Actors Studio in a dispute over the ownership of 1000 audio-tapes of her late husband Lee's coaching sessions

DEATHS	French playwright **Jean-Paul Sartre**
	American actress and playwright **Mae West**
	British photographer and set-costume designer, **Sir Cecil Beaton**
NOTABLE PREMIERES	Blythe Danner, Roy Scheider and Raul Julia lead Broadway cast of Harold Pinter's **BETRAYAL**
	At the National Theatre, Howard Brenton's **THE ROMANS IN BRITAIN** brings prosecution from Mary Whitehouse for scenes of homosexual rape
MUSICAL NOTES	Movie composer John Williams replaces Arthur Fiedler as conductor of the Boston Pops
HIT SONGS	Funkytown
	Turning Japanese

Noises Off

If you had to list the ten most critically and commercially successful British playwrights of the late 20th century Michael Frayn would undoubtedly be around the middle of that list. Yet such has been his endearing, shambling approach to the business of being a playwright that he seems almost to have managed to convince himself, though precious few others, that somehow he doesn't really deserve to be there.

Just as Chekhov, of all of whose major plays Frayn has been the most brilliant adapter, was always maintaining that he was really a country doctor, so Frayn has wonderfully managed to convey to his fellow journalists the idea that even after more than thirty years in the business he never really thinks of himself as a dramatist at all.

He was born in London on September 8th 1933, and after a grammar school education he went up to Emmanuel College, Cambridge. Before that, having been required to do his National Service, he discovered (like his contemporary, friend and fellow playwright, Alan Bennett) that the best place to do this was in the Russian Interpreters division where, instead of eighteen months' pointless square-bashing, it was possible to lead an intellectual collegiate life in uniform which was, in fact, the perfect preparation for Oxbridge.

Frayn then started his career in 1957 as a reporter on the (then) *Manchester Guardian*. From there he moved as a columnist to the London office, and thence to the *Observer* where his satirical views on the new 1960s trendies were perfectly timed to coincide with *Beyond the Fringe* on stage and *That Was The Week That Was* on television.

Next came *The Sandboy* (1971), Frayn's first full-length play, about a city planner having his homelife invaded by an army of television cameras. Here at once were two themes that were to run on almost throughout his later and more successful work – the intolerable territorial imperatives of the media, and the responsibility (seldom acknowledged) of town planners and architects to make our lives more bearable.

But it was in 1975, with *Alphabetical Order*, that Frayn really made his name and came into his own for the first time. He had already published, in 1967, a novel called *Towards The End of Morning*, about what journalists were then still calling a travel 'jolly' abroad. *Alphabetical Order* is also a comic tribute to the utter futility of journalism. Brilliantly staged at Hampstead by Michael Rudman, it was set in the press-cuttings library of a derelict regional paper, where the librarian

Michael Aldridge, Jan Waters, Patricia Routledge and Paul Eddington at the Lyric, Hammersmith in 1982

was a den mother, offering sustenance both sexual and otherwise to a bunch of reporters who seemed urgently in need of the kiss of life.

All in all, *Alphabetical Order*, is a splendidly gossipy play about people living in a verbal junk-yard, full of useless knowledge, and about the fact that journalists are the last people ever able to come to terms with reality, possibly because they see altogether too much of it.

This may be a small point, but Frayn made it quite magically and, in 1977, was to return to his most familiar territory with *Clouds*, a play about three reporters trying to make some sort of sense of a press trip to Cuba.

But it wasn't until in 1981 that Frayn wrote the farce for which he will forever be famous. *Noises Off* is undoubtedly the most technically brilliant comedy written in Britain since the heyday of the Aldwych and Whitehall farces. The frame is simplicity itself – we simply see, first on-stage and then backstage, a total implosion of a seaside repertory company going to pieces in perfect timing with their stage plot. Only Peter Shaffer's one-act *Black Comedy* (1965) ever even began to rival Frayn's agility in understanding that there is nothing quite as funny as watching lives or careers in a chaos brought about by extraneous happenings which are less and less under their control or of their making.

Make and Break (1983) was another ambitious idea. Set in a high-rise hotel in Frankfurt during a business convention, it was concerned with the makers of a display of movable office walls which perfectly provided the frenzied action for a Feydeau-like farce.

Frayn's other major hit of these 1980s in London and New York was the infinitely more serious *Benefactors*, in effect a modern *Master Builder* about the South London architectural wars of the late 1960s.

But it was in 1997, with *Copenhagen*, that Frayn wrote his most ambitious philosophical work, an extraordinary three-cornered study of the origins before and during World War II, of the atomic bomb. The idea here that atoms fall apart and come together much after the fashion of treacherous human relationships, was a dazzling theatrical attempt to cross the border into the higher science, and its long West End and Broadway runs have indicated that Frayn, alone of his generation, and perhaps of his century, is capable of that curiously complex cross-over.

CALENDAR

• Because of the epic nature of *Nicholas Nickleby*, Broadway producers ask for it to be given a Tony category all its own. Request denied, and it wins both the Tony and the Drama Critics Circle awards

• Claus von Bulow, a major Broadway investor this season, is accused of attempting to murder his wife. He is acquitted and Jeremy Irons subsequently makes the movie

• *Deathtrap* overtakes *Arsenic and Old Lace* as longest-running Broadway thriller

• Rodgers and Hammerstein star John Raitt marries Rosemary Yorba, forty years after their parents withheld consent because of their youth

DEATHS Broadway and Hollywood dancer **Vera Ellen**
Gloria Grahame Broadway actress
Broadway lyricist **EY (Yip) Harburg**
Lotte Lenya German singer/actress

NOTABLE PREMIERES On Broadway, the RSC transfer of NICHOLAS NICKLEBY runs eight hours and sets price at $100

Lauren Bacall triumphs in Kander and Ebb's WOMAN OF THE YEAR, based on the Katharine Hepburn movie

In London Elaine Paige replaces an injured Judi Dench at the opening of Andrew Lloyd Webber's record-breaking musical CATS

MUSICAL NOTES Simon and Garfunkel perform before 400,000 people in a Central Park reunion concert ten years after they have split up

HIT SONGS Tainted Love

Don't You Want Me?

Master Harold...and the Boys

Ramolao Makhene, Duart Slywain and John Kani of the Johannesburg Market Theatre Company at the RNT in 1983

Harold Athol Lannigan Fugard, born in the Cape Province of South Africa on June 11th 1932, is undoubtedly the greatest and most significant dramatist and director ever to have come out of that troubled land. The son of an Africaaner mother and an English father, he was educated by monks and then at the University of Cape Town. He served as a merchant seaman before starting out as a journalist with the South African Broadcasting Corporation, and by the late 1950s was a stage manager and press agent with the South African National Theatre Organization.

On first coming to London in 1960 to further his theatrical career, the only job he could get was that of a cleaner and he rapidly went back home before making an international life for himself in Belgium, America, and eventually back in London, where, during the 1970s, he was able (as the critic Ned Chaillet has noted) to harness his multiple accomplishments as actor, dramatist and director to fashion plays, often in collaboration with the black African actors John Kani and Winston Ntshona, which spoke to foreign audiences with humour and force of the furnace of conflicts in his native land.

Not since Alan Paton had written *Cry, The Beloved Country* 30 years earlier had any voice come out of South Africa with more dramatic intensity. Among his earliest plays, *The Blood Knot* (1961), *Hello and Goodbye* (1965), and *Statements After An Arrest Under The Immorality Act* (1972), all in their very different ways examined the relationship between men and women living under inhuman and racist laws. Like the novelist and essayist Nadine Gordimer, Fugard opened up a dialogue with the Free World, one in which he regularly examined the way in which, even in intense racial strife, humanity can transcend politics.

Working often at the Market Theatre in Johannesburg, with Barney Simon and Percy Mtwa, Fugard wrote such powerful works as the 1972 *Sizwe Bansi is Dead*, which starts with an actual death and then explores the absurdity of a society where access was determined by bureaucracy; where with possession of the right identity, a new card could create a new life.

When Kani and Ntshona brought *The Island* back to the National Theatre in 1999 (and then the West End in 2000) it was clear that even after the release of Nelson Mandela and a liberalisation of the South African laws, this play had lost none of its strength or relevance.

Fugard has often said that his influences range from Greek myths to the work of the Polish director Jerzy Grotowski, and he has always been keen to explore the physical and vocal range of actors. The theatre, he once said, is about space, silence and action. But since *A Lesson From Aloes* (1978) his work has seemed more personal and intimate, dealing either with friends caught in the closing trap of apartheid, or else with the lives of people who have tried to find a new life abroad but discovered that the ties of the homeland are always strongest.

Fugard seems now in these later plays to be conducting a dialogue with himself about what it means to be South African in a radically changing time. *Master Harold…and the Boys* (1982) is an even more personal exploration of the social, political and familial conflicts within Fugard himself. It tells what he admits is the true story of his own temptation, when a little boy, to assert his racial superiority and the title contains the greatest irony of all – the Master Harold is a spoiled and insensitive boy, while The Boys are adult Africans of wit, generosity and sympathy.

Now that Fugard has a flourishing career in London and New York (and even still sometimes turns up as an actor in such movies as *Gandhi*, *Meetings with Remarkable Men*, and *The Killing Fields*), it is easy to forget what a tough time he had as a young dramatist and director, perpetually trying to dodge racist rules.

But it is precisely because Fugard has always written of his native land with a sly, subversive wit, that his plays will long outlive the immediate politics of their birth. From the time that Fugard and his wife, the actress Shiela Meiring, started in 1963 to form an amateur group of non-white actors in the African township of New Brighton, Fugard has always been at the forefront of his nation's fight for equality. He has recognised that a writer's job is to remember and to reflect as well as to reform, and through the often bleak and minimalist prose-poetry of his work there can be heard, as clearly as in the speeches of Mandela, the authentic voice of freedom in a country where the word itself was often turned into denial.

CALENDAR

• After a century, falling box-office returns and the expiry of copyrights forces the closure of the D'Oyly Carte company (Gilbert & Sullivan)

• In London, after 11 years building, the Barbican Arts Centre is finally opened by the Queen

• Following the death of Lee Strasberg, Eli Wallach takes over temporarily as the director of the Actors Studio

• Richard Burton and Elizabeth Taylor, twice married, twice divorced, open on Broadway in catastrophic revival of *Private Lives*

• John, Ethel and Lionel Barrymore become first actors to feature on an American stamp

• Variety, reviewing Christopher Walken as *Hamlet*, "complete with blonde goatee beard, he is sullen, crazed and unprincely"

DEATHS

Austrian actress **Romy Schneider**

American actor **Henry Fonda**

Ingrid Bergman Swedish actress

British comic **Arthur Askey**

Jacques Tati French actor and director

Legendary choreographer and founder of the Ballet Rambert **Dame Marie Rambert**

Celia Johnson British actress

British actor **Kenneth More**

NOTABLE PREMIERES

Off-Broadway, Harvey Fierstein opens long-running gay` TORCH SONG TRILOGY

Opening off-Broadway of Tim Rice and Andrew Lloyd Webber's JOSEPH AND THE AMAZING TECHNICOLOR DREAMCOAT

On Broadway, Cher, Sandy Dennis, Kathy Bates and Karen Black star for Robert Altman in COME BACK TO THE FIVE AND DIME, JIMMY DEAN, JIMMY DEAN

LITTLE SHOP OF HORRORS opens long run off-Broadway

Sam Shepard's now approved production of TRUE WEST with Gary Sinese and John Malkovich, starts 800-performance run off-Broadway

MUSICAL NOTES

Ellen Zwillich's THREE MOVEMENTS FOR ORCHESTRA

Eugene Ormandy leaves the Philadelphia with THUS SPAKE ZARATHUSTRA

HIT SONGS

House of Fun

Thriller

Do You Really Want to Hurt Me?

Abracadabra

Run for Your Wife

In the whole 20th century history of British farce, there are really only four names that matter: Ben Travers, who (as a dramatist) effectively invented the form at the Aldwych Theatre in the 1920s, Brian Rix who (as an actor-manager) took it up at the Whitehall immediately after World War Two, Ray Cooney who (as a dramatist and actor-manager) came up through Rix's company and took it on to the Garrick Theatre when Sir Brian went to run Mencap, the Mentally Handicapped organisation, and Sir Alan Ayckbourn, relatively few of whose prodigious number of stage plays could really be classified in the traditional sense of farce, rather than black comedy.

Raymond George Alfred Cooney was born in London in May 1932; educated at Alleyn's School in Dulwich, home of the National Youth Theatre (and also once amazingly the school of Raymond Chandler), and served his National Service in the Royal Army Service Corps.

Soon after he left the army, Cooney began writing farces with Tony Hilton, notably *Dickory Dock* (1959) and the one that first made his name, *One for the Pot* (1960). Over the next quarter-century, often with John Chapman, Cooney was to deliver a series of long-running hits whose titles tell you most of what you need to know about them: *Who were You With Last Night?*, *How's Your Father?*, *Chase Me, Comrade*, *Bang Bang Beirut* (or *Stand By Your Bedouin*), *Not, Now Darling, My Giddy Aunt, Move Over, Mrs Markham, Why Not Stay for Breakfast? Come Back to My Place, There Goes the Bride, Two Into One, Wife Begins at Forty* and of

The
Aldwych
Theatre in
1983

course *Run For Your Wife*, which was based on the magically simple idea of an amiable, bigamist cab-driver married to two separate wives at two separate addresses.

One or two of these have been filmed, and most have been in near-constant stage revival at home and abroad; lately Cooney has even been gainfully employed turning others of them into Hollywood screenplays, having somewhat late in his career been 'discovered' by the Americans. Individually, they do not bear too much critical examination; like the mythical *Knickers Off Ready When I Come Home*, they are designed on intricate floorplans of mistaken identity, or men getting ritually caught in pursuit of women not their wives.

In an age of political correctness, Cooney's later plays stood accused of making fun of foreigners, gays and other minorities; but the women in his farces often come off in the end better than the men, and he can sometimes surprise you with an eccentric kind of liberalism.

He has also very occasionally ventured into other fields, contributing to the book of the long-running musical *Charlie Girl* in 1964, and then in 1986, by which time he had formed a Theatre of Comedy at first the Playhouse and then the Shaftesbury, a careful adaptation of the Labiche farcical comedy *An Italian Straw Hat*.

As the critic Geoff Sadler has noted, Cooney's plays all start from a relatively 'normal' situation – a wedding, the collection of a mink coat, the interior decorating of a flat-from which they spiral into chaos and a maze of misunderstanding. Like Travers before him, Cooney has always understood that comedy is a serious business, and farce even more so; his characters and situations are always, if only for a moment, perfectly plausible and their motives immediately understandable and even reasonable, if only to themselves.

Because, unlike the other 20th-century giants of farce, Cooney has been for most of his career an

actor, producer, director and playwright, he has covered all the territory and his farces exist on a high level of technical brilliance, that of a man who has worked at every backstage and on-stage job the theatre has ever offered. He also began to produce the work of others, notably his great predecessor Ben Travers (*Banana Ridge*), and it was with his ultimate withdrawal from regular farce management in the early 1980s that the genre could be said to have reached its natural conclusion. Not that individual farces, including his own, will not go on being revived, occasionally in London and more often still at every surviving seaside theatre in the country; but we are unlikely ever again to see a resident company at one single theatre performing them on a permanent repertoire basis, as in the great days of the Aldwych in the 1920s and the Whitehall in the 1950s.

CALENDAR

- At the closing performance of *Annie*, its lyricist Martin Charnin tells the audience in a curtain speech that he is already working on a sequel. It will be a memorable disaster
- Producer Zev Bufman fires Andy Gibb of the Bee Gees from the title role in *Joseph and the Amazing Technicolor Dreamcoat* for missing 21 of 51 performances without a good excuse
- The Clarence Derwent Award for Most Promising Actor of the season goes to John Malkovich; his Steppenwolf colleague, Joan Allen, wins it for Most Promising Actress
- Arthur Miller goes to Beijing to direct the first production in Chinese of *Death of a Salesman*
- The dispute between producers and playwrights turns nasty; the Dramatists Guild and the League of New York Theatres and Producers sue one another for monopolistic practices

DEATHS American playwright **Tennessee Williams**
Russian born American choreographer
George Balanchine
British leading ballet dancer **Anton Dolin**
Veteran Vaudeville star **Eddie Foy Jnr**
Howard Dietz American Broadway and
Hollywood lyricist
Lynn Fontanne widow and long-time stage
partner of Alfred Lunt
British classical actor **Sir Ralph Richardson**

NOTABLE PREMIERES Simon Gray's drama **QUARTERMAINE'S TERMS**
about British academic life stars Remak Ramsay
and Kelsey Grammer
The ballerina Natalia Makarova stars in the veteran
director George Abbott's revival of **ON YOUR TOES**
BRIGHTON BEACH MEMOIRS is the first in a
trilogy of autobiographical plays by Neil Simon,
about his childhood
The 1936 Kauffman and Hart comedy **YOU CAN'T TAKE IT WITH YOU** stars Jason Robards Jnr and
Colleen Dewhurst
For the first time, in **LA CAGE AUX**, a Broadway
musical's two leading characters are gay men

MUSICAL NOTES In Denmark, a manuscript of Mozart's **1ST SYMPHONY**, composed in 1764/5, is found

HIT SONGS Let's Dance
Every Breath You Take
Down Under
Billie Jean
Total Eclipse of the Heart
Uptown Girl
Karma Chameleon

Breaking The Silence

Jenny Agutter at the Mermaid in 1985

In a crumbling, rat-infested railway carriage at the back of the Moscow shunting yards sometime in 1924, a Jewish inventor of considerable and starry eccentricity is about to invent talking pictures, some five years ahead of the Warner Brothers in California. The idea itself has a certain fascination, leading as it presumably would have done to a musical remake of *Battleship Potemkin*, not to mention an all-Soviet *Jazz Singer*. But Stephen Poliakoff's best play to date was not in fact another trip down the might-have-been byways of modern history; it was all true, and the inventor was his grandfather who, (due to a little local difficulty involving the death of Lenin and its effect on railroad employment prospects in the new Soviet Union), then had to flee across the border in his stockinged feet, leaving his revolutionary new invention behind him.

In the end, the Poliakoffs didn't fare too badly in exile; the son went on to become the inventor of hospital bleepers, and the grandson to be one of the best playwrights of his generation. *Breaking The Silence* (the title reference wasn't really to the Talkies at all, but to that of the inventor's wife who, in his hour of need at the border, at last finds her voice and saves his life) was also a play about female liberation and the shift in family power structures that came with Communism. Then again, it was about a son in revolt against his father, a man of Tsarist wealth and influence ("I am not the right person to watch telephone poles being erected.")

Stephen Poliakoff was born in London in December 1952, and educated at Westminster and King's College Cambridge. After ten precocious early plays had been produced on the London fringe and at various Edinburgh Festivals, he made his name at 23 with *Hitting Town* and *City Sugar*, two 1975 plays about respectively the tackiness of the new inner-city developments and the inanity of pop radio disc jockeys, two topical issues of the time.

But Poliakoff is not really a journalistic writer; his territory (at least in these early plays) was the nightlife of an anonymous city, where lonely and often shell-shocked survivors would crash into each other in casinos, bars and restaurants. In his 1978 *Strawberry Fields* we are in a wasteland of motorway service stations, where a latter-day English Bonnie and Clyde try to shoot their way out of personal difficulties, and in his 1980 television play *Caught on A Train* an old lady (memorably played by Peggy Ashcroft) crosses Europe meeting a cross-section of representative football hooligans and ugly Americans.

After *Breaking The Silence* came *Coming In To Land* (1987) and then *Playing With Trains* (1989), another railroad piece, this one a savagely waspish indictment of the ritual British terror of inventors and inventions. In the 1990s, Poliakoff's stage luck has not been so great, though on screen his *Close My Eyes*

(1991) was a highly acclaimed account of an incestuous brother and sister in a hot London summer. Gainfully occupied with television, radio and screenplays, Poliakoff may have only temporarily been lost to the theatre; at the time of this 2000 writing, he is after all still only in his late 40s.

CALENDAR

• Joseph Papp co-produces, on Broadway, with the Shubert Organisation, for the first time, *The Human Comedy*

• It's the end of an era when Vincent Sardi Jnr sells the top theatre restaurant to a chain; it will be nearly 20 years before theatre people go back to Sardi's

• The Minetta Lane Theatre, which will become one of Greenwich Village's premier off-Broadway spaces, opens in a former tin can factory

• In San Diego, the old Globe theatre has half a million dollars' worth of damage from its second arson fire in six years

• For the first time, the New York City Department of Consumer Affairs cites a theatre producer for deceptive advertising when they quote New York Times critic Frank Rich as saying, "The kind of play we hardly see on Broadway any more" because what he also wrote was that it was "quite awful"

• The estate of Tennessee Williams bans the Playhouse from being re-named after the playwright, claiming that this would be commercial exploitation of his name

• The Kennedy Centre appoint Peter Sellars, famous for his modern dress production of Mozart operas, as artistic director despite his having graduated from Harvard only four years earlier. He begins his tenure by announcing a new American National Theatre

• Variety takes the New York Times to task for their perceived favouritism for the work of Stephen Sondheim and August Wilson

• When JoAnne Akalaitis' production of Samuel Beckett's *Endgame* is produced at Harvard, Beckett's disclaimer calling the production a parody and saying that "Anybody who cares for the work couldn't fail to be disgusted" is inserted in the programme

DEATHS

American comic **Jackie Coogan**

Tito Gobbi Italian opera singer

American playwright **Lillian Hellman**

Diana Dors British actress

Welsh stage and screen star **Richard Burton**

JB Priestley British playwright

Brooks Atkinson New York Times theatre critic

NOTABLE PREMIERES

Mike Nichols directs Tom Stoppard's **THE REAL THING** starring Glenn Close, Christine Baranski and Kenneth Welch

Ian McKellen's **ACTING SHAKESPEARE** opens on Broadway

Chita Rivera and Liza Minnelli play mother and daughter in **THE RINK**, a musical by Kander and Ebb with a book by Terrence McNally

David Mamet's real estate play, **GLENGARRY GLEN ROSS**, stars Robert Proski and Jo Mantegna

John Malkovich directs and stars in Landford Wilson's **BALM IN GILEAD**

HURLY BURLY, David Rabe's off-Broadway hit, moves to Broadway starring William Hurt, Harvey Keitel, Sigourney Weaver and Christopher Walken

MUSICAL NOTES

Michael Jackson, aged 26, has record-breaking album **THRILLER**, which sells more than 37 million copies

HIT SONGS

Do They Know it's Christmas?

I Just Called to Say I Love You

Footloose

Time after Time

Ghostbusters

Let's Hear it for the Boy

What's Love Got to Do with It?

Les Miserables

If *Show Boat* and *Porgy and Bess* were the stage musicals of the first half of the 20th century, then *Les Miserables* is undoubtedly the stage musical of the second. Originally written in Paris as an epic pageant by two young French and Algerian writers and record-company executives who, deeply impressed by Rice and Lloyd Webber's *Jesus Christ Superstar* on Broadway, could never understand why the French theatre had so totally ignored the musical form, it was brought to London by the producer Cameron Mackintosh, who hired the former theatre and television critic Herbert Kretzmer to work with Boublil on an English book and lyrics, and then gave the show to the RSC directors Trevor Nunn and John Caird who (with *Nicholas Nickleby*) had shown that they alone were capable of stage-managing a vast, sprawling, mid-nineteenth-century dramatised novel.

The result was breathtaking: despite considerable critical apathy, *Les Miserables* became an immediate hit at the Barbican in 1985, transferred to the Palace in the West End and has been running there and in more than fifty other productions around the world ever since.

The greatness of *Les Miserables* is that it starts out, like Sondheim's *Sweeney Todd* and Benjamin Britten's *Peter Grimes* and for that matter Verdi's *Rigoletto*, to redefine the limits of music theatre. Like them it is through-sung, and like them it tackles universal themes of domestic and social happiness in terms of individual despair. There is an energy and operatic intensity here which exists in the work of no British theatrical composer past or present; that sense of a nation's history being channelled through trumpets and drums and violins and cellos. The score has maybe forty numbers, all of which fit like jigsaw pieces into a huge revolutionary pattern; there are songs of love and war and death and restoration; patter songs, arias, duets and chorus numbers of dazzling variety and inventiveness.

This is not the musical *Nickleby*, nor yet a French *Oliver*, though it owes a limited debt to both; rather is it a brilliantly guided tour of the 1200-page eternity that is Hugo's text; there's a *Third Man* chase through underground sewers, an autumnal ending worthy of *Cyrano de Bergerac*, and even occasional lurches into loveable-orphan echoes of *Annie* and, of course, the result is episodic, fragmentary and sometimes evocative of earlier hits, just as John Napier's amazing set, made up of old tables, chairs, cart-wheels and water barrels looks like a tribute to the Sean Kenny setting of Lionel Bart's *Oliver*.

The Palace Theatre in 1990

Les Miserables is in short everything that musical theatre ought to be and almost never is; Boublil and Schonberg followed it in 1989 with *Miss Saigon*, a brilliant update of *Madame Butterfly* to the Vietnam war, which also went on from London to Broadway and then worldwide hit status, and five years later still to the very underrated *Martin Guerre* which, despite three totally revised new productions in Britain and America, never made it to Broadway, nor to the triumphantly long-running status of the other two.

The problems of period style and syntax were much greater than in Boublil-Schonberg's previous hits, and Cameron Mackintosh had inadvertently created another difficulty, which was that by elevating both the scale and the costs of the post-war British stage musical out of all recognition, he had effectively raised the financial and critical stakes to the point where touring became impossible and anything less than a smash hit was counted as a failure.

Characteristically, he devoted the best part of three years of his life to *Martin Guerre*, which finally came good in much smaller-scale American and British repeats. Since then, Mackintosh has been principally concerned with two scores (*The Fix* and *The Witches of Eastwick*) by the young American team of John Dempsey and Dana Rowe, but as his only biographers we suspect it will not be that long before he is reunited with Boublil and Schonberg for a fourth score.

CALENDAR

• With the death of her friend Rock Hudson, Elizabeth Taylor takes on her most demanding role – that of spokesperson and fund-raiser for the battle against AIDS

• New York Magazine drama critic John Simon is overheard to say, in public, "Homosexuals in the theatre! My God, I can't wait until AIDS gets all of them". He subsequently apologises. However, reviewing *The Octet Bridge Club*, he describes it in print as "faggot nonsense"

• In its final week *The King and I* raises its prices to a (for Yul Brynner's last night) $75 top, and thereby sets a new one-week record box-office take

• In *The Normal Heart* the playwright Larry Kramer alleges that the New York Times suppressed early news about AIDS. Alongside the review for the play's opening is a denial by the paper

DEATHS
English actor **Sir Michael Redgrave**
French actress **Simone Signoret**
American producer, actor, director and writer **Orson Welles**
Broadway star **Yul Brynner** of lung cancer
Broadway playwright/ humorist **Abe Burrows**
Audrey Wood legendary American agent

NOTABLE PREMIERES
The MAHABHARATA, Peter Brook and Jean-Claude Carriere's work based on the great Hindu legends begins in Paris, travels to London and thence to the rest of the world

In London and then in New York, Christopher Hampton and the RSC have a major success with LES LIAISONS DANGEREUSES starring Alan Rickman and Lindsay Duncan

William M Hoffman's play about AIDS, AS IS, opens on Broadway starring Jonathan Hogan and Jonathan Hadary

Lily Tomlin opens her one woman Broadway show, THE SEARCH FOR SIGNS OF INTELLIGENT LIFE IN THE UNIVERSE

Anthony Hopkins stars at the National as a Murdoch-like press mogul in David Hare's PRAVDA

AUNT DAN AND LEMON opens at the Public starring the author, Wallace Shawn

MUSICAL NOTES
For its first repertory season at Lincoln Centre, the Joffrey Ballet performs works by Jiri Kylian, Pilobolus and Paul Taylor

HIT SONGS
I Know Him So Well
Dancing in the Street
Crazy for You
Careless Whisper

Broadway Bound

It was with this play that Neil Simon completed the autobiographical trilogy (*Brighton Beach Memoirs*, 1983, *Biloxi Blues*, 1985) which first alerted audiences in America and around the world to the idea that here perhaps was a darker and more complex playwright than might have been suggested by an admittedly unprecedented sequence of urban comic blockbusters.

It has never quite been decided whether Simon is the American Alan Ayckbourn, or Ayckbourn the English Neil Simon. What the two men have in common is tremendous difficulty in crossing the Atlantic; Simon has really only had a commercial life in England as the writer of such musical books as *Sweet Charity*, *Promises Promises* and *They're Playing Our Song*, while on Broadway Ayckbourn plays usually last as many weeks as Simon's plays in the United Kingdom.

What they also have in common is a darkening across the years; having really only written comedies or musical comedies until then, it was in the 1980s that both dramatists started to surprise their audiences with much more chilly or black family sagas, in Simon's case more often than not drawn from his own childhood.

There was, as far as he was concerned, nothing really new in this: from the very beginning, such hit Broadway comedies as *Come Blow Your Horn* (1960), *Barefoot in The Park* (1962), and *The Odd Couple* (1965) had all been based on the early New York experiences of himself or his older scriptwriter brother Danny. But then, after the death of a beloved first wife, Simon turned suddenly to vastly darker territory, adapting for instance the late stories of Chekhov (*The Good Doctor*) or the Book of Job (*God's Favorite*) into plays which came as a considerable shock to his laugh-seeking audiences and were therefore major commercial and even critical flops.

With an account of his second marriage to the actress Marsha Mason, *Chapter Two* (1977), Simon recovered his commercial form, and then continued a sequence of short plays set in a single hotel room (*Plaza Suite*, *California Suite*, *London Suite*, *Hotel Suite*), before starting on his childhood autobiographies with *Brighton Beach Memoirs* (1983) and the above-mentioned trilogy.

Known as 'Doc', not because of his legendary talents as a play-doctor, often called in at the last minute to rescue plays and musicals in trouble immediately pre-Broadway, but because of his earlier intention to pursue a career in medicine, Neil Simon has been over the last forty years as centrally and crucially plugged into the heart of Broadway, where a theatre bears his name, as was another comic dramatist and director, George S Kaufman, in the forty years around World War Two.

In terms of his royalties from stage, screen and television, Neil Simon is also almost certainly the most commercially successful dramatist who has ever lived, and it has been by no means rare for him to have three or four plays, films and musicals running side by side in New York as well as on the road. Nobody has better or sometimes more bitterly chronicled the changes in American domestic life from the 1940s into the 1990s, and no writer (with the possible exception of Woody Allen on film) has ever been as expert at noting the minor details of changing relationships and power structures within the post-war suburban Jewish-American family.

The Simon brothers started out in television, as gagwriters for Phil Silvers and Sid Caesar (the latter of whom Neil immortalised in his 1990s *Laughter on the 23rd Floor*), and he has always been essentially a gagwriter, and yet when he writes of Judy Garland in *The Gingerbread Lady*, or the two old vaudevillians bickering their way through a farewell routine in *The Sunshine Boys*, it is clear that he has a passion for the showbiz traditions from which he comes.

At a time when comedy had grown curiously unfashionable, Neil Simon almost alone brought it back to the head of the Broadway agenda, and unlike Noël Coward or Alan Ayckbourn or indeed Kaufman and Hart, he has never been afraid of exposing his own life and loves to the footlights, whether in terms of laughter or tears.

CALENDAR

• Andrew Lloyd Webber's Really Useful Group goes public, on the London Stock Exchange
• Director/choreographer Michael Bennett withdraws from Tim Rice's *Chess*, citing "angina". He in fact has AIDS, and will soon die of it
• In Hyde Park, New York, Margot Kidder plays in a rare revival of *Sex*, the play that sent Mae West to jail in the 1920s
• Madonna and Sean Penn are in a workshop at Lincoln Center of David Rabe's *Goose and Tom-Tom*
• When Variety reviews Gretchen Cryer and Nancy Ford's new show in a try-out in Massachusetts, it calls it "The most misconceived, misdirected, and mis-acted new musical ever to see the light of day"
• The heads of the Shubert Foundation, Gerald Schoenfeld and Bernard Jacobs, are investigated by the New York State Attorney-General because the Foundation is a charitable trust; the result is that they are, concludes the Attorney-General, "uniquely qualified" and justify their salaries of $840,000 per year, plus bonuses
• The League of New York Theatres and Producers tries to have, like London's West End, a single opening night for reviewers with no legal attendance for review purposes at previews. Following responses from editors, next month's meeting declares it "a dead issue"
• The Pasadena Playhouse re-opens after 20 years
• The Nobel Prize for Literature goes to an African writer, playwright and novelist Wole Soyinka

DEATHS Broadway composer **Howard da Silva**
Jean Genet French playwright
Broadway composer **Harold Arlen**
Broadway tap dancer **John W Bubbles**
Alan J Lerner Broadway lyricist
Comic actress **Hermione Baddeley**
Siobhan McKenna Irish actress
British stage actress **Dame Anna Neagle**

NOTABLE PREMIERES Eric Bogosian writes and performs **DRINKING IN AMERICA**, the first of his well-received series of stage monologues
At the Public Kevin Kline stars in **HAMLET**, and receives rave reviews
At the Public, Vaclav Havel's **LARGO DESOLATO**, an autobiographical play about Havel's persecution in his native Czechoslovakia
First at the Mitzi Newhouse and then on film, writer and editor Spalding Gray's monologue **SWIMMING TO CAMBODIA**
Robert de Niro returns to Broadway in a sold-out run of Reinaldo Povod's **CUBA AND HIS TEDDY BEAR**
The new Marquee theatre in the Mariott Hotel in Times Square opens with the British musical **ME AND MY GIRL**, with Robert Lindsay in his Broadway debut

MUSICAL NOTES World-wide celebration of the centenary of the death of Franz Liszt
After 61 years in America, Vladimir Horovitz returns to the USSR and gives two recitals

HIT SONGS Don't Leave Me this Way
Live to Tell
Addicted to Love

Serious Money

The most widely published, researched and taught female dramatist of her generation, Caryl Churchill has managed (like certain contemporary female American novelists) to become most famous not for her individual titles, but for what they collectively represent. In that sense, at least to a certain Royal Court audience, she has always been totemic, iconic and symbolic of a certain kind of off-centre feminist writing, philosophic rather than immediately or contemporaneously political.

The most readily accessible of all her plays is *Serious Money*, a scabrous comedy of Big Bang dealings which does for the old City of London roughly what *Pravda* did for the old Fleet Street; Max Stafford-Clark's frenetically choreographed Royal Court production was like a ballet of corrupt trading, in which a central cast of eight doubled and redoubled as increasingly shady fixers of rubber futures and criminal pasts. The contemporary Guinness and Boesky banking scandals gave it street-cred immediacy, but Churchill opened her play as a Restoration comedy in rhyming couplets, and made it a timeless everyday story of greed, corruption and all else.

Caryl Churchill was born in London in September 1938, and started her career as a radio playwright in the middle 1960s. In the following decade she moved to television and the stage, though it wasn't until *Light Shining in Buckinghamshire* (written in collaboration with the Joint Stock company, as was her 1979 *Cloud Nine*), that she really made her name with a play about workers in the early seventeenth century.

Cloud Nine was still more ambitious, and precisely the kind of exploration of sexual politics past and present for which Churchill was to become best known. The first half is a farce set in Victorian colonial Africa, from where we move forward a hundred years to a somewhat loose-limbed debate about sexual morality now and then.

A year later *Top Girls* was not so much one as three plays, the first of which was a round-table discussion between such legendary feminists as Pope Joan and the Victorian explorer Isabella Bird about the precise nature of female survival and at what cost through the ages. Then came a tough little latter-day semi-documentary set in a secretarial agency, and finally there was a tight, taut and marvellous domestic drama about two sisters, one of whom abandons her baby to the other in a bid for professional and personal freedom.

But *Top Girls* is not a stridently feminist work of propaganda; instead, it is an immensely carefully weighted argument, starting in epic Shavian terms and gradually narrowing down to the domestic present, about the cost of emancipation and equality, and all written with a curious kind of passionate detachment.

Later Caryl Churchill plays have included *Softcops* (1984), based on the memoirs of a policeman and a criminal in nineteenth-century France, and *Fen* (revised 1986), again written with and for the Joint Stock company and telling the story of a bleak, barely surviving rural community in East Anglia.

As Micheline Wandor has noted, Churchill was the first to pioneer a link between feminism and the London fringe theatre; she writes about often working-class women in a wide political context, and she has always also been interested in the way that the imagination can provide an escape into another and better world.

CALENDAR

- The Tony and the Pulitzer Best Play goes to August Wilson for *Fences*
- Richard Eyre named to succeed Peter Hall as director of Britain's National Theatre
- In Chicago Gary Sinese steps down as Artistic Director of Steppenwolf
- The New York Times reports that the crates of unpublished manuscripts by Jerome Kern, George Gershwin, Richard Rodgers and many others, discovered in a Secaucus warehouse in 1982, are far richer than was first thought

• According to Variety, one out of every three tickets now being sold on Broadway is for one of four London musical imports – *Cats*, *Les Miserables*, *Starlight Express* or *Me and My Girl*

• In Britain, Andrew Lloyd Webber writes the theme tune for the re-election campaign of Prime Minister Margaret Thatcher

• George Abbott celebrates his 100th birthday in Cleveland, rehearsing a revival of the classic play, *Broadway*

• Actor Kevin Marcum, understudying Colm Wilkinson in *Les Miserables*, and about to replace him, is found dead in his apartment of "acute cocaine intoxication"

• Broadway actor Matthew Broderick fined for his involvement in an Irish road crash in which two women died

• The Actors Studio announces temporary closure, amid rumours that the organisation has run adrift

DEATHS   **Danny Kaye** American stage and screen star

Broadway musicals star **Robert Preston**

Broadway actress **Geraldine Page**

Legendary stage and screen star **Frederick Austerlitz** better known as Fred Astaire

Broadway choreographer **Michael Bennett**

Bob Fosse Broadway choreographer/director

French playwright **Jean Anouilh**

NOTABLE PREMIERES   Iain Heggie's **A WHOLLY HEALTHY GLASGOW**, the start of a run of Scots and Irish drama which was to dominate new plays of the 1990s

Alan Rickman and Lindsay Duncan bring Christopher Hampton's long-running **LES LIAISONS DANGEREUSES** to Broadway

Derek Jacobi and Michael Gough bring London's hit, **BREAKING THE CODE**, about Alan Turing and the wartime codebreaking success with Enigma, to Broadway

Bernadette Peters and Joanna Gleason lead the cast of Stephen Sondheim's dark fairytale musical **INTO THE WOODS**

The Yale Rep has this season three shows on Broadway – **FENCES, JOE TURNER'S COME AND GONE**, both by August Wilson, and **A WALK IN THE WOODS**

Robert Harling's **STEEL MAGNOLIAS** opens 1200-performance run off-Broadway. It will later be a hit film

Madonna opens on Broadway in David Mamet's **SPEED-THE-PLOW** which views Hollywood as "a sinkhole of slime and depravity"

Opening at the Brooklyn Academy of Music of Peter Brook's three-part Sanskrit epic **THE MAHABARATA**

Patti Lupone opens 800-performance run at Lincoln Center of Cole Porter's **ANYTHING GOES**; Elaine Paige will star in London

John Malkovich and Joan Allen, founders of Steppenwolf, bring Lanford Wilson's **BURN THIS** to New York

MUSICAL NOTES   Luciano Pavarotti and Yo Yo Ma are among the musical luminaries who play in Music For Life, a concert to support AIDS relief

Leonard Bernstein wins both Schweitzer and the McDowell Award

HIT SONGS   I Should Be So Lucky

La Bamba

Pump Up the Volume

Our Country's Good

Lael Louisiana Timberlake Wertenbaker, of British and American parentage, was brought up in the Basque country, educated in France, and started out as a journalist and teacher before her first play, *This is No Place for Tallulah Bankhead*, was produced in London in 1980.

Ten other plays followed before she first made her name in 1985 with *The Grace of Mary Traverse*, about a young woman of the 1780s who, witnessing the rapist Lord Gordon of the Gordon Riots, decides in self-defence to move through Georgian London as a gambler and prostitute while also hiring men and women to provide sexual services. If you can't beat them, join them before they beat you up, would seem to be the message here, and as Wertenbaker herself once noted:

"My plays often start with a very ordinary question – if women had the power, would they behave the same way as men? Why do we seem to want to destroy ourselves? Is the personal more important than the political? If someone has behaved badly all their lives, can they redeem themselves? Parallel to this will be some story I may have heard, some gossip about somebody, a sentence heard or read. A friend of mine once told me her mother had been taught to be a good hostess by being made to talk to empty chairs. I used that as the opening scene of *The Grace of Mary Traverse*. I once heard about a young couple where the woman, for no apparent reason, had come out of the bath and shot herself. That became *Case to Answer*...everything gets collected and used at some point...A play is like a trial;

it goes before the jury, the audience, and they decide to like or not like the people, to agree or not to agree. If you really have the answers, you shouldn't be a writer but a politician, and if you are only interested in slice of life, then you should make documentaries. The theatre is a difficult place, because it requires an audience to use its imagination. You must accept that, and not try to make it easy for them…in ancient Greece, the number of seats corresponded to the number of adult males with voting rights. I think that makes sense: theatre is for people who take responsibility. There is no point in trying to attract idiots. Theatre should never be used to flatter, but to reveal and disturb."

As the critic Ned Chaillet has noted, there is something askance about nearly everything Timberlake Wertenbaker writes. Of American heritage, educated in France and long resident in England, she comes at the theatre from unusual angles, and juggles both cultures and influences in a way not familiar to most of the all-American or all-British writers of her generation. She takes a world view, and one which transcends cultures or centuries.

Alongside Caryl Churchill and Pam Gems, Wertenbaker remains the most important female playwright of the 1980s and 1990s, though her only worldwide hit has been the 1988 *Our Country's Good*, written for her regular director Max Stafford-Clark at the Royal Court, which told the story of a group of eighteenth-century convicts and their captors in Australia performing the first-ever play in that country, an amateur staging of *The Recruiting Officer*.

Among Wertenbaker's later plays, *The Love of the Nightingale* (written before *Our Country's Good* but then rewritten in rehearsal) was based on a Greek myth about the violence that erupts in societies where women have been silenced for too long; *Three Birds Alighting on a Field* (1991) was a plea for the survival of the beauty of landscape painting in a world where art galleries have gone mad, and *The Break of Day*

(1995) was an at least partially autobiographical account of the agony of international adoption.

Between writing plays of her own, Wertenbaker has been a prolific translator and adapter of the Greeks, Marivaux, Anouilh and Ariane Mnouchkine, and *Our Country's Good* enjoyed a long-running and award-winning Broadway production in the early 1990s.

CALENDAR

- To celebrate the January opening on Broadway of *The Phantom of the Opera*, composer Andrew Lloyd Webber is on the cover of Time Magazine
- Norman Keane, co-producer of the Broadway *Oh, Calcutta!* kills his unfaithful actress wife and then himself
- Publication of stage and screen director Elia Kazan's memoirs revives the controversy over his having "named names" to the House Un-American Activities Committee in 1952
- Director Frank Corsaro (*Hatful of Rain*, *Night of The Iguana*) takes charge of the Actors Studio
- Columnist Jimmy Breslin comes under fire for describing Lanford Wilson's *Burn This* as "that fag play"
- A century after its foundation, the Players Club in New York votes to admit women
- Rocco Landesman, starting his presidency of the Jujamcyn Theatres, announces an annual $50,000 budget to encourage regional theatres to develop more Broadway shows
- In the first annual Equity Fights AIDS week, nearly $100,000 is raised
- Cast of *Me and My Girl* complain to Equity that although the Broadway Marquis Theatre is less than a year old, "it stinks backstage and is cold enough there for you to see your breath"
- New York Times reports that because real estate

development around Broadway is pricing rehearsal spaces out of the market, new applications must allow 5% to be reserved for such use
- Having examined the records of Equity for a century, playwright Peter Stone estimates that the odds against any playwright having more than one Broadway hit in an entire career are 10 to 1
- Advice given by playwright David Mamet to actors requesting stage amplification, "Get off the stage and go home"
- Maggie Smith's broken shoulder, suffered in a bicycle accident, postpones for six months her opening in Peter Shaffer's hit *Lettice and Lovage*

DEATHS	Broadway composer **Frederick Loewe**
	Joshua Logan Broadway director
	Broadway playwright **Rose Franken**
	Kenneth Williams British actor/comedian
NOTABLE PREMIERES	Athol Fugard's **THE ROAD TO MECCA** opens long run at the Promenade
	The musical **CHESS**, already in trouble in London, only survives 68 Broadway performances
	John Lithgow opens on Broadway in David Henry Hwang's long-running **M BUTTERFLY**
	On Broadway, comics Robin Williams and Steve Martin star in **WAITING FOR GODOT**
MUSICAL NOTES	At Covent Garden, Sir Peter Hall directs his wife Maria Ewing in **SALOME**
HIT SONGS	**I Owe You Nothing**
	Never Gonna Give You Up

Aspects of Love

What mattered most about Andrew Lloyd Webber's *Aspects of Love* was that it marked the coming-of-age of the English stage musical. For this was not an American import, or a scenery show, or a dance extravaganza, nor yet an anthology of rock-pop hits cobbled together along a vaguely biographical storyline, preferably ending in violent or drug-driven death (eg *Buddy*, *Elvis* etc).

Instead, it is a lyrical, heartbreakingly romantic chamber piece, through-sung and deeply faithful to David Garnett's 1955 novel from which it derives its slender plot and more importantly, its mood of adult, adulterous, bittersweet regret for dangerous and sometimes impossible liaisons.

Aspects of Love tells of a young man bringing a penniless actress to the home of his uncle in the South of France, only to have the uncle fall in love with the girl, while he eventually falls for the uncle's daughter and then his mistress. Stated so briefly, the story has the darkly uneasy aspect of relative values gone horribly adrift, but the brilliance of Lloyd Webber's score here is the way it returns time and again to themes of lost and betrayed and restored and rediscovered love among an incestuous group of people often separated by at least one generation and one marriage, but all locked together by their passionate belief in passion itself.

Andrew Lloyd Webber was born in London in March 1948, the elder son of a Professor at the Royal College of Music and a mother who was a music teacher; his younger brother is the cellist Julian Lloyd Webber. He was educated at Westminster and then Magdalen College Oxford, which he left after a year to complete his musical studies at the Royal College of Music. In 1966 the agent David Land brought him together with the lyricist Tim Rice, and together they wrote a trio of major hits which effectively brought the London stage musical back to life, and made it for the first time an international force.

The first of these, originally meant only for an end-of-term concert at a small boys preparatory school was *Joseph and the Amazing Technicolor Dreamcoat*

(1968) which mixed American rock, French chansons and small-scale English nostalgia into a curious hybrid of the rock group Slade and Julian Slade. After considerable expansion and re-working, this ended up as a long-running West End and Broadway hit.

Alone, Lloyd Webber then went on to write the scores for two British movie thrillers of the early 1970s, *Gumshoe*, and *The Odessa File*, before coming back to Tim Rice to work on a controversial LP of *Jesus Christ Superstar*, a reworking of the Crucifixion which caused a considerable scandal, not only on disc but when it was

The Prince of Wales Theatre in 1989

first seen in a somewhat unsatisfactory Broadway staging.

After drastic revision, the show opened at the Palace Theatre in London, in August 1972, with Paul Nicholas as Christ and Dana Gillespie as Mary. This was to survive at the Palace until August 1980, a total of 3358 performances, making it (after Lloyd Webber's other hits *Cats* and *Starlight Express*) the third longest-running musical in London theatre history until it was overtaken by *Les Miserables* in January 1994.

Next came a short-lived musical of *Jeeves* in 1975 (with Alan Ayckbourn), revised and revived more successfully twenty years later, and after that, the last of the Rice collaborations, this one also starting out as a triumphant recording.

Evita went on to long stage runs in London, New York and all over the world before becoming, with Madonna in 1997, the first Hollywood musical hit in more than 20 years. But this, for various personal and professional reasons, marked the end of Lloyd Webber's partnership with Tim Rice.

His next lyricist was the late TS Eliot, on whose *Old Possum's Book of Practical Cats* Lloyd Webber based his single most successful and universal score. In a production by Trevor Nunn, and significantly, choreographed by Gillian Lynne, with the original star of *Evita*, Elaine Paige, substituting at the last minute for an injured Judi Dench, *Cats* opened in London on May 11th 1981 at the New London Theatre where it would still be playing twenty years later, after a 17-year Broadway run.

After *Cats*, in 1982, came the double bill *Song and Dance* (Lloyd Webber's first partnership with his brother Julian and the lyricist Don Black). It was joined in the West End and on Broadway two years later by *Starlight Express*, (a train epic locally known as "Squeals on Wheels" because the cast, loosely disguised as trains, races around the audience on roller skates), lyrics by Richard Stilgoe.

The death of Lloyd Webber's father inspired in 1985 the infinitely more serious *Requiem* and, in the following year, for his second wife, Sarah Brightman, Andrew wrote the musical of Gaston Leroux's century-old best-seller, *The Phantom of the Opera*. This opened in London with Michael Crawford and Sarah Brightman in October 1986. The lyrics were by Richard Stilgoe and a young newcomer, Charles Hart. After considerable Broadway union opposition, the same cast then opened there in January 1988 to mixed reviews but, in that season, eight Tony Awards; since then, audiences around the world have added more than another billion dollars to the Lloyd Webber coffers.

In 1989, came *Aspects of Love*, and then, in 1992 (with a book and lyrics by Don Black and the playwright Christopher Hampton), Andrew's musical adaptation of Billy Wilder's movie *Sunset Boulevard*, which opened in London with Patti LuPone in July 1993 and, five months later, in its native Los Angeles with Glenn Close.

Knighted in 1992, Lloyd Webber is the only theatrical composer ever to have had three scores running simultaneously in the West End and on Broadway and, for a while, he also had the three longest-running scores in all British theatre history, before the French invasion of Boublil and Schoenberg.

After *Sunset Boulevard* and the revival of *Jeeves*, came two of his most interesting, dark and smaller-scale scores. First, the 1997 *Whistle Down The Wind* (lyrics by Jim Steinman from the novel and film by Mary Hayley Bell) which, after a major Washington flop, cancelled its Broadway opening but, in a much revised production (again by Gale Edwards) has been running at London's Aldwych Theatre since 1998. *Whistle Down The Wind* was the story of a teenage girl from a dysfunctional (now relocated) Bible Belt family mistaking a killer on the run for Christ one Christmas Eve, and the other of Lloyd Webber's latest scores (*The Beautiful Game*, 2000, book and lyrics Ben Elton) is also about young people in trouble, in this case a team of 1969 Belfast footballers on the brink of the Irish Troubles.

CALENDAR

• In Britain, knighthood for actor Rex Harrison
• Former child star Shirley Temple becomes American Ambassador to Czechoslovakia
• As Sam Wanamaker still fund-raises for the new Globe, the remains of Shakespeare's original theatres, the Rose and the Globe, are unearthed on Bankside
• Broadway composer Stephen Sondheim is appointed first Visiting Professor of Drama and Musical Theatre Studies at Oxford University

DEATHS   British actor, director and producer **Laurence (Lord) Olivier**
Irving Berlin American immigrant composer
American actor/director **John Cassavetes**
Lucille Ball Broadway comedienne
Irish playwright **Samuel Beckett**
Sir Anthony Quayle British actor/director

NOTABLE   On Broadway, Robert Morse revives his career in
PREMIERES TRU, Jay Presson Allen's play about Truman Capote
Boublil and Schoenberg's MISS SAIGON, an
updating of Madame Butterfly to the Vietnam War,
opens a 10-year run at Drury Lane
On Broadway and the West End, Peter Hall directs
Dustin Hoffman in THE MERCHANT OF VENICE
Pauline Collins opens 300-performance run on
Broadway of Willy Russell's one-character play
SHIRLEY VALENTINE

MUSICAL   Eleonor Cory's HEMISPHERES
NOTES   William Albright's CHASM

HIT SONGS   Ride on Time
Voodoo Ray

Racing Demon

The first and best of David Hare's "State of the Nation" National Theatre trilogy, Racing Demon was the story of the Church of England in total moral and spiritual breakdown. It was almost immediately followed by Murmuring Judges about the British judiciary in a similar crisis of conscience, and then by Absence of War which looked at the melt-down of the old Labour Party in the wake of Neil Kinnock's annihilation by the Conservative forces of Margaret Thatcher.

But the reason that Racing Demon was the most critically and commercially successful of the three was that, while nobody could quite agree on what at the beginning of the 1990s was really to blame for the breakdown of Britain's Law Courts or Socialist ideals, virtually everyone was agreed as to what had gone wrong with the Church – it had simply lost its faith and, as a result, its congregation.

Through three very different men of the church, Hare managed to consider nearly all the major questions that have over the last twenty years virtually paralysed the Church of England – who should run it? For whom? And how? Is there really any point, any longer, in organised religion and if not, what should replace it? In an age of sceptical non-Believers, what should be done for the diminishing numbers of True Believers? And in an age of Church vandalism, is there really anything to be said for trying to maintain the Altar?

Not for the first time, Hare here showed himself one of the very few major playwrights of his generation willing to examine the way we live now, be that political, religious or sexual.

Although Hare is now one of our most established and Establishment writers, his early years in the theatre were conditioned by agit-prop, small-scale regional tours and the founding of Joint Stock, a road company dedicated to new plays. In these years, 1971-75, his plays were mainly translations or joint ventures with such contemporaries as Tony and Nick Bicat and, of course, Brenton.

But, in 1975, he alone wrote Knuckle, a stunning transposition of the mean streets of Raymond Chandler's Los Angeles to downtown Guildford, where Hare amazingly found the same mixture of corruption and dark sexuality. A plot about the corrupting effects of Capitalism starred an international arms dealer (suavely played by Edward Fox) who comes home to investigate the mysterious disappearance of his sister and finds, in a labyrinthine thriller, his own true love, only to lose her by his own treachery.

In the same year, an already prolific Hare also wrote Fanshen, about the transformation of a tiny Chinese village after Mao's Revolution, and a viciously funny near-musical Teeth 'n' Smiles. The premise here was simple enough: into the privileged, cloistered world of Cambridge undergraduates shambles a pop group led by Maggie, a singer whose ambition it is to reach a San Francisco bar, preferably on a tide of Johnny Walker scotch. Played in the performance that made her name by Helen Mirren, this was really about a new generation of twenty-somethings who feel that they are trapped on the Titanic without much chance of getting the Captain to change course.

What Hare first did in this early play, and was often to do later (not least in Plenty and Licking Hitler, both 1978) was to bridge the past, present and future, so that here were characters who remembered being at the Café de Paris the night they dropped the bomb on Snakehips Johnson, as well as kids reflecting the sheer bloody awfulness of being stuck in a third-rate minor cult pop group – "The louder we play, the sooner we can go deaf". But in the end, none of Hare's characters is either waving or drowning, they are just trying to make up their minds about the depth and temperature of the water.

Three years later, at the National Theatre, Hare's Plenty was the most ambitious new play of its era. Set across two decades, from 1943 to 1962, it remains a mordantly funny, savage and cynical play about the betrayal of whatever complex ideals may once

Oliver Ford-Davies at the RNT in 1990

have been symbolised by an English girl in the French Resistance.

Time and again, here, as in such later plays as A Map of the World (1983) and Secret Rapture (1989) Hare writes with coherent and committed rage of a national failure of guts and truth. Time and again, he delivers amazingly impressive packages and, if you listen very carefully, you can usually hear them ticking.

But, in the 1990s, he began also to turn his attention to major plays about one single individual; first for Michael Gambon in Skylight and then for Judi Dench in Amy's View, he created two larger-than-life characters with whom it was very hard not to fall in love, despite their many and explicit failings as lovers and parents. At the end of Amy's View, in one of the most bleak closing lines of all modern theatre, Dench, as the actress who can only really exist on stage, notes "Finally, we are alone", and there perhaps lies one of the messages Hare was sending out at the end of the century. But he is never that predictable, and when he took to the stage himself, to recount his own voyage of discovery in the latter-day commercialised Holy Land Via Dolorosa (1998), a project which, like many others of his, is now being turned into a screenplay, one suddenly saw him for the first time as a current-affairs monologuist in the tradition of Spaulding Gray.

Hare's most recent work has included The Blue Room, an updating of Schnitzler's La Ronde which became a tremendous success for Nicole Kidman in London and on Broadway in 1998/9, and then in the autumn of 2000 he wrote and directed for the Royal Court My Zinc Bed, a new play about the state of contemporary Britain in which an Internet mogul invites a young poet to work on his web site.

CALENDAR

- Neil Simon's Jake's Women is only his second show in 30 years to close on the road pre-Broadway
- British producer Cameron Mackintosh starts near-riot among theatre-party agents by suggesting that for his forthcoming Miss Saigon they will not get the usual 10% commission but a sliding scale starting at 5%
- Variety summarises "Broadway this winter is more like the Sahara Desert than a theatrical capital"
- Actor David Carroll leaves the cast of Grand Hotel and dies of AIDS a few days later
- Director Jerry Zaks (Lend me a Tenor, Six Degrees of Separation) leaves Lincoln Center to become director-in-residence of Jujamcyn Theatres

DEATHS American cabaret star **Sammy Davis, Jr**
Max Wall British actor and comedian
British actress **Jill Bennett**

NOTABLE PREMIERES Eric Bogosian opens long-running off-Broadway solo show **SEX, DRUGS AND ROCK AND ROLL**, a follow-up to his successful **DRINKING IN AMERICA**
Kathleen Turner scores major Broadway success in the revival of the Tennessee Williams' **CAT ON A HOT TIN ROOF**

MUSICAL NOTES Birth of The Three Tenors as Domingo, Carreras and Pavarotti sing on worldwide television

HIT SONGS Nothing Compares 2 U
Black Velvet
It Must Have Been Love

Six Degrees of Separation

Like AR Gurney but precious few others of his American generation John Guare has fought a lonely battle to restore to an increasingly eclectic, eccentric and even wayward New York theatre, some semblance of the elegance, charm, and even language which we associate with the major playwrights of his immediate past. His interests have very often been nostalgic, taking us back to an almost Chekhovian world where people, or at least those who can afford to do so, are somehow trying to escape the realities of a modern world with which they can really manage only a very limited connection.

John Edward Guare was born in New York in February 1938, educated at Georgetown University in Washington DC, transferred to Yale School of Drama and then the University of Washington. He had started writing plays as early as 1959 (*Theatre Girl*) but instead of focusing on his writing, he became an assistant to the manager of Washington DC's National Theatre.

Always active in academia and criticism, his plays in these early years, many written for television, and often produced at the O'Neill Center, did not really tempt major managements from New York. By 1964 he had formed his own playwrights unit in New York, was a founder member of the Eugene O'Neill's Playwrights Conference in Waterford, Connecticut and playwright-in-residence at the New York Shakespeare Festival. From there he went to teach at Yale and, perhaps because of this considerable amount of administrative and academic work, his own plays were slow in coming.

But in just twelve years, he had written twelve plays, and although one or two of these had been briefly seen off-Broadway, none of them had the 'legs' to carry them any further and, for a while, Guare thought that he might settle for the life of a theatre professor or historian.

That all changed in 1971 with a play called *The House of Blue Leaves*. Already it was clear that there was a contradiction at the heart of Guare. Editorially he sided with Gurney and Richard Nelson and the more conservative writers of that time. But artistically he was always a rebel with a strong sense of the Theatre of the Absurd and even if one could now find where precisely mainstream American drama was, the chances are against Guare being anything near the centre of it.

In *The House of Blue Leaves*, as the critic Steven Gale has noted, Guare brilliantly moved from fantastic images capturing the essentials of American life to the merely bizarre surface nature of his immediate society. What Guare is looking for, in this and other plays of the period, is some kind of a metaphor for the decline of American spirituality. It was as though he had discovered, like O'Neill before him, that a family which stays together also slays together.

On the face of it a light comedy, *The House of Blue Leaves* takes place on the day the Pope visits New York for the first time. He's there, just over the Brooklyn Bridge, a few minutes and a million miles from the Shaughnessy flat where the admittedly peculiar family is unhinged by even the prospect of the visit. Among the older generation, Artie the mailman dreams of a life as a showbiz celebrity, writing ditties which he plays to anyone who will listen, while his wife, Bananas, a Guare comic invention of infinite subtlety, having given up on reality, feeds him on Brillo burgers. Their son is nowhere to be seen, having gone over to Manhattan to try to blow up the Pope, but Artie's mistress, she who believes in the gospel of *Modern Screen* magazine, is very much in evidence until she runs off with the Hollywood producer who Artie thinks is going to make him a star. Then there are the nuns who are watching the Pope on television with the Shaughnessys. Or are they? *The House of Blue Leaves*, especially in its Lincoln Center production with Swoosie Kurtz as Bananas and John Mahoney as Artie, precisely nailed Guare's central preoccupation with the conflict between belonging and alienation, fantasy and reality, closeness and distance.

His next major success came a year later when, spreading his wings into the Broadway heartland, he wrote with Mel Shapiro a rock musical adaptation of Shakespeare's *Two Gentlemen of Verona*. Already established as a master of the wacky and the weird,

Guare found here a wonderfully legit basis, with Shakespearean characters always on the extremity of experience and worlds which could be destroyed or made magical by nothing more than words.

And then came *Six Degrees of Separation*: the title refers to the theory, commonly held at the time, that everybody in the world is related to everyone else through not more than six connections and, in a New York riven by class, colour, and fiscal divisions, Guare had not only tapped the vein of just about every concern common to the NY theatregoer, he had also integrated his long-held obsessions with fantasy, reality, alienation and family.

CALENDAR

• In Chicago, Steppenwolf move into their new $8million 500-seat house, just south of the Loop. The inaugural production at the first theatre ever built for itself by a Chicago troupe is Ronald Harwood's *Another Time* starring Albert Finney
• Brian Friel's *Dancing at Lughnasa* wins both Tony for Best Play and the Drama Critics Circle awards. Frank Rich says, "It does exactly what theatre was born to do"
• Nicol Williamson, in a curtain speech at *I Hate Hamlet*, a troubled ghost story in which his co-star has more than once had to leave the stage injured, criticises the Tony judges who failed to nominate him for an award, "As Irving Berlin once wrote about show business, everything about it is appalling." He fails to mention that during an on-stage swordfight he has actually and deliberately abandoned the choreography in order to hurt his co-star/opponent

DEATHS American choreographer **Martha Graham**
Tom Eyen American playwright
American touring actress **Eva Le Gallienne**
British actress **Dame Peggy Ashcroft**
Broadway director and founder of The New York
Joseph Papp Shakespeare Festival
British director **Tony Richardson**
Lee Remick American stage and screen actress

NOTABLE PREMIERES On Broadway, Mandy Patinkin and Rebecca Luker open in the Lucy Simon-Marsha Norman musical THE SECRET GARDEN
Opening of very brief Broadway run of Timberlake Wertenbaker's OUR COUNTRY'S GOOD
Opening at Manhattan Theatre Club at City Center of McNally's LIPS TOGETHER, TEETH APART
Eileen Atkins opens successful solo show about Virginia Woolf A ROOM OF ONE'S OWN
Four major stars triumph in the West End this year in new plays and revivals: Fiona Shaw does the remarkable double of HEDDA GABLER and ELECTRA; Juliet Stevenson was devastating in DEATH AND THE MAIDEN; Nigel Hawthorne brought back to life a long-lost monarch in Alan Bennett's THE MADNESS OF KING GEORGE III; and, after a long road tour, Derek Jacobi brought Anouilh's BECKET back to London

MUSICAL NOTES The rock group Nirvana emerge from Seattle with the newly popular grunge music
Pavarotti sings in the rain in Hyde Park and Domingo in Windsor Great Park

HIT SONGS Everything I Do I Do for You
One More Try
Never Mind

Adrian Lester and
Stockard Channing at
the Royal Court in 1992

Dancing At Lughnasa

The invasion, or so it seemed, of the London and New York theatre by Irish dramatists in the 1990s was really fathered by one single writer, Brian Friel. After George Bernard Shaw and Sean O'Casey, although Brendan Behan and several others were to have individual hits, no really sustained career abroad was achieved by anybody from across the Irish Sea until Friel and even he has had a curiously divided career with major successes in the 1960s, especially in America, but then a long gap before his rediscovery 20 years later.

Bernard Patrick Friel was born in County Tyrone early in January 1929. He has four daughters and one son by Anne Morrison and throughout the 1950s made his living as a teacher in primary and intermediate schools in Derry. In 1960 he decided to become a full-time playwright and four years later his fourth play, *Philadelphia, Here I Come*, immediately struck at the heart of thousands of NY Irish theatregoers. It tells the story of Gareth O'Donnell who is torn by conflicting emotions as he prepares to leave his Irish family and, like so many thousands before him, seek his fortune in the United States.

From now on Friel was to write almost a play a year and, until very recently, almost each one was greeted with greater enthusiasm in New York than in

Anita Reeves, Catherine Byrne, Brid Ni Neachtain and Brid Brennan at the Phoenix Theatre in 1991

London. Friel's apparently random decision to give up the security of a teaching career for the riskier life of the dramatist was justified almost from the very beginning. After *Philadelphia, Here I Come*, in rapid succession *The Loves of Cass McGuire*; *Lovers*; *Crystal and Fox*; *The Gentle Island*; and then, in Dublin, London, Chicago and New York in 1973/4 came *The Freedom of the City*. Here, for the first time, in a fluid and agile production by Albert Finney, was the first full-scale attempt to deal in a play as opposed to a tract about the contemporary political and religious situation in Northern Ireland. Friel's thesis here is that the new Troubles are caused by poverty rather than religion, confusion rather than rebellion, and accident rather than design.

At a time when IRA bombs were still going off with some regularity, Friel's cool and wry writing was less than popular at least in London. His play took a cool and detached look at the whole ghastly mess and concluded that no good could ever come out of a situation already invaded by university lecturers, television reporters, and High Court judges.

His next major play was, although a success in London, the one that ended his run of Broadway successes as rapidly as it had begun. As played on Broadway by James Mason in his last (and one of his very few performances there) *The Faith Healer* was a haunting, and in our view, brilliant set of three monologues delivered across three acts by a wandering and possibly suspect medium and the two people unwise enough to get caught up in his web which, predictably, tears apart roughly as they do.

By now it was clear that Friel was never going to be interested in the daily political struggle and treachery which were tearing up his native land. Instead, in play after play, he seemed to pull back into his own inner landscape while trying there to work out in historical or familial terms just what had gone so horribly wrong.

True, *The Freedom of the City* (1973) did come briefly back into the fray in considering Ulster's anguished political scene. But for Friel's next success, *Translations* (1981), he takes us back to 1883 and the town of Baile Beag, known to the English as Ballybeg. A party of initially friendly English Redcoats has come over to chart the countryside and anglicise the local place names. Ireland is to be conquered not by the sword but by the map. There is to be a process of 'erosion' whereby English will replace Gaelic first as a language and second as a way of life.

It would be hard to deny that this is the most important drama, theatrically and historically, to have come out of Ireland since long before the death of O'Casey in that it deals not only with the roots of the on-going conflict but also with the cornerstones of the Irish character which condition it. What begins as a John Ford comedy of Irish misunderstanding becomes by the end of the play an epic tragedy which is to last at least 150 years. What matters here is the way Friel takes the old Abbey Theatre stereotypes – the drunken schoolmaster and his Joxer friend and the young lovers of folk comedy – and creates for them a tapestry altogether new and terrifying.

In recent years, all over the world, Friel's greatest hit has been *Dancing at Lughnasa* which opened this year on Broadway after successful runs in London and Dublin. Set back into the middle 1930s, at a time when radio was first penetrating even rural Ireland *Dancing at Lughnasa* was again set in the playwright's beloved Ballybeg and was again a lyrical Chekhovian story about a family of sisters and a mysterious brother with a terrible secret whose return from Africa is much anticipated.

In one sense, not a lot happens here except for a ritual rustic reunion down on the farm. On the other hand, everything happens; Friel somehow manages with his extraordinary mix of subtlety and subversion to tell us everything we need to know about the roots of modern Irish discontent. As usual, however, the audience as well as the cast have to dig deep to work out precisely what those roots really mean.

Angels in America

Although there is considerable doubt in some critical minds as to whether or not Tony Kushner's epic, sprawling, two-part *Angels in America* is really the best play of the 1990s, there cannot be a lot of doubt that it was certainly the major dramatic event of the decade.

Tony Kushner was born in New York City on July 16th 1958, but his mother and father, both professional musicians, soon moved their family out to Lake Charles, Louisiana, where Kushner grew up, watching his mother act in a considerable range of local amateur productions. When he returned to New York for college at Columbia he began theatregoing almost every night and went on to the graduate programme in directing at New York University.

His first play, *A Bright Moon Called Day*, was successfully premiered in San Francisco in 1985 when Kushner was already 27 but the New York production at the Public Theatre survived less than two weeks. Kushner then turned to the comparative safety of an adaptation of Corneille's *L'Illusion Comique* which was produced in several regional theatres and brought him sufficient acclaim to be invited to teach playwrighting at Princeton University and to become a playwright-in-residence at New York's Juilliard Drama Department.

So, even before *Angels*, Kushner had started to make his name in the New York Shakespeare Festival and in San Francisco, Chicago, London (*A Bright Moon Called Day*) and with a musical *Widows*, co-written with Ariel Dorfman.

But nothing in his past really prepared us for the sheer ambition of *Angels In America* in which Kushner highlights a group of characters living according to a set of millennial moral absolutes but then (as Giles Croft has noted) conjures up a complex and contradictory world where the good and the bad angels that are in us all attempt to seduce them into compromise.

The plays were originally commissioned by the Eureka Theatre in San Francisco through a special grant from the National Endowment for the Arts and as befits a somewhat rambling piece, its original stage history is nothing if not complex.

Part One: *Millenium Approaches* was first produced at the Eureka in May 1991, was further developed at the Mark Taper Forum in Los Angeles and reached the National's Cottesloe Theatre in yet another revision in the January of 1992. From there it went to Broadway where in 1993 it won four Tony Awards as well as the Pulitzer.

Part Two: *Perestroika* also premiered at the Eureka before again going to the Mark Taper Forum and reaching the Cottesloe in London in November 1993 whereupon, for the first time in Europe, both plays could be seen in sequence in a six-hour production by Declan Donnellan.

Angels In America views the journey of four gay men through the Reagan Presidency – a WASP (White Anglo-Saxon Protestant) drag queen named Prior Walter and his Jewish lover, Louis Ironson who flees when he can no longer cope with Walter's AIDS, a married Mormon lawyer named Joe Pitt who tries to use his religion to ward off his homosexuality and Pitt's mentor, Roy Cohn, the real-life, famously corrupt, Red-baiting lawyer who made his name as the hatchet-man for Senator Joseph McCarthy at the time of the Communist witch-hunts of the 1950s.

Though the spread of *Angels* is vast, most of the scenes consist of two or three characters fighting out moral issues of considerable philosophic complexity. By the end of Part One, one of the men is on a symbolic trip to the Antarctic, Joe and Louis have started their affair while Prior, already at death's door, is visited by an Angel who crashes into his room through the ceiling and announces, "Greetings, Prophet; The Great Work begins. The Messenger has arrived." In Part Two: *Perestroika*, at least some of these many loose ends are tied up and the play ends on a note of surprising poetic optimism.

"When I sat down to start *Angels in America* in 1988," Kushner told the *New Yorker* drama critic John Lahr, "it was supposed to be a two-hour play about five gay men, one of whom was Mormon and another was Roy Cohn. I was not trying to write a gay problem play, nor a plea for homosexual tolerance, nor anything very overtly political. All I was trying to do was to honour the gay community by telling a story that sets it in the larger historical context of American political life. As Louis says in the play, 'There are no angels in America, no spiritual past, no racial past, there is only the political.'"

CALENDAR

• Poet and playwright Toni Morrison becomes first African-American to win Nobel Prize for Literature

• In Paris, the Folies Bergère comes back to life after a year-long bankruptcy closure

• Circle in the Square, off-Broadway, announces a deficit for this season of nearly $2million

• Variety headline on its review of *Aint' Broadway Grand*: a life of the flamboyant producer Mike Todd is: "No, It Ain't"

• Natasha Richardson, daughter of Vanessa Redgrave, makes her Broadway debut in *Anna Christie* opposite Irish actor Liam Neeson for whom she will soon leave her husband, British producer Robert Fox

• British actress and singer Julia Mackenzie makes her New York directorial debut with a Stephen Sondheim anthology *Putting it Together* starring Julie Andrews

• In London, Patti LuPone opens *Sunset Boulevard* but is told by Andrew Lloyd Webber that Glenn Close is now the star of the Broadway production

• Playwright Israel Horowitz, Artistic Director of the Gloucester Stage Company denies charges by several women that he has sexually harrassed them

DEATHS

Russian-born ballet star **Rudolf Nureyev**

Audrey Hepburn Dutch-born actress

Broadway actress **Lilian Gish**

Cyril Cusack Irish actor

American stage and screen star **Vincent Price**

Ruby Keeler American stage and musical star

Veteran actress **Helen Hayes**

Pioneering Broadway and ballet choreographer **Agnes de Mille**

NOTABLE PREMIERES

Willy Russell's long-running London musical **BLOOD BROTHERS** opens on Broadway to poor reviews but survives there for almost two years

Lynn Redgrave opens on Broadway her own one-woman show **SHAKESPEARE FOR MY FATHER**

Michael Cerveris opens 900-performance run of a revival of the Pete Townshend rock opera **TOMMY**

It is being rumoured around Broadway that the premiere of Tony Kushner's **PERESTROIKA**, the second half of his **ANGELS IN AMERICA** is being rushed into opening so as to catch Frank Rich, a known admirer of Kushner, before he leaves his critical column

MUSICAL NOTES

Domingo and Pavarotti celebrate 25 years at the Met

HIT SONGS

Can't Help Falling in Love

All that She Wants

That's the Way Love Goes

Both Sides

Mr Blobby

Love! Valor! Compassion!

Of all contemporary American playwrights it is Terrence McNally whose antecedents can most clearly be traced, not only by the mixture of tartness of language and political polemic which characterised G Bernard Shaw, but by the deftness of stagecraft and the broadness of comic intention that has informed farceurs from Feydeau to Travers.

What differentiates McNally from most others is that his plays cannot be (with a few exceptions) characterised as 'comedies', 'dramas' or 'tragedies' but are always hybrids, usually heavy on the comedy in the first act and moving inexorably darker and deeper into drama and often tragedy in the second. McNally is one of those rare playwrights whose first acts can often, literally, make you fall off your seat with laughter and an hour later have you leaving the theatre with tears in your eyes.

At just over three hours, Terrence McNally's *Love! Valor! Compassion!* is at times overlong, rambling and even shapeless. But as it slowly tells the story of eight gay men across three long summer weekends, before, during and just after the plague of AIDS, it comes to be seen as the great American play of its difficult times.

His characters bitch and bicker, flirt and flounce, and generally carry on like *The Boys in the Band*, except that this time it is all for real; AIDS is waiting for them on Fire Island, and this may well be the last of the summer reunions before the light goes out on at least some of the group. So how shall it be spent?

Not in grieving, that's for sure; McNally's widely-assorted gay characters are not going gently into that good night, they are waving not drowning, and they are still for the most part convinced that the deadly killer is not going to get them, regardless of how many friends

Ramon de Ocampo, Floyd King, Sean Pratt, Michael Russotto amd Christopher Wilson at the Studio Theatre, New York

and neighbours are forced into a far too early grave. But this year that killer was AIDS, and all other bets are off.

Back in 1973, after he had written some twenty plays for off-Broadway and elsewhere, McNally really made his name off-Broadway with *The Ritz*, one of the most hilarious farces in post-war American stage or screen history. Essentially it was about a Mafia family trapped in a gay bathhouse, but like all great farces it spun off from there into the private and public lives of its individual characters and only very occasionally came back to base.

In 1984 he wrote the book for John Kander and Fred Ebb's *The Rink*, a musical about a mother and daughter closing down an Atlantic City skating rink and with it a part of their lives. His book, as usual about opposites trying to form some kind of bond despite their differences, tended to just stop when it was time for a song, a problem he was to solve some years later when he was to work again with Kander and Ebb adapting the movie for the musical of *Kiss of the Spiderwoman*, which opened to rather better reviews but thinner houses.

Then came a none-too-successful backstage farce, *It's Only a Play*, which, in common with the later *The Lisbon Traviata* (1985) a latter-day tragicomedy, suffered from a cracking first act, leaving nowhere much to go in the second, a McNally problem which later plays, particularly *Love! Valor! Compassion!* managed to solve.

McNally has always fought typecasting; his more recent work has ranged from *Frankie and John at the Clair de Lune*, which ran lengthily off-Broadway (with Kathy Bates and Kenneth Welsh) and then as a movie (starring Michelle Pfeiffer and Al Pacino), telling the tale of an ordinary working-class forty-something man and woman groping towards some sort of life together.

Then came, after the group collaboration of *Kiss of the Spiderwoman*, a solo triumph with *Master Class*, a savagely accurate account of Maria Callas' famous master classes at Juilliard in New York.

In 1997 he returned to adaptation with an immensely ambitious book from EL Doctorow's novel *Ragtime*, and captured on stage an entire social, racial and artistic history of 20th-century America, without losing the subtlety or delicacy of the original, while still allowing room for Lynn Ahrens and Stephen Flaherty's score and the performances of a huge and accomplished cast.

Most recently (1999) there has been *Corpus Christi*, an account of the Last Supper which caused predictable Religious-Right picketing on Broadway and a rather more muted protest in London, where it seemed rather too often to resemble *Godspell* without the songs. Sadly, the controversy about the production overshadowed the play itself.

CALENDAR

- Edward Albee wins a Pulitzer Prize and the Drama Critics Circle Award for *Three Tall Women*
- The Actors' Centre announces that, for the first time, it is to offer classes to non-professionals
- The number of musical revivals on Broadway persuades the Tony Administration Committee to split the Best Revival category into two parts – Best Revived Play and Best Revived Musical
- The Disney Company, expanding its Broadway interests, buys the New Amsterdam theatre on 42nd Street
- The same day that Jessica Tandy dies, her husband and frequent stage partner, Hume Cronyn, receives an Emmy Award for his performance as a man trying to come to terms with the recent death of his wife
- Shortly after *Beauty and the Beast* sets a record for one day's box-office takings for a show, it is broken by Andrew Lloyd Webber's *Sunset Boulevard*

DEATHS

Jessica Tandy American actress

Romanian playwright **Eugene Ionesco**

Martha Raye American singer and dancer

Playwright and original 'Angry Young Man', **John Osborne**

NOTABLE PREMIERES

Terry Johnson's comedy about a group of Benny Hill fans, DEAD FUNNY

David Mamet's drama, THE CRYPTOGRAM

Arthur Miller's latest play, BROKEN GLASS, starring Ron Rifkin, Amy Irving and David Dukes

Robert le Page's THE SEVEN STREAMS OF THE RIVER OTA

STOMP, a percussion-based dance show, starring Luke Cresswell, opens at the Orpheum

A revival of DAMN YANKEES starring Victor Garber is a smash hit, and eventually transfers to the Adelphi Theatre in London, with Lewis reprising the role of the Devil

Diana Rigg repeats on Broadway her London success as MEDEA

Disney's BEAUTY AND THE BEAST at the Palace

Edward Albee, THREE TALL WOMEN on Broadway

Glenn Close opens Andrew Lloyd Webber's American production of SUNSET BOULEVARD

MUSICAL NOTES

Peter Maxwell Davies' SYMPHONY NO 5

EMI's cd Chant revives the popularity of Gregorian chant, recorded at a Spanish monastery

HIT SONGS

Parklife

Love is All Around

New England

David Burke holds court in the RSC's production at the Pit in 1994

Although an American, no latter-day dramatist from either side of the Atlantic has written more consistently about the uneasy relationship between the English and the Americans either in their own or each other's territory. Having just written (for the RSC, his most constant London home) a savage attack on a strolling band of American Shakespeare scholars scavenging Britain for information that might help their careers back home (*Some Americans Abroad*), Richard Nelson then turned the tables and for *New England* looked at a bunch of derelict British teachers trying to make some sense of the American academic system and its followers.

From here he went on (again for the RSC) to an epic account of the travels and travails of Christopher Columbus which did not entirely work, although it continued Nelson's interest in writing about travellers in some kind of moral or physical chaos. Latterly came *The General From America*, an account of the treachery of Benedict Arnold, once again Nelson's favourite theme about the culture clash of England and America.

Richard Nelson was born 17th October 1950 in Chicago: after working as an associate with the Goodman there and the Guthrie in Minneapolis, he started playwriting in Los Angeles while also adapting a number of foreign writers such as Moliere and Brecht.

He first came into his own as a writer in 1984 with *Between East and West* and then two years later with *Principia Scriptoriae*, both of which dealt in various ways with the artist and the intellectual foundering in a world which has no more use for them.

In *Principia Scriptoriae* they are two young writers thrown into gaol by the right-wing regime of some unnamed Latin American country, only to meet fifteen years later across a conference table negotiating the freedom of a poet imprisoned by the country's now Leftist authorities. Flashed across the back of the set were writers' text book homilies like "Choose your setting carefully" and "Always like your characters" which are in bleak contrast and ironic counterpoint to the events taking place here.

Some Americans Abroad was an elegantly satirical look at the annual migration patterns of American scholar abroad; beneath the witty, bantering surface something rather nastier is in fact going on here. One of the professors is about to be unseated, another charged with making politically incorrect advances to one of his female students in a direct forerunner of the much tougher *Oleanna*.

With the possible exception of Alex Finlayson, an American linked to the Royal Exchange, Manchester for over a decade, no American playwright has ever been taken to the heart of a classical British company in the way that Nelson has regularly been commissioned and supported by the RSC; and although the results have sometimes been variable, the twenty-year relationship (often under the direction of David Jones) has paid off in a kind of continuity of thought and production which has been granted to all too few other American writers in the London theatre.

CALENDAR

• Austin Pendleton takes over the Circle Repertory Theatre

• Off-Broadway producers decide not to enter their shows for the Tony Awards as the required two free tickets for the hundreds of voters will be uneconomic for theatres of their size

• Tennessee Williams, one of America's greatest playwrights, is the subject of a US Postal Service commemorative stamp

• Broadway dims its lights as a sign of respect on hearing of the death of one of its most distinguished directors, George Abbott, a man who was directing on Broadway even before Broadway got its name. He was 106

DEATHS

British playwright **Robert Bolt**, husband of actress Sarah Miles

Arthur English, veteran British actor and comedian

NOTABLE PREMIERES

Carol Burnett returns to the stage in Ken Ludwig's **MOON OVER BUFFALO** at the Martin Beck

Harold Pinter's **MOONLIGHT** opens on Broadway, starring Jason Robards and Blythe Danner

Tom Stoppard's **ARCADIA** transfers to New York after a successful London run

Ralph Fiennes brings his performance of **HAMLET** to Broadway after starring at the Hackney Empire in London. Gertrude is played by Francesca Annis, who later becomes his real-life partner

VITA AND VIRGINIA stars two of the stage's most accomplished actresses, Vanessa Redgrave and Eileen Atkins

Sarah Kane makes her reputation – albeit a somewhat savage one – with **BLASTED**, which opens at the Royal Court's Theatre Upstairs

Patrick Marber's **DEALER'S CHOICE** at the National (Cottesloe) reveals a new playwriting talent

CELL MATES at the Albery becomes better known for the offstage events than for the play itself: Stephen Fry, stung by some wounding notices, absconds to Bruges, Simon Ward is brought in to replace him, the show, nonetheless, closes, and Simon Gray writes a furious denunciation of Fry's behaviour, which is published in book form as Fat Chance

Tom Stoppard's **INDIAN INK**, starring Felicity Kendal, opens at the Aldwych

BURNING BLUE, DWM Greer's play about gay relationships among the American military, opens at The King's Head and is later to transfer, with less success, to the Theatre Royal, Haymarket

Roger Michell's production of Dylan Thomas' **UNDER MILKWOOD** is a hit at the National Theatre (Olivier)

David Hare's **SKYLIGHT** also opens at the National (Cottesloe) and stars Michael Gambon

Rodney Ackland's **ABSOLUTE HELL**, a drama set in Soho just after VE Day in 1945, stars Judi Dench at the National (Lyttleton)

At the Cottesloe, Fiona Shaw scores a personal triumph in a cross-gender playing of Shakespeare's **RICHARD II**

Leo McKern and Nicola McAuliffe fight a generational battle in a revival of **HOBSON'S CHOICE** at the Lyric, Shaftesbury Avenue

Diana Rigg is **MOTHER COURAGE** in Brecht's sombre masterpiece, at the National (Olivier)

Toby Stephens plays the title role in a well-received **CORIOLANUS** at the Barbican

Jude Law, a rising theatre actor, appears in Cocteau's **INDISCRETIONS** on Broadway

MUSICAL NOTES

The New York Met introduces surtitles on special monitors

Luciano Pavarotti stars in **ANDREA CHENIER**

Premier at Houston of opera on the life of the murdered gay San Francisco mayor, Harvey Milk

HIT SONGS

Gangsta's Paradise

Back for Good

All I Wanna Do

Two Trains Running

No other 20th-century American playwright has so quickly achieved and held onto the high ground of the New York theatre as has August Wilson. While there has been some inevitable unevenness between plays, he has managed to win both critics and audiences to his cause with each of his long-running and loosely connected series of meditations on the black experience in his century.

Born in Pittsburgh in 1945, the son of working-class black parents, August Wilson dropped out of high school and began writing poetry, only turning to drama in his early 20s. Early in the 1980s both the O'Neill playwriting conference and the Yale Rep began to take an interest in his work, and the sequence of plays which followed all made his name, won him the Pulitzer and several other awards.

All treated of the black experience in transition, whether moving from town to town or job to job: *Ma Rainey's Black Bottom* (1984) is set in the 1920s; *Fences* (1987) in the late 1950s; *Joe Turner's Come and Gone* (1988) in 1911, and *The Piano Lesson* (1990) in the 1930s.

In an extraordinary achievement, each of these five plays has won the Pulitzer or the New York Drama Critics Circle Award or both, and each has enjoyed a long New York run, playing often to black audiences who had seldom ventured onto Broadway before, because it had somehow seemed so totally irrelevant, as well as to the white middle-class who are the mainstay of more traditional theatrical fare.

Never, since Lorraine Hansberry's *A Raisin in the Sun*, has a black playwright managed on a sustained multi-play basis to include record numbers of his own constituency in his audiences without either inciting them or soothing them with musical pablum. In all his plays he has managed to maintain the tricky balance between telling some serious stories about prejudice and cowardice and conflict, and driving white audiences out of the theatre convinced that the villains are not them.

He pulls no punches but his characters are believable and often lovable, and his issues, while specific to the black world, are the universal problems of a society not always clean and tidy and instantly resolvable. There is anger in August Wilson but it finds its way to the surface in ways that find resonance in us all.

Wilson uses realism, mysticism, and eccentricity in a curiously random search for style or technique; yet like no other black writer of his time, he is able through

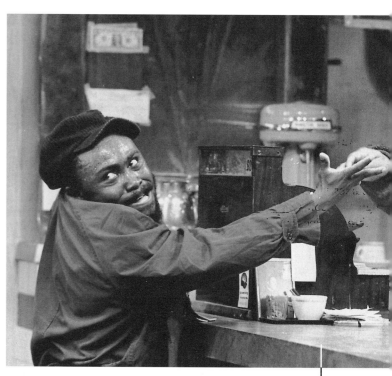

James Brown-Orleans and Michael Howe at the Studio Theatre, New York

mood and motion to capture the black experience as it has seemed to him across almost a century.

In that sense he is the dramatic voice of his people, and if his plays seem a little unstructured and even random in their quest for black happiness and fulfilment, we might do well to remember that he is, unlike many of his Broadway and London contemporaries, not in fact writing just for a rich, white, middle-class audience. His triumph, and that of his director Lloyd Richards, has been to find and prove that there was such a thing (in New York and elsewhere) as another kind of audience interested in the historic dramas of their own ancestors.

As Wilson himself has noted: "I write about the black experience in America, and try to explore in terms of the life I know best those things which are common to all cultures. I see myself as answering James Baldwin's call for a profound articulation of the black experience; which he defined as that field of

manners and ritual of intercourse which can sustain a man once he has left his father's house. I try to concretise the values of the black American, and place them on stage in loud action to demonstrate the existence of the above 'field of manners' and point to some avenues of sustenance."

Wilson himself is quick to give credit to Lloyd Richards for the process by which these values are placed on stage. It is well known that each of the plays have been developed with Richards over a very long, sometimes years-long, and tortuous process. They go through many drafts and many workshops before they see the light of day on a real stage, usually that of Yale Rep where Lloyd Richards has for many years been Dean of the Drama Department.

Within this sympathetic and academic framework Wilson's plays have been nurtured as have no other playwrights of our experience, and it is surely this protection from the frantic hot-house of Broadway that gives them their cohesion. While Lloyd Richards has been criticised for the amount of Yale's resources he expends on Wilson, the efforts are, we think, justified by the strength and popularity of the results.

Though the sequence has not been written chronologically, it was *Ma Rainey's Black Bottom* which, in 1984, made Wilson's name in New York. The story of an imperious blues singer about to record for her white bosses was set against that of her band, trying to come to terms with racial prejudice and wondering whether to break out towards a new, all-black sound of their own.

As Richard Christiansen has written, "Wilson's plays are always notable for their determination to capture the causes and effects of the rage, alienation frustration and despair of black men and women in America; there is also the power and beauty of Wilson's language, which transforms the speech of the poor and the ignorant into flights of amazing grace."

It is possible that, finally, Wilson's legacy will be to have painted for future audiences a true picture of what it meant to be black in the 20th century.

CALENDAR

• Actress Zoë Caldwell suffers post-prandial reaction to oysters and has to be hospitalised after collapsing on stage during an evening performance of *Master Class*

• The League of American Theatres and Producers initiate a Tony Awards website on the internet

DEATHS

Bernard B Jacobs Shubert Organisation executive

Walter Kerr, drama critic

NOTABLE PREMIERES

MOLLY SWEENEY, Brian Friel's play about a woman who regains her sight after years of blindness, opens at the Roundabout starring Catherine Byrne

Opening of Jonathan Larson's **RENT** at the New York Theatre Workshop

Martin McDonagh's **THE BEAUTY QUEEN OF LEENANE** signals the arrival of a highly talented young playwright

David Hare's **SKYLIGHT**, starring Michael Gambon and Lia Williams, opens on Broadway after its successful London season

Mark Ravenhill's **SHOPPING AND FUCKING** opens at the Royal Court Upstairs

Peter Hall's production of Oscar Wilde's **AN IDEAL HUSBAND** reaches Broadway after a successful London run, and stars Martin Shaw and Anna Carteret

The Broadway production of Ronald Harwood's **TAKING SIDES** stars Daniel Massey, Ed Harris and Elizabeth Marvel

Stephen Sondheim's **PASSION** opens at the Queen's Theatre, starring Michael Ball and Maria Friedman

MUSICAL NOTES

Opening of the Lincoln Center Festival, which includes 11 world premieres

HIT SONGS

Macarena

Wonderwall

Stanley

The Cookham artist Stanley Spencer, he of the primitive church paintings, was a rich subject for biography, not least because of his complex matrimonial and domestic arrangements, and Antony Sher's performance at the Barbican (and subsequently rather briefly on Broadway) made this the latest in a long line of Pam Gems's hugely theatrical stage biographies.

But by no means all of her career has been about writing footlights lives of the famous. Born in Dorset in August 1925, she was educated at Manchester University and began writing plays for children in 1972. Her first hit came in 1976 with *Dusa, Fish, Stas & Vi*, which as Micheline Wandor has noted was the first major exploration of contemporary women's experience. The four women of the title are sharing a flat, and we follow each of their less than perfect lives – Fish commits suicide when yet another love affair collapses, Dusa has her children effectively kidnapped by their father, Stas takes to the life of a prostitute and Vi turns into an anorexic neurotic.

What Gems is saying here is that Britain in the 1970s was simply not officially geared to deal with women who had finally found a voice but no roles in a still male-dominated society, and in much of the rest of her work she was to go back through time, looking at

Anna Chancellor and Antony Sher at the RNT in 1996

the lives of strong women in history to see whether things were any better for them.

Her *Queen Christina* (1977) was admittedly not much helped by the fact that the title character seems to be the head prefect at some especially seedy transvestite academy, rather than the old Garboesque heroine at the prow of her ship, and in cobbling together a chronicle of her celebrated abdication Gems fell into rather too many lines like "Can Poland give me a son?" and, our own especial favourite, "Shall I call for the leeches, Madam?"

But then, in 1978 for the RSC, came *Piaf*, a brilliant account of the Little Sparrow, seen not through the eyes of the usual sentimental showbiz biographies but instead through her own, as a tough little female survivor in a man's world. Several years later, as with her *Marlene* for Sian Phillips, Gems was to take her play, cut it back to effectively one act, and then have act two as a prolonged musical concert, and although this was a much more commercial idea it meant that inevitably some of the detail got lost. Gems' point about Piaf was that she simply wanted economic independence and the right to her own sexuality – a right hitherto reserved for men only. Her success had to be on her terms, and her refusal to be dominated by managers or husbands or even audiences made her in a sense the first truly modern icon.

All Gems' major plays have had a woman at their centre, and her themes have remained constant over thirty years: working-class survival, motherhood, and the need for women not to be handicapped from the start by their gender. Gems does not advocate separatism or destruction of the old power blocks; she simply suggests that in a man's world, women should fight as they do and fight moreover to win.

CALENDAR

• The decade-old industry magazine, Theatre Week, ceases publication
• Continental Airlines offers a corporate sponsorship deal that results in it becoming Broadway's 'official airline'
• The director of the National Actors Theatre in the States, Tony Randall, proves that work keeps you young by becoming a father, aged 77

DEATHS

American composer **Burton Lane**

Sanford Meisner, drama coach and original member of the Group Theatre

NOTABLE PREMIERES

Christopher Plummer stars on Broadway (at the Music Box) in **BARRYMORE**, his one-man show about the great American theatre star. The New York Times says that he is undoubtedly "the finest classical actor of North America"

Tim Rice and Elton John's musical **THE LION KING** opens on Broadway, to rave reviews

Peter Bowles stars in a revival, at the Piccadilly Theatre, of Ranjit Bolt's version of Molière's **THE SCHOOL FOR WIVES**, in which the show is stolen by veteran comedian Eric Sykes, playing a servant

Arnold Wesker's new play, **WHEN GOD WANTED A SON**, opens at the New End, Hampstead

Ruthie Henshall and Ute Lemper star in **CHICAGO** in the Encores! production which has transferred from New York

Richard Briers and Geraldine McEwan star in Theatre de Complicite's **THE CHAIRS**

Ralph Fiennes stars in a revival of Chekhov's **IVANOV** at the Almeida. Among the rest of the cast are Oliver Ford Davies and Harriet Walter

Ben Elton's **POPCORN** is a considerable hit at the Apollo, Shaftesbury Avenue

Ian Holm's **KING LEAR** at the National Theatre (Cottesloe) is a triumph

Disney's **BEAUTY AND THE BEAST** arrives at the Dominion in a larger-than-life, lavish, pantomime style musical

Patrick Marber's **CLOSER** transfers to the Vaudeville

Conor McPherson scores a hit with **THE WEIR**, which proves the continued appeal, for English audiences, of Irish plays

Hugh Whitemore's play about Harold Macmillan and the Profumo scandal, **A LETTER OF RESIGNATION**, stars Edward Fox and opens at the Comedy

David Haig's play about Rudyard Kipling, **MY BOY JACK**, opens at Hampstead Theatre. Haig is better known as an actor but this moving piece proves him a skilled playwright as well

MUSICAL NOTES

This is a bumper year for musical anniversaries, including Brahms, Mendelssohn, Schubert and Donizetti

David Helfgott, the Australian pianist whose life story was told in the film SHINE, undertakes an American concert tour

HIT SONGS

Wannabe

Men in Black

Art

If you had been asked in 1996, when *Art* first opened in London (this was the year of its Broadway premiere) what would turn out to be the most-produced play of the 1990s in the whole of Europe, not to mention the most commercially successful worldwide dramatic hit in more than two decades, you might not have selected a 90-minute play in which three men stand around in front of a blank canvas debating what is really meant by modern art and male friendship. Then again, you might not have believed that *The Mousetrap* would still be running rapidly toward its half-century.

Still more unusually, *Art* has come out of Paris which, since *Waiting for Godot* in the early 1950s, had not been exactly a hotbed of world hits on stage, and the author Yasmina Reza was largely unknown in Britain. But the producers, Sean Connery and his wife Micheline who had seen the play in Paris, were taking no chances: they hired Christopher Hampton to write the English version, assuming not unnaturally that the dramatist who had made such a triumph of *Les Liaisons Dangereuses* could deal with another essentially monologue-heavy piece.

Then they reunited Tom Courtenay and Albert Finney from *The Dresser* and much else, and brought in Ken Stott as the only other character. What they soon also realised was that the play could stand frequent recasting, especially if internal connections were made; thus three actors from the same British or American TV series could alternate the roles across the Atlantic, never having to commit for more than a few weeks and thereby making the roles attractive also to film stars with a horror of leaving Hollywood for a full-length run.

Art thus became a Euro-American event, with more than fifty productions already up and running within a couple of years of the Paris and London premieres. But the play remains, in our view, a phenomenon rather than a classic; it has very little to say about the world of modern art that wasn't said better in Timberlake Wertenbaker's *Three Birds Alighting on a Field*, or even in Noël Coward's old 1956 *Nude with Violin*.

ALBERT FINNEY

TOM COURTENAY

KEN STOTT

WYNDHAM'S THEATRE

The original cast

The reason that *Art* has triumphed all over the world, and this admittedly is a minority dissenting view, is that it is coffee-table theatre; the snob hit at its most snobbish, nicely short so that tired businessmen and their clients can make it into a restaurant by 9.30pm. It is as vogueish as a *Vogue* cover, and just about as meaningful in its high-chic emptiness; a half-arted evening, so generalised and non-committal that, like the blank canvas, you can read anything you wish into it. Do-it-yourself theatre, in fact, and I suspect that the comparative West End failure of Reza's next play, *The Unexpected Man*, despite Michael Gambon and Eileen Atkins (1998, Broadway 2000) may be due to her audience tiring of conversation pieces in which very little happens, and very slowly.

Nevertheless Reza is currently Europe's most successful dramatist, and we need perhaps, as we roll towards the next theatrical century, to wonder what that really means: does an audience really now feel happier watching three stars bickering elegantly and eloquently for ninety minutes on a virtually bare stage than getting involved in what might be called a real drama with all its untidiness and sprawl and challenge? *Art* is Eurodrama for the EuroStar generation; neat, clean, speedy, multinational and with no real shocks or surprises along the route.

The final irony here is that *Art* is just like the white canvas at its heart; you can read anything you like into it, or just tick it off like Tate Bankside as one more artefact of the new world culture that has to be seen for dinner-party conversation, but need not really take up too much of our ever-more limited time and attention span.

DEATHS

Frank Sinatra American singer and actor

British satirist and playwright **John Wells**

Patricia Hayes Veteran British actress

NOTABLE PREMIERES

David Hare's play about Oscar Wilde, **THE JUDAS KISS**, starring Liam Neeson, opens on Broadway after transferring from London's Playhouse Theatre

In the States, Kathleen Chalfont has a hit in **WIT**, Margaret Edson's play about a tough English teacher coping with the fact that she is dying of cancer

David Benson's extraordinary recreation of the late actor, comic performer and diarist Kenneth Williams, **THINK NO EVIL OF US**, transfers to the West End for a limited run at the Vaudeville

David Soul appears on stage at the fringe New End theatre, Hampstead, in a revival of Nick Darke's play **THE DEAD MONKEY**

Sebastian Barry's play about Irish family life, **OUR LADY OF SLIGO**, opens at the Cottesloe to consistently good reviews, confirming his reputation that he established with his earlier **THE STEWARD OF CHRISTENDOM**

Jonathan Larson's **RENT** finally arrives in London. Although it is a very New York piece and receives mixed reviews, it strikes a chord with younger audiences and settles in for a decent run

Andrew Lloyd Webber's latest musical opens. **WHISTLE DOWN THE WIND** is based on the novel by Mary Hayley Bell (Lady Mills), which was in itself filmed some forty years earlier, starring the Mills' daughter, Hayley

Leslie Bricusse's musical **DR DOLITTLE** opens at the Labatt's Apollo in Hammersmith, directed by Stephen Pimlott and starring Phillip Schofield

David Hare's **THE BLUE ROOM** opens at the Donmar Warehouse, starring Ian Glen and Nicole Kidman

Tom Stoppard's **THE INVENTION OF LOVE** is a highly intelligent voyage around the life and times of English poet AE Housman, which transfers to the Theatre Royal, Haymarket after an early start at the National Theatre

Film star and heart-throb Ewan McGregor returns to the stage in a revival of David Halliwell's 1960s play **LITTLE MALCOLM AND HIS STRUGGLE AGAINST THE EUNUCHS** at Hampstead Theatre

Harold Pinter's play about the breakdown of a marriage, **BETRAYAL**, gets a welcome revival at the National Theatre

Natasha Richardson (Sally Bowles) stars with Alan Cumming (as the MC) in **CABARET** in New York, in the Donmar Warehouse production which, in London, had Jane Horrocks as Sally

MUSICAL NOTES

The Gershwin and Ellington centenaries are marked by a variety of events, and there is a special concert to mark Elliott Carter's 90th birthday

Anne-Sophie Mutter performs all 10 Beethoven sonatas in three concerts before setting off on an international tour

Matthew Bourne's **SWAN LAKE** opens on Broadway, a moving and witty reinterpretation

HIT SONGS

Bitter Sweet Symphony

Truly Madly Deeply

Summerfolk

It may seem deliberately perverse to close this 20th century chronicle of World Theatre (even in the interests of also closing the circle) with a play written in 1903; but it was in 1999 that Trevor Nunn's magnificent ensemble company at the National Theatre, one of the

Chekhov's *Cherry Orchard* of which this, in its own wonderful way, is essentially the tabloid, populist version. Where Chekhov gives us a fundamentally aristocratic elite in personal or financial meltdown, Gorky gives us the much broader picture of an entire society in millennial and pre-revolutionary change; if

finest achievements ever realised in that building, brought the play back in triumph more than a quarter of a century after it had last been seen in London in a somewhat lacklustre production by the RSC at the Aldwych.

 While Gorky was writing *Summerfolk*, for a cast of thirty, the Moscow Art Theatre was rehearsing

Chekhov wrote of a closed society behind the railings of their private estates, Gorky writes of what was going on in the public parks and streets of the same period.

 Here we get not only the doctors and the lawyers, but a vast range of others, from millionaires to nihilists, all drifting into a 20th century about which the

Jim Creighton, Roger Allam, Henry Goodman and Michael Bryant at the RNT in 1999

only thing they really know is that it is unlikely to live up to any of their private or public hopes.

Where Chekhov has idealists and villains, Gorky just has ordinary people muddling through unhappy marriages and unsatisfactory careers; in a sense, they could be refugees not from the coming bloodbath, but from a latterday comedy of bad marital manners by Michael Frayn. *Summerfolk* is about life at an endless picnic where nobody really wants to be, except that going home is no alternative either.

As for Gorky himself, born in 1868 and orphaned at an early age, he became a wandering tramp, attempted suicide at 19 but then in 1892 began to publish the first in a sequence of novels and short stories which brought him to Chekhov's attention and thence to the Moscow Art Theatre under Stanislavsky. For a while he became their house dramatist, most notably with *The Lower Depths* (1902), but his outspoken defence of the people against the Tsarist police sent him to exile, where he first met Lenin.

After the revolution, the men returned in some triumph, but Lenin's wary jealousy caused Gorky to spend most of the 1920s in Italy. When he did return home to the USSR his later plays were flawed by discursiveness and preaching, though his passionate moral commitment to improving man's lot was never in doubt. By now persona non grata with the Kremlin, he lived on until 1936 when he was given a full state funeral, though the precise circumstances of his death or murder have never been adequately established. Stalin later announced that he had been poisoned, though not by him. His birthplace was renamed Gorky, as was the theatre in Leningrad where many of his plays were first seen.

In a way, while written at the beginning of our century, *Summerfolk* also encapsulates the whole of it – the relentless drive towards reflecting the world as it is rather than as we would want it to be, the incorporation of realism into our myths and myths into our realism, the recognition that audiences are reverting to what they were in Shakespeare's time, no

longer only Lords and Ladies but also groundlings with money to spend in the pits (with bear-baiting and dog-fighting to compete with); and the belief that if the theatre is about anything, it is about the universal truths and conflicts of the world we live in now, in the past, and in the future. It is about us.

DEATHS **Anthony Newley** British actor/songwriter/singer

British actor **Oliver Reed**

British stage composer **Lionel Bart**

Derek Nimmo British actor and producer

NOTABLE PREMIERES Three classic revivals, MONEY, SUMMERFOLK and CANDIDE open at the National this year, and all have Simon Russell Beale, in lead roles

Another outstanding performance at the National is Henry Goodman's playing of Shylock in THE MERCHANT OF VENICE

SPEND, SPEND, SPEND, a musical on the life of pools winner Viv Nicholson opens at the Piccadilly Theatre

MAMMA MIA! is a musical inspired by the songs of Abba, the Swedish pop group of the 1970s and early 1980s

Richard Greenburg's THREE DAYS OF RAIN opens at the Donmar Warehouse in a production featuring Colin Firth, Elizabeth McGovern and David Morrissey

Rufus Sewell heads a stylish revival of Shakespeare's MACBETH at the Queen's Theatre

Dick Vosburgh and Denis King's witty tribute to Molière and '40s musicals, A SAINT SHE AIN'T, appears first at the King's Head and then in the Apollo, Shaftesbury Avenue

Robert Lindsay, who first proved himself a major stage star (as well as an undoubted television one) with ME AND MY GIRL in the 1980s, proves the fact once more in the title role of the RSC's RICHARD III at the Savoy Theatre

One of London's liveliest fringe theatres, the Bridewell, hosts a rare revival of George and Ira Gershwin's OF THEE I SING

At the Old Vic Peter O'Toole reprises his 1980s triumph In JEFFREY BERNARD IS UNWELL

Julian Barry's play LENNY is given a revival at the Queen's Theatre, starring Eddie Izzard

QUARTET, a new play by Ronald Harwood, set in a home for retired opera singers starring the combined talents of Stephanie Cole, Alec McCowen, Donald Sinden and Angela Thorne, opens at the Albery Theatre

SONG AT TWILIGHT, Sheridan Morley's production of Noël Coward's last play, starring a company of Redgraves (Vanessa, Corin, and Corin's wife Kika Markham), transfers to the Gielgud after opening at the King's Head

Terrence McNally's gay play about Christ and his disciples, CORPUS CHRISTI opens, to great controversy, at the Pleasance Theatre in London

At the Queen's Theatre Alan Bennett's THE LADY IN THE VAN tells the story (already recounted in print) of how Miss Shepherd, an eccentric semi-tramp, parked her camping van outside his house and, in effect, became a sort of lodger for the next fifteen years

HIT SONGS Let Me Entertain You

That Don't Impress Me Much

ACKNOWLEDGEMENTS

1900 Uncle Vanya
©John Haynes
1901 The Dance of Death
©Performing Arts Library
1902 The Importance of Being Earnest
©Henrietta Butler/Performing Arts Library
1903 Man and Superman
©The Mander & Mitchenson Theatre Collection
1904 Peter Pan
©The Mander & Mitchenson Theatre Collection
1905 The Voysey Inheritance
©The Mander & Mitchenson Theatre Collection
1906 Major Barbara
©The Mander & Mitchenson Theatre Collection
1907 The Playboy of the Western World
©The Mander & Mitchenson Theatre Collection
1908 Peer Gynt
©The Mander & Mitchenson Theatre Collection
1909 Strife
©The Mander & Mitchenson Theatre Collection
1910 Grace
©The Mander & Mitchenson Theatre Collection
1911 Trelawny of the Wells
©The Mander & Mitchenson Theatre Collection
1912 Hindle Wakes
©The Mander & Mitchenson Theatre Collection
1913 Mary Goes First
©The Mander & Mitchenson Theatre Collection
1914 Pygmalion
©Ronald Grant/Arena Images
1915 The Widowing of Mrs Holroyd
©The Mander & Mitchenson Theatre Collection
1916 Hobson's Choice
©The Mander & Mitchenson Theatre Collection
1917 Dear Brutus
©The Mander & Mitchenson Theatre Collection
1918 Exiles
©The Mander & Mitchenson Theatre Collection
1919 Heartbreak House
©Performing Arts Library
1920 The Skin Game
©The Mander & Mitchenson Theatre Collection
1921 The Circle
©The Mander & Mitchenson Theatre Collection
1922 Six Characters in Search of an Author
©The Mander & Mitchenson Theatre Collection
1923 Anna Christie
©The Mander & Mitchenson Theatre Collection
1924 Juno and the Paycock
©The Mander & Mitchenson Theatre Collection

1925 Hay Fever
©Angus McBean/The Mander & Mitchenson Theatre Collection
1926 On Approval
©The Mander & Mitchenson Theatre Collection
1927 Thark
©The Mander & Mitchenson Theatre Collection
1928 Showboat
©The Mander & Mitchenson Theatre Collection
1929 Rope
©The Mander & Mitchenson Theatre Collection
1930 Private Lives
©The Mander & Mitchenson Theatre Collection
1931 Of Thee I Sing
©Opera News/Arena Images
1932 Dangerous Corner
©The Mander & Mitchenson Theatre Collection
1933 A Sleeping Clergyman
©Swarbrick Studios/Mander & Mitchenson
1934 Murder In The Cathedral
©Donald Cooper/Photostage
1935 Waiting For Lefty
©The Mander & Mitchenson Theatre Collection
1936 French Without Tears
©The Mander & Mitchenson Theatre Collection
1937 Amphytrion38
©The Mander & Mitchenson Theatre Collection
1938 Our Town
©Donald Cooper/Photostage
1939 The Little Foxes
©The Mander & Mitchenson Theatre Collection
1940 The Corn Is Green
©Angus McBean/The Mander & Mitchenson Theatre Collection
1941 The Man who Came to Dinner
©The Mander & Mitchenson Theatre Collection
1942 Antigone
©Andrzej Klimowski
1943 Oklahoma!
©Michael Le Poer Trench/Arena Images
1944 Galileo
©Dominic Photography
1945 Perchance to Dream
©The Mander & Mitchenson Theatre Collection
1946 All My Sons
©Ivan Kyncl
1947 A Streetcar Named Desire
©The Mander & Mitchenson Theatre Collection
1948 The Lady's Not For Burning
©Angus McBean/The Mander & Mitchenson Theatre Collection
1949 Lost in the Stars
©The Mander & Mitchenson Theatre Collection